Rahel Varnhagen

Sketches of german life and scenes from the war of liberation in Germany

selected and translated from the memoirs of Varnhagen von Ense

Rahel Varnhagen

Sketches of german life and scenes from the war of liberation in Germany
selected and translated from the memoirs of Varnhagen von Ense

ISBN/EAN: 9783742875273

Manufactured in Europe, USA, Canada, Australia, Japa

Cover: Foto ©ninafisch / pixelio.de

Manufactured and distributed by brebook publishing software (www.brebook.com)

Rahel Varnhagen

Sketches of german life and scenes from the war of liberation in Germany

CONTENTS.

PART I.

CHAPTER I.

Page

Parentage and early Life. — State of Germany towards the close of the Eighteenth Century. — Düsseldorf. — The Convent of St. Barbara Garten. — The Convent of La Trappe, at Dusselthal. — The French Revolution.—Voyage up the Rhine.—Strasburg Cathedral. — The Costume of the Women. — State of public Feeling in Strasburg.—Public Rejoicings.—National Guards.—French Emigrants in the Brisgau. — Viscomte de Mirabeau. — Reckless Conduct of the Emigrants. 1785—1792. 1

CHAPTER II.

Return to Düsseldorf. — War with Republican France. — The Emigrants on the Rhine. — Execution of Louis XVI., and the Impression it produced.—Lutheran School at Düsseldorf.—Journey to Hamburg. 1792—1794. 17

CHAPTER III.

Hamburg. — Klopstock. — The Emigrants in Hamburg.— The Expedition to Quiberon. — Bookstall in Hamburg. — The "Turkish Spy."— Lafayette in Hamburg. — Death of my Father.— Berlin Medical Academy. — Chamisso. — Fichte. — Louis Goldsmith. — Rahel Levin. — Poetical Club. — War between France and Austria. — Peace with Prussia. 1794—1806. 25

CHAPTER IV.

The University of Halle. — Manners of the Students. — Their Clubs. — Warlike Movements. — Prussian Troops in Halle. — Vacation Time. — Field Marshal Von Müllendorf. 1806. . . . 37

CONTENTS.

CHAPTER V.

War declared between France and Prussia. — General Enthusiasm. — Death of Prince Louis Ferdinand. — Departure of the Court from Berlin. — General Schulenburg. — Battles of Auerstadt and Jena. — The French in Leipsic. — Plundering of Halle. — Their Entrance into Berlin. — Bivouack in the Lustgarten. — Napoleon in Berlin. — Fall of Magdeburg. — Desperate Condition of Prussia. 1806. 40

CHAPTER VI.

Fichte's Lectures in Berlin. — Schleiermacher. — Meeting with Rahel Levin. — Description of Rahel. — Her Character. — The Society at her House. — Her Letters and Journals. — Rahel at Charlottenburg. 1807. 47

CHAPTER VII.

Jean Paul Friederich Richter at Baireuth. — His Manner and Conversation. — Jean Paul's Wife and Children. — His Opinions on Rahel, Goethe, Schlegel, and others. — Jean Paul's Manner of Writing. — The Romantic School. — Tieck and Bernhardi. 1808. 56

CHAPTER VIII.

The Battle of Aspern. — State of Silesia. — Deutsch-Wagram. — The Camp. — Archduke Charles. — The French cross the Danube. — Storm in the Marchfeld. — Position of the Austrian Army. — Archduke John at Presburg. — Failure of the first Attack of the French on Wagram. — Archduke Charles's Plan of Action. — Napoleon's Arrangements. — Attack upon Atterkla and Wagram. — Defence of Atterkla. — Advance of the Imperial Guard. — Defeat of the Left Wing of the Austrian Army. — Retreat of the Austrians upon Bockfliess and Gerasdorf, 5th and 6th of July. 1809. 65

CHAPTER IX.

Personal History. — The Hospital at Zistersdorf. — Wounded Austrian Officers. — Absolution given to One of my Companions. — The Franciscan Monk. — Arrival of the French in Zistersdorf. — State of the French Army. — Character of the Colonel. — The wounded Austrians declared Prisoners of War, and sent to Vienna. 1809. 99

CONTENTS.

CHAPTER X.

Paris. — Prince Charles Schwarzenberg. — Count Metternich. — Hostility to Napoleon. — Life in Paris. — Preparations for Prince Schwarzenberg's Ball. — The Emperor and Maria Louisa. — Arrival of a Courier. — Fireworks. — The Ball. — Sudden Fire. — Napoleon quits the Ball. — The Queen of Naples. — The Queen of Westphalia and Princess von der Leyen saved. — Return of the Emperor. — The Bivouack. — Discovery of Princess Pauline Schwarzenberg's Corpse. — Gloomy Impression produced by the Fire. 1810. 108

CHAPTER XI.

Berthier. — The Battle of Marengo. — Denon. — Cardinal Maury. — The Salle des Ambassadeurs. — Reception at Court. — Napoleon's Manner. — Sudden Outbreak of Temper. — The Emperor's Departure. — General Relief. 1810. 124

CHAPTER XII.

Paris. — Musée Napoleon. — Musée des Monumens Français. — The Luxemburg Palace. — The Hall of the Senate. — Prix décennaux. — Musée d'Artillerie. — The Imperial Library. — Versailles, St. Cloud, and Malmaison. — Talma. — The Empress Josephine. — Jean Jacques Rousseau. — Life in Paris. — Parisian Advertisements. — State of Parties. — French itinerant Mountebank. — Pulpit and Bar Eloquence. — The Comedian Brunet. — Epigrams on Napoleon's Marriage. — Breakfast at Count Metternich's. — Scene in the Café de Valois. — Madame de Genlis. — Boulevards des Italiens. 1810. . . . 131

CONTENTS.

PART II.

CHAPTER XIII.

The Castle of Steinfurt. — The reigning Count. — Life at the Castle. — The old Castle of Bentheim. — Torture Chamber. — The white Lady. — Superstitions in Westphalia. — The Castle Seer. — Münster and the Anabaptists. — Arrival of the French in Steinfurt. — The French Police. 1810, 1811. 171

CHAPTER XIV.

Garrison Life in Prague. — The Prussian Minister Stein. — His Outlawry and Escape into Bohemia. — Stein's Character. — Vienna. — State of Public Opinion. — Prospect of War between France and Russia. — Birth of the King of Rome. — Ball at the French Ambassador's. — Festival at Prague. 1811. 183

CHAPTER XV.

Töplitz. — The princely Family of Clary. — The Prince de Ligne. — Life at Töplitz. — Troop of Bohemian Actors. — The French Spy. — The Disappearance of Mr. Bathurst. — The Englishman and the French Courier. — Beethoven. — Prague. — The Emigrants and Exiles at Prague. — Justus Gruner, the Head of the Prussian Police. — Napoleon at Dresden. — Arrest of Gruner, and Consternation of the others. — Arrival at Berlin. — News of the Burning of Moscow. — The Cossacks enter Berlin. 1811, 1812. . . 189

CHAPTER XVI.

Tettenborn's early Life. — The Electoral Court at Mayence. — Flight of the Elector to Aschaffenburg. — Tettenborn joins the Army in the Netherlands. — Hohenlinden. — Tettenborn at Ulm. — Tettenborn at St. Petersburg. — The Retreat from Moscow. — The Taking of Wilna. — The Advance of the Cossacks. — Failure of the Attack on Berlin. — Advance of the Russian Infantry, and Retreat of the French. 1812, 1813. 200

CHAPTER XVII.

State of the North of Germany in 1813. — Riots in Hamburg. — Executions. — Excitement of the People. — Tettenborn at Ludwigslust. — Encounters General Morand. — Arrival of the Cossacks in Hamburg. — Tettenborn's Triumphal Entry into the Town. — Joy of the Inhabitants. — Tettenborn's Measures for the Defence of Hamburg. — Spread of the Insurrection. — Inefficiency of the Hamburg Authorities. — The Approach of the French. — Their Defeat at Lüneburg. — The French quit the Elbe. — Negotiation with Denmark. — The French advance upon Lüneburg and Haarburg. — Fresh Preparations for the Defence of Hamburg. — Attack upon Wilhelmsburg. — The Danes enter Hamburg, but receive Orders to withdraw again. — They are succeeded by the Swedes, who are likewise ordered to withdraw. — Desperate Condition of Hamburg. — Tettenborn retreats to Lauenburg.   .   .   .   209

CHAPTER XVIII.

State of the North of Germany. — Tettenborn in Mecklenburg. — Newspaper started in the Camp. — Johanna Stegen, the Maid of Lüneburg. — Eleonora Prochaska, of the Lützen Free Corps. — Tettenborn's Expedition against Bremen. — Difficulties of the March. — Bremen is invested. — Death of Colonel Thullier, the Commandant, and Surrender of the Town to Tettenborn. — The Fortifications destroyed and the Town evacuated. — The Battle of Leipsic, and its Effects. — The Crown Prince of Sweden enters Bremen. — Campaign in Holstein and Schleswig. — Armistice with Denmark.   250

CHAPTER XIX.

The Allies enter France. — Napoleon's Resources. — The Allies at Chalons and Rheims. — State of Affairs. — The Army of Silesia under Blücher and the Main Army under Schwarzenberg. — Blücher's Advance upon Meaux. — The Battle of Laon. — Excitement of the French Peasantry against the Allies. — Difficulty of Communication. — The Attack upon Rheims. — The French retake it. — Tettenborn evacuates Epernay. — The Action at Arcis-sur-Aube. — Epernay is retaken by Tettenborn. — Junction of Blücher and Schwarzenberg. — Determination of the Allies to march upon Paris. — They encounter and beat Marshals Marmont and Mortier. — The Battle of Saint Dizier. — Napoleon learns the Advance of the Allies upon Paris. — The Allies enter Paris, 1813-14.   .   .   262

CHAPTER XX.

State of Paris in 1814. — Rapid Change in the Parisians. — Scheme to seize upon the Emperor of Russia and the King of Prussia. — Defeated by Count Schlabrendorf. — The Count d'Artois enters Paris. — Plan of a Constitution. — Chateaubriand, Benjamin Constant, and Count Gregoire. — Louis XVIII. enters Paris. — Ballad on the King. — Madame de Stael. — Death of the Empress Josephine. 287

CHAPTER XXI.

Viennese Life and Society. — The Prince de Ligne. — Cardinal Consalvi. — Stein. — Baron Cotta. — Dr. Bollmann. — The Opening of the Congress. — Difficulties and Impediments. — The Influence of France. — Entertainments in Vienna. — Lord Stewart. — Death of the Prince de Ligne. — Prince Metternich. — Baron Wessenburg. — Gentz. — Frederick Schlegel. — Prince Hardenberg and Baron William Humboldt. — Counts Stackelberg and Nesselrode. — Lord Castlereagh. — Prince Talleyrand. — Sir Sidney Smith and the Knights of Malta. — The Question touching Saxony and Poland. — French Intrigues. — Life in Vienna. — The Collection in the Castle of Ambras. — Difficulties in Congress. — Funeral Service for Louis XVI. — The Arrival of the Duke of Wellington. — Murat and Sicily. — Napoleon's Escape from Elba. — Its Effect in Vienna. — Napoleon's Progress. — Murat defeated. — War with France inevitable. — Termination of the Congress of Vienna. 299

SKETCHES OF GERMAN LIFE,

AND

SCENES FROM THE

WAR OF LIBERATION IN GERMANY.

CHAPTER I.

Parentage and early Life.—State of Germany towards the Close of the Eighteenth Century.—Düsseldorf.—The Convent of St. Barbara Garten. —The Convent of La Trappe, at Dusselthal.—The French Revolution. —Voyage up the Rhine.—Strasburg Cathedral.—The Costume of the Women.—State of public Feeling in Strasburg.—Public Rejoicings.— National Guards.—French Emigrants in the Brisgau.—Viscomte de Mirabeau.—Reckless Conduct of the Emigrants. 1785—1792.

FAMILY records have generally been collected and published either from motives of vanity or for the sake of worldly advantage, but they might undoubtedly be made to serve more important purposes if properly directed. The successive generations, the increase and duration of a family, their intermarriages and changes of place and country; their altered circumstances; the varieties of character and talent; all this, treated with due discrimination, would afford materials for useful reflection. The threads of private life, followed through several generations, would exhibit the course of events in a new and peculiar form. In this manner a method of genealogical study might be pursued, having for its object higher views and nobler purposes than at present: every thing, however, would depend upon the intelligence and good sense of the author. I do not undertake to give an example of such a method myself, but I will prefix a short account of my ancestors before I begin to relate my own life.

The race from which I spring has been settled in Westphalia from the very earliest period. "The old, famous, and noble family of Von Ense," as it is called by the Westphalian chronicler, Von Steinen, separated in early times into two branches, one of which took the name Von Ense from an old castle near Arensberg; and the other that of Schnidewindt. In the records of the thirteenth century we find the Von Enses frequently mentioned as knights, lords of castles, high bailiffs, privy councillors, canons, &c.; at one time holding military, at another civil, offices. In the course of time the Von Enses gradually quitted the career of arms, and devoted themselves more exclusively to the learned and clerical professions, in which equal honours were to be acquired, combined with profit and intellectual advantages.

This tendency was further promoted by a certain Conrad Von Ense, surnamed Varnhagen, a canon of Cologne cathedral, and pastor at Iserlon, who, in the year 1520, founded an hereditary vicariate at the church of St. Martin, and endowed it with a considerable income. This still remains the exclusive property of the Varnhagen family. The first incumbent, Johann Von Ense, likewise called Varnhagen, took an active part in the Reformation, and, after great opposition, introduced the Lutheran form of worship into Iserlon. The next step was the marriage of the vicar. His first wife—for he subsequently married a second time—was a Von Kettler, the sister of the Duke of Courland; and from her sprung my immediate ancestors, who nearly all of them followed the learned professions, and were either clergymen or physicians. The family now belonged by position and profession to the burgher class, and held the liberal opinions which are often to be found in that station of life.

Meanwhile an event had taken place which caused a great severance of the family ties. My great-grandfather, who had settled as a physician at Paderborn, was converted to the Catholic religion by the Jesuits, a body which has always offered considerable attractions to men of learning. His descendants naturally were of the same faith, but, although outwardly separated from their Protestant relations, they always retained a freer spirit of inquiry, which was increased by the spirit of the times and by their devotion to the study of medicine.

My grandfather, after studying at the Protestant University of Leyden in Holland, travelled over Prussia and Austria, and selected Vienna as his home: his intention, however, was frustrated by a quarrel with the famous physician Van Swieten. He came to Dusseldorf, and, contrary to the usual habit of the family, took as his wife a foreigner—the daughter of a merchant at Petersburg.

My father received the usual instruction from the Jesuits, without, however, being much influenced by their views and doctrines. He then, following the example of his ancestors, studied medicine, first at Heidelberg, subsequently at Strasburg and Paris. He married a Protestant of Strasburg, to whom he had been engaged while at the University, and finally settled at Dusseldorf where I was born on the 21st of February, 1785.

Great changes had taken place during the eighteenth century: the most toilsome and thankless part of the work was done, and people were expecting to reap the fruit of their labours: a rapid development was taking place, but its results were still to come. France was the centre whence radiated a complete change of feelings and opinions: religious views, the constitutions of states, education, society, all was to be altered: old forms were to be abolished; the very government appeared to be willing and pliant, and the excitable, clever, and accomplished French nation had a prodigious effect on other countries: the influence of its talents and activity reached as far even as Poland and Russia. The new impulse was communicated to the heads of the nation,—emperors, kings, princes, and men in the higher ranks of life were subject to its influence long before it had descended to the middle and lower classes. North America had already adopted an independent form of government compared with which the degree of freedom enjoyed by England, Holland, Switzerland, and parts of Germany was nothing.

It would, however, be a great error to suppose that Germany had not an equal share in the comprehensive labours of that century: the glory, indeed, was all with the French; but Germany had not been behindhand. The last years of Frederick the Great shed a lustre over the Prussian monarchy, and the reforms of the Emperor Joseph II. were working great changes in the Austrian hereditary dominions and in the whole German empire. Principles of humanity, freedom of thought, and toleration, had a strong hold upon those who sat on thrones: prosperity, commerce, and a general thirst after knowledge had taken root during an interval of many years' peace. All classes were actively engaged in the pursuit of instruction, and in ridding themselves of their several prejudices: in short, the whole nation had made rapid progress in general intelligence.

This was remarkably the case on the lower Rhine. This district, composed of princely states, free imperial towns, archbishoprics, electorates, and other spiritual dominions, united within itself the most various elements: moreover, it enjoyed free trade with Holland and England, was in constant communication with France, to which it looked for intellectual culture, manners, and fashions, besides being influenced by its immediate contact with Prussia, and more remotely with Austria through Belgium.

Dusseldorf had made greater advances than other towns. It had formerly been a royal residence, and was still considered as such, although the court had removed to Manheim: as the principal town in the dukedom of Juliers and Berg, it was the seat of government, and its position on the Rhine gave it great commercial advantages: it was a well-built thriving town, full of intelligent inhabitants, military and civil officers, provincial nobility, and strangers who flocked to see its famed gallery of pictures.* Add to this that a good company of actors performed during the winter season, and sufficient reasons have been given to entitle Dusseldorf to be considered one of the most agreeable towns on the Rhine.

My earliest impressions and recollections, however, are not associated with a town life, but with the garden and with the Rhine. The back of our little house in a by-street looked out on the river, and just enough ground was saved from the Rhine

---

* Now forming part of the collection at Munich. — *Transl.*

by means of piles and stakes to form a little garden. Steps led from a window of the drawing-room down to this space, which was laid out in grass-plats and flower-beds: its bright sunny prospect up the river, the strong running stream, the view of the opposite banks, and the wholesome fresh air, made it a perfect paradise for us children. I still remember the pure pleasures, the happy spirits, and the bright days we then enjoyed. From my third to my fifth year this garden is associated in my recollections with pictures of an unbroken summer.

During my early childhood I paid a visit to my father's sister, who was a nun in the convent of St. Barbara-Garten in Rheinberg. She had been admitted into this convent, which was intended only for noble maidens, by the favour of the court, and, young and inexperienced, she eagerly seized this opportunity of ensuring salvation. During her noviciate she regretted her determination, but shame and helplessness induced her to persevere. We found her in the beauty of youth, kind, composed, and tolerably contented. She played well on the organ, wrote and drew beautifully, and busied herself worthily and agreeably in her spiritual duties. My father, whom she treated with some ceremony, spoke to her without witnesses, inquired into her circumstances and views, and offered to assist her in quitting the convent if she wished it. He promised to do it by force if he could not succeed by fair means: the Prussian frontiers, which were close at hand, offered a secure retreat. She rejected his proposal with many thanks: she had got used to her mode of life, and could conceive none other.

All this was told to me afterwards. I was then full of the impression which the beautiful rooms, the good food, and the numerous company made upon me. The court and garden in which we passed the evening in the open air offered me every inducement to play. Nevertheless an impression of awe and seclusion which prevailed in the place, and the few words of pity and commiseration which I heard bestowed upon the poor nuns, made me exceedingly glad to leave the convent.

My good aunt's history had a most melancholy termination. She grew blind, and lost her senses. Whether it was that the nuns thought her condition in itself required stern treatment, or that she uttered expressions which showed her former dislike to monastic life, and which the nuns held to be ungodly, obstinate, and deserving of punishment,—I know not what were the reasons,—but my unfortunate aunt was most cruelly shut up in a remote dark sort of cellar, where she passed many years subject to the hardest privations. Her younger brother, who was a professor at Cologne, frequently went with the intention of seeing her, but could never obtain an interview. He took advantage of the French being in possession of the country, and, accompanied by some gens-d'armes, he one day unexpectedly demanded admittance in the name of the civil authorities, who were not to be resisted. The nuns had no time to make any preparations; and, on following them closely, the most miserable spectacle presented itself to his sight. His unfortunate sister was seated totally naked on the bare earth; she had neither a blanket nor straw, neither table nor chair! When they brought her something to eat, the nuns offered her a spoon and a fork: she took no heed of them, but seized the food with her fingers, plainly showing that she had for years lost the habit of using any thing else, much as the cruel nuns wished to conceal the fact. When her brother spoke to her she recognised his voice, wept, and lamented her condition; accusing no one, but only hoping that she might be better treated in future. She was weak in intellect and stupified, owing most likely to her long years of terrible suffering; but by no means raving mad, which alone could have excused such treatment. Her gentleness continued unchanged, and works of charity and devotion were her constant occupation. She lived for some years in a religious community at Cologne at the expense of the nuns, in a weak but placid state of mind, perfectly quiet, and died at an extreme old age in 1814.

I had another opportunity of seeing conventual life, and this presented itself under a very cheerful aspect. Not far from Dusseldorf there was a convent of La Trappe, the severest of all orders of monks. This order has few followers: there are only this one convent in Germany, another in Italy, and the famous one in France, established by the founder of the order. People gave the most horrible account of the hard, deadening mode of life of the wretched brethren; upon whom, besides deep silence and a perpetual contemplation of death, the most toilsome field labours were imposed. If these miserable men were the subject of commiseration, and were considered as sacrificed to the most absurd system of superstition, they also gave an opportunity of praising the spirit of enlightenment, which had even penetrated the walls of the darkest of all convents, and must eventually destroy them. My memory retained some circumstances of which I did not understand the import until my riper years explained them. The monks had selected my father as their medical attendant; and as there were many sick, I frequently went to Dusselthal with him. We never penetrated into the dark interior of the convent — this may have been dismal enough — but the rooms set apart for the reception of the sick, and the refreshment of visitors, had nothing repulsive about them. Here, moreover, the strict rule of silence was not enforced; the monks chatted, and drank wine with the visitors to their hearts' content: cakes and fruit were laid before us, of which a large share fell to my lot, and my pockets were filled with good things to eat on my way home. They put no restraint on their conversation before a child, who seemed occupied with rosaries and pictures of saints, and troubled their heads no more about me. Thus, without intending it, I heard things, the full import of which I did not quite understand, but which sounded as if they were not quite right, and gave me the idea that these holy men were full of roguery and tricks. When the words told me little or nothing, the look, the sarcastic self-satisfied laugh, or the repulsive impudent gesture with which these words were accompanied, explained them all. On my way home, I asked my father when a certain monk, who was particularly kind to me, would be ill again, so as to talk and drink wine. It was clear that I conceived the poor creatures looked upon illness as an advantage, and settled among each other who was to enjoy his turn. I saw that I was not far wrong, from the good-humoured way in which my father muttered some words, laughing to himself, without giving me any further answer.

When I was about six years of age, my mother and sister visited Strasburg, the sight of which awakened in my mother the strongest affection for her native town, with which so many tender recollections were associated, and what she said to my father recalled his old love for the university in which he had studied. He compared the brilliant and agreeable life of the capital of Alsace with the small and dull society of Dusseldorf, and he finally determined to leave the latter, which was rapidly becoming more and more a mere provincial town, and to settle at Strasburg. But there were other motives stronger than these.

The French Revolution of 1789 had every where produced great excitement: the friends of improvement, freedom, and humanity expected a new and general diffusion of prosperity from this great movement. My father had been among the first to hail and to record his opinion of these glorious prospects. It is true that he recoiled with horror from the scenes of violence and cruelty which took place at first, and occasionally recurred; he wished to see the object of his hopes obtained only by gentle means. But these cruelties were lost sight of in the great stream of innovation and improvement. Moreover, the movement now appeared to be taking a direction favourable to order; the National Assembly was busily employed in framing a fresh constitution, and to belong to the new state of things in which freedom, law, and brotherly love were recognised, seemed to be the happiest lot which could fall to the share of a well-thinking man.

The voyage up the Rhine to Manheim was the pleasantest event in my youthful life. The cabin was large and comfortable; but the deck was most agreeable to us, in spite of the restraint put upon our actions for fear of falling overboard. We made acquaintance with the sailors, learnt the use of much of the gear of the vessel, and had our attention called to the remarkable objects and towns on the shore. There was no lack of tales and old legends; but what captivated us most was to look for hours on the deep green water, and to follow with our eyes the ripples and eddies of the stream. The voyage was long and slow. On the towing-path, at a distance, we saw the team of horses dragging our vessel with some difficulty against the current. The middle of the rope, which was tied to the top of the mast, was generally hidden in the water; but when a stronger current than usual, or the act of rounding some point, caused the dripping rope to jump out of the water, and to shine and glance in the air, our joy knew no bounds, and we waited a long time for such a sight.

We stayed some time in Mayence, and also in Manheim, whence we went by land; and the change from the easy mode of travelling in a ship to that by a carriage was very disagreeable to us. After passing Rastatt we saw the huge Strasburg Minster in the distance, and rapidly approached the wonderful apparition, which grew larger and clearer every moment: the road made a turn, and what had hitherto appeared a dark mass suddenly became transparent — a magic network of delicate threads stood out in bold-relief against the sky, and was every where open to the flood of light. — No other is equal to this first impression of the Minster: it overpowers the senses while it quickens the imagination: it satisfies, yet it creates a feeling of impatience. The effect of this sight is so powerful, that it is impossible to recede: you are irresistibly drawn on, and all other objects fade before this one, which changes at every step, and keeps the whole attention fixed upon itself alone.

Every Strasburger naturally enough looks upon the Minster as the pride and ornament of his town, — a treasure and glory, of which the meanest inhabitant has his share. The sight of the enormous, open worked, but excessively strong wall which rises perpendicularly from the principal entrance up to the platform whence springs the tower; the glorious view from the platform over the town, and the green landscape watered by the silvery Rhine; the sight of the snake-like staircase which winds round the outside of the tower, gradually tapering, and then losing itself in the ball and cross, whither the eye scarcely dares to follow it — all this is so striking, that even the uncultured mind of a child cannot fail to appreciate it.

The women still wore the peculiar costume which Goethe so charmingly describes; but it was rapidly disappearing: during the course of the Revolution it became rarer, and then totally ceased to be worn. The picture of my mother as a bride represented her in a French dress, but with her hair plaited in the old burgher fashion, in long braids. But this mode of dressing the hair, and the short full petticoats, were now only to be found in the lowest classes, and in full perfection in the small country villages. This costume and the native dialect were much laughed at by the enlightened reformers of Strasburg: as even these scoffers could not always speak the purest German, they took refuge in French: in talking this language, however, the pitch of voice peculiar to the Upper Rhine, and to a portion of Switzerland, always betrayed their Alsatian descent.

Owing to the Revolution, the French tongue was rapidly gaining the upper hand. Up to this time all had felt the influence of their German origin, and endeavoured to keep up old habits and old customs. The language, the religion, the costume, the civil form of government, all were opposed to the catholicism and absolute power of the French court. But when notions of civil and religious liberty were brought from Paris, fear and dislike vanished, and were replaced by the most brilliant hopes. The Strasburgers unhesitatingly joined hands with those who preached freedom and civil liberty, and desired to make one people with these regenerated Franks. The feeble ties of old habits could not resist the new and stronger impulses.

It was impossible to walk a step in Strasburg without coming upon some trace of this altered feeling. The revolutionary movements in Paris had immediately found ready sympathy in Alsace, and the Strasburgers had gone all lengths: every where we heard the new watchwords of freedom spoken, and saw trees of liberty planted: the cockade was on every hat,— the tricolor on every public building:—even the women wore tricolor gowns; day and night nothing but patriotic songs were to be heard. The famous *ça ira* sounded in all directions: every little blackguard knew some of the words, and sang them at the very top of his voice. Praise of the patriots and destruction to the aristocrats were the two themes of this and many other popular ballads.

The feeling of civil liberty was best exhibited in the Strasburg national guards: every man capable of bearing arms was enrolled,—had arms and an uniform given him, and was regularly drilled: my father, like the rest, took the prescribed oath. This body of men made a better appearance than the troops of the line. The ease with which burghers may be converted into soldiers has always excited surprise, but never more than in the first days of the revolution. The storming of the Bastile, the occurrences in La Vendée, and at Saragossa, the Spanish guerillas, the Austrian and Prussian landwehr or militia, and, lastly, the Parisians in the three days of July, have since then sufficiently proved the innate strength of the masses: but at that time it was held absurd to imagine that a promiscuous rabble of tinkers and tailors, as they were called, could make any stand against regular soldiers. The Strasburgers knew that they were laughed at by those on the other side of the river, but they did not mind that: they persevered in their drilling, enforced strict discipline, and in a short time the national guard was thought quite sufficient for the protection of this important fortress. The citizens had raised a few troops of cavalry and a remarkably effective corps of artillery, which kept on the best terms with that belonging to the regular army. The royal artillery was distinguished here, as in the rest of France, for its zeal in the popular cause.

Enthusiasm had reached its height, and a golden age seemed at hand, for news had come from Paris that the King had accepted the constitution sent up to him from the National Assembly. This day, the 14th of September, 1791, was celebrated as a holyday all over France, and in no town was it better kept than in Strasburg. The cannon were fired at break of day, the troops of the line and the national guard were early in motion; there was no end to the marching and counter-marching of the separate divisions, with their bands of music. At length they all united on parade, and, after going through their several exercises, the muskets were fired into the air, and, amid loud shouts of " *Vive le roi, vive la nation!*" the troops fraternized with the people. Suddenly long rows of tables were spread, and all dined together. When this spectacle was at an end, all adjourned to the minster, to view the preparations made for the evening. The corporation had arranged all sorts of amusements for the people:—for the poor there were dinners at the public expense;—many distinguished and rich burghers dined in the open air, and invited the passers-by to join them. After dinner the crowd went out into the fields, sang patriotic songs, and danced. In the evening the whole town was illuminated, but nothing was comparable to the tower of the minster, which reared its gigantic structure towards heaven covered with thousands of lamps. People crowded close to it to see the glittering mass in detail, and then they went to a distance to enjoy a better view of the whole. Fireworks were discharged from the neighbouring villages, and bonfires were seen in the distant Vosges. Streams of people filled the streets all night. In the midst of the general joy, however, there were occasionally heard voices inciting the people to acts of violence. It was said that the houses of several aristocrats were not illuminated, and the people were exhorted to revenge this mark of contempt. On reaching these houses they were found to be lighted up, and their owners, instead of ill-treatment, received loud applause. Late at night, however, the mob broke a few of the mayor's windows, and burnt him in effigy as a devoted adherent to the king.

But in these joyous days no one could listen to such dark forebodings: on the contrary, the newly proclaimed constitution promised a succession of prosperous days: quiet and order seemed to gain ground in the interior, and the recently awakened spirit of freedom had little to fear from foreign foes. It was known that all foreign courts viewed the proceedings in France with anxiety, and that the Germanic empire made strong representations against the doings in Alsace, by which it thought that German interests were affected; that the Emperor had talked of a crusade against France, in which the King of Prussia, the Elector of Saxony, and other potentates,— even Catherine of Russia,— had promised to assist him. But the jealousy which these several powers felt of each other made this junction more than doubtful. The French emigrants, of whom there were many in the German frontier towns, especially at Coblentz, were the subject of more immediate alarm; but they were powerless without foreign assistance. These men were forming bodies of troops with which they intended to restore the old state of things in France. The highest aristocracy, the best generals and officers, those most distinguished about the Court for birth and rank, were there assembled, and the names of the royal Princes gave weight and dignity to their cause: it was impossible to say what relations they might have with Paris and the provinces.

But the blind fury which they vented upon every thing not on their side, the impossibility of coming to any terms with the nation, the inanity of all their previous plans, and their insane and hateful conduct, — all this caused them to be considered as enemies who could really create no serious alarm. They were laughed at, caricatured, and lampooned. The Strasburgers had one subject for ridicule close at hand. On the other side of the Rhine, in the Brisgau, the Viscomte de Mirabeau, the brother of the revolutionary hero, was busied with a free corps which he was drilling, with the intention of attacking and subjugating Alsace to the old régime. There were a certain number of old officers with him, but the rest were the merest rabble. The proximity of this enemy afforded the Strasburgers daily amusement: every one inquired, with malicious fun, about their numbers, and made excursions across the river, to Kehl, to see them at parade. Viscomte de Mirabeau was very fat; the urchins at Strasburg made a point, every evening, of burning or drowning an effigy, which they nicknamed Mirabeau-Tonneau.

My father was dissatisfied with the turn which affairs were taking, and thought that years would elapse before the troubled waters of the revolution would run clear: these years he determined to pass in some quiet spot. Impressed with these ideas, he refused a very good appointment on the medical staff of the army, and made his preparations for returning to Germany.

My mother felt very differently. She was in her native town, among her own relations, and with her old father, whose death could not be very far distant. She therefore wished to remain in Strasburg, at any rate till it could be settled what our future life was to be. I know not what took place between my parents, but it was arranged that I was to travel with my father, while my sister was to remain with my mother at Strasburg. The last week was passed in the midst of tears and tenderness: at length the day of departure came, and, torn almost fainting from my mother and sister, I found myself by my father's side in the carriage which was carrying us rapidly out of the town on our way to Landau, where, however, we did not remain longer than was required to prepare for our further journey. This strongly fortified town, which was looked upon as the bulwark of France on that frontier, was filled with troops of the line, with whom the national guard vigorously co-operated: the citizens and the authorities were full of zeal for liberty and war. The people crowded round our carriage. "These traitors," said they, "should not be allowed to go over to the enemy's camp. Only aristocrats could wish to fly from the land of freedom." The postmaster refused to give us fresh horses without a special order, the mayor did not choose to be troubled, and it was with some difficulty that we obtained the necessary passports from the commandant; we were then allowed to proceed.

We reached Neustadt and then Manheim without further impediment. Here every thing was in greater excitement than before. The French emigrants, more numerous than ever, were in high favour with the upper classes, and fanned the flame of hatred against revolutionary France. Nevertheless they made themselves disliked, and many people regretted having received them into their houses as guests. They, however, had considerable political influence: it seemed certain that they would shortly become masters of France. It was not to be expected that the French nation, deprived of its leading men, of its aristocracy and best officers, could resist the united arms of Austria, Prussia, and the French princes. The expedition against France, and the destruction of the revolutionary party, were looked upon as certain. My father thought otherwise. He held the revolution to be firmly established, and its principles recognized, and he thought the national guard far more formidable than the troops who were advancing to attack them. No one, however, dared to utter such opinions; the contrary only were listened to.

We took ship and sailed down the Rhine. The company on board was mixed, and divided into the same factions which were shaking the world to its centre. Several emigrants talked very big: no one was disposed to contradict them, although their violent language was most disagreeable to others. On a sudden one of them perceived on my coat a ribbon, which he recognized as a tricolor. He stared at it as if he could not believe his eyes, then summoned his fellow travellers, and uttered a torrent of words which I could not understand, but which I clearly saw annoyed my father. He was equally voluble; but what was one against so many? They decided that we were concealed revolutionists, and should not be allowed to proceed further: they therefore ordered the sailors to put us ashore. As these showed no inclination to obey their commands, and the emigrants persevered in their noise, the scene suddenly changed. The rest of the company — Germans from the Palatinate, from Worms and Mayence, who had been until now quiet spectators of the scene, — instantly took our part, and declared that if the Frenchmen did not hold their tongues, they themselves should be thrown into the river, a threat which the sailors expressed their readiness to carry into execution. The French were compelled to be silent, for they saw that the deed would soon follow the threat, and the eddies of the Rhine were curling under the boat. The Germans were perfectly contented with having reduced the emigrants to silence; and the matter was soon forgotten. Some of the men were very kind to me, and a charming lady quietly cut off the fatal ribbon and gave it laughing to my father, telling him that he might, if he liked it, wear and defend it himself, but that he should leave his child neutral. He quite agreed with her: he was averse to any thing that might give offence to others, but had not himself observed this objectionable ribbon, which the tailor sewed on being the first that came to hand. I was glad to get rid of it, for the furious looks of the emigrants frightened me, and I was somewhat alarmed for my father.

The emigrants were the first to leave the ship at Mayence, and we saw no more of them: we stopped for two hours, changed boats, and went down the river with a totally different company. The people of Mayence had a much stronger dislike to the emigrants than those of Manheim, and we heard them spoken of on our way to Coblentz with perfect hatred. Hundreds of stories were told of their pride, their extravagance, their violence, and their laughable vanity. Coblentz was overrun with them: they had there established their headquarters, and played the part of lords and masters. The Elector of Treves, who had received them into his territory, had not a word to say in the matter: his magistrates were treated with contempt by these strangers, his troops supplanted; French courts of law were established, before which Germans were forcibly dragged whenever the French had any complaint to make against them. All civil order was at an end; men's homes were invaded; young nobles quartered themselves wherever a pretty woman struck their fancy: their gallantry took the coarsest form, and the grossest immorality prevailed. The inhabitants complained to the Elector; and when he expressed his inability to assist them in their necessities, they asked his permission to drive the foreigners out of their country: he begged them, for God's sake, to have a little patience. This was a terrible predicament for any German prince; and one not likely to make him respected by his own people. The only hope was, that war would soon break out, whereupon their troublesome guests would be forced to pass the frontier. The emigrants themselves looked upon the triumphant march into France as so certain, the acquisition of power and wealth as so infallible, that they did not think of husbanding their resources: on the contrary, they threw away their money in the most reckless manner, as if they wanted to be rid of it, so as to have more room for what they were so sure to obtain. I saw gold pieces, which had been used as marks for pistol shooting, thrown among the people to be scrambled for. A peasant girl, who was selling flowers, had gold showered into her hands, because she was pretty. The most luxurious feasts took place: it was an amusement to make every one, even the school-boys, drunk; and to send them reeling to their homes. But nothing excited greater disgust than the contempt with which the emigrants treated the rye bread: they took out the crumb, and kneaded it into pellets, with which they pelted passers-by or broke windows: they hollowed out the crusts, which the young viscounts or abbés put upon their feet, and danced about in the streets amidst loud laughter, until the bread was broken by the stones and lost in the mud. The manner in which they treated God's gift was the one sin which the Germans would least forgive, and upon which they called down the vengeance of the Lord: and, whenever they could, they laid violent hands on the offenders. If any emigrants were thrown into the water, or otherwise maltreated, it was more owing to the rye bread than to any thing else. The effect produced on the minds of the people by the conduct of the emigrants along the whole course of the Rhine should not be overlooked in the consideration of subsequent events: it was one reason why the revolutionary armies were so well received when they entered these countries.

CHAPTER II.

Return to Düsseldorf. — War with Republican France. — The Emigrants on the Rhine. — Execution of Louis XVI., and the Impression it produced. — Lutheran School at Düsseldorf. — Journey to Hamburg. 1792—1794.

ANOTHER year was now past, which had brought with it many changes; the success of the French had been such as to silence the menaces of the opponents of liberal ideas, and to inspire others with greater courage. My father's friends the liberals, who were numerous and active, unanimously called upon him to join their ranks once more. He learned that the authorities would not oppose his return, — the chancellor, Count Nesselrode, told him that he might come back with perfect security, as all Germans who had entered France carried away by revolutionary doctrines had been invited to return, that their past offences would be forgotten, and every protection afforded them in their native land.

The war against the French still continued, always to the disadvantage of the Germans; party zeal for and against the revolution manifested itself more and more strongly the nearer the war approached Düsseldorf. The opponents of the revolution had on their side the advantage of the power in the hands of government; but the majority of the people was inclined to the French, at any rate to their opinions, and the victories and progress of the French were considered as a triumph. The time did not seem far distant when the arms of freedom would reach us, and old established forms be broken up. Every fresh piece of intelligence in favour of the French brightened our countenances, while dismay and confusion were depicted in those of the upper classes, of the officials, and the clergy. The people with whom we lodged merely cared about their own peculiar gains: they declaimed against the times, but made the best use of them. They obtained from emigrants and refugees many articles of value, besides money, in payment for lodging. Until now there had not been many emigrants in Düsseldorf; but on a sudden, owing to an advance of the French troops, a whole horde of them passed the Rhine and stopped in Düsseldorf, where they hoped to find safety. The town was filled with them to overflowing, — they went in large bodies through the streets and market-places, and French seemed to be the only language spoken. Our landlady took this opportunity of letting every hole and corner at six times the value.

Although I looked upon the emigrants as enemies, I could not help being attracted towards them. With joyous vivacity they quickly supplied my broken phrases with the words which were wanting, and declared me a perfect French scholar. Great lovers of society, they soon made themselves at home every where, especially with pretty women and girls, even without a knowledge of their language. Cruelly disappointed hopes and pressing necessities had subdued the overweening pride which had given such offence at Coblentz : they were now remarkable for gentleness, courtesy, and good-humoured drollery. Their society afforded me incessant diversion, and I learned not only their language, but their manners; I saw arms and accoutrements of all sorts, court dresses, hunting costumes, watches, time-pieces, crosses, and rings, most of which were sold for a quarter their value. I beheld, with astonishment, fine gentlemen cooking their dinners and making their beds with a zeal and care which no other person could hope to equal.

The news of Louis XVI.'s execution made a deep impression on all men : the emigrants were horror-stricken, and wild with passion. I saw some tear their hair, scratch their faces, and call down execrations on the murderers, and on the whole nation, as accomplice in the murder. Others laughed convulsively, uttered loud shouts, and were ready at once to rush to the young King's rescue. There were, however, some zealots who rejoiced at the event, saying that Louis deserved his fate for having been one of the chief causes of the misery of France : it was he who had fostered the revolution by concessions, and betrayed the crown and the aristocracy. Now all would be well : neither the young princes nor the allies would now be restrained by false ideas of leniency.

While some of them kissed the portrait of their King with tears in their eyes, others flung it to the earth and trampled upon it: all this in the same family — in the same room! The horror inspired among Germans by the spectacle of a King publicly executed was no less strong than among the French: my father especially lamented the unfortunate Louis. The party of the emigrants was now distinct from that of the King, and many said that he had fallen a sacrifice to their mad designs.

The dangers of war had disappeared, but we now felt its effects. There was a general complaint of the dearness of every thing, of heavy taxation, and of stagnation of trade. A division of the Elector's troops left Düsseldorf to join the imperial army; we regretted this, and wondered why the emigrants had not been sent against the enemy. After all, it was their cause for which we were fighting, and it was upon their false representations that the war had been undertaken. They were to be seen daily in the market-place sauntering up and down, taking up the whole length and breadth of the pavement, and pushing aside children, maid-servants, and others who wished to walk there. This was speedily put down by the townspeople; several emigrants were severely beaten, and many were threatened with a ducking in the Rhine, after which they behaved somewhat more prudently. But their unpopularity daily increased. Most of them had exhausted all their resources, lived in a retired manner, or were much in debt: some endeavoured to gain their livelihood as they best could. The authorities sent many out of the town, and others were ordered to cross the frontier, for disturbing the peace of families. All this tended to promote the spread of liberal views, and Pichegru was now as much in favour as Lafayette and Dumouriez had been, and his name was toasted at public dinners associated with the freedom of France. It was in vain that the higher orders and the officials opposed this by all the means in their power; public opinion was too strong, and too well supported by circumstances, to be so easily put down.

Political circumstances forced my father to quit Düsseldorf, and it was not without deep emotion, and accompanied by numerous friends, that, leading me by the hand, he crossed by the flying bridge to the other side of the Rhine. We were now in the dominions of the Elector of Cologne, and found a carriage ready to convey us to Neuss, where we were received by our friends with open arms. The opinions for which my father had been exposed to the hatred and persecution of those high in office, were here so honoured and loved, that we experienced nothing but kindness and sympathy. To be treated in this manner, and to be praised and made much of by all parties, seemed to me no bad fate; and I thought that if this were banishment, there was not so much in it to complain of after all.

One of the chief causes of anxiety to my father now was, in whose charge he should place me: my education was interrupted; he wished it continued, and did not like me to be exposed to all the accidents of his uncertain life. Two elderly women of good family offered to take me in, promising to treat me well, and to take care that my education should be the best that the town of Düsseldorf could afford. They were Lutherans, and intended to send me to the Lutheran school, which was highly praised, and with justice. My father determined to try this plan.

When I heard that I was to be separated from him I thought I should have died. I was already separated from my mother and sister — I scarce ever heard of their existence, and now I was never to see my father again. I was to be sent to the one place which he could never visit. I clung to him, and asked in my grief whether he no longer loved me? His tenderness appeased me, and his arguments silenced my objections. We parted, and I thought it a hardship of which I did not dare to accuse my father, but I accused some dark powers, for the word fate was not yet in my vocabulary.

Every thing was admirably arranged for me in Düsseldorf: the two ladies were most kind, and the servants attentive: the house was clean and agreeable, the rooms tastefully furnished. I had a separate apartment: my desk was most temptingly laid out with all the pretty nick-nacks of a lady's writing-table. Moreover, many visitors came to the house, and I was frequently taken to the play — in short, every thing seemed perfection. I honestly expressed my gratitude, but still something was wanting: I longed for my father, — for his love, — for the open air in the pleasant garden at Herdt, between Neuss and Düsseldorf.

But I found relief from that which was expected most to annoy me — going to school. Here were life, activity, and such pleasures as I wished for and wanted. The Lutheran community at Düsseldorf had always had their rights secured to them, but being a weak minority, had, with tact and discrimination, endeavoured to maintain their position against Catholic influences by means of the admirable manner in which they conducted their church discipline and managed their schools. No sooner had I entered the school than I felt perfectly at home; my schoolfellows were my dear companions, the teacher commanded my attention, and I learned easily and willingly under his guidance: the histories we read, the poems we wrote out, the elements of natural history, geography, and arithmetic, — all pleased me. The school inspector Hartmann gave us religious instruction, and I listened with pleasure to his lectures, although they contained much that I did not quite understand. I attended his sermons on Sundays, and the Lutheran service made the most agreeable impression upon me. The preacher's animation and sympathy with his fellow-creatures — expressed moreover in German — strongly contrasted with the impression of strangeness and awe with which the celebration of mass in Latin, and the pomps and ceremonies of the Catholic church had filled me. Besides, I was pleased with the idea of being brought nearer my mother and sister by this connection with the Lutheran church, and I pictured to myself in vivid colours their wonder and joy.

People soon observed the change in me. My father's opponents found new grounds to accuse the religious principles of one who could invite his child to renounce his faith, who could deliver to eternal damnation — to the instruction of heretics — the soul of one who, by birth and baptism, belonged to the Catholic church. They were vehement in their abuse of Hartmann and those who lent a hand to such a proceeding, nay, forwarded it to the utmost in their power. This was constantly the subject of conversation between my two protectresses and those who visited them. Occasionally the Catholics took my father's part, on the plea that doctrinal differences were of small importance, that the moral views were the same in both religions, that Protestants had the advantage of a purer and simpler faith, and that any enlightened Catholic could listen to Hartmann's sermons with edification. They thought my father perfectly right in not allowing a few Lutheran prayers and psalms to interfere with his sending his son to the best school in the town: I might still remain a Catholic. I was delighted to hear this, for the idea of conversion was odious to me from what I had heard my father say; and something within me whispered that one might throw off the old fetters without submitting to new ones.

The ease with which I learnt, and the zeal with which I went to school, turned out to my disadvantage. At the end of a few weeks it was found out that I was fit for better things, and I was promoted from the lower or German, to the upper or Latin school. This was honourable enough, but the consequences of the change were by no means agreeable. The head master of the Latin school, Rector Reiz, was a learned man, but rough in his manners. He did nothing to render the change easy. I sat the youngest boy in the school, on the lowest bench, with the strange books open before me, and while the master explained the lessons to the older boys — on the upper benches were boys from sixteen to eighteen, — I conned over my task: when I asked the boy next me to explain some difficulty, he made me signs to hold my tongue, while the master, who had perceived this, said, sarcastically, that he saw I wanted to make acquaintance with a couple of canes to which he pointed, and which were lying near him! All further desire of learning vanished.

I wholly lost my spirits. In agony lest I should not know my lessons, I repeated them incessantly, but as they were beyond my comprehension, it seldom happened that I knew them by heart, and when I did, the stern face of the rector put them entirely out of my head. I now had no time for amusement or recreation: the distress of learning took up every moment of my time, and as my two protectresses understood nothing of all this, and did not doubt of my abilities, they naturally attributed to perversity and folly, that, whereas I could formerly learn every thing, I now did nothing. They, therefore, held it to be their duty to show me, by their displeasure, what they thought of my conduct.

How often did I look back with regret to the short but happy time which I passed in the German school! There every thing went well; the day was properly divided between study and recreation, and both in moderation. I was praised — at any rate, not scolded — I saw others contented, and was so myself. With still greater regret did I look back upon those days which I passed by my father's side: these, however, seemed too far distant ever to recur.

My father had insisted, to the great annoyance of my two protectresses, that I should be allowed to pay him a few visits. The first time he found me looking well, happy, and talking in high terms of the German school. What I told him of my life perfectly satisfied him. The zeal which was shown in converting me to Protestantism made him shake his head, but every thing else was so satisfactory that he thought little of this. But the second time that I visited him after an interval of a fortnight, every thing was changed: I was pale, thin, and melancholy, and my short answers provoked fresh inquiries. This was when I was in the Latin school, and subject to all sorts of miseries. His face darkened as he listened, and I at last confessed with a flood of tears that I was thoroughly wretched. We sauntered up and down the banks of the Rhine until the hour came for my return home. My father let me go, but desired me to take leave of my two protectresses, and to join him on the following day: in future I was to remain with him. They suspected what was coming, as they knew that my father had to take a long journey, and would not leave me behind. They were kind in their manner to me, and exhorted me to cherish my Lutheran inclinations.

I was now happy beyond measure by my father's side. Throughout all the vicissitudes of my life, in all trials, and under all circumstances, he alone was my fast support. Under his guidance, I readily devoted a couple of hours a day to study; the rest of the time was passed in happy idleness, which, however, was not without its fruits.

My father's friends visited him daily from Düsseldorf, and many were the discussions as to his future plans. It was agreed on all sides that Hamburg alone offered every thing that he could desire; there he would find free German institutions, and complete exemption from the bickerings and quarrels of the narrow society in which he had lately lived. Our preparations were soon made; and after stopping at Driesberg, we pursued our journey to Munster, thence to Osnabruck and Nieuburg, where we staid a few days, and continued our journey without further adventure to Haarburg on the Elbe.

CHAPTER III.

Hamburg.— Klopstock. — The Emigrants in Hamburg.— The Expedition to Quiberon. — Bookstall in Hamburg. — The "Turkish Spy."— Lafayette in Hamburg.— Death of my Father.— Berlin Medical Academy.— Chamisso. — Fichte. — Louis Goldsmith. — Rahel Levin. — Poetical Club. — War between France and Austria. — Peace with Prussia. 1794—1806.

FROM Haarburg we sailed with a favourable wind among the green islands of the Elbe, and soon had a forest of masts with Hamburg in the distance before our eyes. We gradually worked our way through large and smaller vessels, and landed safely at the Baumhaus, where we were met by crowds of busy men and curious idlers. They took us for French emigrants, looked at us sullenly, and threw all sorts of impediments in our way. But my father soon convinced them of their error, and we were shortly on our way to one of the hotels on the Buten Quay. My father and the driver of the cart which conveyed us and our luggage became excellent friends; the latter made excuses for his mistake. I perceived that the emigrants were disliked by the common people as much here as elsewhere.

The most brilliant star in the intellectual world of Hamburg was Klopstock. He lived a very retired life, seeing only a few old friends. I was shown his house in the Königstrasse, and he himself was pointed out to me as he was going out for a walk. He had a dignified, almost solemn air, but seemed shy and suffering: his features were not good; they might almost be called ugly—were it not for a certain noble expression. As he walked quietly through the streets all who recognised him took off their caps. The people of Hamburg treated those who were any way remarkable with the most genuine respect.

Most of the distinguished men in Hamburg were more or less inclined to the French Revolution; they abhorred the cruelties which were practised, but held the principles on which the movement was founded. Wealth visibly increased, and it naturally followed that no one was averse to a party from which so much advantage was derived. But even this was scarcely sufficient to account for the evident sympathy which not alone the middle, but the lower classes showed for the French liberals. All seemed to feel that this party in France was essentially that of the middle class, while the other was wholly devoted to the cause of royalty: a sentiment of comprehensive German nationality was not yet dreamt of.

The French emigrants did much to assist this view of the case. No longer tolerated in many countries whither they had fled, they had come in great numbers to Hamburg as a last refuge, whence the sea offered them escape, if necessary. Some among them were doubtless distinguished and honourable men, but the majority were a wretched crew, intolerable from their vanity and boasting. These garrulous idlers speedily became objects of intense hatred to the plain honest Hamburgers, who, on the other hand, felt a great interest for the republicans, some of whom they had seen in Hamburg in diplomatic or commercial capacities, and whom they had learned to respect.

It struck me, however, as strange that my father, who was zealously devoted to liberal views, for which, moreover, he had endured persecution and banishment, did not attach himself to the party in power; he had no connexion with the republican French, — on the contrary, whether by accident or design, he lived much more with the hated emigrants. He liked the cultivated minds and good manners of the French aristocracy. He thought that a true friend of the people ought to endeavour to raise the standard of the lower classes, and not to descend to their roughness and ignorance: whoever did this he looked on as a mere vulgar agitator.

But my father was not so dazzled by fame or by brilliant talents as to prefer these to more solid qualities. What he best liked was the honest, hard-working, middle class, among whom sufficient cultivation of mind is to be found, and whose straightforward sense and good humour teach them the simplest and easiest way of making life agreeable to themselves and others.

It was impossible to find better specimens of honourable upright men than some of the higher artisans and tradespeople of Hamburg,— a most important and numerous class. Many of the richest merchants sprung from this class, and still belonged to it, as far as their thoughts, manners, and customs were concerned.

The unfortunate emigrants were shipped off in crowds to England to take part in the attack on the coast of Brittany, for which great preparations were being made. They said that their leaders had merely to step on the French shore, and that thousands would flock to the royal standard: they blamed the English government for their delay in sending ships and arms: they wanted nothing else. My father tried to dissuade some of them from going, but they would not listen to him, and hurried off so as not to be too late for the honours and advantages which they were afraid others would obtain before them. With these vain hopes they sailed for England, whence they went to Quiberon. At the end of June the landing was effected; by the end of July the whole thing was at an end. One portion fell in battle, a greater number were taken prisoners and shot. But a short time before this we had seen these same men full of zeal and confidence,—we knew many by name and some of them intimately, — and in a few weeks the newspapers were full of their failure, their death-struggle, and their execution.

We lived close by the churchyard of St. Nicholas; there was a side door into the church, which was shut on week days; but a space was left open in which the laudable eagerness of a Hamburger to turn every vacant space to account had caused a circulating library to be established—this was winked at for a trifling consideration by the sexton. Here I found all that my heart panted for — tales of knight errantry, ghost stories, romances, love adventures, and wondrous tales of all sorts. I had plenty of books at home which I read with pleasure, but none like these. I could not resist the temptation, and procured myself the coveted and forbidden pleasure. Although my father had not expressly said so, I knew that he would not approve such reading. I therefore read in secret with all the eagerness of youth, and revelled in the world of fancy which was open to me. If I broke off in the middle of a story I was miserable when I could not procure the second part. For many years the titles of those romances which I had been unable to finish dwelt in my memory. The worst was that I could not afterwards procure them, as circulating libraries of higher pretensions had a better selection of books. It was not till twenty years later, in Bohemia, where such rubbish still existed, that I could obtain the sequel of a romance, the beginning of which I had never forgotten, and I did not deny myself this pleasure. Hence I learnt the magic power which fancy exercises, how it changes the meanest thing into gold; mine had drawn nourishment from the most wretched materials; truly it is a good proverb, that a black cow will give white milk. — I cannot say that this empty reading, which ended in three months, when it was discovered, did me any harm. I did not perceive what was bad, and, contrary to Tischbein's ass, which ate pine-apple, thinking it was thistle, I ate thistles, and believed them to be pines. I agree entirely with Rousseau, that whoever can be spoilt by bad books is already corrupt. I was equally diligent at my lessons; indeed every thing went easily, as I always had a pleasure in store; besides, conscious of deserving blame, I did not wish to heap up other causes of complaint against myself. Among other books which fell into my hands was "The Turkish Spy," a book which was most popular in its day. It gives a vivid account of the times of Louis XIII. and XIV., as if written by a Turkish spy then living in Paris. The author, Marana, is less famous than his book: though he possesses neither critical skill nor the art of presenting his subject dramatically, he has this great merit,—like his contemporary Gregorio Leti—of having brought a mass of historical matter in a readable form before the public. The form he has chosen allows him to place the customs of the East in strong contrast with those of Europe, and treating the events as if they were contemporaneous gives them a certain interest: moreover, the author has the art of weaving the occurrences closely into his fiction. The Turkish Spy speedily became a favourite, and I read his despatches with great eagerness.

My mother and sister reached Hamburg in the spring of 1796. When I went to the Baumhaus to meet them, my heart beat so thick that I was obliged to stand without speaking a word. My father was already there, and I embraced him and the new comers by turns. The lapse of many years had not estranged us, and after the first quarter of an hour we were as intimate as if we had never parted.

In 1797 an event occurred which had long been hoped for in Europe and America, namely, the release of General Lafayette from his prison at Olmutz. His arrival created the greatest commotion in Hamburg, where he had enthusiastic admirers, who loved him not only for his political opinions, but for his sufferings and his virtues. My father and I waited at the Baumhaus to see him get out of his carriage with his two daughters: his companions in captivity, Bureau de Puzy and La-Tour-Maubourg, followed him. At every step he had to receive fresh embraces, and he blessed the land of freedom which now welcomed him: to this place he had been accompanied by an Austrian officer.

My father was now busily employed: his position daily improved, and promised ultimate wealth. His zeal won for him the confidence of the poor, and he had to make exertions beyond his strength. Hitherto he had always had excellent health, but he now sickened with a liver complaint. He was his own physician, and believed his complaint to be mortal.

During his long illness, we perceived with astonishment a great change in him. It had struck us, even before he left us, to try the effect of the waters of Schwalbach, that his views with regard to France had been much modified,—that he cared less for their victories, and blamed their political and military proceedings. This change of opinion had become much more pronounced. The demands made by France on Germany at the Congress of Rastatt, the doings in Switzerland and Italy, nay, Bonaparte's expedition to Egypt, excited his bitter animadversion. But still more remarkable was another change in him: he had before made me read to him the Psalms in Latin, St. Augustin, and Boethius; but with illness his love for such books increased, and he now read Thomas à Kempis and Hermann Hugo's *Pia Desideria*. The latter book, composed by a Jesuit, struck me as childish in thought and tone, and I was surprised to see my father condescend to read it. But his earliest associations were bound up with this book: he had forgotten it until it was now suddenly presented to him. All the pictures of his youth, all the delightful and pure sensations of early piety were recalled by these pages: a strong-minded man may well be allowed to give way to such sweet impressions. He drew consolation from Protestant as well as from Catholic sources; and I frequently saw Wankel's *Precationes Piæ* in his hands: the only thing he required was, that the books should be in Latin.

A change of lodging somewhat fatigued my father; he visibly declined in strength, and during the night of the 5th of June he felt suddenly worse, summoned us to his bed-side, and expired without a word. He died in his forty-third year. He was buried according to the Protestant form, and on his tomb were engraved the words "Vir probus et sapiens."

In the year 1800 I entered the medical college at Berlin, where I spent two years and a half in unbroken study — even the holydays were no loss of time. But a circumstance occurred which put an end to the good understanding between me and the principal. I was subjected to an arrest for some trifling cause: after a few days I was released, but told to leave the college.

Before I could select some new profession I was taken ill: the excitement had been too much for my strength. The illness took the form of a nervous fever; after some days, during which I had death constantly before me, I gradually recovered.

During my recovery, my friends and acquaintances were busy in my service: from all sides I received offers of assistance, and, instead of wanting every thing after such a catastrophe, I found myself with all that I could desire. My friends exhorted me not to over-exert myself, and endeavoured to discover some mode of life which would offer me quiet and moderate occupation. They asked me if I had any objection to become a tutor, for a time, — not to select this as a profession: they described to me a rich family with two boys of six and seven years of age, the parents well-informed, the society agreeable, where music and foreign languages were to be heard — in short, just what would be useful to me, — an agreeable life and sufficient occupation. The scheme pleased me, and I paid my visit of introduction. I was still weak, and leant on a friend's arm. I was conducted into a library which looked on the garden: the books were every thing I could wish — German, French, and English. After a few minutes the master of the house entered. The house, the society, the scheme of life, all seemed most inviting: my letters of introduction were good; my youth, and my recent recovery from illness, inspired sympathy, and the agreement was soon made. After a few days I became an inmate of the house, and I began a happy period of my life, removed from care and anxiety.

It is very seldom that time passes so agreeably as mine did from the month of May till far into the summer; I entered into all the pleasures of life with the energy and zest of youth. My occupations were just sufficient to make me enjoy my hours of freedom: my duties did not lower me in my own estimation; and I had, for the first time in my life, a feeling of individual existence. No one measured with a foot rule what I did, thought, or wished: no one interfered with my objects or views. The qualities which I possessed had hitherto been repressed and guided by others; I was now free to exert them as I pleased. This feeling, which arose partly from the change in my position, was much increased by other fortunate accidents, such as do not often occur together.

I must first mention my dwelling-place, which could not be more agreeable. The house itself — large and roomy — provided with every thing which could insure comfort, was built between a court and a spacious garden: all the best rooms of the house looked out upon the garden: shady walks, mown lawns, high trees and shrubberies, flowers and fruit trees gave the place great diversity, and this green and blooming spot afforded daily and hourly opportunities for the purest enjoyment.

At this time I made acquaintance with a Prussian officer at Charlottenburg. M. de Chamisso * had left France at the breaking out of the French revolution when quite a lad, and had come to Berlin as an emigrant. He was first one of the

---

* The author of "Peter Schlemil, the Shadowless Man."

widowed Queen's pages, and then joined Götz's regiment, while his parents, like many other emigrants to whom it was permitted, eagerly returned to France. Chamisso could not conceal his nation: his language, manners, and ideas betrayed his origin. There was withal something strange in his ways: all sorts of things annoyed him: his long legs and tight uniform, his hat, sword, and pigtail, stick and gloves, were constant sources of indignation, but, above all, he was incessantly struggling with the German language, which he mastered with great difficulty. He had composed German elegies and songs, and had begun a Faust in iambics, and I listened with wonder and admiration to the passages which he recited to me with his strange pronunciation, in a doorway, where he stood impeding people's entrance into the room. I immediately spread abroad a report of this new poet, who was, moreover, the best fellow in the world, and became my most intimate friend. German literature was the object of his deepest veneration, and we worked very much together: we interchanged our views and opinions, and discussed our favourite authors. I began less to admire Klopstock, Voss, and Wieland, but Schiller rose daily in our estimation, and Goethe above all, whose writings, especially "Wilhelm Meister," were our chief study. We took every opportunity of being together, — the most indifferent visit — every walk and occupation — afforded us an opportunity for improvement.

I was also introduced to Fichte, whose high intellect and character I looked on with profound reverence. In him I beheld a wise man, whose actions corresponded with his words and doctrines, whose thoughts and character were equally pure. He willingly gave to us, who needed it so much, his instructive advice, entered into my pursuits, recommended me strongly to study Classical antiquity, told me that I must learn to know the history of Rome and of Greece thoroughly, pointed out the means of acquiring such knowledge, urged me to lead a strict and diligent life, and advised me as yet to have nothing to do with purely philosophical studies. I thought him almost a divinity while he spoke thus to me; sincerity beamed in his eyes, while kindness dictated his expressions. Although neither opportunity nor my own wishes allowed me strictly to follow his advice, still it had a great effect upon me, and I constantly had recourse to Fichte in my difficulties. Chamisso and my other friends were no less influenced by their intercourse with him: he was the star whose light guided us through all the mists and dangers of life, and to which we looked with confidence for strength to pursue what was true and good.

To turn to far different matters — an English Jew, Lewis Goldsmith, notorious first as the writer of certain political pamphlets, then as the editor of the Argus, an English newspaper published at Paris, and afterwards as the author of a scandalous libel against the court at St. Cloud, came during the summer of 1803 to Berlin, and was received as an old acquaintance in our house. He seemed to be well provided with money, and to enjoy all the comforts of life: he could relate many remarkable stories of political men and passing events, and declared himself vehemently for the First Consul, less apparently from conviction than from boastfulness and self-interest: for he did not conceal the fact that he had staked his fortune on Napoleon, and still less that his happiness consisted in living at his ease. His conversation was animated, but offensive and malignant: much as this displeased us, it amused the master of the house, upon whom the bold confident tone of the fellow had as much effect as the mission on which he was sent, and which he did not conceal from an old acquaintance. Goldsmith was on his way to Warsaw, with full powers to treat secretly with the pretender to the French crown, afterwards Louis XVIII., and to endeavour to prevail upon him to renounce his claim to the throne in consideration of a large sum of money which Napoleon offered to pay. This was told to me shortly after Goldsmith's departure, with the idea that my opinion of the man would be much raised thereby. In fact, the mission was important, and gave an early insight into the then carefully concealed projects of the First Consul: all this, however, was afterwards denied. Goldsmith came back from Warsaw after a while, but made no stay in Berlin; his haste proved that he had failed in his negotiation, as indeed he himself confessed. I was then perfectly indifferent to political matters: a poem had far greater charms for me than the whole state of Europe, and an affair of the heart than all battles and treaties put together.

Here I must mention one person who made a first impression on me at this time. One evening, while I was reading some extracts from Wieland to those assembled round the tea-table, a visitor was announced, whose name caused a commotion, in which surprise and pleasure had an equal part. This was Rahel Levin, or Robert, for she once bore the latter name. I had frequently heard her mentioned in various quarters, and always in such terms that I was prepared to see a most extraordinary person. What I had heard from others had led me to expect an union of intellect and simplicity of nature in its purest and most original form. The blame which I had heard cast upon her frequently redounded to her credit. There was much talk of some passion which, according to common report, far surpassed in vehemence and misfortune any thing that had ever been sung by poets. To the amusement of the company, I watched with nervous impatience for her appearance. A light, graceful figure, small, but vigorous, with delicate well rounded limbs, entered the room: the hands and feet were peculiarly small. The forehead, shaded by a profusion of black hair, announced intellectual superiority; the quick determined glances left one in doubt whether they were more disposed to receive impressions or to communicate them, and a settled expression of melancholy added a charm to her clear and open countenance. She moved in her dark-coloured dress almost like a shadow, and her greeting was easy and kind. But what most struck me was the rich soft voice which seemed to come from her inmost soul, and the most extraordinary conversation that I ever heard. Simplicity and wit, quickness and the charm of softness, were blended in the easy, unassuming manner in which she expressed the most original thoughts and fancies, all based upon such deep truth that few found any thing in what she uttered that they could gainsay. Her generous warmth and goodness rendered her presence welcome even to the most commonplace people. The whole visit lasted but a short time, and I could remember no particular word or phrase worth repeating; but I deeply felt the general impression she had produced, and was so full of it that after she had left the room, I could talk and think of nothing else. I did not see Rahel Levin for many years, but her name remained like a talisman impressed on my soul. I little thought that this first meeting would be followed by many others, and that the most important event and the most lasting engagement of my life would be bound up with hers.

Chamisso introduced me to the poets of the Musen Almanach, none of whom I knew. I saw Hitzig, Robert, and Theremin, who appeared to me a very superior man, and who captivated me by his rich noble language. As we all had our several occupations during the day, we settled to meet in the evening. These poetical tea-parties, at which literature and poetry formed the chief subject of conversation, were first given by Hitzig, whose rooms were the largest, and whose agreeable and social qualities rendered them the pleasantest place of union: we here enjoyed pure pleasures, after the various occupations of the day. The subsequent tea-parties given by Theremin and Robert lost the charm of simplicity; there was more pretension, and other objects came into play: our society likewise increased. A clever good-humoured companion of Hitzig, Adolph von Uthmann, and Chamisso's fellow-countryman, a certain Count de Lafoye, made no change in our habits. But our evenings became more noisy and distracted by the introduction of Koreff, a young physician from Breslau, who was practising his studies at Berlin, and who was inexhaustible in fun and humour. At the same time George Reimer, and several other real or pretended lovers of poetry, joined our parties, which now were more sumptuous. Eventually, however, they again became more modest as the society got smaller: Koreff's tone grew more earnest as our intimacy increased. We occasionally sat with Chamisso when he was on duty at the Potsdam or Brandenberg gate, and, amid various military interludes, passed whole nights discussing poetry, our plans of study and of life, the execution of which was, alas! far distant.

Meanwhile a violent war raged in the south of Germany between France and Austria; even in Hamburg, whither I had now gone, there were warlike preparations, and every one was waiting to see what Prussia would do. There I heard that Chamisso's regiment had received orders to be ready to march on a particular day: we could see our friend if we started immediately. To reckon up the time, pack up a few things, and get into the diligence was the work of a few minutes — we saw Chamisso, and found his rooms already nearly full — one lay on a sofa, another passed the night on a cushion, in a corner of the room. During the day not a soul was to be found in his apartments, but at night we assembled like owls. The march was delayed, and we spent several weeks in Berlin with Chamisso very happily.

The slow process of arming was now nearly completed, the troops were rapidly assembling, and Chamisso was aware that at any moment his regiment might be ordered to leave Berlin. We had not attained that true zeal which could employ itself all day exclusively on political matters: the incessant discussions on war and the state wearied us, and we in vain endeavoured to return to the old habits and subjects of conversation which we had before enjoyed at Berlin. Chamisso was soon to leave us: his studies must be given up, and poetry neglected. However, the marching of the troops was delayed, and, as we could remain at Berlin no longer to the neglect of our own studies, we returned to Hamburg and set to work again with renewed diligence.

We had been in Hamburg but a short time, when the long-expected march of the troops from Berlin took place, and an animated correspondence with Chamisso fixed our attention more and more upon the movements of the troops and the events of the war. Napoleon's victories alarmed us, but we could not then wish success to his opponents;—indeed, when we thought of the French soldiers as the promoters of freedom, our sympathies were with them. The enigmatical conduct of the Prussian government held us for some time in suspense; but it eventually threw aside its threatening attitude and made terms of peace. Meanwhile the troops did not immediately return to their former post: instead of Berlin, after much marching and countermarching, Chamisso found himself destined to protect Hanover, and his regiment garrisoned the fortress of Hameln.

CHAPTER IV.

The University of Halle.—Manners of the Students.—Their Clubs.—Warlike Movements.—Prussian Troops in Halle.—Vacation Time.—Field Marshal Von Müllendorf. 1806.

WE were now prepared for a higher sphere of action, and determined, in the spring of 1807, to go to the university of Halle. Our road was by Hamburg to Hanover, thence to Hameln, where Chamisso was expecting us. Great was the joy at our meeting: we recapitulated all that we had seen, read, and thought, and speculated much on our future plans of life. We passed a few weeks at Hameln very happily, and then went in the diligence by Brunswick to Halle.

It was early on the 21st of April that we entered Halle. The rattling and jolting of the carriage over the rough pavement disturbed us out of our deep sleep, and the old-fashioned quiet town, with its silent streets and closed windows, instantly roused and interested us. I felt the importance of the moment in which I was about to begin the new life for which I had so ardently longed, and even now doubted having obtained my wishes. It appeared to me as if I had entered a sanctuary: the silence seemed so ominous and solemn.

This first sight of an university town struck us much: the manners of the students interested and amused us: their behaviour, dress, and language showed their freedom, which, nevertheless, was kept within due bounds by their own laws, by poverty, and by other influences. The greater number of the students lived after the manner hereditary to the race; they had their fencing-rooms and duels, as well as their clubs, drinking-bouts, and tobacco-smoking; but they by no means interfered with those who did not live after their fashion, and even allowed them to walk on the broad pavement in the middle of the street: this was only contested with the Philistines, viz. the town people. The number of students was considerable, at least fifteen hundred, who were divided into several clubs, and no small number belonged to none. We naturally kept clear of such things, and could not conceal from ourselves that, although we lacked the true student spirit, in many respects we had advanced beyond our companions.

During the whole summer we had heard of warlike movements interrupted by hopes of peace: but after Napoleon had obtained a firm footing in Germany by means of the Rhenish Confederation, all idea of peace was at an end, and every one in Prussia who had a voice called loudly for war. Prussian troops were to be seen in and near Halle on their way to the south and west, and the desire for war grew stronger every day. Some hot-headed fellows were furious if peace was hinted at, or if the superiority of the Prussians over the French was not at once acknowledged. I distinctly remember meeting an officer who asserted that the war was as good as ended,—that nothing could now save Bonaparte from certain destruction. When I attempted to talk of French generals, he interrupted me by saying, "Generals! whence should they spring? We Prussians, if you like it, have generals who understand the art of war; who have served from their youth up: such men will drive the tinkers and tailors, who date only from the Revolution, before them like sheep. For God's sake, do not talk to me any more of French generals, indeed!" This put me out of temper, and I answered bluntly, that a man became a general not by the accident of birth, but by actual service; that a man's former condition was nothing; a tinker or a tailor might make as good a general as a drill serjeant.

The vacation meanwhile commenced. Several of my companions made an excursion into Saxony, while, by Theremin's invitation, I went to join him at Berlin. In a few weeks we expected to return to Halle; no one dreamt that any thing would prevent this. I was, however, reminded all along the road, that we were on the eve of some great event; in every direction we met soldiers in larger or smaller detachments, with artillery and baggage waggons. In Treuenbriezen I saw old Field Marshal von Müllendorf on his way to join the army; war was no longer doubtful, and it was thought that the presence of one of Frederick the Great's heroes would fill the troops with the enthusiasm of that period, and incite them to fresh victories. I saw him with a smiling countenance making the most confident promises of victory out of his carriage window to the surrounding crowd; he then drove off amid the loud huzzas of the assembled multitude. The soldiers were singing jovial songs, and rejoicing that at last they were to be led against the enemy; every where were to be seen stragglers and others rushing to join the army. The noise died away after leaving Potsdam, — an unusual stillness prevailed, and the fine summer weather soon banished from my thoughts all save the objects and expectations which more immediately concerned myself.

CHAPTER V.

War declared between France and Prussia. — General Enthusiasm. — Death of Prince Louis Ferdinand. — Departure of the Court from Berlin. — General Schulenburg. — Battles of Auerstadt and Jena. — The French in Leipsic. — Plundering of Halle. — Their Entrance into Berlin. — Bivouack in the Lustgarten. — Napoleon in Berlin. — Fall of Magdeburg. — Desperate Condition of Prussia. 1806.

I ARRIVED at Berlin towards the end of September, in anxious expectation of news from the army. We had seen the reserve, under Prince Eugene of Würtemberg, pass through Berlin on its way to the Elbe; our only fear was, that peace would again restore the sword to the scabbard. All Berlin shared the general enthusiasm, and scarce any one ventured to express doubt, or even anxiety as to the results. At length the declaration of war appeared, dated Erfurt, the 8th of October, and we rejoiced that, at any rate, this step had been taken. This was received as an instalment. But now the desire for further news, for accounts of victories — of which no one entertained a doubt — became almost intolerable: this violent impatience of the public contrasted strangely with the unbroken silence maintained by those at the head of affairs. Days passed without news; nothing was to be gathered from letters or travellers. Not a sound was heard from the mysterious district in which the armies were supposed to be engaged: the metropolis seemed cut off from all communication with the camp, where the whole strength and the rulers of the state were to be found. This intolerable state of suspense, — during which the idle boasting of several military men gradually ceased, — gave occasion first to melancholy forebodings, then to the most contradictory and inexplicable reports, and was at last relieved only by the most terrible news. The first certain intelligence which reached us was the death of

Prince Louis Ferdinand: it was said that he did not choose to survive the unfavourable issue of the battle of Saalfeld. It is impossible to describe the sensation caused by the death of this prince, who was loved and honoured by all men. Many taxed him with imprudence, reproaching him for his untimely and useless death; but subsequent events proved but too well that he could not have chosen a more worthy destiny, and that his fate was more irreproachable, and more worthy of envy, than that of most of his comrades.

This beginning did not augur well. Nevertheless, every one continued to have perfect confidence in the Prussian arms. When the report of a lost battle reached the town, no one would at first believe the news: people ran here and there, and assembled before the houses of the Ministers. They forced their way into the house of General von Schulenburg, and asked eagerly for information, from friends and strangers, from high and low. They went in large bodies from one place to another, as chance or vague rumour guided them. At length a printed notice was posted up in all the corners of the streets, in which Schulenburg made known in a few words that the king had lost a battle, and that the first duty of the inhabitants of Berlin was to be quiet. This well-meant but foolish notice was poor consolation in the increasing bitterness of public feeling. The first impulse of the people was one of courage and action. A number of young men, headed by bold spokesmen, went to Schulenburg, and offered to form a company of volunteers: they only wanted to be supplied with arms and to be led at once against the enemy. When Schulenburg in evident embarrassment denied their request, and at last, with some harshness refused their offer to serve as common soldiers, saying, that he did not know what to do with the soldiers he already had, much less with raw recruits,—then every one clearly saw that nothing was to be done but to let ruin come and bear it quietly.

Berlin now saw its former pride and strength cut down, its hopes destroyed. The royal household, the highest officials, and other persons of high station, hastily packed up their valuables, and departed. Afterwards the muskets were all taken from the armoury and placed in boats, but something delayed their being conveyed to a place of safety. Finally, Schulenberg went with all the troops he could muster, some thousand strong, towards the Oder, after giving the town into the charge of his son-in-law, Prince von Hatzfeldt. The people impeded Schulenburg's departure:—"I leave you, my children," said he, and they let him go.

Meanwhile fame had announced a succession of disasters without magnifying them, as is usually the case; on the contrary, the misfortunes proved to be actually greater and more numerous than were reported. We were told of the battle of Auerstädt and of Jena, of the Duke of Brunswick and General von Rüchel being mortally wounded, and of the retreat of the troops who were to have assembled at Magdeburg. We still hoped that the passage of the Elbe would be defended, and we knew that the reserve, which had not yet been in action, was stationed at Halle. But this comfort speedily vanished: the remainder of the army fled beyond the Oder; Prince Eugene of Würtemberg was attacked and beaten on the 17th of October by Marshal Bernadotte. First, the queen, then the king had fled towards Prussia proper: the French had appeared in Leipsic, had passed the Elbe at Dessau and near Magdeburg, and were advancing on all sides in triumph. It is impossible to describe the state of dull despair and anxious expectation in which the town of Berlin was plunged. The worst was, that not a Prussian soldier was to be heard of. We had seen the army go forth in all its pride and glory: it seemed as if the earth had swallowed it up, and we now saw in its stead the hated and despised enemy enter the town. No stragglers of the army ever reached Berlin; they had all fled further northwards or had been made prisoners of war,—some of them basely, without striking a blow, as at Prenzlau,—others after a stout resistance, as at Lubeck.

All was now care and anxiety at Berlin: the magistrates did nothing, but left things to take their own course. Prince von Hatzfeldt had shown himself wanting in vigour, and already incurred great censure. Many people, having a thought to the future when an army would be quartered upon them, laid in a store of wine and good things, in order to appease the fury of the soldiers by good feeding, while others, mindful of themselves, got in a provision of potatoes to meet their own private wants. A few still hoped for the advance of Russian troops, and a yet smaller number, who still thought that they would find in the French the old soldiers of liberty, rejoiced in their approach. It was reported that Hessen-Cassel had separated itself from Prussia, and declared its neutrality; and one man hastily adorned his doorway with the arms of that power, having obtained licence for so doing from the Hereditary Princess of Hessen. This however availed him nothing, as the French did not respect his neutrality, and made no difference between Hessians and Prussians; thus, besides the annoyance of having soldiers billeted upon him, he had the additional mortification of seeing his fellow-citizens exceedingly pleased that his device had failed.

I myself was much moved, not only by the events of the day at Berlin, but by what had happened at Halle. The latter town had been plundered; the university had been shut up by Napoleon's command, all the students ordered to leave the place, and I was again thrown on the world without a home.

The French, who were not far off, did not come quite so quickly as was expected; they had gone considerably to the north of Berlin, and could scarcely have been aware that it was ready to receive them. At length, on the 24th of October, the enemy appeared. I saw the first French who entered the town. At about midday an officer, in a blue uniform, accompanied by three or four chasseurs, rode into the town: they stopped their horses, hurriedly asked the way towards the municipality, or the mansion-house, told the idlers to stand off, and galloped away again. There they were then! Many people still maintained that these were not French, but Russians. This was evident, said they, from their green uniforms. But in a quarter of an hour there was no longer room for doubt: large bodies of cavalry and infantry entered the town, and on the following day Berlin was filled with Marshal Davoust's troops. And now began a totally new life among the half-stupified inhabitants of Berlin. We breathed again; for, instead of wild unprincipled plunderers, we found a well-disciplined gay soldiery, who were disarmed by being addressed in French, and whose officers were, for the most part, remarkable for courteous manners. This first favourable impression was not effaced by subsequent rough conduct, although it was difficult to satisfy the pressing wants of so many people. We still found that we had to thank God, if we were to have enemies quartered upon us, that they were not worse than these. Nevertheless, the slovenly, dirty, ragged appearance of these little, mean-looking, impudent, witty fellows, was a strange sight for eyes which, like ours, had been used to the neatness and admirable carriage of the Prussians, and we were the more astonished how such rabble—for they almost deserved the name—could have beaten such soldiers out of the field.

Some few days later, on the evening of the 27th of October, Napoleon himself left Charlottenburg, and entered the town at the head of his guards. It had been said that he would not trust himself in Berlin.

On the 27th October, I was taking my usual evening walk by the so-called Lustgarten, or park, when I was struck by a new sight. The whole space in the middle, which had been always kept carefully mown, and even the side-walks towards the palace, were covered with innumerable watch-fires, round which the soldiers of the imperial guard were grouped in all sorts of attitudes. The huge fires shone upon these handsome men and their glittering arms and accoutrements, and the eye was attracted by the incessantly recurring national colours of red, blue, and white. About 10,000 men were moving about in this glowing bivouac, near the gloomy-looking palace in which Napoleon had taken up his abode. The whole scene made a strong impression upon me, and when I examined the small details,—for every one was allowed to go among the troops,—my wonder was increased: each soldier, in appearance, manner, and authority, was like an officer,—each man seemed a commander, a hero. The men sang, danced, and feasted till late in the night, while every now and then small detachments in an admirable state of discipline, marched to and fro with drums and music. It was such a sight as I had never beheld. I staid there for hours, and could scarce leave the spot. The imperial guard remained there for some days, and all eyes were riveted by the beautiful but hated spectacle. But no subsequent impression equalled that of the first night: the fires burned more dimly; part of the troops had been detached elsewhere; and at length, small bodies of cavalry, with their horses ready saddled and bridled for instant service, were the only troops left in this encampment. The numerous body-guard in the court of the palace was quite sufficient for Napoleon's personal safety.

Meanwhile the position of Prussia became worse every day. The lost battles, the bad measures, the want of activity, the carelessness of the government, were bad enough; but the capitulations and surrenders of strong places were beyond belief. The fall of Magdeburg was like a dream: a garrison of above 20,000 men laid down their arms without striking a blow. One could scarce believe that this strong bulwark of Prussia could be taken without firing a shot. It appeared fabulous, that the cowardly panic of their commanders should yield two places like Stettin and Custrin, which were reckoned impregnable, to the first handful of French cavalry that galloped up to the walls. The boundless corruption which had been gradually sapping the foundations of the state now became notorious. We sank under the shame which had fallen upon the Prussian arms, without at once comprehending its full extent. In the excess of their grief the Prussians themselves were the most bitter against their countrymen. In former days a Prussian officer was the ideal of all that was honourable, brave, and accomplished; the name now implied cowardice, boastfulness, and incapacity. All looked with anger upon the enormous power which the army had gradually acquired; men were only disposed to forgive this when it proved itself the steady defender of the country, and secured its lasting glory and conquest. Many now rejoiced at the rapid progress of the French, as a means of overthrowing this domestic tyranny. No one who did not live in these times can conceive the expressions which Prussian patriots used against the military authorities, nor the bitter contempt with which names once held in high respect, but to which attached a suspicion of treason, were now mentioned. The abuse of the Prussian soldiery was universal, and often unjust: in many instances the enemy were fairer than the Prussians, and occasionally took the part of those men; but in those times it was almost impossible to stem the current. A perfect flood of pamphlets was poured forth: the secretary-at-war of Cologne was the first to disclose without shame the weaknesses and crimes of his own government: others wrote hastily and foolishly, endeavouring to fasten their own political abstractions upon the victorious party, and to show their wisdom by the fulfilment of their prophecies of victory.

The sights, impressions, interests, and experiences of this period filled and excited my mind, and gave me much cause for thought. The state of Prussia was important and worthy of observation. But the French soldiers were in their way most remarkable; the mixture of refinement and savageness gave them a peculiar character, which was not without its charm; and I had a decided liking for many officers whose acquaintance I made. I looked upon Napoleon with all the hatred which was due to the oppressor of freedom in France, and to the enemy of improvement in Germany; but I could not avoid admiring his great qualities, and when I saw him inspecting the troops in the Lustgarten, in the midst of his generals, as I frequently did, and allowed the whole scene to make its due impression upon me, I well understood why his soldiers followed him with enthusiasm in his never-ending career of victory.

Until now, the most beautiful weather, in spite of the lateness of the season, had made life more tolerable. But suddenly the weather became gloomy, wet, and cold, and the appearance of every thing was changed. The French troops had almost all advanced into Poland or Prussia, and Napoleon joined them with the few that had remained behind. Berlin, now almost a desert, sank under the accumulated burdens and vexations which daily became more oppressive; want and misery were everywhere visible. General von Zastrow had been sent by the King to Napoleon to sign a treaty of peace; but it did not take effect, as the Emperor's unparalleled success made him reject the terms which he had formerly been disposed to grant. Nothing remained for us under these disheartening circumstances, but to look forward to a series of wretched days and to a miserable future.

CHAPTER VI.

Fichte's Lectures in Berlin. — Schleiermacher. — Meeting with Rahel Levin. — Description of Rahel. — Her Character. — The Society at her House. — Her Letters and Journals. — Rahel at Charlottenburg. 1807.

MEANWHILE the interval of a year had produced some change, and a new career was opened to me. The shutting up of the university of Halle was perhaps a greater loss to me than to any one else. Every thing was to be found there of which I stood in need: but at Berlin, where I now was, I occasionally saw Fichte, Wolf, and Bernhardi. Towards the end of December Schleiermacher and his sister left Halle, and came to settle permanently in Berlin. Fichte now commenced giving lectures in the hall of the academy before a numerous company, and I did not fail to attend them. It was curious to hear a German professor exhorting his hearers to keep up their nationality, in the midst of a French army: many of his audience thought of Palm, the bookseller, and felt some fear lest a similar fate should await the bold lecturer. I likewise attended Schleiermacher's lectures on ethics. These and other persons in Berlin formed a select society, and made an agreeable interruption to our studies.

Among the various persons whom I frequently heard mentioned in this society were some of the most remarkable men and women in Germany; the brothers William and Alexander von Humboldt, Frederick Schlegel and his wife, Ludwig Tieck, and others of like eminence, with whose names every high interest is associated. But no one was more often quoted and described than Rahel Levin, and I soon conceived the greatest desire to know her. The lady of the house in which we met spoke of her as something without parallel, and when occasionally some blame interrupted the general flow of praise — for instance, when it was said that if Rahel paid more attention to outward appearances, or could manage to assume a tone more consonant with the general views of society, it would be better, — our hostess did not deny that in all matters of real importance, she acknowledged Rahel's superiority. It struck us as remarkable, when we heard a woman whom for intelligence and accomplishments we looked upon as the pattern of her sex, speak of another in such terms, placing her above compare, and we requested her to ask her friend to the house, that we might judge for ourselves of their respective merits. The visit was promised. Rahel appeared; but staid only an hour, as she was not well, and indisposition had unfitted her to appear to advantage in a small society where the impression was not altogether in her favour. All further talk with her was impossible, when Schleiermacher appeared, sat down, and entered into earnest conversation with her. We were not a little surprised to see Schleiermacher play a subordinate part, and apparently with a good will; indeed, he several times stopped short in his conversation. When her carriage was announced and she went away with a promise to come again, Schleiermacher accompanied her to the door, and when he returned, his praises of her knew no bounds. But his excitement, which lasted during the whole evening, proved her power more than any thing he could say. We were doubly astonished; for we had never seen Schleiermacher second to any one, and seldom so excited. I ardently wished to become better acquainted with this wonderful creature, before whom all others paled, and I felt that I must soon be more intimate with her than with any other person.

With a mind prepared to receive new impressions, and thirsting for fresh stimulus and support, I happened to meet Rahel one cold spring morning under the lime trees. I knew her companion, to whom I spoke, and while I walked a short distance with them, Rahel, to my delight, joined in the conversation. I found myself attracted towards her to an extraordinary degree, and exerted all my wit not to let this good opportunity pass unimproved. Among other things, I managed to make use of one of her peculiarly expressive phrases which had reached my ears, in such a manner as to convey at the same time a compliment and a playful attack. She perceived both, looked penetratingly at me, as if to measure the extent of my boldness, and answered that she could endure to hear her words quoted, but not in a false sense: there was, indeed, something in the expression which had been incorrectly repeated. I excused myself by saying that I could not vouch for the accuracy of quotations which I heard only by accident, and I was rewarded by her permission in future to come to the fountain-head at once. I availed myself of this favour the very next day. Rahel then lived in the Jägerstrasse, opposite to the Admiralty, under the care of her mother, whose old-fashioned and admirably-arranged house was open to the most agreeable society. I had occasionally visited Ludwig Robert in this very house; but with what different feelings did I now cross the threshold!

I have a few times in my life felt myself suddenly raised by the influence of congenial minds into a higher sphere, where the very air which I breathed, and the impressions which I received, at once opened to me a new existence. I had more especially marked three such periods in my life,—the dawn of my intellectual life, at the commencement of my studies at Berlin,—my first entrance into an independent and active existence,—the inauguration of my student life at Halle, and eight years after the first epoch I took my fourth step in life,—my acquaintance with Rahel,—which united in itself all the elements of the former periods. I do not hesitate to affirm that during the four-and-twenty years which have passed since my first acquaintance with Rahel, in which time much that is new, great, and unexpected has occurred, there has been nothing in my varied life which will bear the slightest comparison with that event. Rahel is still to me * the newest and freshest feature in my existence; and whilst I trace the circumstances and feelings which accompanied our early connection, I need not draw upon my imagination to call up the warm and delicate perfume of those happy days: I feel and enjoy their influence now as I did then. But I fear that my description will be tinged with the sadness which, even while I write this, fills my soul when I think upon the manifold, deep, and passionate sorrows of my dear and early friend.

I cannot attempt to describe my beloved Rahel: to know and appreciate her thoroughly was possible only to those who held daily intercourse with her. Even her letters, full of genius and

---

* This was written in 1832. Rahel died on the 7th March, 1833. — *Transl.*

originality as they are, give but an imperfect picture of her mind, the chief quality of which was that natural, unborrowed vivacity which throws upon every subject new lights and shadows of its own, and lends a freshness and a charm to all things, which no pen can describe. I will only attempt to give a slight idea of the impression which she then made upon me.

First, I must say, that while in her presence I had the full persuasion that I beheld a real creature—the work of God in its purest and most perfect form. She was full of life and soul; of a nervous, excitable organisation, in complete harmony with nature; her expressions and emotions were unaffected and original, and had a certain grandeur from her native simplicity and sense; she was, moreover, quick, exact, and determined in word and action. The purest goodness, the most active benevolence, the deepest sympathy with her fellow-creatures, pervaded her whole nature. In her all the excellences which I had seen separately in others were united: she possessed intellect and wit, penetration and a love of truth, imagination and humour. She combined with force of character and acuteness of mind a womanly grace and gentleness, which gave to her eyes and to her noble mouth an expression of the greatest sweetness, without at all disguising the vigour and impetuosity of her passions.

I almost doubt whether my description will enable any one to form any idea of such an union of conflicting elements. It was after some doubts and many errors that I at length came to a right conclusion: for a long time I was confident of but one thing; that I saw before me the most extraordinary and admirable object. I had no prejudice against her, spite of the disadvantageous terms in which I had heard her described by various people; and even if I had, it would speedily have vanished in her presence. Her simple, natural address, the unaffected ease and sincere kindliness of her conversation, which at first turned only on indifferent subjects, immediately dispelled all unpleasant feelings, which were soon succeeded by others—the offspring of the moment: the freshness of her language gave a charm, and a character of truth and originality to the most indifferent subjects, and invested the most commonplace ideas with a certain elevation. In her presence I felt myself in a new atmosphere of poetry, unlike what commonly bears that name, inasmuch as it was true instead of false, real instead of apparent. Before long, however, our conversation turned upon more important matters; books, persons, and social relations afforded us various subjects for discussion. We talked of Frederick Schlegel, Tieck, Madame de Stael, and Goethe, and expressed our sentiments and opinions with as much openness as was consistent with the reserve of a first visit.

We were not long alone; other people came in, and the conversation soon became animated and free from restraint. Every one showed himself in his true colours—there was nothing to be gained by hypocrisy. Rahel's simplicity, good humour, love of truth, and desire to give every one fair play, had its due effect. I declaimed with youthful exaggeration against the French; another brought out his store of theatrical news; a French officer received sarcastic advice about his love affairs from Major Von Schack, a witty Prussian; every thing passed off lightly and agreeably. When the tone of conversation grew harshly earnest, it was interrupted by wit and humour, and this again by serious topics: it was thus animated, and at the same time restrained within due bounds.

My impatience allowed only a few days to intervene between my first and second visit; and so rapid was the growth of our intimacy, that I then became a daily visitor. I was anxious to gaze upon this new appearance, to approach nearer to these peculiar truths, to these disclosures of high import which at every step unfolded themselves more and more brilliantly before me, and to enjoy these new sensations the existence of which I had never before suspected. To my astonishment, I found that in the same degree in which others try to dissemble their feelings, Rahel revealed her inmost soul, and spoke of her sensations, woes, wishes, and expectations, even when they might bear an unfavourable interpretation, and when she herself looked upon them as failings and errors, with as much freedom and truth as if she were saying what was favourable and flattering, and had to boast of the most undisturbed peace and felicity. This degree of openness, which I have never seen in any other human creature, and of which Jean Jacques Rousseau was only capable in writing, at first caused me some uneasiness, as her passionate confessions often betrayed a certain harsh, inconsiderate vehemence, and a degree of peculiarity which would have been repulsive if, as it is usually the case, there had been something still left unsaid. But with Rahel it was otherwise: with respect to herself she spoke the whole truth without reserve. She never attempted to extenuate or conceal her errors, for she expected from others the candid and indulgent sympathy for perfect truth which she herself always felt, but, unfortunately, seldom met with.

I now saw Rahel by degrees in every relation of her life. I soon perceived that there was an immeasurable gulph between her and those about her. She stood alone in the midst of a wide circle, neither understood, cherished, nor loved as she required and deserved, but regarded with indifference, or selfishly made use of for the moment, and then thrown aside. None denied her extraordinary gifts; it was conceded that she was endowed with remarkable powers of mind, wit, and humour: but others thought themselves possessed of the same qualities, with the addition of a greater share of prudence and repose, — thus they called their insipid selfishness and languid dulness. With what Rahel, in her generosity, bestowed upon them of her abundance, they thought themselves her superiors. Few could understand her noble aspirations, her generous impulses, her sacred love of truth. I felt myself all the more strongly attracted towards her by the consciousness that I could offer her a sympathy and an acknowledgment of her merits, which she too seldom received.

Our intimacy strengthened daily. I told Rahel all my most secret thoughts, and nowhere could I have found truer sympathy, or more useful advice. Far from receiving unconditional praise, I was blamed for much, and could perceive that Rahel felt more disapprobation than she expressed. But her interest in me rather increased than diminished, and this made up to me for the mortification. In her circle, too, I enjoyed the society of most remarkable men, Prince Louis Ferdinand, Gentz, Schlegel, the two Humboldts, Tieck, the Prince de Ligne, and many other diplomatists, artists, and learned men, who frequented her society.

But this rich collection of important portraits, to which she gave me the most lively explanations, was not all; another treasure was unfolded to me, which excited my interest still more strongly. Rahel was one of those rare natures to whom is given the gift to love. A poet might, indeed, picture to himself a mind like Rahel's, shaken or elated by the strongest passion of noble natures. But the insight which was afforded to me far surpassed any thing that I could have imagined. The fire of passion had here fed upon the noblest nourishment — other passions and other sorrows appeared trifling in comparison with hers. The letters and journals which I was permitted to read, in the strictest confidence, displayed a vital energy, which even such writings as those by Goethe and Rousseau seldom reach. The letters to Madame de Houdetot, which Rousseau mentions as incomparable, may possibly have glowed with as ardent a flame. These papers, after being long in my possession, were unfortunately lost or destroyed in 1813, with the exception of some few which give no sufficient idea of their worth. It would appear that productions of this nature are destined never to see the light, but to perish with the persons to whom they belong. I sat whole nights reading these letters, which opened to me a class of feelings of which until then I had had no idea. It appeared to me like a dream that I had obtained these papers, and had acquired so close an interest in the existence therein described.

The beauty and elevation of poetry and philosophy were fully felt by Rahel. Long before it was the fashion to praise Goethe, she had been struck by his extraordinary genius, and had placed him above all other poets. In philosophy, she gave the first place to the noble Fichte. She was intimately acquainted with the works of Schlegel, Novalis, Schleiermacher, Schelling, and Steffens, and knew most of them personally. Gluck, Mozart, and Righini were her favourites in music. She was fully alive to the demerits of Kotzebue and Iffland, who then kept complete possession of the stage, long before literary criticism had ventured to direct its attacks against these idols of the public.

I had not stood long in this new relation, before I gave my friends an animated account of my good fortune. At first it was doubted and treated as a joke. One of my female acquaintances was astonished, and could not comprehend how Rahel and I could long understand one another: she at the same time admitted, however, that after her no other woman would seem interesting or original to me. My college companion, Harscher, was her most obstinate opponent: he was quite capable of recognising and wondering at Rahel's varied qualities, but he could not endure her healthful independence of mind, and envied the ease with which she produced what was true and beautiful without art or trouble: he grew in a manner jealous of her, and tried by every means in his power to separate me from my new friend. He occasionally went with me to Rahel's, was most kindly received, enjoyed her conversation, and could scarce find words to express his surprise and admiration. But this very feeling angered him: he would not be overcome, and remained away in order, as he said, that he might not yield to her fascination. At length he saw that his sarcasms and exhortations were thrown away, and let me go my own way, happy to find that my new passion did not interfere with our old friendship.

During the summer months Rahel inhabited a small house at Charlottenburg, and I visited her there as often as I possibly could. The solitude in which I here found my friend gave leisure for more interesting and confidential conversations. The quiet, shady place before the door of the small house in a retired street, the cool walks in the fragrant garden, or in the broad shady roads round this retired village, and the beautiful moonlight evenings, are closely associated in my recollection with the highest pleasures of the intellect, and the tenderest and most passionate feelings of the heart.

The summer had passed away, and the time approached when the plans upon which we had determined were to be carried into effect. The nearer the time for our separation approached, the more strongly did Rahel and I feel the value and the happiness of our connexion. We endeavoured to conquer our grief, but melancholy thoughts crossed us in the midst of our joys. It now seemed folly to part, and yet our previous resolutions remained unchanged. We had the courage to separate; I had still much to learn, and should only have been miserable in a life of pleasure and idleness. I was forced to go in order one day to return an altered man, after having endured trials and withstood temptations. But the treasure I had won remained secure to me: the vicissitudes of life, the world's variety would have no influence over her. When the day of separation arrived, and I bethought me that I should no longer see those eyes, kiss that hand, or hear that voice, I grew faint-hearted, and the idea of leaving Rahel filled me with a despair, which even the prospect of a future meeting could scarcely soothe.

I was at this time twenty-four, and Rahel more than half as old again, a circumstance which might possibly have prevented our union had it been apparent. But this noble creature who had already seen so much good and suffered so much evil, still looked young, and was strong. Our marriage, however, could not then take place. I had not finished the term of years appointed for study at the university, and I had others of trial still to go through. I had scarcely entered life when internal troubles, and the oppression of the times carried me along with them in their course. Military service, journeys, dissipations, the temptations of vanity, other passions, and the misunderstandings which are incidental to a long absence—nothing could break that strong tie which bound me to Rahel; I felt a deep conviction that I had found that which alone could make my life happy, and I never ceased for one moment from my struggle to attain my object. Six years passed in this manner, only broken by some few intervals when I saw Rahel, and renewed our plans and hopes. At length, after various turns of fortune, after peace had been restored, I returned from Paris, and found Rahel in Bohemia, and after passing a delightful summer with her, I joined my lot in life with hers in Berlin, on the 27th of September, 1814.*

---

* For a further account of this remarkable woman, see "Rahel, ein Buch des Andenkens für ihre Freunde," 3 vols.; "Varnhagen Von Ense's Gallerie von Bildnissen aus Rahel's Umgang und Briefwechsel," 2 vols.; the "Revue de Paris," for November, 1837, and "Carlyle's Miscellanies," vol. v. p. 314. — *Translator.*

CHAPTER VII.

Jean Paul Friederich Richter at Baireuth.— His Manner and Conversation.
—Jean Paul's Wife and Children.— His Opinions on Rahel, Goethe,
Schlegel, and others. —Jean Paul's Manner of writing. — The Romantic
School.— Tieck and Bernhardi. 1808.

BAIREUTH, Sunday, the 23d of October, 1808.—This forenoon I went to visit Jean Paul. I immediately recognised in a pleasant, civil, inquisitive woman who opened the door, Jean Paul's wife, from her likeness to her sister. One of the children was sent to call his father, who soon came: he had been expecting my visit, owing to letters from Berlin and Leipsic, and received me most kindly. As he sat down near me on the sofa I nearly laughed in his face; as he bent down a little he was so exactly like the description which Neumann had jestingly given of him in our joint novel of Versuchen und Hindernissen.* Moreover, his way of speaking and what he said made the impression stronger. Jean Paul is a large man, with a full, well-shaped face, small eyes, fiery and glowing at one moment, and soft and heavy the next; his mouth has an agreeable expression, and is mobile even when he is silent. His speech is rapid and almost hasty; he occasionally stutters, and he has a peculiar dialect, which I should find some difficulty in describing, but which appears to me to be half Franconian, half Saxon, although his language is tolerably correct nevertheless.

I had, first of all, to tell him all that I knew of his Berlin acquaintances, and to repeat all the messages with which I had been charged. He recalled with pleasure the time he spent as Marcus Herz's neighbour, in Leder's house at Berlin, where, seven years before, I had seen him walking in a garden near the Spree with papers in his hand, which I was

* See further, p. 63.

told in secret were a part of the "Hesperus." These personal reminiscences and subjects connected with literature, which arose during the conversation, excited him extremely, and he soon had much more to say than to hear. His conversation was pleasing and good-humoured, always full of meaning, unaffected and simple. Although I was perfectly aware that his wit and humour belonged only to his pen, and that while he could scarce write a note without giving proof of both, his conversation seldom betrayed either, I was, nevertheless, much astonished to hear nothing of the sort from him during the whole time in which he was so excited and allowed himself to be carried away by the vehemence of his feelings. His manner was like his conversation; not very polished, but no ways strained or pretentious; it was unstudied, and just what might be expected from a person of the middle classes. His courtesy arose from kindness, his manners and bearing were patriarchal, full of consideration to others, but perfectly unconstrained. Even in the heat of conversation he was true to his character; he uttered no sharp word, he made no false representation, he never watched for an opportunity to take an unfair advantage: he was invariably gentle, but allowed his own comprehensive nature to run riot. He first praised every thing that had lately appeared, and when we entered more fully into the subject, then there was blame and more than enough. So of Adam Müller's Lectures, of Frederick Schlegel, of Tieck, and others. He thought that German authors should always hold to the people and not to the upper classes, among whom all was corrupted and spoilt, and yet he had just praised Adam Müller for understanding how to speak a true word to the well-instructed men of the world. He was convinced that nothing could be gained from the gleanings of the Indian world, but the addition of perhaps some new form of poetry to those which we already possess — no increase of ideas; and yet he had but a few minutes before praised Frederick Schlegel's studies in Sanscrit, as if some fresh salvation were to come of it. He could not conceive any one but a Protestant being a real Christian, and asserted that it was sheer perversion of intellect when a Protestant turned Catholic, and yet with these views he had shortly before expressed a hope that the

Catholic spirit in Frederick Schlegel, fused with the Hindoo, might work out great good. He spoke of Schleiermacher with great respect, but said he could not enjoy his translation of Plato, and thought he could trace much more of the godlike and wise ancient in the enthusiastic Jacobi and Herder, than in the learned and acute Schleiermacher. I did not allow these observations to pass without contradiction. He could not bear Fichte, of whose address to the German nation, delivered at Berlin amidst the noise of the French drums, I told him much ; the determined energy of the man oppressed him, and he said he could only read this author as a school exercise; that the import of his philosophy no longer interested him.

Jean Paul was called out of the room for something, and I stayed a while alone with his wife. I had now to begin afresh about her native town of Berlin : such was her interest in the persons and in what was going on there, that I had to add much to what she had already heard. She pleased me exceedingly : she was gentle, lady-like, and modest, and united to domestic qualities of the highest order, greater talents for society and conversation than Jean Paul appeared to possess. However, she willingly considered herself inferior to her gifted husband in this respect as in others. It was evident that theirs was a most happy life. Their three children were beautiful, captivating, and lively creatures. A boy of about five, Max, was the favourite of his father, who saw in him a future hero: the boy was full of strength and courage, and well-formed. Two girls, Emma and Ottilie, the one older the other younger than the boy, seemed charming ; and showed that, however different they were in many ways, they inherited the quality of kindliness which was common to both parents. All three were devoid of awkward shyness, perfectly free and easy, and thorough children : you could see that their good qualities were more the result of nature than of education. When Jean Paul returned it was late, and I was about to go ; this was only permitted on condition of telling my companion that I should not dine at home ; I had no hope of bringing Harscher to dinner with me, as Jean Paul requested.

Jean Paul was in excellent spirits, and expatiated on all manner of subjects. Among others, I had brought a greeting from

Rahel Levin, with the modest question, "Whether he still remembered her?" His face lighted up with pleasure. "How could one forget such a person," said he, impressively: "she is unique in her way: I liked her much, and should like her more every day; the impression she made upon me strengthens with my strength: she is the only woman in whom I have found genuine wit and humour!" (Jean Paul had forgotten Madame de Sévigné, or did not call her peculiar characteristic by its right name: for what the French praise in her so much as simplicity, is exactly what, in most cases, we should call humour.) He then proceeded to enumerate her several good qualities. When I interrupted him in the midst of his praises, and said that all the intellect, acuteness, and wit which he admired so much in Rahel, were in my eyes as nothing compared with the real goodness of her disposition, he was not astonished, but immediately believed my assertion, merely repeating that the other qualities for which he had praised her still were very great. He set great value upon two letters which he had received from Rahel, and said that one of them from Paris was worth ten volumes of travels; that no one had understood and described the French and the French world so admirably at first sight. "What eyes must those be," he exclaimed, "which could see the whole truth and only the truth so clearly and so quickly! When I told him the number of her letters which I possessed, not all written but given to me, he envied me greatly. He said that if we lived in the same town, I must read him at least a sentence or two out of each letter: that I had a great treasure: that Rahel wrote admirably; but that it was necessary for her to have some one in whom she was much interested to write to,— she never could sit down and write a book. "I am more capable of understanding her now than I was in Berlin; I should like much to see her again. The more I hear of the remarks and expressions she throws out here and there, the more astonished I am! She is an artist, and is from a different sphere than ours; she is quite an exception, always at war with the world, and far beyond its ken; she will, therefore, always remain single!" He said I was very lucky in having such a friend, and asked, as if to prove me and measure my value, how one so young had deserved such good fortune? I visibly rose in his estimation through my connexion with Rahel.

By Jean Paul's invitation, I again went to see him in the afternoon of the 24th of October. He had just returned from a walk; his wife, with one of the children, was still out. We talked about his writings, a most difficult chord with most authors, some of whom will not bear to have it touched, while others will play upon nothing else. He was more admirable on this subject than I could have expected — open, unprejudiced, and rational in all he said. What brought on the discussion was the last annual published by Cotta, in which Goethe's "mad wanderers" and Jean Paul's "dream of a madman" appeared. No copy had yet reached Baireuth, but I had brought one with me from Dresden. Jean Paul wished to have my copy, and referred me to Cotta, at Tubingen, for another. "Such phantasies as these," said he, "I could write for ever, as long as I am well and in the mood. I sit down to the pianoforte, allow my fingers to run wildly over the notes, give myself completely up to the impressions of the moment, and then I write down the images that flit before me, in a certain predetermined order, it is true, but with so little connexion that I frequently change the arrangement afterwards." In this manner he once began to write a "hell" such as no mortal ever yet dreamt of; much is already done, but is never intended to see the light.

We then talked a good deal about literature and its objects, and touched upon descriptions of scenery. In this Jean Paul was a great master, and no wonder, for he has always passed much of his time in studying nature; in his youth he spent half his days in the open air, watching the clouds, the air, the land and water, the shape of every leaf and blade of grass, every thing, in short, great and small, keeping accurate notes of all that was worth describing. He was a little staggered when I ventured to assert that Goethe was inferior in this respect, and he quoted two passages from "Werther" descriptive of scenery, which certainly were most masterly. But we discussed the matter some time before we could agree as to the technical manner in which the subject should be handled. At length, Jean Paul remarked, that, in order to give a poetical description of any scenery, the poet should begin by making a sort of camera obscura of another man's breast, and endeavour to see the object through this medium: this would be most effective; while nothing could be less life-like than an inquisitive traveller's exact description of the mere material scene. Jean Paul maintained that a poet should never describe scenery except through the medium of the imagination, which alone could give the real and the true. For example, he himself, in his "Titan," had described particular Italian and Swiss landscapes most correctly—at least so said the best judges—without ever having seen the places; and he never was in Nürnberg, which he has so accurately described in the "Paliægenesion," even to the minutest detail, except for half a day, and that long after he had written the description. A deep truth is no doubt contained in this apparent paradox. It requires something more than the compasses and a foot rule to draw a portrait; and the imagination, in order to describe what is actually seen in nature, should draw upon its own resources for familiar images.

The conversation then turned on public events, on the condition of Germany, and the oppressions of the French. I dislike political discussions, but I was delighted to hear Jean Paul's patriotic sentiments. What he said was profound, sensible, brave, and thoroughly German. I had much to tell him: of Napoleon, whom he knew only by portraits; of Johann von Müller, of whose character and life he was most anxious to hear; of Fichte, and of the Marquis de la Romana and his Spaniards, whom I had seen in Hamburg. Jean Paul never doubted that the Germans would one day rise against the French as the Spaniards had done, and that Prussia would revenge its insults, and give freedom to Germany. All he hoped was, that his son would live to see it: he did not conceal that he was educating him for a soldier. What I told him strengthened his convictions; I brought forward plenty of witnesses to prove how hollow and weak was Napoleon's power; how deeply rooted and strong, on the other hand, was the opposition to him in public opinion. Many facts had not penetrated into this remote province, and Jean Paul listened with avidity to what I had to say. He warned me not to keep a copy of Stägeman's "Ode to Napoleon," which I had recited to him, but shortly afterwards, forgetting his own warning, he begged me to give him one. We shook hands as persons having a community of sentiments, and freely expressed our individual opinions. The Spaniards were the refrain to every thing, and we always returned to them.

One of my last evenings in Baireuth was spent in Jean Paul's company. I stayed to supper contrary to my intention, as I had promised Harscher not to be late, having to leave Baireuth early the next morning. Jean Paul was so pressing, and his wife so thoroughly kind, that I could not resist their joint entreaties. The best humour prevailed at this meal, which, though simple, was ample enough to support its South German reputation. Among other things, Jean Paul made us laugh heartily by offering to give me a letter of introduction to one of his dearest friends—at least so he called him—at Stuttgart, but he was obliged to let me go without it, as he could not recollect his friend's name. Of a more serious turn, however, was our conversation about Tieck, Frederick and William Schlegel, Bernhardi, and others, of the so-called romantic school. Jean Paul had recognised the talent of these men in one of his works, but he did not like them. He was especially angry with Tieck on many accounts. He accused him of stealing a great part of his comic descriptions from Bernhardi, some more from his, Jean Paul's writings, and much from Shakespeare. What was serious and touching, he said, was taken partly from old popular tales, and the witty story of the tailor Tunelli was almost a paraphrase of some old author. Thus Tieck was subjected to a *concursus creditorum* similar to that which the Schlegels had held upon Wieland. But I opposed Jean Paul in his unjust and excessive depreciation of Tieck. Bernhardi himself had told me that the best parts of a work which appeared in his name, had been really written by Tieck, and I asserted that the working up of old materials was an author's acknowledged privilege. This could never be made a subject of reproach against a poet, and Tieck's "Genoveva," "Octavianus," and others, were almost new creations. Lastly, I told him Bernhardi's opinion was, that—whether he would or no—he was forced to confess that of all the leaders of the romantic school, Tieck was incomparably the most truly original. Jean Paul thought awhile, balanced the evidence, his heart at once recognised Tieck's merit, and it happened, as before, that he arrived at a different conclusion from what one could have anticipated at the beginning of the conversation. His dislike and depreciation of Tieck disappeared, and the latter was installed at once as a great and remarkable poet.

From these conversations I learned to know more of Jean Paul himself than of those persons whom we discussed. His was a great and noble nature : there was no guile or meanness in his character. He is altogether as he writes,—kindly, hearty, strong, and brave.

While I thus considered the real worth of this excellent man, my conscience suddenly smote me. I could not help thinking of Neumann's and my joint novel, and of the absurd figure under which Jean Paul appears in it, under his own name, and in his own most peculiar manner. Although the chief part was Neumann's, still it appeared false in me to leave Jean Paul without confessing our crime. I therefore told him all about the novel, how it originated, and how Johannes Von Müller and Johann Heinrich Voss were represented as well as himself. He heard me complacently to the end, said the joke was a good one, hoped it was well executed, and praised me for having told him of it. He understood how it was meant, and said that he knew that those soldiers of Julius Cæsar who sung satirical songs against him during his triumphal processions were yet the bravest and truest in his army. It all depends, said he, upon how your work is executed. He thought that Müller and Voss would not take it well as they did not understand a joke as he did. He expressed some annoyance and fear when he heard that we had dared to laugh at Goethe, and bring Wilhelm Meister on the scene. "Children," said he, "what have you done." Goethe's "is an anointed head : he is unlike the rest. I am more unwilling to give him up to you than myself." He spoke of Goethe for some time, with increasing admiration, nay with a species of awe and reverence.

The most beautiful fruit was brought for dessert. Jean Paul rose from the table, gave me his hand, and said, "Pardon me,

I must go to bed! But, as it is still early, stay here in God's name and chat with my wife: you have much to tell her which my talking has kept back. I am an old-fashioned citizen, and it is my hour for going to sleep." He took a candle, and said good night. We parted with the utmost cordiality, and with mutual wishes to meet again in Baireuth.

CHAPTER VIII.

The Battle of Aspern.— State of Silesia.— Deutsch-Wagram.— The Camp.
— Archduke Charles.— The French cross the Danube.— Storm in the
Marchfeld.— Position of the Austrian Army.— Archduke John at Pressburg.— Failure of the first Attack of the French on Wagram.— Archduke Charles's Plan of Action.— Napoleon's Arrangements.— Attack
upon Atterkla and Wagram.— Defence of Atterkla.— Advance of the
Imperial Guard.— Defeat of the left Wing of the Austrian Army.— Retreat of the Austrians upon Bockfliess and Gerasdorf, 5th and 6th of July,
1809.

AFTER the signal reverses in Bavaria, the taking of Vienna, and the failure of so many plans from which so much had been expected, the fate of Austria, and indeed of all Germany, appeared to be sealed. Suddenly, at a time when it seemed hopeless, the Austrians obtained a most glorious victory. The worn-out and beaten troops, labouring under the disadvantage of a rapid retreat, had disputed the passage of the Danube, and after a contest which lasted during the 21st and 22d May, succeeded in driving the French across the river. The victory of Aspern resounded throughout Germany, and stirred up every heart. Until now Napoleon had never been beaten: this was the first battle that he had lost; it was a great battle utterly lost in the open field. Archduke Charles was the first to gain so important a victory over the greatest conqueror of modern days: Napoleon in after times repeatedly lost greater battles, but he never left the crown of victory so undisputed to one opponent.

In Berlin, and in Silesia—where we then were,—the enthusiasm was general. The spell was broken, Napoleon was no longer invincible, he had been stopped in the full career of victory, his army had been beaten, and he himself might be crushed as he had hitherto crushed others. When his dangerous position in the heart of an enemy's country and the distance which separated him from France were considered, his downfall might well be expected; he had predicted his own fate when he told his soldiers at the beginning of the war that this would be his last campaign in Germany. The Tyrol was in open hostility, the north of Germany, and Prussia, were ready for any outbreak, England was making active preparations, confederate princes, his allies on the Rhine might desert, and the people rise against him — in short, all the favourable prognostications with which the Germans had flattered themselves at the beginning of the war, seemed more likely now than ever to prove true.

Filled with these hopes and impressions we continued our journey. Two of my companions were forced to stay in Silesia, and the remaining four entered Moravia, there to begin our new life. Here the tone of mind of the people struck us much; they were neither vehemently elated by the victory, nor yet without a due perception of its importance. A tranquil confidence in a right cause, and a steadfast determination to defend it faithfully, seemed to pervade all classes, and to place them above the vicissitudes of fortune, without inspiring any unusual enthusiasm. The old-fashioned system of government in connection with a population formed chiefly of Sclavonian elements, explained this apparent anomaly. Nearly all those capable of bearing arms were already engaged in active service; the possessors of land, the youths of the towns and villages, and even civil officers had been enrolled in the regiments of the line or the militia; and it was only here and there that a few weak divisions of raw recruits were to be seen in a state of half equipment, previous to joining the main army.

At Olmütz we found the detailed official printed report of the battle of Aspern. We eagerly seized this complete account of so important an event. The statement was read aloud, commented upon, and made a strong impression upon us: many were the thoughts of the past and of the future which crowded upon our minds. When we compared the loss of the Austrians with the number engaged, and found that one in four had been either wounded or killed, we could not help remarking, that in the event of a similar engagement, one of ourselves was fated to fall.

We hurried on, full of anxiety lest we should miss some important action. It was a wonder that the truce had lasted until now: it could not continue many days more.

My companions wished to enter cavalry regiments, but I intended to serve in the infantry, and in order to find for myself some regiment which would suit me, I had purposely brought no letters of introduction. We parted with light hearts, and I proceeded with post-horses to head-quarters.

I offered a place in my carriage to a drill sergeant who happened to be going the same road, and his conversation was most useful to me on many points on which I wanted information. The ideas which I had until now entertained of the French and Prussian soldiery gave way to others of a totally different kind.

I reached Deutsch-Wagram early on the 21st of June, and before I had shaken off the torpor produced by the chill of the night, the postillion drove to the Archduke's house, which I recognised by the flag and the guard of honour. They took me for a courier, and were about to awaken the Archduke, a proceeding which I with difficulty prevented, by repeatedly assuring them that I had no despatches to deliver, but had come on purely personal business; at last, I made them understand that Archduke Charles was on no account to be disturbed. I found myself, however, in a curious predicament. Every house in the village was filled to overflowing with staff officers or others connected with the army, and sentinels stood before nearly every door. An inn, therefore, was out of the question. As the whole place seemed profoundly quiet, and no one took the smallest heed of me, I tried my luck in the nearest house, where some people appeared to be stirring. Here I found several quartermasters, who took compassion on me, and asked me to share their breakfast. I now gave myself up to the strange impressions produced by the scene, and to a further consideration of my venture. A few officers entered, and, after a short conversation, they considered me as already their companion in arms, and gave me good advice, by which, however, I profited the less as they were by no means unanimous. I then wrote a memorial, stating, as shortly as I could, the object I had in view, and sent the letter to the proper authorities.

As the sun rose, the head-quarters were full of life, and I went out into the fields. I surveyed Deutsch-Wagram, and the camp, and wondered how it was that a stranger,—probably the only civilian among so many thousand soldiers,—was allowed to wander about unchallenged: no one questioned me as to my name or occupation, and my passport had not been asked for since I left Olmütz. A confused mass of human beings was in motion before my eyes. The huge encampment was full of soldiery, and in Wagram itself the various streams seemed to unite. All sorts and conditions of men in different costumes, in and out of uniform, at work or on duty, in search of news or of pleasure, buying and selling, were hurrying to and fro. Some of the uniforms of the Austrian regiments are extremely beautiful; the hussars, the lancers, and the Hungarian grenadiers are the finest among them: in comparison with these the German foot soldiers look mean, although in large masses their appearance is impressive. The dress of the generals is remarkable; their stone-blue coats and red breeches offering the strongest contrast between what is almost invisible and most staring. Similar contrasts were presented by their figures and the expression of their faces: perfect ease and pedantic stiffness, light humour and deep fixity of purpose, comfortable dulness and wild passion; all these were depicted in their countenances. The eye was not so much struck by individual Germans, Frenchmen, Walloons, Sclavonians, Italians, and Magyars, as by the general mixture of all these nations. The most curious characteristic of the Imperial army was not that the individuality of so many different nations, languages, forms, and manners remained, but that they were all held together by some strong attractive power. I almost fancied myself in the midst of the soldiers described by Schiller in Wallenstein's camp; and, indeed, this army consisted for the most part of the same materials. The strange scenes which met the eye, the old-fashioned phrases which caught the ear, brought back to my recollection the once-popular novel of "Simplicissimus;" and when the provost-marshal was pointed out to me, going his rounds, I thought I saw before me the Rumor-meister, or queller of disturbances, in the wild times of the Thirty Years' War.

In head-quarters was great excitement, and a certain degree of splendour and gaiety; but in the camp itself every thing looked quiet and serious. The ground was accurately measured out, and strict order maintained in the spaces left for passage. A careful watch was kept over all: no noise, no disputes, were permitted: the troops were busily employed in cleaning their arms and accoutrements, or in other routine work; but most of them were at drill. From early dawn the several divisions, large and small, were on parade; the blanks left by former heavy losses were filled by raw recruits, who were drilled as well as haste would allow. This active drilling and the regularity and precision with which the various duties were performed, imparted to this warlike activity a character of peaceful order.

Three times a day the troops were drawn up under arms for prayers; the beat of drum summoned the sergeants and corporals to receive orders; at a given signal the soldiers silently formed in line: numerous outposts kept constant watch at their several stations, and when darkness came on, their challenges alone broke the stillness of the night. The troops lay in the open air; in the midst of each regiment was a single tent, which served as a chapel, and afforded shelter for the colonel. All the other officers, like the common soldiers, contented themselves with a trench dug in the ground, which some of them covered with twigs and grass, as some protection against the weather. The remarkable energy, tranquillity, moderation, and obedience of this army, was an exact type of the German character: and, compared with the restless and dissolute life of the French soldiers, gave every promise of success, more especially under the command of the best Austrian general of the day. A few instances may serve to show what these Austrian soldiers were in those days. A man badly wounded was brought to the rear, and in answer to the inquiries of his comrades how he felt? said, "Oh, very well — the enemy is in full retreat towards the Danube." A grenadier's musket was bent double in his hand by a cannon ball, he looked with amazement at the damage, saying in a tone of regret, " 'Twas such a good gun!" An officer asked a troop of grenadiers who had been in the thick of the battle, where the batallion was? "We are the batallion," was the short answer:—the rest had been killed.

This and the following day I passed in endeavouring to form an accurate idea of the nature of the country and of the camp. Since the battle of Aspern the Austrians had remained almost on the same spot, only slightly drawing back and spreading their line. Aspern and Esslingen well fortified, and filled with troops, were in our front. The Danube flowed between us and the French, who were posted and protected by strong works on the island of Lobenau, or, as it was more commonly called, Lobau. Higher up by Nussdorf, and even further, the right wing of the Austrian army rested on the Danube; thence it stretched towards Stamersdorf and Wagram, and the left wing which was furthest from the Danube extended as far as Markgrafen-Neusiedel, in the Marchfeld. Deutsch-Wagram was the centre of our position. To the left of this spot the ground rises and forms on the east a high table land, which falls in terraces towards the south. Some hundred paces in front a brook, called the Russbach, planted with willows, flows down from Wolkersdorf towards the plain of Marchfeld through Wagram, Baumersdorf, and Markgrafen-Neusiedel. In the far distance, across the plain beyond the Danube, the tower of St. Stephen's church at Vienna stood out against the hazy horizon. It was strange thus to have the capital occupied by the enemy ever before us, and to be able only to reach it with the eyes. The Austrian head-quarters were not fortified, as the position offered great natural advantages. In the event of a second engagement the Marchfeld offered a fine arena for the movements of cavalry. On the other hand, all along the Danube, especially by Aspern and Esslingen, which were the best places for crossing the river, very strong and extensive works had been thrown up. Both armies had ceased firing, and lay observing each other from their positions. The longer this cessation of hostilities lasted the greater would be the advantage to the Austrians. Napoleon was in an enemy's land, in the midst of a hostile people; the passes over the Danube were guarded, Vienna already felt the want of provisions, the Tyrol was in arms, Styria by no means secure, and Hungary daily becoming more formidable. The Austrians endeavoured, by sending troops to the Upper Danube, still further to impede the French in their operations, and to increase the insurrection in their rear; while lower down, on the right bank of the Danube, Archduke John bravely defended the strong tête de pont at Pressburg against the daily attacks of the French troops. Well might Archduke Charles say that every day that he staid there and kept the French army inactive, might be considered a victory: besides, delay was of further importance in a political point of view.

I had wished to see the Archduke, and an opportunity soon occurred. In the evening I had heard him for an hour playing on the pianoforte in which he was a master; shortly after he mounted his horse and rode about the camp: he then returned and walked afoot. His appearance was most engaging; he looked like a brave, honest, kind-hearted man; his commanding eye and earnest manner inspired confidence, as well as respect and awe; his small slender figure was by no means deficient in strength, but gave tokens of that nervous temperament for which he was remarkable. The rude fatigues of war had not deprived his limbs of a certain soft grace, but what most distinguished the Archduke were his simple and natural manners, and the total absence of all affectation. The languor of his movements would lead one to suspect in him want of energy, but the fire of his eye forbade the thought. His undaunted courage, that tender care of others which made him always sacrifice himself, his honest firm sense, and the glory of his former victories, had won for him the love of the army. The officers and men alike, especially the Bohemian troops, were devoted to him. Wherever he appeared he was greeted with loud cheers, which betrayed his presence to the enemy: and it was with difficulty that this cheering could be prevented. As commander-in-chief his power was greater than any Austrian general had exercised since Wallenstein. He had immediate command over every thing connected with the army: he could promote and dismiss, reward and punish without appeal; the conduct of the war was left entirely to him, and the finances of the state were placed at his disposal. There was, however, some difficulty with regard to Hungary in this respect, and other secret motives interfered with his power from the very beginning.

For two long days I had wandered about head-quarters and the camp, and my dreary lack of occupation became more unbearable every hour. By some misunderstanding a direct negative had been given to my memorial, and I had lost all hope of getting a commission when I was referred to the colonel of the regiment Vogelsang, stationed on the high plateau to which I have before alluded, to the left of Wagram. This colonel was Count Von Bentheim from Westphalia, a handsome young man of captivating manners, who had been appointed to the command of this regiment as a reward for his distinguished bravery at Aspern. A few words explained my wishes, and Count Bentheim welcomed me into his regiment, which I entered as ensign in the first company, under the brave Captain Von Marais. I bought the accoutrements of an officer who had been killed at Aspern, exchanged the hat for the schako, girded on the sword and the broad belt clasped with the Austrian eagle, made acquaintance with the officers, and slept with them in a trench, dug in the earth, next to my captain and another officer, as if I had done so all my life.

The following days passed heavily enough. The excessive heat had burnt up the grass and the leaves: the willows by the Russbach were long since leafless, and even stripped of their bark; not a shadow was to be seen upon the endless plain, only thick clouds of dust, raised in eddies by sudden gusts of wind for a moment veiled the glaring sun, and covered us with a shower of hot sand. The drilling had to be suspended, and we crept back into our mud hut. With the best intentions my fellow officers were but sorry companions. The views taken by northern Germans were incomprehensible to the Austrians, who saw in war merely a trade from which to gain all the advantage they could, and who looked forward with pleasure to garrison life in Prague. The colonel was the only one who knew Gentz, and had heard of Frederick Schlegel; to the rest these were names like any others. Moreover, the regiment consisted chiefly of Bohemians, who spoke only their own language. There was no enthusiasm, no poetry: even the excitement of danger was denied us: not a shot was fired, and profound quiet reigned around. It was rumoured that there would be no further engagement; peace was talked of and even wished for. There could be no doubt that some negotiation was going on, as French employés were constantly seen in Wagram: it was even said that Napoleon's confidant, Duroc, had been sent with proposals to the Archduke.

The worst trial was now over. On the evening of the 30th of June, after a hot, wearisome, wasting day, which promised just such another for the morrow, we were cheered by the welcome sound of a cannonade on the Danube. We soon learned that a party of French had come across from the Lobau in boats to a meadow called the Mill Island, which was only separated from the left bank by a small arm of the Danube. They had thrown a bridge over this arm, and protected it with outworks. Our batteries at Esslingen opened upon the French to hinder their passage: they replied with their guns on the Lobau. It was said that the negotiation was at an end, that the Emperor Napoleon had concentrated his troops, and meant shortly to pass the river with his whole force, and to give battle. This showed how rightly the Archduke had judged in thus obstinately keeping his position, as it proved that the enemy could find no better place for his passage than the one which had been fortified and prepared for his reception. During the night we saw the alarm fires in the plain below us, and the whole camp was in motion. The cannonade ceased for a time, but about one in the morning the regiments quartered on the heights near Wagram were ordered to break up their quarters, and to advance five or six miles nearer the Danube, towards Wittau and Rasdorf. We expected the enemy's attack every moment: the cannonade was renewed at intervals. However, the French did not advance, but contented themselves with completing the works at the bridge. Archduke Charles went first to Rasdorf, thence to Stadt-Enzersdorf, where he surveyed the enemy's operations from the church tower; he then took up his quarters in Breitenlee. Meanwhile, it became evident that the preparations for passing the Danube at this spot were too insignificant to be in earnest, and that the enemy merely wanted to divert our attention from his real object, which was to pass the river higher up, either at Nussdorf, or lower down at Ort, by which movement the right or the left flank of the Austrian army, as it was then posted, would be threatened. It was therefore deemed more advisable in this state of uncertainty as to which point the enemy would select, to fall back again into a position where our troops might meet either contingency. In consequence of this determination we unexpectedly received orders, on the 3d of July, to occupy our former position at Wagram. This march forwards and backwards is not mentioned in the Austrian despatches, and yet our advance was by no means unimportant, as, if adhered to, it would have forced the enemy to fight under circumstances precisely similar to those of Aspern, while our falling back again gave him, instead of a narrow field, the advantage of an extended line of attack. As we lost the battle of Wagram, we may deplore having given up the advantage of the narrow field of action nearer to the Danube.

We had no longer the prospect of having to pass another day with no further amusement than that of being burnt up by the sun or smothered in dust. We had no distinct idea of the enemy's intention, but could guess from their movements that some great plan was in preparation. The fortifications on the island of Lobau, the repairing and protection of the bridges over the Danube, the building of new bridges between the several islands and the shore, the continued labour of carpenters and shipwrights, the arrival of artillery and powder waggons—none of this escaped our notice. Our suspicions were confirmed by the movement of the troops who kept pouring in from the upper and lower Danube. From Bisamberg we saw the so-called Italian army advance towards the Danube. Archduke Charles determined to destroy Napoleon's plan, to begin the attack himself, and to cut off Napoleon from his reserved point at Lobau. The Austrian divisions on the Upper Danube had received orders to give the enemy no rest, while Archduke John was told to leave the tête de pont at Pressburg, and to march along the right bank of the Danube. At seven o'clock on the evening of the 4th of July, these orders were countermanded, and he was directed to transport his troops over to the left bank of the river, and to advance immediately as far as Marcheck, so that in the event of a battle he might act upon the enemy's right flank. We too were ordered to be ready for action. On the evening of the 4th of July we were told, if we heard a cannonade, to remain quiet till break of day, and then to be in marching order. Accordingly, as soon as it was dark we heard heavy firing on the Danube in our front: the sky was lighted up with the incessant flashing of cannons, bombs, and grenades. The contest lasted two hours on both sides. At the very moment while we were endeavouring to destroy their works on the Lobau, the French were striving to ruin ours and to burn Stadt-Enzersdorf. The Austrian artillery had little effect upon the strong works of Lobau, and the French at Mühlau, against which point our cannon was directed, from an idea that they intended to cross there, suffered but little from our shot, as they lay down on the ground. On the other hand, the enemy's shot told fearfully upon us: their artillery was more numerous and better served, their plan better laid and carried out with greater energy. In a short time Stadt-Enzersdorf was in flames, and our batteries availed little against their superior force. The horizon had been lighted up for a time by the conflagration of this village, when the sky suddenly grew black with thunder clouds, the rain fell in torrents, the flames slackened, the artillery fired seldomer,—a storm so frightful as no one remembered to have seen burst over the Marchfeld, which rocked with the crash of the thunder; and, what with the pouring of the rain and the howling of the wind, there was such a war of the elements that artillery could scarce have been heard in it.

The enemy, who were prepared for all ventures, were singularly benefited by this storm. They had selected as their point for crossing the river, the open country on the left bank of the Danube, by Mühlleithen and Wittau, nearly opposite the Lobau. The French troops made good their landing, and the blaze of the burning village of Stadt-Enzersdorf facilitated their falling into line, unmolested by us. The Austrians thought the French extremely unlikely to select this point for their passage. The attempt was bold, and would have been full of danger, had the fourth division of the Austrian army remained at Wittau, or had it immediately returned there. The success which crowned the French attack displayed Napoleon's masterly skill and admirable arrangements, the certainty with which his orders were executed, and the precision and rapidity of his movements. He reckoned upon carrying his point before the Austrians could stop him. By ten o'clock at night General Oudinot had established on the other side of the river 1500 voltigeurs, under General Conroux: their landing was protected by the fire of ten gun-boats. The Austrian outposts retreated without much loss from the works they had erected, and the enemy obtained a firm footing on the plain before Mühlleithen. Meanwhile Colonel Sainte-Croix, Massena's adjutant, had landed with 2500 men near Schönau. Six bridges, for which the materials had long been ready, were now thrown across the Danube. First the infantry crossed the river, and over the next bridge the cavalry, and artillery of Marshal Massena; a little lower down, the troops of Marshal Davoust and of General Oudinot passed over, taking up their positions in an orderly quiet manner. Before three in the morning above 40,000 were concentrated near Mühlleithen, and many more were following. The rearmost troops had crossed by mid-day, while the foremost had been already some time engaged with our troops. The following was the original order of battle. The fourth division, under Massena, was placed, as the left wing, on the Danube: the second division, under General Oudinot, formed the centre; while the third, under General Davoust, formed the right wing, abutting upon Wittau. Behind these the troops of Marshal Bernadotte, or the ninth division, the Italian army under Eugene Beauharnais, and the eleventh division, under Marmont, formed the second line. The guards and the cuirassiers brought up the rear, as a reserve. Napoleon's army consisted of about 160,000, of which 15,000 were cavalry: he had 600 pieces of cannon. The passage of the river and the getting into line was accomplished, in the midst of the storm, with extraordinary rapidity and precision : it commenced during the night, and was finished by broad day.

The first dawn of day, on the 5th of July, showed us what had happened: the storm had subsided, the sun gave promise of a hot day, and at about four the cannonade recommenced with increased fury. Volumes of smoke rose again from Stadt-Enzersdorf, which, in spite of the brave efforts of a battalion of the regiment Bellegarde, was carried by assault after a short resistance. The castle of Sachsengang, between Mühlleithen and Wittau, shared the same fate. A portion of the Austrian troops, under General Von Nordmann, for a moment threatened the right flank of the French near Rutzendorf, but General Oudinot quickly repelled the attack, and the French soldiers deployed, supported by a large park of artillery. Marshal Davoust drove the Austrian outposts out of Grosshofen, and advanced from Rutzendorf against Markgrafen-Neusiedel, his extreme right being covered by two dragoon regiments under Grouchy and Pully, and by a division of light horse commanded by general Montbrun. The centre, under Bernadotte, advanced against Pysdorf and Rasdorf: Massena's right rested on Breitenlee, while his left was protected by the Danube, and he took possession of our works at Esslingen and

Aspern as fast as the Austrians quitted them. The fortifications raised against the Lobau were open in the rear, and being outflanked, were no longer tenable. The Austrians therefore slowly quitted them, one by one, taking even their heavy guns with them.

Archduke Charles had been unable to prevent the French from passing the river under cover of the stormy night. The enemy had not only gained a firm footing, but had formed into line, and were advancing to attack us. All the divisions of their army were in motion, their communication with each other secure and perfect. The several divisions of the Austrian army, on the other hand, were too much separated to be able to meet so formidable and rapid an enemy, much less drive them back over the Danube. The whole Austrian force was under 100,000 men, with 410 pieces of artillery; the troops were distributed in the following manner:—A vanguard consisting of artillery, cavalry, and infantry, under Field Marshal Von Nordmann, had been stationed on the Danube, supported by the sixth division under Count Von Klenau. In his rear, the fifth division under Prince Von Reuss-Plauen, held the country about Bisamberg. To his left, near Hagenbrunn, were placed the third division under Count Kolowrat, then near Säuring, the grenadiers, under Field Marshal Von Prochaska, and at Breitenlee the mass of cavalry under Prince Liechtenstein. Further, at Wagram, the first division was commanded by the cavalry officer, Count Bellegarde, and in the same direction, close by Baumersdorf, was the second division under Prince Hohenzollern, while the fourth division was at Markgrafen-Neusiedel, under Prince Rosenberg. For this purpose, only the three divisions behind the Russbach, and the cavalry, were handy for action; the grenadiers were not so, and both the divisions at Bisamberg were nearly eight miles from the scene of action. Under these circumstances, Archduke Charles found himself compelled not to give battle by the Danube, but to draw back his forces from the river; and while the French were advancing, he was employed in concentrating his troops. He determined to stand the first brunt of the action in an advantageous position between Stamersdafe and Markgrafen-Neusiedel, and then to become the attacking party himself; by directing his whole force against the left flank of the French, he hoped to cut off their communication with the bridges they had built over the Danube, while Archduke John should unexpectedly fall upon the enemy's right flank and rear, and strike the decisive blow. In this spirit all his arrangements were made. The outposts as well as the detachments of the sixth division, which had been pushed forward along the Danube, were ordered to fall back gradually before the French, fighting the while; the former were to join the left, the latter the right wing of the main position. The fourth division and the grenadiers were ordered up from their positions, which were too distant, so as to reduce to a smaller compass the wide half circle formed by the army. The troops on the Danube at Linz and Krems were too far off to be sent for; moreover, in the event of the French being defeated, they might render most efficient service in those districts. On the other hand, a message was sent early on the 5th of July to Archduke John at Pressburg, directing him to march with all speed and with such troops as he could get together, by Marcheck, so as to take part with the left wing in the approaching action. A second order to this effect was despatched later, as from the exposed condition of the left flank, which had no point on which to rest, it was feared that it could not stand its ground till the decisive moment. The courier despatched during the evening of the 4th, as well as those sent later, arrived safely at Pressburg. They announced on their return to the camp, that the troops from Pressburg could not possibly arrive the same day, but that nothing was likely to impede their presence on the battle field on the 6th of July. It seemed probable, considering the large number of troops engaged, and the great extent of the field of action, that the battle could be made to last until then.

A portion of Prince Liechtenstein's cavalry had been ordered to advance from Breitenlee towards Rasdorf and Pysdorf, to observe the enemy's motions; for a long time it stood its ground under a murderous fire, which swept off a sixth of the Hohenzollern regiment of cuirassiers, and so many officers, that a young Prussian ensign of the name of Gustavus Von Barnekow found himself next in command to the colonel. The young man had shown such bravery as to attract Archduke Charles's especial observation. About midday, this body of cavalry had a serious engagement with Marshal Bernadotte's division, near Rutzendorf, and several times forced the Saxon cavalry under his command to retreat. In this encounter, it so happened that two regiments fought hand to hand, one of Austrian cuirassiers, the other of Saxon dragoons, both of which regiments had been raised by, and named after, Duke Albert of Saxe Teschen. The Austrian cavalry for some time maintained their ground, but were forced to give way before the advancing foot and the artillery. Napoleon directed his chief attack against the central position of Wagram and the Austrian left flank, the extreme point of which was marked by an old square tower, near Markgrafen-Neusiedel. The Austrians guessed Napoleon's plan, planted a battery on the mound, and would have thrown up some entrenchments had the enemy given them time. By mid-day Napoleon's right wing had reached Glinzendorf; his centre was at Rasdorf; the left wing had made less progress, and had only advanced as far as Aspern. Stronger batteries continued to advance, larger masses of troops were brought into action: the whole line blazed with fire. From our high position, the movements of the enemy had resembled those of a chess-board, but the battle approached nearer, and the cannon-balls came whistling over our heads in lavish profusion, while we replied from our batteries. The foot were now ordered to lie down, and the balls at first did little execution: but as the enemy approached, we stood to our arms. Archduke Charles and his staff rode along our line, drew bridle in front of us, looked over the plain along which the enemy was rapidly advancing, gave out his commands in a manner that showed his disregard of death and danger, and his complete absorption in his duties. The battle gave to his manner a remarkable enthusiasm,—an air of high joyous courage, with which again he inspired his soldiers. The men looked on him with pride and confidence: many cheered him. After he had ridden on towards Baumersdorf, one of his adjutants galloped up, saying, "Volunteers, forward!" In an instant the whole company of Captain Von Marais was in motion; we thought that we were to storm a French field battery which was advancing through the corn fields in front, and we hastened joyfully down the slope of the hill. Then came a second adjutant with orders that we were only to occupy the Russbach, and to prevent the enemy from crossing it. We were to reserve our fire until they were close upon us. Dispersed in skirmishing parties, and concealing ourselves as well as we could from the enemy's shot and musketry behind the willow trees and in the standing corn, we remained ready for action. For above an hour we continued on this spot with the shot whistling in every direction over our heads. We soon perceived the enemy's superiority: they fired double the number of shots, although their guns were not so well served, but we admired the active zeal and enduring valour with which the unequal contest was maintained. As our guns were in batteries, the French could more easily avoid the shot, while their artillery, being planted in all directions along the line of the Russbach, served them more effectually than our skirmishers served us. General Oudinot had at least forty cannon directed against Baumersdorf, but as often as his troops entered the burning village, they were driven out by the brave General Count Ignatius Von Hardegg.

Napoleon saw with impatience that the day was drawing to a close and nothing decisive done. He had calculated on striking the blow at once, and was resolved not to have directed all his force upon a single point in vain. He rapidly arranged his troops for a general charge. Marshal Bernadotte was commanded to advance upon Wagram by Atterkla, and by taking this place to force the centre of the Austrian line. At the same time two close storming parties were to cross the Russbach to the right and left of Baumersdorf, to scale the heights, and to drive the Austrians from their post.

Meanwhile, the enemy's foot were already close upon us, the skirmishers were ordered to fall back into line, and a tremendous fire was opened along the whole front. The loud reports, the sharp cracking noise caused by the incessant fire of small arms, the rattling jingle made by the handling of above 20,000 muskets, all crowded together in so small a space, was the only thing that made a new and strange impression upon me in this my first battle. The rest partly accorded with what my imagination had already pictured to me, and partly even fell short of it. Every thing,—even the thunder of the artillery,— appeared to me insignificant in comparison to the incessant cracking of the small arms — that weapon by which even modern warfare is rendered so murderous. While this continued, and Archduke Charles galloped to Wagram, where the firing began likewise to be heavy, there came a report that the left flank was attacked by French cavalry. It proved, however, to be a body of infantry, who had climbed the heights, under cover of the smoke from the guns and from the burning village of Baumersdorf. The enemy, however, were soon forced to retreat beyond the Russbach, while General Count Ignatius von Hardegg dashed out of Baumersdorf; and falling upon the retreating French, drove them with great loss far into the plain towards Rasdorf.

The enemy who had crossed the Russbach from the left of Baumersdorf, consisted of two divisions, led by Generals Macdonald and Lamarque, in conjunction with two other divisions, commanded by General Grenier, and led by Eugene Beauharnais in person; they took advantage of a ravine which quickly led them up to the height between our first and second divisions. The French attacked the flank of the first division, and threw it into disorder; a fierce contest ensued; both parties fired point blank, and then crossed bayonets. The enemy's attack on our left flank was too vehement to be resisted; the line was broken, and some of our regiments were forced back upon the second line. At the first onslaught, a shot hit me in the thigh, and from that moment I could only be an idle spectator of what was going on.

For some time the confusion was very great, and threatened serious consequences. Archduke Charles came up with his staff, tried to establish order, and put himself at the head of the troops, who eventually recovered their lost ground. Prince Hohenzollern now returned with his light horse, and charged the enemy, who thus attacked on all sides, suffered severely. They were without artillery, which they had been obliged to leave on the other side of the Russbach, and the cavalry after passing the brook with difficulty, attempted to retrieve the lost ground, but they were entirely cut to pieces by Prince

Hohenzollern's light horse and four squadrons of hussars. But few escaped. Wherever the battle was hottest Archduke Charles was foremost. Captain Weitenfeld of the regiment of Vogelsang, cut down a Frenchman in the very act of discharging his piece at the Archduke. A French officer who thought to make a good prize, was shot down as he called to the Arch duke to surrender. The Archduke was slightly wounded, which did not, however, prevent him from remaining on horseback or for a moment interrupt his attention to his duties. The Prince of Orange (the present king of the Netherlands), who held the rank of general in the Austrian army, had two horses shot under him. Both sides suffered severely.

Meanwhile Marshal Davoust had crossed the Russbach at Markgrafen-Neusiedel with a portion of his troops, and had brought forty guns to bear upon the Austrian position, with great effect. At the same time the two divisions of Morand and Friant attacked the Austrians from the left bank of the Russbach, while the light cavalry under General Montbrun endeavoured to turn our left flank. Prince von Rosenberg however repelled all these attacks: the French retreated back over the Russbach before dark, and encamped that night beyond Glinzendorf.

Somewhat later than these failures, the attack against Wagram itself began. Marshal Bernadotte led the Saxons against this position, which was bravely defended by Colonel von Oberndorf at the head of the regiment Reuss-Plauen. After this officer had been wounded the French succeeded in reaching the middle of the village, but were received by so murderous a cross fire from two battalions which advanced from both sides, that they retreated with great loss. Darkness prevented any further attempts. The country was lighted up with burning villages; close by us flames burst from Baumersdorf and Wagram. This scene and the welcome sight of our colonel with the colours in his hand were the last which I saw.

Whilst I and the other wounded were being carried to the rear, the balls were flying over and about us, and we heard the thunder of the artillery until late in the night, when it gradually ceased, and we carried away with us the impression of having won the battle. Napoleon's bold attempt to break the Austrians' line by one grand charge, had entirely failed, and had ended in his own partial discomfiture.

He could not conceal his anger and annoyance, and attributed his want of success partly to the unhappy accident that the French and Saxons had by mistake fired upon one another, and partly to the negligence of Bernadotte, whom he hated and wished to lower in public estimation. Nevertheless, he had reason to thank fortune, even though she denied him the victory on that day, for defending him from a greater misfortune. For had Archduke Charles been able to bring fresh troops into action, had he had at his disposal a numerous body of cavalry with which to have followed up his advantage, it would have gone hard with the French army. The four French divisions which had been driven back from the heights, involved those behind them in their retreat; the whole line was in confusion, and kept falling back all night. The imperial guard alone maintained their ground at Rasdorf, and formed a rallying point for the rest. The Austrian divisions which had not yet been engaged, were too far off; nor could they have left their positions without danger. Archduke Charles had not above 10,000 horse in the whole army, and some of these were dispersed about in various divisions, the others had been engaged all day. The night was passed by both armies in making preparations for battle.

This time the Austrians seem to have arranged their plan of action with greater skill and boldness than the French, who were affected by the unfavourable issue of the last night's contest. Napoleon contented himself with concentrating his troops round Rasdorf during the night so as to be able to bring them to bear upon any direction, and it was not till daybreak that he determined upon renewing the attack. Archduke Charles had again taken up his quarters in one of the few houses left standing at Wagram, and before midnight he had planned and sent the following order of battle to all his generals.

His right flank, consisting of the sixth and third divisions and the grenadiers, was to attack the enemy's left; their right would rest upon the Danube, and they were to advance along the course of the river from Stamersdorf towards Breitenlee and Süssenbrunn; their left was to be covered by Prince Liechtenstein's cavalry. The advance of the centre was planned in connection with this movement: the first division to proceed to Atterkla, defended on the left by the Russbach, and still keeping possession of the heights to the left of Wagram; this last position was likewise assigned to the second division. The left flank, consisting of the fourth division, was directed to occupy the attention of the French, and keep them in check until Archduke John, who was on his way from Pressburg, could fall upon the enemy's rear. The fifth division was to remain as a reserve at its post on the Upper Danube, where some French troops had showed themselves. One brigade of the third division, with a battery of guns, was placed on the heights near Stamersdorf. The sixth and third divisions were to leave their ground at one, the grenadiers at three, and the first and fourth divisions, at four o'clock. The troops were ordered to keep perfect silence, and not to throw away their shot. The infantry were drawn up in battalions with skirmishers in front. Archduke Charles had introduced this system into the army, and it had succeded admirably at Aspern. The battalions, consisting generally of six companies each, formed into squares, twelve or eighteen deep, and planted at regular intervals, opposed an impenetrable mass. In this array they marched, repulsed and even attacked bodies of cavalry, and were not easily broken in a retreat; but it is true that they laboured under great disadvantage when exposed to the fire of artillery.

The Archduke's intention was to cut off the communication of the French with Lobau, and then to beat them in the plain of the Marchfeld. But, alas! the execution by no means equalled the vigour and brilliancy of the plan. Some time elapsed before the troops received their several orders, owing to the darkness of the night, and even then they did not move with sufficient quickness to reach their destinations in due time. Fresh orders were despatched to Archduke John at two o'clock on the morning of the 6th of July, urging him to hasten his advance.

Napoleon, whose plan was by no means so prudent or so well-laid as it was afterwards represented, determined on the 6th of July to renew with greater vigour the attack which had failed on the previous day. He appears to have wavered once or twice and to have acted upon the spur of the moment, by which he several times ran great risk of losing the battle. To render the attack more successful, he concentrated his army in the fields round Rasdorf, which formed his head-quarters, and where, at the head of his guard, he intended to await the issue of the battle. Marshal Davoust, with the right wing, came nearer the centre of the position, and placed himself near Grosshofen; Marshal Massena, with the left wing, was ordered to quit the Danube and to approach Atterkla, leaving only the division of Boudet at Aspern to protect the bridges at Lobau. These arrangements had been made, and Napoleon was impatiently awaiting the execution of his orders, when the firing of cannon and musketry unexpectedly resounded along the whole line from Markgrafen-Neusiedel to Wagram, and by its increasing noise showed that the Austrians were already advancing. Struck with the boldness of this attack, Napoleon paid greater attention to the disposition of his troops, lest he should expose some weak point to his determined foe. For the first hour or so, the French attack was conducted without much courage or impetuosity — on several points they were beaten back, and it was some time before they at all recovered their usual temper. If Napoleon intended to have renewed his attack against Wagram, it would have been impossible at this moment, as the Austrians clearly had the advantage at that point.

The first division of the Austrian army, where Archduke Charles had taken up his quarters, had the smallest distance to march. Captain von Tettenborn, who commanded a body of light horse of the Klenau regiment, which formed the vanguard found Atterkla deserted by the Saxons, who had fallen back during the night upon Rasdorf. He took possession of the village, which was filled with wounded Saxons; several officers, some of them belonging to Bernadotte's staff, were taken prisoners. Tettenborn drove back several advanced posts of the enemy, and then joined some regiments which meanwhile had advanced, in order to cover two batteries, the fire of which forced the French division of Dupas, forming the right wing of their advanced guard on the Russbach, to retire towards Rasdorf. The chasseurs and infantry under General Karl von Stutterheim took possession of Atterkla. The whole of this division of the

Austrian army then advanced between Atterkla and Wagram, the leading troops in squares at regular intervals, those behind them in close line. This was the first real encounter of the day; and while many of the Austrian divisions were still advancing to take up their positions, the French were able to bring the cannon belonging to all the troops that were concentrated at Rasdorf to meet this attack. The Austrians soon lost the advantage they had gained, as with far inferior artillery they had to contend with the superior force of their adversaries. Nevertheless they fought for several hours with great firmness and courage.

Meanwhile the fourth division of the army had left the heights near Markgrafen-Neusiedel at about four o'clock, and advanced to the attack of Grosshofen and Glinzendorf, both of which villages were held by Marshal Davoust with artillery and infantry, while two bodies of cavalry were formed in double lines just behind. The third division of the French army was at that moment in the act of making for the centre of Napoleon's position, according to his orders. The French skirmishers had retired, and the Austrians, in spite of a murderous fire, had advanced close to the villages above named, and were preparing to storm them. This attack kept the French to their original position. General Puthod remained with his troops at Grosshofen, and General Friant at Glinzendorf, while Marshal Davoust threatened to attack our flank with the Gudin division. Napoleon himself at the head of a portion of his guards, and followed by the heavy cavalry under Generals Nansouty and Arrighi, galloped up to this position. He brought a heavy train of artillery to bear upon the Austrians, while he sent strong detachments of every description of troops to Loibersdorf, where they passed the Russbach, and then directed their march upon Ober-Siebenbrunn. This side movement along his and the whole flank, compelled Prince von Rosenberg to keep back his cavalry, which was to have supported the infantry, in order to observe the enemy's motions. Just as the Austrians were in the act of charging the enemy, the Archduke sent orders for the left wing to halt, for the right wing was too far off to take part in the engagement, and the left would thus have had to bear the whole brunt of the action, especially as nothing was yet seen of Archduke John's division. This delay, which arose from no local disadvantage on our side, but which was considered necessary, was the first bad symptom as to the ultimate issue of the battle. The enemy saw the advantage to be gained, and was not slow to profit by it. On the heights above Stamersdorf glittered the bayonets of the Austrian troops intended to act against the left wing of the French army, but the contest had not yet begun, and Napoleon saw that he should have time to beat our left wing before his own right could run any danger; he could afford to reinforce the latter from his centre before it was actually beaten. He gave Arrighi's cuirassiers to Marshal Davoust, ordered him to persevere vigorously in the attack against Markgrafen-Neusiedel, and then returned to Rasdorf. The rest of Napoleon's guards, which had been directed to advance to the assistance of the right wing, were ordered to march back upon Rasdorf. Meanwhile Marshal Davoust had sufficient force at his disposal to be able to spread out his troops to the right, and to press more and more upon the Austrian left flank. The French continued to bring up more artillery, and destroyed several of our batteries by their murderous fire. The Austrian left wing was thus reduced to act merely on the defensive.

The grenadiers of Säuring advancing by Gerasdorf against Süssenbrunn, now made their appearance on the field of battle; the first and second divisions were supported on both flanks and in the rear by cavalry. At length the sixth division also commenced an attack upon the left wing of the French between Breitenlee and Hirschstätten. Their numerous infantry was at Aspern, and the plain between Aspern and Stadelau was covered with parties of skirmishers. A general charge completed the confusion produced by the effective fire of the Austrian guns, which at this particular spot were more numerous than the French. General Augustus von Vecsey cleared the plain of the French skirmishers: Major Michailowich at the head of the battalion St. George, stormed the village of Aspern and advanced against the left wing of the enemy, while General Count von Walmoden at the head of Liechtenstein's hussars, charged the right wing, killed a large number of men, and took nine guns. The French retreated with the loss of many prisoners, some by Aspern towards the Mühlau, the others by Esslingen to Stadt-Enzersdorf. Count von Klenau then took possession of Aspern and Esslingen, and of the works which had been erected within this district. The troops drawn up in squares between Aspern and Breitenlee, waited to see what would happen to their left. It was now ten o'clock, and the battle had continued without intermission in the other parts of the field.

Meanwhile, the third division had advanced in two lines from Gerasdorf to Süssenbrunn; its right rested on Breitenlee, which was held by three battalions. Count von Kolowrat did not wait for his left wing to come up, but boldly attacked the enemy's left wing near their main position at Rasdorf, and advanced as far as Neuwirthaus: for some time, he had the advantage, but could not maintain his ground, and was obliged to fall back with his right wing upon Breitenlee.

The Emperor Napoleon galloped along the whole extent of the French line, encouraging his troops, who received him with loud cheers. Nearly opposite Atterkla he met Marshal Massena, who came up with three divisions. Massena was in a carriage, as a fall had prevented him from riding. Napoleon embraced him, ordered him to attack Atterkla without delay, and then galloped back to Rasdorf to see what Prince Eugene's and General Oudinot's divisions were about. He was incessantly occupied in giving orders as to the movements of the troops. He continued to send fresh bodies of men towards Markgrafen-Neusiedel, so as to turn the Austrian left flank. He felt confident that he was strong enough to attack our left wing and our centre at the same moment. The first and most important object was to take Atterkla, so as to secure his own centre already endangered by the impetuous advance of the Austrians.

Marshal Massena ordered a strong body of cavalry to draw up in the plain near Rasdorf, and to advance against Atterkla and Breitenlee: he put himself at the head of two strong divisions of infantry and stormed Atterkla right and left, as he conceived that General Carra Saint-Cyr's division did not carry on the attack with sufficient vigour. Neither the constant fire of the Austrian grenadiers, nor the murderous discharge of artillery, stopped the determined advance of the French; whole ranks were mown down at every step; but they continued to press forward to the charge. The Austrians gave way before their impetuous attack, the French succeeded in taking Atterkla, and forced their way into the Austrian line. The danger was imminent: success at this point would be decisive. The French thought their victory secure, and threw themselves between the Austrian squares, with the intention of separating and beating them by turns. But just at this moment the disorder produced by the impetuosity of the attack was injurious to the French. Archduke Charles, Count von Bellegarde, and other generals and staff officers, by great exertions, restored order among the scattered troops, formed them into squares, and charged the enemy at the point of the bayonet. The French could not speedily collect their forces, were driven back in disorder, out-flanked, and cut down in great numbers before they could reach Atterkla. Two French regiments, the 24th and the 4th, were nearly exterminated,—more than 1000 men fell, above 500 were made prisoners, and four colours were taken. One of Count Kolowrat's battalions led by Major Haberein, and the three grenadier regiments, Scovaux, Putheany, and Brzezinski, stormed Atterkla, and retook it from the enemy after a severe contest. General Charles von Stutterheim was here wounded by a cannon ball, whereupon the Archduke entrusted the further command of this village to his brother, Archduke Louis. The French several times renewed their attack upon this position with fresh troops, but their attempts to retake Atterkla were repulsed every time by General Merville with the sacrifice of many men killed and wounded, besides the loss of two more colours. The Austrians likewise lost a considerable number of men; and General Merville, after twice driving the French out of the village into which they had penetrated, was at length struck down by a musket shot. The French cavalry had meanwhile remained drawn up on the plain; they were kept in check by a body of Austrian cavalry on their flank under Prince Maurice von Liechtenstein. The two cavalry regiments, Kron Prinz and Rosenberg, had saved the artillery planted in front of Atterkla, which in the first moment of the enemy's attack had been given up as lost. When Napoleon saw that his troops were flying in confusion, he rode up to the spot, and with Massena's help succeeded in restoring some sort of order. It was high time, for new measures were presently required to meet other contingencies.

The successful defence of Atterkla frustrated Napoleon's hopes of breaking the Austrian line at that point. Not knowing that his troops had once actually taken this village, he repeatedly exclaimed, " Oh, that I had but been in possession of Atterkla, even for a few minutes!" The bravery of the Austrian troops had averted a great danger. Meanwhile the attack of the French on Atterkla had impeded the advance of the Austrians. The several divisions of our army had not been able to draw nearer to each other, nor were our troops sufficient to cover the extended line of action. It is true that the two remaining grenadier brigades of Murray and Steyrer joined the line from Atterkla and Breitenlee, but their battalions could only form the advanced guard, and the cavalry had to be drawn up behind them to protect their rear. This induced Prince John von Liechtenstein to advance further, and with the aid of the third and sixth divisions to attack the main position of the enemy in the flank and rear. Massena's march from the Danube on Rasdorf and Atterkla, which we have mentioned above, had given freer scope to the right wing of the Austrian army; and by this movement Prince von Liechtenstein hoped to cut off Napoleon's communication with the Lobau. The third and sixth divisions had only to bend to the left, when they would be in the rear of the French army, and would thus place it between a cross fire.

Napoleon not only saw the danger which threatened him, but turned it to good account. He drew considerable bodies of troops from his centre, and ordered them to prepare for an attack: meanwhile Massena advanced his division to the left, towards Neuwirthaus, against the third division of the Austrians. General Macdonald, with three other divisions, took Massena's place, and Prince Eugene, with the guards, followed to support this movement. A tremendous fire of artillery opened the way for them. Marshal Bessières led on to the attack six regiments of the heavy cavalry of the imperial guard: Napoleon spoke a few encouraging words to each regiment, and recommended the men to use the point, and not the edge of the sword. This body of troops charged the Austrian grenadiers and the third division before they had formed. Prince John von Liechtenstein drew back his right wing again, towards Süssenbrunn, thus leaving a space open to the enemy, which, however, was exposed to the cross fire of the Austrian grenadiers and of the third division. Some infantry regiments were drawn up close behind, and beside the French cavalry; they advanced in spite of the cross fire, and charged the battalions St. George and Fisch with the bayonet. The Austrians stood their ground firmly, and poured a murderous fire upon the French infantry each time it advanced, while the grenadiers of Porter and Leiningen repulsed the French cavalry. One body of the enemy which advanced up to the very bayonets of the regiment of St. George, lost their leader, who was pulled from his horse, taken prisoner, and moreover was exposed, in our ranks, to two charges from his own cavalry and to a tremendous fire from the French artillery. Count von Leiningen took a French staff officer prisoner single-handed in front of his battalion.

But Napoleon had other plans in reserve. "The artillery of the imperial guard shall advance," said he; and sixty pieces of artillery, under Colonels Drouot and Daboville, were brought from beyond Rasdorf. Forty other guns joined these, and proceeded in the midst of a tremendous fire from the Austrians. These 100 pieces of artillery, covering about a mile of ground, poured a fire of grape and canister shot, more deadly than any of our people had ever seen before; the Austrians suffered severely, and their great guns were shattered. Several battalions repeatedly charged in the midst of this murderous fire, with the view of taking the French artillery; but they were driven back or cut down by the iron hail. The French likewise suffered severely, and lost a good many artillerymen and horses.

Napoleon had ordered Marshal Massena to turn back towards the left, but suspended his further advance. He himself remained between Rasdorf and Atterkla, perfectly unmoved in the midst of the heaviest fire, watching every incident in the battle, and giving his orders accordingly. By repeated marches and counter-marches the order of battle in his centre had been broken several times; but he restored it by bringing up fresh troops. Meanwhile accounts reached him from Massena that the right wing of the Austrians was gradually gaining ground, that Boudet's division had been driven back upon the Lobau with the loss of its cannon, that the Austrians were close upon the bridge, and that their guns would shortly be directed against the rear of the French army. Until now, Napoleon had received all reports without a word in reply, contenting himself with looking eagerly towards Markgrafen-Neusiedel. When he saw that Marshal Davoust had secured the heights above that spot, and that his fire would shortly bear upon the Austrians' flank, he exclaimed "Now is the time!" He ordered Massena to attack the Austrian right wing, and he formed the divisions of Lamarque, Broussier, and others into line, and directed General Macdonald to advance at their head by Atterkla upon Süssenbrunn, against the third division of the Austrian army, whose left wing received the first shock. The Archduke who was present in that division, led on his troops and changed the defence into an attack. General Vukassovich during the advance received a mortal wound, Count Saint Julien and General Lilienberg charged the left flank of the enemy who begun to waver. Napoleon ordered up the cuirassiers of General Nansouty and the cavalry of the imperial guard, under General Walther, to support the infantry, but they too were driven back by the heavy fire. Whereupon the French division of Serras and the Bavarian division of Wrede advanced, and were followed by the young guard under General Reille. The divisions of Pachtod and Durutte moved on either side of Macdonald, to make room for him, the one towards Wagram and the other towards Breitenlee. The battle had now raged on both sides with great fury and obstinacy for some time, but the Austrians had decidedly lost ground.

It was mid-day, and the battle continued along the whole line. Where the troops had not been in actual action—as was the case with the whole second division of the Austrian army appointed to guard the Russbach near Baumersdorf, or where they had stopped in their advance, and this was the predicament of the sixth division of the Austrians at Aspern, where they were waiting for the others—they were nevertheless exposed all the time to a tremendous fire from the French artillery extending in an unbroken line from the Danube to beyond Markgrafen-Neusiedel. Indeed, the number of guns and the weight of metal seemed to increase every moment.

Meanwhile the left wing of the Austrian army was equally hard pressed. At about ten o'clock the French troops which had crossed the Russbach at Loibersdorf, drove back General von Frelich's corps of observation, placed near Ober-Siebenbrunn, and thus turned the left flank of the fourth division of the Austrian army, which they proceeded to attack. To meet this threatened danger Prince von Rosenberg ordered up two of his regiments to the flank, and formed the rest into squares. But three other bodies of French marched from Ober-Siebenbrunn and Glinzendorf, covering their advance with the fire from a large number of guns. The Archduke hurried to this quarter and placed the troops in order. He directed the Hohenzollern cuirassiers to charge and drive back the French infantry. Seeing the impossibility of succeeding, and perceiving the imminent danger in which his left flank was now placed by the enemy's cavalry he ordered the cuirassiers to attack the latter, while he himself galloped up to the infantry where his presence seemed most necessary. Markgrafen-Neusiedel was bravely defended against several attacks from the enemy.. But at length, after the Archduke had been summoned elsewhere by the danger which now threatened his right wing, the weary Austrians gave way to the superior force of the French, and left them in possession of the village. The brave General Peter von Vecsey was here mortally wounded. The appearance of Archduke John in the rear of the French army was now most anxiously looked for; this alone could give a favourable turn to the battle. It was already feared that he would arrive too late; but as long as there was any hope, the Austrians were bound to maintain their ground. Meanwhile the French brought fresh troops to their right, and endeavoured more completely to turn our left flank. By this movement but few French troops were left opposite to the second division of the Austrian army. When Prince Hohenzollern saw that his front was in no danger, while the fourth division was hard pressed, he of his own accord sent to their assistance five battalions and four squadrons of horse. This advance of fresh troops to the extreme left flank brought a momentary relief, but did not change the fate of the battle. The contest was too unequal. Marshal Davoust had a third of the whole French army in this quarter. The Austrian troops were all engaged in action; there were no troops reserved for any sudden emergency, while the French had a constant supply of fresh men ready to be sent in all directions from their reserves at Rasdorf. General Oudinot again advanced against Baumersdorf and attacked the second division of the Austrians. But the battle continued to be most furiously contested at Markgrafen-Neusiedel. The French divisions Gudin and Puthod in six solid masses with a numerous park of artillery, and with a number of skirmishers in front, frequently stormed this position; while the divisions Morand and Friant kept extending their line to the right. The Austrian cavalry under Field Marshal Count von Nostitz, General Count von Wartensleben, Colonel Sardagna, and Prince von Coburg, who was wounded by a bullet, repeatedly charged the enemy. They several times drove back the cavalry of Generals Grouchy and Montbrun, but were too weak to make any impression on the French infantry, and were eventually compelled to fall back. Mayer's infantry brigade, at the head of which Field Marshal von Nordmann had placed himself, stood several of the enemy's charges; but when this brave leader was killed, General Mayer wounded, and more troops were brought against them, the Austrians were forced to give way, and the enemy gained ground. It was now that the division Morand attacked and carried by storm the tower of Markgrafen-Neusiedel. During this attack, or according to some accounts earlier in the day, or on even the day before, Colonel Oudet of the seventeenth regiment of the line fell, whose charms of person and character Charles Nodier mentions in such high terms. The right wing of the Austrian army, placed near the heights, still kept its ground; at their head Field Marshal Prince von Hohenlohe-Bartenstein, and the brave Prince von Hessen-Homburg, who was here wounded by a ball, repulsed several attacks of the French. Prince von Rosenberg endeavoured to retake the tower of Markgrafen-Neusiedel, but the cross fire which mowed down his men, and the superior force of the enemy, compelled him to give up the attempt. The

Austrians could no longer reckon upon or wait for Archduke John's arrival: the last moment at which his troops could have effected a diversion in our favour on the rear of the French was past. The right wing of the Austrians had until now been victorious, the centre had stood its ground, but the left wing was outflanked and beaten, and its fate decided the issue of the whole battle.

At about one o'clock the fourth division received orders from the Archduke to retreat. Once more the Austrian cavalry charged and repulsed Arrighi's squadrons, and gave the infantry time to fall back; but the enemy still continued to press upon the Austrians, who retreated in good order towards Bockfliess.

Had the wooded heights of Hohenleithen been sufficiently fortified to afford a resting-place for our troops, the left wing of the Austrian army might have stood its ground some time, and perhaps have repulsed the enemy with considerable loss. We had commenced throwing up some intrenchments in the forenoon; but before the work had made any progress, it was given up as useless: it was too late. The fourth division of the Austrian army remained all night on the heights, and kept possession of Bockfliess. The regiments of Hiller and Sztarray protected the rear, and kept the enemy at a proper distance. A weak body of troops maintained their position at Bockfliess against the French cavalry, until four squadrons of Archduke Ferdinand's hussars came to their assistance, charged, and drove off the enemy. A few battalions and some hussars, under Field Marshal Count von Radetzky, guarded the fords over the Weiden-bach, near Schweinwart and Hohen-Ruppertsdorf. The second divison of the Austrian army, the left wing of which was completely exposed, was now vigorously attacked, and suffered most severely from a murderous discharge of artillery on its flank: it now commenced its retreat. The enemy likewise attacked the Austrians in front, and did great execution upon them with a most destructive cross fire. General Count Ignatius von Hardegg defended Baumersdorf against all attacks, and only gave up possession of the village to the French on receiving orders to that effect. Behind Wagram the troops were obliged to turn back a little and to break, in order to cross the Russbach, which here makes a bend towards the west: the

French cavalry seized this opportunity to attack them, but were driven back by the unexpected fire of several battalions in some outworks on the Russbach, and by the charge of Vincent's regiment of light horse. The Austrian artillery was safely carried across, and the whole division marched without loss, by Säuring, towards Enzersfeld. One brigade of the first division, which had been placed on the heights near Wagram, followed this movement: the remaining troops of this division still kept their position at Atterkla, where Lieutenant Löffler's battery, on the left wing, caused great annoyance to the French; it was, however, soon silenced by their guns. It was past two o'clock before this division of the Austrian troops received orders to retreat, which it effected slowly and in good order. When the enemy pressed too much upon the Austrian troops, Colonel Count von Bentheim, at the head of the regiment Vogelsang, charged, and thus kept them for some time at bay. The march was thus continued in the best order towards Gerasdorf. We were compelled to leave a great number of wounded in Atterkla, Süssenbrunn, Gerasdorf, Baumersdorf, and other villages. Few of these were saved, as the fire, which had partly consumed these villages the day before, and which had been nearly extinguished, broke out afresh. It was now the turn for the grenadiers and the cavalry to commence their retreat, which they did towards Gerasdorf. They suffered severely, and a cannon-ball killed Field Marshal D'Aspre as he was leading the grenadiers through the burning village of Atterkla. The third division fell back upon the heights of Stamersdorf, by the way of Süssenbrunn, in such good order that the French for some time made no attempt to impede their retreat; but when it became dusk the French guards made a sudden attack upon them, took a battery, and attempted to follow up their advantage: the French cavalry meanwhile endeavoured to cut their way into the infantry of the first division of the Austrian army; but this division formed into squares, and drove them back three successive times. The Austrian cavalry now galloped up; Liechtenstein's cuirassiers charged the flank of the enemy, while the Schwarzenberg lancers and the Klenau light horse made repeated attacks upon the French; Captain von Gallois, at the head of his regiment, recovered the lost battery from the enemy's hands, while Tettenborn, with his squadron of light horse, drove back the French cuirassiers. The sixth division quitted Esslingen at one, and Aspern at two o'clock; it continued to retreat towards Stamersdorf, keeping up an incessant running fight with the enemy. Here, again, our infantry formed into squares; and, supported by the Kienmayer hussars, repelled the French attacking parties. The retreat was so well conducted, that all the attempts of the French commander, in which he was zealously seconded by his troops, failed in throwing our men into the disorder of a regular flight. Napoleon admired the strict discipline kept by the slowly retreating Austrian divisions, and gave the Archduke full praise for the obstinacy of his resistance, and for his admirable conduct of the retreat.

Both armies had been strained to the utmost, and the loss was great on both sides. The French had concentrated all their forces; and during the battle they had brought all their troops from the other bank of the Danube, so that they must have had about 200,000 men, of whom 160,000 had been actually engaged. On the side of the French above 14,000 men were killed and wounded, and 7000 made prisoners. They likewise lost twelve eagles and colours, and eleven cannon. Of their leaders Lasalle and Duprat were killed; Bessières, Wrede, and fourteen other officers were wounded. The Austrians were deprived of the assistance which they expected from Archduke John's detachment; it was not till past four o'clock that his advanced troops reached Ober-Siebenbrunn, and made a few prisoners in the rear of the French army. But, as the battle was already lost, and the French could bring a sufficient force to meet this unexpected attack, Archduke John retraced his steps. The enemy showed no inclination to impede his march. He did not come upon the traces of any forces sent to keep him in check, or even to watch his movements. His approach had not been expected or observed, and the French army had been exposed to the greatest danger from this quarter. It is in vain that General Pelet, in his otherwise admirable work, attempts to make us believe that, at the commencement of the battle, Napoleon foresaw and prepared to meet this contingency. The facts are clearly against him. Archduke John was much blamed for the lateness of his arrival. His talents and his courage no one would think of disputing; but we must observe in general that the Austrians do not shine in moving large masses of troops with ease and expedition, and even Archduke Charles, much as he improved the Austrian army in other respects, could not compete in this with the enemy. On the side of the Austrians, at most 100,000 men fought at Wagram, and they lost above 20,000 killed and wounded, and about 8000 made prisoners. Four generals were left on the field of battle; among them General von Nordmann, whom the French bulletins designated a traitor, as he was of French extraction and had served under Dumouriez; the Archduke and ten generals were wounded. The Austrians lost nine cannon, and only one standard. "It is one of the most remarkable accidents of this battle," says the Austrian report, "that the victors lost more trophies than the conquered."

The events of the following day proved how little the courage and moral force of the Austrians or their leader were affected. With the exception of the fourth division, which, however, shortly rejoined the others, the Archduke had, with great skill and prudence, directed the retreat of his army upon Znaym, and not upon Brünn as was expected. He then formed his troops into line behind the Taya, and offered battle to the victors on the 10th and 11th of July, which likewise, after various changes, ended in favour of the French. An armistice, which was shortly followed by the treaty of Vienna, put an end to further hostilities. Personal motives meanwhile had induced Archduke Charles to resign the command of the army. The terms of the treaty of Vienna were remarkably disadvantageous to Austria. Nevertheless, this campaign of 1809, especially the battles of Aspern, Wagram, and Znaym, inspired Germany with a feeling of courage which did not perish. This war made a deep impression even on the French, and when their soldiers talked of the battle of Wagram, a feeling of respect damped their natural boastfulness; and all Germans, who had at heart the cause of their country, and the glory of their fellow countrymen, looked upon Archduke Charles and the Austrian army of 1809, with pride and confidence.

CHAPTER IX.

Personal History. — The Hospital at Zistersdorf. — Wounded Austrian Officers. — Absolution given to One of my Companions. — The Franciscan Monk. — Arrival of the French in Zistersdorf. — State of the French Army. — Character of the Colonel. — The wounded Austrians declared Prisoners of War, and sent to Vienna. 1809.

To return to my own personal history: when the ball struck my leg, I felt a blow that went through me; on looking, I saw two streams of blood running down my thigh—the ball had gone clean through it. I had, however, no time for thought; the regiment, the left wing of which was vigorously assaulted by the enemy, was in full retreat, carrying with it the right wing, and I had to exert all my remaining force not to be left behind. Two soldiers took me under the arms, and half carried, half walking, I managed to reach the rear. Several cannon-balls plunged about us, one of them so close to us as to cause one of my supporters to fall—luckily without a wound; the other conveyed me a few hundred paces further, and then returned to the battle, which was now pretty equal. I could not walk alone, and stood looking towards the battle-field. It was then that I saw the colonel on horseback, with the colours in his hand, leading on his men. Their charge and the clouds of smoke arising from our burning camp, prevented me from seeing any thing further. To the right and left of Wagram and Baumersdorf I likewise saw flames and columns of smoke, while the roar of the artillery increased every moment. Several wounded men who came by, rendered me some assistance; one soldier carried me a little way until we reached a broken powder-waggon which, being empty, was driven to the rear. Upon this I found a seat, and was driven slowly along in the cool of the evening with a whole train of wounded men, who groaned and complained bitterly. The jolting of the cart gave me excruciating pain, and when the flow of blood, which had continued until now, ceased, my whole leg grew cold and stiff. Like the others, I suffered from extreme thirst, and the chill of the night air was hard to bear. By a lucky accident my Bohemian servant, who was slightly wounded in the hand, followed this waggon; he found me out in the dark, and remained constantly at my side. During the course of the night we reached Bockfliess, where a surgeon looked hastily at my wounds, and I shortly afterwards fell into a profound sleep.

About daybreak the noise woke me; not only the room in which I lay, but the whole house, and even the street, was full of wounded men: we were to be conveyed still further as soon as possible. The roar of the cannon announced that the battle had begun again.

My wounds had opened again during the night: as I could not raise myself, I was carried on my straw mattrass, which with a pair of sheets I had bought for a considerable sum, to the waggon. My own servant and two other wounded men were placed upon the same waggon, and in this company we went on, I neither asked nor cared whither. The day was oppressively hot: the sun poured its flood of light over the cloudless sky, and every thing glowed around me. The roar of the artillery accompanied us: it sometimes appeared to come nearer, and the sight of some straggling fugitives caused us some alarm lest we should fall into the enemy's hands; but we went never the faster for this. The Sclavonian peasant does not alter the pace of his team, besides every stone which the wheel went over made us exclaim—"Pomali!" for the jolt went to our very marrow. There was not a tree, nor even a bush, to afford us a momentary shade; no refreshment save very bad water to be got. By the time we reached a place where we were to stay for one hour, the mid-day sun had raised blisters all over my face and neck. A young officer, who had been ordered to this spot to superintend the wounded, pitied my condition, and ordered the cart to be covered with the boughs of a filbert tree which grew near: this was done in spite of the remonstrances of the proprietor. I found such a relief from the shade and the sight of the green boughs, that I no longer felt the torture of my wounds, and occasionally fell into a sort of pleasant dreamy state, in which I even made verses in honour of the tree which had done me such signal service. I cannot now remember the actual words, but the sensations which gave rise to them are still present to my mind. Unluckily these feelings were frequently broken by the cry of pain wrung from me by the stumble of the horse, or the jolting of the rough waggon.

In the evening we reached Zistersdorf, a small village, where arrangements had been made for establishing an hospital, even before the battle of Aspern. However, I was not taken to the hospital, but to a cottage belonging to some poor people, where, for the first time, my wounds were properly dressed by the village surgeon, as no army surgeon had yet arrived. I had another very tolerable night. On the following day, however, I was seized with fever; for twenty-four hours, I suffered excruciating torture, and could not conceal from myself that it might end fatally. The surgeon had been summoned elsewhere, and the bandage therefore remained unchanged; the wound was much inflamed, and required instant attention. This I only obtained at the end of four days, when I was conveyed to the hospital and placed in a sort of cellar with two other wounded officers; here my leg was bandaged by an assistant; and with the exception of frightening me a little at first, no staff surgeon could have treated me better. As I had been able to walk a little, I believed the thigh bone to be uninjured, and said so to the assistant. But when he saw the wound and the direction that the ball had taken, he confidently pronounced, "There can be no doubt but that the bone is shattered!" This sounded like my death warrant; my knowledge of surgery made me feel certain that in this case I must lose my leg, an operation which was hardly practicable so high up. On the most favourable supposition, I should not be able to leave my bed for six or eight months; whereas, in the case of its being merely a flesh wound, I might be cured in as many weeks. Although I could not but give credit to the assistant's confident assertion, a small voice within me whispered that he might yet be wrong. After many days, embittered by this dread, the assistant confessed that he might be mistaken, and at length said, almost with a tone of regret, that my case would not long be serious. His method of treatment was excellent: he handled the wound as gently and as little as possible, and dressed it only with camphor water with perfect success. My spirits rose, and I was able to sit up and write a little. The assistant at first opposed this; but when he saw how bent upon it I was, and how rapid was my recovery, he at length consented. The time I spent in writing was the happiest in the day, and made up for many long and dismal hours. But as the letters were sent round by Vienna, the uncertainty of their ultimate fate somewhat damped my zeal in writing them.

My interest in public events was at first so intense, as to make me forget my own personal griefs; but this decreased every day, as the accounts got worse and worse. The reports, few and uncertain as they were, all agreed in this, — that after Wagram, we had lost another battle at Znaym, that an armistice had been proclaimed, and that peace would shortly be declared, which all agreed in saying would be most disadvantageous to us. The worst was that on all sides, I heard wishes expressed for peace on any terms; the few officials of the place, the burghers, the clergy, the surgeons, even the officers and the soldiers in the hospital, all wished for peace, and confidently predicted it to be near at hand. There was consequently nothing more to detain me in Austria, and I longed to be well and at Berlin. Meanwhile, my patience was heavily taxed. The two officers who shared my room were but sorry companions, and too dull to understand my feelings. The younger one, who was barely fifteen, and whose foot had been shattered by a cannon-ball, was beyond all hope of recovery. It was impossible now, from want of instruments, to remove the limb, an operation which should have been performed within the first few days. The few subjects we had in common were soon exhausted. The visits of the magistrate, of his wife and daughter, and of a pretty housekeeper, who occasionally brought me some flowers, enabled me to spend a pleasant quarter of an hour or so; the rest of the long summer days passed most drearily. I asked for some books, and received a cargo of trashy novels, into the midst of which I plunged, seizing with avidity upon the stray quotations from Goethe and Schiller which they contained. Luckily I obtained an old edition of Cornelius Nepos, and an equally well-thumbed copy of Cæsar's Commentaries, which I studied with fresh interest derived from my newly acquired knowledge of military affairs.

The wounded lad daily got weaker; and although he firmly believed in his ultimate recovery, he yielded to an old corporal's advice, and asked to see a priest. The priest came, heard his confession, and gave him absolution. Our beds were so placed that both myself and the third officer, in spite of our endeavours to the contrary, could not avoid hearing the greater part of the young man's confession. The sacredness of confession was thus to a certain degree violated. His sins were trifling, and his frank confiding tone touched me deeply; but the whole ceremony — the manner in which it was conducted and ended — produced on me no favourable impression; it was a mere form, and did not pretend to be more. The priest then asked us if we needed his services, and seemed almost relieved by our declining them. Perceiving from my accent that I was from the north of Germany, he entered into more intimate conversation with me. He had formerly been on the banks of the Rhine, where he had had tolerable prospects, but these had been destroyed by the advance of the French; and now that he held good preferment in Austria, there was every chance of the same ruthless persecutors following him even here; the French had already selected his parish wherein to quarter their troops, his parsonage would not be spared, and his kitchen and cellar were sure to suffer. I sympathised with his sorrows, but added that no great harm would be done, provided his housekeeper was of the canonical age. He added, with evident self-satisfaction, that he had foreseen the evil days which were coming, and had already sent the young woman to her friends in a remote part of the country. In return for my sympathy he provided me with books; I obtained through him Schmidt's History of the Germans, and some few volumes of Hormayr's Austrian Worthies, by which means my days passed somewhat more happily.

We were also occasionally visited by a Franciscan monk, who was brought by the priest, and whose kind disposition and knowledge of mankind taught him to understand the necessities and to minister to the wants of man. His scientific acquirements were below contempt; his account of the Reformation, and of Luther, would have made a protestant stare: but his whole conduct was a striking example of perfect resignation and contentment. I could learn little from him touching his convent; and only gathered from his conversation that he had suffered much at first from his fellow monks, but that he now led a tolerably quiet life. Passing events had nearly ruined the convent; and in addition to other hardships, the monks had now to bear the privations of want.

An attempt to walk with crutches fully succeeded; and it was with infinite pleasure that I stepped first into the little garden under my window, next into the castle yard, and thence into the open fields overlooking the wide plain and the woody heights, lately the scene of bloodshed. In spite of my emotions, and a natural longing for peace, I could not help hoping that war might again be declared : there was no solid foundation for peace and quiet. The villagers were full of anxiety and excitement : the French were daily expected, not indeed as enemies, as the treaty had been signed; but their approach was, nevertheless, regarded with dread. The village magistrate hastened the departure of a pretty cousin who had come from Vienna, and invited me to his house: he likewise took in three wounded French officers, of whose presence in the hospital I had until now never heard, and about whom no one had previously cared. I made acquaintance with them; but refused to share their meals, as I dined daily with the village priest. The food was moderate; the wine of the country tolerable; and several guests, among others a Franciscan monk, seemed well pleased with their fare. This monk belonged to the same convent as the Franciscan I have before mentioned ; but how different from him ! He was pale, thin, and haggard; the picture of envy. The position of my host, which he constantly compared with his own, was wormwood to him. He confessed to me that a curacy was the height of his ambition; but that the convent, with all its privations, must for ever be his lot. It was some consolation to him to think that mine host might be ruined by the advance of the French. We talked of various subjects, among others of the French, who were to arrive on the following day: the Franciscan, who knew a few words of French, invited himself to dinner next day, to act as an interpreter. While we were yet talking, trumpets sounded, and we all rushed in alarm to the window. Troops trotted round the corner; and before we could recover our surprise, the colonel and several French officers entered the room. The colonel made the most civil excuses for intruding himself upon us a day before his time, stating that he had been turned out of his former quarters that very day, and that he and his brother officers were easily satisfied. As no one present but myself understood his oration, I naturally undertook the part of interpreter. A second dinner was put on the table in a marvellously small space of time: I wondered whence it all came so quickly; but the priest had prudently laid in a store, and game, fish, and pastry made their appearance: the Franciscan saw all this with increasing envy. After dinner the company were shown the rooms which they considered small; and when the colonel heard that the magistrate's house was larger, he thanked the priest much for his hospitality, assured him that it was against his principles to quarter himself upon the clergy, for whose sacred profession he had the greatest respect, and said that he would take up his abode with the magistrate. The latter functionary was not a little alarmed when he saw these numerous guests enter his house. The wounded French officers were told to stay; and I—the Austrian officer, who was to have been carefully kept out of the way, necessarily became the daily guest of the foreign enemies !

The colonel was one of those men often to be met with in the army, and his character was easily seen through. He had risen from the ranks by his good conduct, and was quite aware that he owed to his courage and military experience the position which he then held, and which he daily felt that he wanted other qualifications to maintain. He therefore endeavoured, by excessive politeness, and great professions of humanity, to give himself an air of superior breeding. On the whole this answered very well, but he sometimes overacted his part, and thus betrayed himself to close observers. He had, at the same time, a keen perception of his own interests and convenience. He abhorred the young men of good education and noble family, who now began to join the several regiments, and upon whom the rank of officer was immediately conferred, and he subjected them to constant petty annoyances, while, at the same time, he made a great display of civility, by which he thought he was imposing upon them, while he was simply laughed at for his pains. "These men, with silver spoons in their mouths," said he, "are the ruin of the army, and the Emperor acts most unwisely in promoting them; their fine education must be wiped out with the sabre, and their pride somewhat let blood, before they are worth any thing as soldiers." There were several such young gentlemen in his regiment, upon whom he, and old blades like him, kept a sharp eye.

My daily intercourse with these people soon inspired them with such confidence as to induce them to lay aside all restraint, and I heard with secret joy that general discontent prevailed in the army together with a liberal tone that alarmed the Emperor. The complaint of the deterioration of the army was universal, which these men attributed entirely to that love of court display which had led Napoleon to forget the main consideration that he was their general and emperor, and that to recognise and reward merit was better than to dispense favours. It was asserted as beyond question that one regiment of Bonaparte's, Moreau's, or Jourdan's republican soldiers was as good as three or four of the Emperor's present troops. I also heard remarkable confessions of which no mention was made in Napoleon's bulletins: here a superior force of French cuirassiers had been beaten by Blankenstein's Austrian hussars, or the infantry had not done their duty; there some particular general had committed some egregious blunder—Napoleon himself was not spared. They did not scruple to call him a rogue, but were ready nevertheless to do his bidding at a moment's notice. Napoleon in one of his bulletins, had called the war carried on against him by the Emperor of Austria, a revolt. The Emperor of Austria was one of the house of Lorraine: Lorraine belonged to France; therefore all denial of the justice of this position was instantly declared to be mere sophistry. A captain of horse from Alsace and a surgeon from Worms, contested the point with me in German so obstinately, that at length the colonel was forced to command them to be silent.

My wounds, favoured by the fine weather, gradually healed, and I was shortly able to leave off first one, then both my crutches. I quitted the small sick room in the hospital and hired one in the master's house, where I received every sort of attention from his family. It was known that a treaty for peace was on foot, but how it would end was far from certain. Meanwhile the Austrian army had retired into Hungary, where it had taken up a strong position: but what rendered the chance of peace still more doubtful, was this—the prisoners were not to be exchanged in masses, as is usually the case when peace is settled, but one for one. This circumstance affected me individually. In consequence of the armistice, the French had advanced as far as Zistersdorf: there was plenty of time to have moved the wounded Austrians further off; but in consideration of those who were severely wounded, and confiding in the protection of the French commanding officer, the hospital had remained where it was. The French, however, now declared us all prisoners of war, totally disregarding our protest against such a measure. I was by no means disposed to submit quietly to this injustice, and made arrangements with an honest burgher to transport me as he had already done several others, across the March into Hungary. I had frequently told the colonel that I considered myself perfectly free, and he would not have thought worse of me had I gone without leave. But, unluckily, he just then received orders to send all those who were well enough to leave the hospital to Vienna, for the purpose of being exchanged. One of my wounds was still open, but this was no impediment, and, amid the good wishes of the colonel and the tears of the magistrate's wife and daughter, I took my place in the carriage under the guard of a French soldier. My servant Lorenz was with me, and early on the 14th of August we reached Vienna, without further adventure.

After passing some weeks in Vienna I received notice that I had been formally exchanged, and might rejoin my regiment, which was then quartered in Hungary. I took leave of my friends, and started on my way to Pressburg, which I reached on the evening of the 23d September, 1809.

CHAPTER X.

Paris. — Prince Charles Schwarzenberg. — Count Metternich. — Hostility to Napoleon. — Life in Paris. — Preparations for Prince Schwarzenberg's Ball. — The Emperor and Maria Louisa. — Arrival of a Courier. — Fireworks. — The Ball. — Sudden Fire. — Napoleon quits the Ball. — The Queen of Naples. — The Queen of Westphalia and Princess von der Leyen saved. — Return of the Emperor. — The Bivouack. — Discovery of Princess Pauline Schwarzenberg's Corpse. — Gloomy Impression produced by the Fire. 1810.

WE travelled with great rapidity across the rich plains between Vienna and Strasburg, and thence to Paris. It was the middle of June, and the dust and heat had nearly destroyed us in the country, when we plunged into the close narrow streets of the French capital. We found rooms prepared for us in the Hôtel de l'Empire, and were soon in the whirl of the gay and busy Parisian world.

We found that what had been told us was true, that being an Austrian was the best possible introduction. Putting aside the Empress Maria Louisa, a name which inspired every Frenchman with respect, the interests of Austria were sustained in a manner it would be difficult to parallel. Prince Charles von Schwarzenberg, the Austrian ambassador, a man of great experience both in war and diplomacy, admirably represented the majesty of Austria. The intelligence and ready kindness of his wife were only equalled by his own; his sons and his whole household were actuated by the same spirit. It was the only embassy at Paris which was treated with marked distinction by the French government — there were none of those impediments to a good understanding which were constantly arising in the relations between foreign sovereigns and Napoleon's court. The several diplomatists and military officers attached to the embassy, made the best use of these favourable circumstances. The house was open to strangers, but all Austrians at Paris were considered members of the family, were received at all hours, and had place at tables always reserved for them.

The number of Austrians then at Paris was considerable. Prince Joseph von Schwarzenberg, the ambassador's elder brother, had taken a house for himself, his wife, and his numerous family; so had Prince von Esterhazy. General Count von Walmoden and Count von Neipperg, who had to conduct some important business with the French government, Count von Bentheim, and many other Austrians of high birth and consideration, had been attracted thither by business or pleasure. Political affairs of the most important nature had induced Count Metternich, the minister of foreign affairs, to come to Paris, and by Napoleon's invitation, he came with his family and a large suite. The personal appearance of Count Metternich was captivating — his manners were free from formality, and there was a vivacity in his conversation which showed that he was as capable of gaining his ends in the drawing-room as in the cabinet. The hotel of Marshal Ney, which looked upon the Seine, was prepared for him as Napoleon's guest, and the Emperor's establishment of servants was ordered to attend him. Every Austrian was welcomed to Count Metternich's table, as well as many foreigners.

We thus had two agreeable homes on each side of the Seine. But the invitations to these two houses were not confined to Austrians only; almost every German in Paris, whether they were ministers from the states on the Rhine, members of sovereign and mediatised houses, people who had claims to make or favours to acknowledge, even the German artists and men of letters — all clustered round the Austrian embassy to take part in its social and other advantages; so that never before or since have German interests had so effective a rallying point.

As an Austrian officer, I had free access to this brilliant and agreeable society, but other circumstances placed me on the most intimate terms with several members of it; and I found that, notwithstanding the apparently friendly relations with the French, there was at bottom a thoroughly German feeling, a decided objection to our new allies, and a strong partiality for every thing German. So determined was the hostility to Napoleon, that men looked with more pleasure to past discomfitures than to the present alliance, and rejoiced in the prospect of future war. It was not difficult for politicians and courtiers, long accustomed to sudden changes, to outward forms, thus to conceal their real feelings. Napoleon himself set them an example; his conduct showed that, although he placed great value upon the Austrian alliance, in as much as it flattered him, and raised his importance in the eyes of the world, he by no means intended it to act as a restraint upon his actions : mere forms of civility were kept up, but in reality he was as hard and determined an enemy as ever. Our hereditary dislike of Napoleon was shared by a large portion of the French themselves — and that the most important and influential — not only by the old royalists, who were about the court, but even by men who owed every thing to the revolution or to Napoleon. They looked to the support of a foreign court to back them up in their opposition and ill-will to the government, and pretended that their zeal for Austria was assumed for Napoleon's service, and from a desire to flatter him. Moreover, they were perfectly confident that, if they went too far, their secret would be kept inviolate. Napoleon's power rested on such frail foundations, that, out of the number of those about his person whom he had promoted and enriched, there were only three or four, such as Duroc, Rapp, and Savary, on whose attachment he could rely.

But other pleasures besides politics and general society occupied my time. On the first evening of my arrival I found my friend Chamisso; afterwards Bekker, the celebrated physician Koreff, Ludwig Uhland, and Sieveking. To these old friends I soon added others, among whom I may mention Dr. Gall, and Alexander von Humboldt. We generally passed the day together, and managed to join profit with amusement. We met every day regularly in the Musée Napoleon, from whence we sallied forth on our expeditions, and passed a life of great intellectual and social enjoyment, avoiding great assemblies as much as we could. Our evenings were usually spent at Frascati's or in a garden in the Rue Richer, where Henriette Mendelsohn, Frederick Schlegel's sister-in-law, lived and assembled round her a small French and German society.

Here we heard the topics of the day discussed, the balls which we had seen, and others which we had missed, and one which was to exceed all others in splendour, to be given by the Austrian Ambassador. No one could help observing the enormous preparations going on at the hotel and in the garden; and we could by degrees form some idea of the gigantic scale on which every thing was to be done. We repeatedly visited the rooms where the carpenters were still employed; in a few days all this rough work would be concealed under the most expensive hangings. The 1st of July was, after several delays, fixed upon as the day for the ball; the Emperor and Maria Louisa had accepted the invitation, so that there could be no further change. The men redoubled their exertions, and worked day and night. Those were lucky whose turn came to work by night, for the mid-day heat was intolerable, and made the stones and the wood almost too hot to touch. The greatest art was required to preserve the trees and flowers to be used at the ball, as every thing was parched up by the heat. We must now describe the site.

The ambassador lived in the Hôtel de Montesson, a large house with a court on one side and a garden on the other, in the Rue de Mont Blanc. But this space was not reckoned sufficient for the extraordinary entertainment to be given, and the neighbouring hotel was expressly hired for the occasion. The necessary communications were made, and the rooms duly arranged for their several purposes. An immense room had been thrown out into the garden, adjoining the reception-rooms, the whole built of planks by artists who had constructed similar works for former entertainments. The roof and the sides were covered outside with cerecloth, and lined with tapestry: mirrors, candelabras, and coloured lamps ornamented the walls. The pillars which separated the centre from a species of gallery which ran round the room, were coated with the richest stuffs, and festoons of artificial flowers, muslin, and gauze were hung in all directions. Gold and silver chains connected by draperies and flowers with the other ornaments of the saloon, supported magnificent lustres. On an elevated stage covered with a gold embroidered carpet, at the further extremity of the room, two thrones had been erected, in front of which the floor had been prepared for dancing. There were three entrances: one towards the back, near the thrones, leading to the interior of the house, was intended for the household; in the front towards the garden on the left, was a long and broad gallery, built of the same materials, and ornamented in the same manner as the saloon, which ran all along the back of the hotel, and served to connect the rooms and the garden. To the right, opposite this gallery, a stage had been erected for the musicians, the only access to which was by a staircase outside. A handsome doorway which led directly from the garden by a flight of broad steps, wide enough to allow the passage in and out of a huge mass of human beings, was the chief entrance into the saloon.

The greatest care was taken that every thing should be magnificent, suitable, and convenient: nothing was neglected that could distinguish this ball from all others. As an inscription was to be placed over the doorway, it was determined that it should be in the German tongue. Should the French wonder and take offence at it, they could not dare to complain too loudly as it was the mother tongue of their Empress, and the Austrian embassy surely had the right, at a ball given in her honour, to use her native language. It was easy to find space for two lines, but not so easy to find the verses. Many prudently declined the invidious office; but at length two most commonplace lines were selected, and were cut, not indeed on stone, but on strong pasteboard. The important thing was the German characters, and these in a transparency shone proudly from their high position:—

"Mit sanfter Schönheit Reiz strahlt Heldenkraft verbunden;
Heil! heil! die goldne Zeit ist wieder uns gefunden."*

The important day at length arrived, every thing was completed, and even those last and most busily employed were able to devote themselves to the adornment of their own persons; and here the Austrians had the advantage, as the richness and

---

* Bright beams soft beauty's charm with might heroic blended;
All hail the golden time wherein our storms have ended.

beauty of their uniforms far surpassed those of the French. The servants, numerous as they were, had been increased by some hundreds, and a portion of them wore the French state livery.

Early in the evening a division of the imperial guard occupied the post assigned to them as a guard of honour. While it was still broad day, the whole hotel, with its garden and outhouses, sparkled with thousands of lamps, and the carriages which brought the guests drove through the masses of people collected on both sides of the street. Parties of Austrians were in readiness to receive the visitors as they arrived: the ladies were presented with flowers, and led into the grand saloon.

The seats round the walls were soon filled, and the middle of the room began to be crowded. Every moment the number of persons remarkable for beauty, birth, and importance increased. Kings and queens were among the company, and were expecting one greater than they. At length the sound of presenting arms, the challenge of the guards, the clash of trumpets and roll of drums, announced the approach of the Emperor and his Empress. Their carriage dashed up to the door between the files of soldiers. The families of Schwarzenberg and Metternich received their illustrious guest at the foot of the stairs. The ambassador made a short speech, while the ladies presented flowers to Napoleon, who handed them to his wife: then giving her his arm, he entered the house, accompanied by Prince Schwarzenberg, and followed by a crowd of people. I was near the Emperor, and looked closely at him: for the first time I was struck by his great beauty, and also by the power of his iron countenance. His air was fixed, unbending, almost cruel; his look steadfast, and directed to the ground; not a trace of kindness in his manner; and his mouth seemed ever ready to pronounce some fearful order.

The Emperor walked through the rooms and the gallery until he reached the saloon, where he remained a few minutes, cast a rapid glance at every thing and every body, refused the proffered refreshments, and spoke a few words to several persons near him. A flourish of trumpets accompanied his entrance. Napoleon and the Empress accompanied Prince Schwarzenberg, at his invitation, into the garden, and the whole

VOL. I.   I

assembly followed them. Singers and musicians, distributed at intervals behind trees and bushes, began to sing as they approached. Other surprises were in store for them.

The party stopped before a well mown lawn, on which seats had been placed for the Emperor and a few others, and where an accurate representation of the château of Laxenburg had been prepared. In order to recall still more vividly to the Empress's recollection the scenes of her home, dancers in Austrian costumes suddenly appeared, and performed dances peculiar to the Austrian peasantry, together with a pantomime, in which scenes of peace and war were enacted, all ending in glory and happiness.

This was scarce over when the attention was excited by another object. The cracking of whips and the sound of a horse's hoofs announced the approach of a courier, who, covered with dust, pressed into the midst of the brilliant assembly, shouldered his way up to the Emperor, and delivered his despatches. There was a murmur of some great victory in Spain, but the Emperor, who was in the secret, immediately said with a smile that the despatches came from Vienna, and handed to the Empress a letter from her father, written for the express purpose of being given at this ball.

After this scene, which was not without interest, a sudden display of fireworks attracted the attention. Art and invention were taxed to the utmost, and no expense had been spared. But in the midst of the explosions, one of the frames caught fire, and caused a momentary alarm; the flames, however, were instantaneously put out. The zeal and ability of the firemen were praised, and no one thought how soon their services would again be required, and that they would not be crowned with similar success.

The brilliant throng was again in motion, and, after several turns in the garden, found itself in the saloon. All were struck by the inscription over the doorway; it was spelt, read, and translated. The Emperor, startled at first, ended by laughing contemptuously, and many were the remarks made upon the German text. The trumpets again sounded as the Emperor and Maria Louisa entered the saloon, and took their seats on the thrones prepared for them. The music now began for dancing. It was about midnight. The most brilliant and difficult part of the evening had passed. The ball appeared to be kept up with great spirit, and promised to last till morning. The Queen of Naples had opened the ball with Prince Esterhazy, and Prince Eugene, the Viceroy of Italy, with Princess Schwarzenberg, the ambassador's sister-in-law.

After the quadrille, the Emperor and Maria Louisa had walked in opposite directions round the room, addressing a few words to several of the company whom they knew, and to those who were presented to them for the first time. Maria Louisa was the first to return to her seat; the Emperor remained at the further end of the room, where Princess Pauline Schwarzenberg, the ambassador's sister-in-law, was in the act of presenting her daughters to him, and Napoleon was addressing a few words to those about him, when on a sudden, in the gallery under the pillars, and near the entrance into the great gallery connecting the saloon with the hotel, a gust of wind brought the flame of one of the numerous candles in contact with a gauze curtain. The fire ran up the curtain, causing an instantaneous blaze, which as suddenly ceased. A few sparks remained, and so unimportant was the incident considered at first, that Count Bentheim extinguished some of the flames by a lucky throw of his hat, and Count Dumanoir, one of the Emperor's chamberlains, clambering up one of the pillars, pulled down what remained of the burning curtain. Several sparks, however, had flown up and set fire to some hangings which were out of reach: the flames spread rapidly among the inflammable materials, and reached the roof. The music ceased, the musicians, who were the first threatened, quitted their stage in alarm; the door communicating with the outward air, let in a blast of wind which fed the flames. The dancers dispersed,—all were in confusion, and sought to discover what had already happened, and how it was all to end.

Napoleon had seen the whole incident, and was, therefore, far from suspecting any treachery; he went up to the Empress and watched the progress of the flames with a quiet countenance. His devoted adherents, who at first suspected treason, hurried round him, and drew their swords. The

Austrian ambassador, who preserved his calmness and dignity, kept close to the Emperor, and when he saw that the flames were rapidly spreading in all directions, urged him to quit the room. Napoleon, without answering, gave his arm to the Empress, and followed the ambassador to the gate leading into the garden, warning the company, as he walked along, to act with order and discretion. Every body behaved well until the Emperor was safe; and then all order ceased, and the struggling mass rushed, panic stricken, towards the door.

When Prince Schwarzenberg learnt that Napoleon intended to go home, he prudently sent an adjutant to desire the Emperor's carriage to draw up at a small side door in a back street adjoining the garden. The greatest confusion prevailed in front of the hotel, whereas the Emperor might go away unperceived by the backway, and frustrate any attempt upon his life, were any such intended. But when Napoleon perceived the direction in which they were leading him, he stopped, asked whither they were going, and not approving of this plan, said shortly and decisively, "No, I will go by the proper entrance." He turned short round and ordered the carriage, which had already reached the back street, to return to its original place. By this means, much time was lost, which Prince Schwarzenberg passed in great uneasiness, although with an outwardly calm countenance, while Napoleon waited with great patience. He thought that any attempt upon his life would be more difficult in the front than in some small back street. The statement in the "Moniteur," that Napoleon entered his carriage by the garden gate, like many other accounts of that event, is quite erroneous.

All these circumstances were told to me by immediate eye-witnesses. I will now relate what I myself personally saw and felt.

The heat was so intolerable in the saloon, that I had gone into the long gallery for fresh air, when the noise of music and dancing suddenly ceased, and I heard screams and loud confused sounds: I turned round, intending to return to the saloon, and saw flames spreading in all directions. There was no time for thought or action,—a mass of human beings, pressing upon me, carried me with them in their flight. Several powerful-looking generals were exclaiming with terror, "My

God,—the Emperor!— the Emperor is in danger:" others were calling out for water; I was so entangled with them, that it was only in the third room that I could extricate myself from the throng, and retrace my steps towards the scene of horror.

Most of the people had already escaped out of the gallery into the garden, the entrance to which was no longer crowded. But the doors of the saloon, which was now one sheet of fire, were still encumbered with people struggling to escape from the flames and stifling smoke. Heavy lustres fell with a crash; the lath and plaster partitions, the boarding and beams, were burning and tumbling in all directions: the whole room was one mass of fire and destruction. The wood and the inflammable materials with which the saloon had been ornamented, caused it to burn with prodigious fierceness, the buckets of water that were poured upon it merely hissed and went off in steam; every thing seemed to add fuel to the flames. All this took place in a shorter time than I have taken to describe it. In a few moments the roof of the gallery was in flames, the draperies, lamps, and lustres were falling close behind me, and scarce time was left to escape into the garden.

The most frightful scenes were here taking place. The new buildings were one mass of flame. The terror was universal: anguish and anxiety had taken the place of all thoughts of pleasure. Men, in search of those nearest and dearest to them, were rushing through the crowd; all had personal objects in view, and recklessly pushed aside every impediment to their search. Husbands sought their wives, mothers their daughters: they had last seen them standing up to dance, or had dragged them some distance, and then been forced to leave their hold. No one knew the other's fate; here were people overcome with grief,—there they were rushing wildly into each other's arms in excess of joy,—some were fainting, others wounded and bleeding. The wooden stairs had given way under the weight of those escaping from the fire; many had fallen down and were trampled under foot, injured by the falling timber, or seriously burnt. The Queen of Naples had been saved by the Grand Duke of Würzburg, the Queen of Westphalia by her husband and Count Metternich. The Russian ambassador had been dragged fainting from the crowd by Doctor Koreff and others; and his burning clothes extinguished with the first water they could find. Many women were dangerously burnt.

In the midst of this turmoil were seen servants and workmen of all sorts; all distinction of ranks was at an end—stars and orders were forgotten—royal birth overlooked. The firemen, summoned from their supper, rudely elbowed the aristocratic crowd; the opera dancers, in their paint and tinsel, pressed forward among noble dames, to gratify their curiosity,—no one remarked this assumption of equality.

Prince Joseph Schwarzenberg had pressed his daughter to his bosom; he found her in the garden, saved, but much hurt. He then, in a state bordering on desperation, sought after his missing wife. His daughter had been by her side, till a falling beam separated them, and she then lost sight of her mother. We cannot do better than quote from Major von Prokesch's "Memoirs of the Schwarzenberg Family" the following circumstances. "Prince Joseph was standing near the Empress when the fire broke out. At the first cry of danger he returned to the room where the dancers were, and pointed out to Prince Eugene and to his wife a side door by which they might escape. The room was already untenable from flames and smoke. He ran up and down in vain—he could not find his wife. He reached the stairs leading into the garden without accident. He asked every one whom he met, whether he had seen his wife: some said they had, others, that she was certainly in the garden. 'There she is,' said one. He rushed to the spot, and found some one strikingly like her. Despair took possession of him. The torture of suspense was beyond bearing; he was almost certain of her fate,—a terrible death by fire. He returned to the saloon. The stairs had given way; the crowd were tumbling one over the other. His child was brought to him terribly burnt. His brother's wife was carried past him, the ornaments trodden from her head. He sees suddenly lighted up by the fitful flames a figure half burnt; it was Princess von der Leyen. A Swede who had saved her assured the bystanders that he had seen a woman wandering about in the midst of the flames, a frightful and ghastly sight. Prince Joseph approached the doorway, and attempted to climb over the burning rafters. At this moment the whole flooring of the room gave way with a dull hollow sound; volumes of smoke and flame burst forth — all was lost."

So ends this account. From the commencement of the fire to this particular moment, barely a quarter of an hour had elapsed, and I was all the time present at the spot. The various services to be rendered to those who were seeking their friends, or who were injured — the rapidity with which the whole scene passed — scarce allowed time to note each particular event. But a tolerably correct account could be got from one's own individual observation, compared and corrected by that of other witnesses. The statement of the "Moniteur," that Princess Schwarzenberg was seen in the garden, talking with the King of Westphalia, Prince Borghese, and Count Regnauld, is certainly not true. It was easy to confound her with others; moreover, the report may have been spread from a kind motive. But when Monsieur de Bausset states, in his "Mémoires," "*On vit s'élancer une femme jeune, belle, d'une taille élégante, ... poussant des cris douloureux, des cris de mère;*" and when he proceeds further to describe the "*désolante apparition,*" he allows his poetical imagination to get the better of him. No one saw or spoke to the unfortunate Princess out in the garden; no one saw her return into the saloon. To return was simply impossible. At first the rush of people flying from destruction, afterwards the scorching heat, would have prevented such a proceeding. Such was the intensity of the fire, that no one could approach within ten feet of the entrance without danger of being stifled; it was scarce possible even to look at the burning mass. At first the Princess's fate was not suspected; it was taken for granted that she was safe somewhere, either in the garden or in a neighbouring house. She was sought and inquired after in all directions by her unhappy husband.

Meanwhile the saloon and the galleries were burnt to the ground, and the fire threatened destruction to the hotel itself. The archives were saved with considerable difficulty. All the Austrians present were busy with buckets of water, or helped to remove papers. Hats and swords were thrown aside, as well as our uniforms, which were completely spoilt by the smoke and water, and were moreover oppressively hot.

Nearly all the company had retired; the Austrians, some few intimate friends, and several French officials, still remained examining this scene of woe. Instead of the well-dressed guests, a strong detachment of Imperial guards took possession of every avenue leading to the hotel, and filled the court and garden. This evidence of military power struck the imagination. The following incident made a stronger impression.

The Emperor went with Maria Louisa as far as the Champs Elysées, where her carriages and suite were waiting to conduct her to St. Cloud; he then returned with an adjutant. His unexpected appearance in his grey great coat produced immediate silence. He ordered all strangers to leave the place, the streets to be guarded, and took prompt measures against the further spread of the fire. The stream of water from one of the engines nearly knocked him down, but he took no notice of it. The most vigilant search was still continued after the missing Princess. At the same time a strict inquiry was made into the conduct and appliances of the officials. The head of the police, Count Dubois, had a hard duty—he was expected to know every thing, to be prepared for every thing, and to give an account of every thing. Napoleon's rough severity sharpened the wily officer's zeal: he attempted to exculpate himself, rushed to all sides with his orders, entreaties, and questions, returned again to the Emperor, and received with extreme humility new reproaches and harsher words. But the chief of the firemen was the worst used of all. Count Hulin, who wished to show his zeal, and to find some object upon which Napoleon's wrath could vent itself, struck the wretched man several times with his fist, and even went so far as to kick him. It ended by the man's imprisonment, and subsequent ignominious dismissal from office. He may have been guilty of some neglect,—the appliances were not ready, or of much service at first,—but it was generally said that even when Napoleon quitted the saloon —and before this the firemen had not even been summoned,— no human power could have saved the burning buildings.

Meanwhile, the endeavours to find some traces of the missing Princess continued unabated. The courtiers and others attached to Napoleon went here and there, messengers were despatched in every direction — not a trace of her could be discovered. The house of every friend and connexion, every corner of the garden was searched; the burning ruins were examined — all in vain. The miserable husband wandered about, the picture of despair; his bodily strength was exhausted, but the torture of his mind urged him to fresh exertions. The attempts to quiet him were fruitless — even the Emperor's presence, and the words he addressed to him, were totally unheeded.

Napoleon, tired out by the fruitless search, and having no further cause to stay, now that the fire was nearly extinguished, returned to St. Cloud. The grenadiers, however, prepared to bivouack on the ground; and seldom does it happen that soldiers fare so sumptuously — the meats and wines prepared for the company were distributed among them.

We likewise, worn out by work and excitement, thought of refreshment, and sat down at the nearest table. Then it was that we compared notes, and filled up from the experience of others the blanks in our own observations. Every one had much to ask and more to tell, — much that was dreadful was known, but more still remained doubtful.

A storm which had been gathering over head, now burst with violence. The lightning flashed, the thunder rolled, the houses trembled, the rain poured down in torrents, and effectually put out the smouldering fire.

After a while the storm passed away, and morning began to break. A certain restlessness drove us out to view the scene of what appeared to have been a horrid dream. We were but few, and separated into several parties. I walked over the spot, which was now a heap of sooty embers, — beams reduced to a cinder, heaps of stone, bits of furniture and crockery, and pools of dirty water, were all that remained of the brilliant ball-room. We found bits of chandeliers, broken swords, bracelets, and other ornaments melted by the heat. Not far from where I was, Count Hulin and Dr. Gall were turning over the rubbish. Suddenly Count Hulin stopped short, looked aghast at something before him, and I heard him say with a low voice, "Doctor Gall, come here: — this is a human body!" I still remember with horror the thrilling tone in which these words were said; every nerve was affected, and my breast heaved with anguish. Gall and I went to the spot in silence, and endeavoured to convince ourselves of the fact. It was only by degrees that we made out the truth. A corpse, blackened and shrivelled up with fire, lay half covered with cinders — the features could not be distinguished; indeed, it required some effort of the imagination to discover that it was a human figure at all: one breast had accidentally lain in a pool of water, and its dazzling whiteness contrasted in a strange and horrible manner with the rest of the blackened corpse. Although accustomed to sights of horror, I involuntarily started back from this. Gall looked more closely into the sort of hole, and thought that he recognised Princess Schwarzenberg. A few rings and a necklace, found on the corpse, were sent to the ambassador, who was in another part of the garden. There could no longer be any doubt; for the necklace bore the names of her children; she had eight, and a ninth, still unborn, shared her fate. When the horrible certainty flashed upon us, our courage left us; we bowed our heads in sorrow, and found relief in tears. Two vivid flashes of lightning, and a long rolling peal of distant thunder, shook the atmosphere — they were the last.

It was now our duty to communicate the fact to Prince Joseph Schwarzenberg, and to give directions for the funeral. The position in which the body was found induced us to hope that the unfortunate princess had not been burnt alive. Seeing no chance of escape by the principal entrance, owing to the dense crowd, it is possible that she may have attempted to reach the inner rooms of the hotel by some side door, — have fallen in her flight, and been stifled by the smoke before the flames came near her. When the flooring gave way, she fell with it into the water in which she was found.

We quitted this scene of woe and destruction; but any attempts to sleep were vain: the most frightful dreams caused us to start up and meet the frightful truth. The streets, which had been crowded during the night, were now filled with people following their daily pursuits.

All Paris was in a state of violent excitement. The glare of the fire had spread the news far and wide. Some suspected that the Emperor's life had been attempted, or that some conspiracy had broken out — the uncertainty made them more anxious. It was very generally supposed that the fire was intentional, and that Napoleon's domestic and foreign foes had intended, by a bold stroke, to get rid at once of their odious ruler, of his whole family, and devoted adherents. So strong was this impression, that it was difficult to eradicate it, and the accounts and witnesses to the contrary were heard with suspicion. It was only at the end of three days that the account in the "Moniteur" appeared, and this even did not quite satisfy men's doubts. But, in the end, these groundless suspicions gave way before the concurrent testimony of so many witnesses and the evidence which Napoleon's subsequent conduct bore to their truth; and the accidental nature of the fire was acknowledged in France as elsewhere.

Now followed a succession of melancholy days, during which nothing but the terrible event and its possible consequences were discussed. Princess Pauline Schwarzenberg was buried with the usual ceremonies. Then followed the funerals of Princess von der Leyen, Made. Touzard, and of several other women of high rank who died in the course of the next few days, after suffering excruciating agonies. Altogether about twenty persons died, and above sixty were more or less injured. The young Princess Pauline Schwarzenberg, who narrowly escaped the fate of her mother, lay dangerously ill for many weeks; and the life of Prince Kurakin, the Russian ambassador, was for some time despaired of. The loss in jewels was reckoned at some millions of francs. The Austrian ambassador, whose own losses were the greatest, took upon himself to replace what was damaged or burnt.

The impression made by the event was deep and pregnant with mischief. Gloomy allusions were made to the misfortunes attending the marriage of the Dauphin, afterwards Louis XVI., and Marie Antoinette, and to their fearful end. This last tragedy at Prince Schwarzenberg's betokened that some fatality attended any union with Austria. Napoleon's subsequent career gave a colour of truth to these superstitious forebodings.

CHAPTER XI.

Berthier. — The Battle of Marengo. — Denon. — Cardinal Maury. — The Salle des Ambassadeurs. — Reception at Court. — Napoleon's Manner. — Sudden Outbreak of Temper. — The Emperor's Departure. — General Relief. 1810.

WE had now been at Paris some time, and as yet there had been no diplomatic reception. One was at last announced, and we were to be presented to Napoleon. Meanwhile Prince Schwarzenberg had introduced us to several men of high rank about the court, among others to Berthier, Prince of Neufchâtel and Wagram, as he was then called. At Berthier's we found a good many people; the men dispersed about the room talking, the women sitting in great state, apparently not much amused. Count von Neipperg and I were the only strangers, and we were seized upon with eagerness. Berthier's manner was most friendly; it was gentle and engaging, with that peculiar repose which so often is found in men of great power. He pleased me exceedingly, and I by no means agreed with those who thought that he was not gifted with intelligence of a high order. Energy, confidence, and experience were engraven on his earnest face, and his language was clear and forcible. General Neipperg turned the conversation upon the battle of Marengo, and some incidents were discussed with vehemence. Berthier had written a special account of the battle, in which there were great blunders of omission as well as of commission, which had evidently been inserted to please the Emperor. It was generally said that much praise had been given to General Desaix, which properly belonged to others who were still living, but whom it would have been inconvenient to Napoleon to have rewarded. Berthier had a hard contest to maintain with the well-informed Neipperg, but he managed very well, and constantly brought fresh statements and arguments to bear upon the subject, and as at Marengo, in spite of the advantages of the Austrians, the victory remained with the French, Berthier clearly had the best of the argument notwithstanding Neipperg's superior knowledge. When he was reminded how doubtful the contest was after Desaix had already fallen, and how Napoleon himself had despaired, Berthier replied, that the general was perfectly right, even if the battle were quite lost, adding:—"*C'est toujours après les succès que je crains le plus dans la guerre, et rien de si dangereux que le commencement d'une victoire.*" Several women now joined us, and the conversation was interrupted.

It was much to Berthier's honour, that in spite of his princely rank and great wealth, he retained his old manners with his former companions, and was moderate in his habits. Although devoted to Napoleon, he was by no means cringing, like Davoust and many others. Bernadotte, on the other hand, was said to laugh with his habitual light-heartedness at the manners of the court, and not to conceal his amusement at Napoleon's assumption of pomp and ceremony. He stuck fast to his republicanism, and lived on the most intimate terms with his old companions in arms.

Berthier asked us how we had amused ourselves in Paris, and whether we had seen all the exhibitions of the works of art. Hereupon an old French general, whose name I forget, began to discuss the Musée Napoléon, and wondered how it was that so few of the works of art had reached Paris; adding, that as he had seen three times the number packed up, a great many must have disappeared on the road. The following example will show how carelessly these things were managed. Napoleon had ordered a monument, commemorating the victory of the Prussians at Rossbach, to be taken from the spot where it stood, and sent to France. The monument itself was worthless as a work of art—a mere column of sandstone—but as a memorial of military glory, it was of the highest value. This column disappeared, and was nowhere to be heard of. Napoleon stormed, inquiries were made on all sides, Chamisso was privately asked what it was like, and the French had even some notion of substituting a false one. At length, the real column was unexpectedly discovered at Brest—no one knew exactly how it got there; and it now stands in its original place, a double monument of Prussian valour.

At Berthier's house I again saw Denon, who, in spite of all his friendliness of manner, made an unpleasant impression upon me; in his *habit habillé*, with a dress sword and laced ruffles, he looked like a dressed-up ape. An adjutant of Napoleon's, whom I had known at Vienna, who now had some civil office about the Emperor's court, and whom in his military uniform I had always thought a very good-looking fellow, seemed to be masquerading, with his red embroidered court dress. But to make the company still more gaudy, a couple of ecclesiastics came into the room with their red stockings, and appeared to rejoice mightily in the few spare minutes of society which were now allowed them. Meanwhile Berthier had gone into the antechamber, and had left the company for a moment. As the ecclesiastics were going away, one of them—who happened to be Cardinal Maury—whispered into my ear, with a peculiar expression,—" *Nous avons beaucoup de joie de vous voir ici!* " I looked at him in amazement; why should he say privately and with secret joy what he might perfectly have said openly as a common-place compliment? But he evidently referred to the circumstance that Austria had lately made strong representations in favour of the Pope.

The first reception after the fire at Prince Schwarzenberg's took place on Sunday the 22d of July; it was expected to be a very brilliant one. I had often seen Napoleon at Berlin, Vienna, and Schönbrunn, but never near enough for his countenance to remain strongly impressed on my memory. The terrible events at Prince Schwarzenberg's ball had obliterated his features from my recollection. I therefore consider that this day of reception was the first time that I really saw him thoroughly and closely. The opportunities I afterwards had of seeing him frequently at the Tuileries, and more especially at the dramatic representations at St. Cloud, where Talma, Fleury, and Mademoiselle Raucourt acted before the court, only confirmed my previous impressions.

We drove to the Tuileries, and made our way, through a great crowd of guards and people, to a room called the *Salle des Ambassadeurs*. The manner in which so many distinguished men were penned up in this small space, was unpleasant but laughable, and was not lost upon the Parisians. Officers in gorgeous uniforms were working their way with great difficulty amid livery servants bearing refreshments. Conversation was loud and animated; every one was trying to find their acquaintances and more room. There was no appearance of dignity or ceremony worthy of the occasion; every one looked uncomfortable and bored. The only people whose appearance did not belie their station were the members of the Austrian embassy. Prince Schwarzenberg especially had a noble appearance; his manners were easy without languor, and earnest without pomposity; his whole conduct made a striking contrast to the ridiculous activity and glib insignificance of so many others, especially of those courtiers who, having followed the popular current, had now been left behind in the race, which was the fate of many present. If these people, with their crosses and smart clothes, and in the circle in which their nature and education intended them to move, made so wretched a figure, what was to be expected of them in the councils of princes, in high offices of trust in the camp? These thoughts struck me the more, because I now found the French court, which had been described as the seat of all that was dignified and imposing, to be the picture of disorder and ridicule.

At length the time approached, and every one rushed towards the doors; ushers, pages, and guards filled the passages and the antechamber. Even here the soldiers seemed to be the only people who knew their business, and these had learnt it, not from courtiers, but from their corporals.

A half circle was formed in the audience chamber, and we waited till the cry of *l'Empereur* announced Napoleon's approach. He was dressed in a plain blue uniform, with his small cocked hat under his arm, and slowly advanced towards us from the end of the room. He had the air of one exercising a strong restraint upon himself, in order to conceal his contempt for those from whom he had some object to obtain. He wished to make a favourable impression, but nature had denied him ease of manner, and it was scarce worth the trouble to assume it. Hence there was an incessant contest going on within him. He first addressed the Austrian ambassador, who was at one end of the half circle, and the conversation turned on the unfortunate ball. Napoleon intended to express sympathy, but failed in conveying his meaning. His manner was less friendly towards the Russian ambassador, Prince Kurakin; and lower down the circle he must have heard or seen something to annoy him, for he lost his temper, and nearly annihilated the minister of some second-rate power, whose name I cannot at this moment recall, by his furious manner. Those who were near enough to witness this scene afterwards asserted that no cause whatever had been given for this sudden outbreak of temper, and that Napoleon had selected this unlucky wight upon whom to vent his wrath, in order to keep the others in wholesome dread.

As he proceeded further down the circle he tried to be more gentle, but his ill-humour was constantly showing itself. He spoke in a short hasty tone, and even when he intended to be kind, he always looked as if he were angry. I scarce ever heard so rough or so unpleasant a voice as Napoleon's.

His eyes were gloomily fixed upon the ground, and occasionally glanced rapidly from one person to another. When he smiled, the smile played only about the mouth and cheeks, the eyes remaining immovably fixed. If by an effort he succeeded in forcing the smile into the upper part of his face, his countenance grew still more repulsive. There was something awful in this union of smiles and sternness. I cannot understand what those people mean who say that they found his countenance captivating from its pleasant and kindly expression. His features, undeniably classical and beautiful, were hard and fixed as marble, and incapable of expressing confidence, or any generous emotion.

What he said, at least whenever I heard him, was insignificant in substance and expression, without force, wit, or clearness,—sometimes it was common-place and ridiculous. Faber, in his *Notices sur l'Intérieur de la France*, has written at some length on the questions which Napoleon was in the habit of asking on particular occasions, and which received an undue share of praise for knowledge and acuteness. I had not then seen the book, but I afterwards found my own views confirmed. Napoleon's speeches were frequently like those of a schoolboy, who, not quite sure of knowing his lesson, is constantly muttering to himself the part he is afraid of forgetting. This is accurately true of a visit he made to the royal library: all the way up the stairs he kept asking for the passage in Josephus in which our Saviour is mentioned, apparently with the view of showing his learning. It looked almost as if he had got his lesson by heart. He once asked some man from the north of Germany whence he came; and on his answering from some country near Holland, Napoleon exclaimed, with a satisfied air, "*Ah! je sais bien; c'est du nord, c'est de la Hollande!*" He was not so fortunate with Lacepède, at the collection of natural history, where, to the consternation of Maria Louisa and of the naturalist, he mistook the cameleopard for a bird. Napoleon's attempts to shine in society were often ridiculous, and his failure in this department was as remarkable as his success in others. His chief pleasure consisted in wounding people's feelings; and when he attempted to say agreeable things, the result was at best utter insignificance. I remember hearing him, at St. Cloud, repeat the same phrase twenty times over to a whole row of ladies,—"*Il fait chaud.*"

It is perfectly true that several strong nervous expressions are attributed to him, and his orders were mostly terse and vigorous; but even these indicate power rather than any other quality, and their importance is derived from the high station of their author. Several happy expressions given to him by the hangers-on at court, properly belong to others, who sedulously repudiated their own property. When he spoke continuously on any question, he was apt, by mixing up too many subjects, to be wanting in method, precision, and clearness. He never, it is true, lost sight of the objects he had in view; but he attained them not by his speeches, but by his unrivalled talents as a commander, and by the power of his iron will. His real greatness consisted in these qualities, and he has no need of others to make him one of the most extraordinary men that ever appeared. The gift of eloquence, common to Alexander, Cæsar, and Frederick, was foreign to Napoleon's nature and intellect.

It was for this reason that Napoleon was so sensitive and angry when any biting and clever satire was published against him. A witty song drove him half mad. About this time a ballad on his second marriage was handed about*; although in

* Vide page 161.

the language of the common people, it evidently was written by a man of education. Napoleon saw his majesty and splendour defiled by a vulgar ballad, and panted for revenge. The police, however, were at fault; they could neither discover the author nor the distributors of the satire. It had been sent to me by the post; I had read it to several friends, and knew it by heart. Exactly as the Emperor came near where I stood, the verses and the tune came unbidden to my memory, and the more I tried to forget them, the faster did the natural agitation of the moment force them to my lips,—when, fortunately, the reception was at an end, and Napoleon left the room. He did not speak to me, but fixed a searching glance on me as he went by.

After the Emperor's departure we all breathed freely again, as if a heavy weight had been taken off. The conversation became loud and general as before, and the loudest of all were the hangers-on of the French court, who made amends for their previous silent dread by loud hilarity. The stairs down which we went resounded with witty observations, and bursts of laughter, having for their subject the reception at court.

Napoleon was great, where he was really himself, at the head of an army. But when he attempted to act a part out of his own peculiar line, he failed signally, and deceived none but the weak and the ignorant. The impression left by his memory on the present generation is far stronger than that which he made on his own. It sounds strange, but it is nevertheless true, that neither the lower nor the upper classes in Paris— not even his own immediate adherents—had any real reverence for him, or considered him a man of the highest order.

CHAPTER XII.

Paris.—Musée Napoleon.—Musée des Monumens Français.—The Luxemburg Palace.—The Hall of the Senate.—Prix décennaux.—Musée d'Artillerie.—The Imperial Library.—Versailles, St. Cloud, and Malmaison.—Talma.—The Empress Josephine.—Jean Jacques Rousseau.—Life in Paris.—Parisian Advertisements.—State of Parties.—French itinerant Mountebank.—Pulpit and Bar Eloquence.—The Comedian Brunet.—Epigrams on Napoleon's Marriage.—Breakfast at Count Metternich's.—Scene in the Café de Valois.—Madame de Genlis.—Boulevards des Italiens. 1810.

ONE of the first people I visited in Paris was Chamisso, whose surprise and joy were great, as he had no idea of my coming, and had no other friend to fall back upon. With him I made frequent expeditions: he knew Paris, and loved it well; and it was a matter of pride with him to be the first to show me all its remarkable sights. We glanced at the principal buildings and monuments; we walked over the Boulevards, Quais, public places, the Palais Royal, and the Tuileries Gardens, before we satisfied our impatience by seeing the treasures of antique art and the pictures. By these we were quite fascinated, and did not quit the Louvre so soon as we had intended. We felt that this was a sight of the greatest interest, not only for Paris, but for the whole world; Paris had nothing to do with it beyond accidentally happening to be the city in which these things were to be seen. We felt constantly more and more strongly attracted to this collection of treasures, and scarce a day passed on which we did not meet there. As those times have now become historical, and great changes have since occurred, I cannot do better than give my impressions as they were written down at the time.

The greater portion of this rich collection, which was here united under the name of the *Musée Napoléon*, had been obtained by plunder from Italy, Germany, Holland, and some few pictures from Spain. Our first impression was, that we stood before some great monument of Victory, or were witnessing a triumph of ancient Rome, for every thing here was arranged more with a view to glory than to art. Many were the proofs of how little these inestimable works were valued for themselves. The rain was allowed free entrance, and had injured several pictures; but many more were spoilt by whitewash and dust, as the pictures were neither removed nor covered up while bricklayers and carpenters were at work close by them. Many of the pictures were cracked by the action of the sharp air which penetrated through the thin walls and ill-fitting windows, and in several places the surface had been injured. A still larger number were ruined by the process of cleaning; among others, the celebrated Madonna della Sedia, from which the colours had nearly disappeared, and which those who had previously seen, could scarcely recognise. Above a thousand pictures, and these some of the greatest and best, stood by dozens covered with dust, and leaning one against the other in a room where some workmen were employed sawing, planing, and hammering, while whitewash and stones were lying about in all directions, and thousands of men were daily passing to and fro. It was perfectly right, no doubt, that every one should have free access to this gallery; but I own that it caused me a bitter pang when I saw whole swarms of fishwives, soldiers, porters, and peasants in their sabots, with their hats on their heads, and their tobacco-pipes in their mouths, coarsely jesting, shouldering and pushing each other among these works of genius. As if to spare this collection no indignity, Denon had undertaken a series of engravings, which showed total ignorance and misconception on his part, accompanied with a great parade of learning. For a display of booty all this was well enough; but a sanctuary of art required care, and far different management.

Of the nine rooms opening one into the other, which formed the long gallery of the Louvre, one was filled with French, four with German and Dutch, and four, besides a large antechamber, with Italian pictures. Most of the French pictures belonged originally to France, still some few were obtained by plunder: for example, the four glorious Claude Lorraines from Cassel; these, however, were not in the Louvre, but at Malmaison. The pictures of the Dutch school came chiefly from the Hague; the German, from Nürnberg, Augsburg, Vienna, Cassel, Berlin, Potsdam, Dantzick, and other towns; and the Italian pictures were plundered from various cities in Italy, where for ages they had been the pride and object of reverence of the whole nation. Some of these pictures were the highly-prized treasure of the community, or of the municipality, by whose order the artist had especially painted them for some particular niche, in which they had remained ever since. With what sad feelings did I now stand before these pictures, when I compared the noble simplicity and quiet grandeur of the German school, and the genius, power, and glowing colouring of the Italians, with the coarse minds of these people, who merely felt their vanity gratified, and a vulgar astonishment excited by this spectacle! Truly these elect children of a godlike art would not have done amiss, had they suffered their life-like colours to melt away into the paleness of death, and thus rescued themselves from profanation.

This feeling of profanation struck me with still greater strength at sight of the ancient statues on the ground-floor of the *Musée*. Perhaps among all the objects which one had rather not see in Paris, there were none the effect of which was so spoilt, I may almost say annihilated, as these highest productions of ancient art. The narrow, dark, dirty rooms, the hateful ceilings, covered with gaudy allegorical or mythological paintings, the bad light, the ill-placed statues, — all this produced the very worst effect, which was further increased by the masses of vulgar people who crowded in on the public days, and crawled about like worms in the presence of these deities. Statues never affected me less than in Paris. I have still a vivid recollection of the powerful manner in which the first sight of such things moved me two years before in Dresden, how small the pictures were in comparison with the sculpture, and how exquisite I thought the marble itself. I felt no such effect here! I stood without pleasure, nay, almost suffering, dull and unmoved before this concourse of divinities; before the Apollo of Belvidere, the Venus of

Medici, the Laocoon, and other celebrated statues; the mere mention of whose names in worthless books of travels, the sight of which in wretched engravings, had formerly awakened in me the strongest emotions: moreover, I was punished by the conviction that if I did not feel duly excited, the fault was not in the statues of the gods, but in me. I appeared to myself as one of the barbarians who had so angered me. I walked about the rooms daily with Chamisso, with Bekker, with Sieveking, and with Bartholdy, without being able to find the right feeling for the statues, and I perceived that these several men did not bring to this wonderful collection of ancient art any more feeling than I did; I was not to be deceived by Chamisso's exaggerated expressions, nor by Bartholdy's more quiet artist-like sentences. Bekker alone seemed by education and feeling more just in his appreciation of this antique world, and far more devoted to it than we were. The Apollo, above all the others, overcame the influence under which we suffered, and his god-like beauty and anger shone out in their full glory. The famous Venus of Medici had less effect upon me; in this place she seemed no goddess, but a shameless courtezan. The glorious Diana, the noble Juno, the gigantic Muse,—to all these we paid due worship. But next to the Apollo, the two colossal river gods, the Tiber and the Nile, attracted me most; and I could never take my eyes off these works, so full of wondrous beauty, and of deep and powerful expression.

We were told that the beauty of the Apollo had taken such complete possession of a young girl's senses, that she sank down at his feet, and knelt in rapture before the statue as long as she was permitted to remain. She could scarcely be torn from it, but wished to stay day and night, until they were obliged to remove her by force. She had a conviction that in time she could, by her love and earnest prayer, move the god to hear her, and to step living from the marble. Chamisso dearly loved this story, and told me that he should have put it into verse, had not Helmina von Chézy already done so.

The paintings, great and magical in their way, likewise affected us more; they addressed themselves more plainly to our senses than the dreamy and half-mutilated divinities of a world far removed from ours. In the gallery we were soon at our ease, and perfectly at home. As a rendezvous for other excursions, I daily visited the gallery, and was always certain to find my friends in the rooms devoted to Raffaelle: we then and there arranged our further schemes for the day. The painter Unger was copying the Madonna della Sedia, and we gladly stood near his easel, listening to his conversation: technical and historical notices are always acceptable in the presence of pictures; but I must confess that my attention was by no means devoted exclusively to the history of art, or to the acquirement of a knowledge of pictures. My stay in Paris was to be short and uncertain: my pursuits, and even my inclinations, lay in another direction. I wished simply to enjoy the best specimens of art as an amateur; to see only what was agreeable to my eye, and what most excited and pleased my fancy. I would not suffer the criticisms of the learned either to influence my taste, or to disturb my enjoyment. I discovered that by keeping to this maxim I did perfectly well, and had the pleasure of finding that my taste was frequently confirmed by high authorities, and that I had the good fortune to be generally attracted to those pictures, which were most worthy of constant admiration. Thus in the course of the first day I had selected out of the mass of pictures a certain number of favourites, which formed a little gallery of my own, and to which I remained constant to the end. Of Raffaelle's pictures, of which never before was such a collection seen, not one was excluded; Leonardo da Vinci contributed largely; then came Julio Romano, Titian, Pierugino, Guido Reni, Fra Bastiano, Fra Bartolomeo, Domenichino, Giorgione, Cristoforo Allori, and Garofalo; Correggio and Murillo attracted me less; and least of all the two Caraccis. Among the German and Dutch school my favourites were Holbein, Albert Dürer, Van Dyck, Rembrandt, Ruysdael, the so called Van Eyck of Dantzick; and among the French I liked Claude Lorraine, Poussin, and Lesueur. The sight of Rubens's pictures pained me: I was fully sensible to his merits; but, if I dared not blame, still less could I admire him.

But in this selection, to which Chamisso, Bekker, and Uhland the poet gave in their adhesion, there were some pictures which attracted me, as much for personal reasons as for their artistic merit. Two portraits had struck me from the very first: the one was the Mona Lisa of Leonardo da Vinci, a painter whose especial faculty it is to represent modesty of expression; and the second was Joan of Arragon by Raffaelle, the greatest painter of pure beauty. The latter picture had a peculiar charm for me, as it was extraordinarily like the young Countess von Bentheim: the longer I looked at it, the more convinced I was that it was her portrait also. The living may well be proud of having been painted by Raffaelle. A Madonna by Leonardo da Vinci, Herodias's daughter, by Solari, and a small picture of St. John, by Luini, especially attracted my notice: I was much affected, but in a different manner, by Titian's master-piece, the murder of Peter martyr, from Milan. Allori's Judith, in which character the artist had painted his mistress Mazzafirra, while her mother is represented as the maid, and he himself figured as Holofernes, struck me much from the tragic expression of the countenances; the idea, too, was poetical, although the picture itself is not so.

Not only have the Germans and Italians, the Dutch and the Spaniards, great cause to turn away with sorrow when they see the most precious monuments of their country collected in Paris, but a melancholy feeling must occasionally come across even the Frenchman, and Paris must appear to him in the light of a monster that swallows every thing. It is true that the accumulation of treasures of art is so enormous, that the superfluity flows off into the provinces, and museums are erected in the departmental towns; but the treasures originally taken away never return to the place whence they came. This struck us very strongly on entering the *Musée des Monumens Français*. During the course of centuries, France had become exceedingly rich in monuments and works of art, erected partly from a spirit of religion and love, partly from vanity; churches, castles, abbeys, market-places, and private dwellings served as storehouses of ancient works of art, which were scarce known beyond their own immediate neighbourhood. How rich the provinces were, as well as the metropolis, was only discovered when these ancient treasures were directed to be destroyed by the savage order of the National Convention. Nothing in any way connected with royalty, religion, or the aristocracy, was suffered to exist; all the past was to be obliterated. Great was the company of the destroyers, inexhaustible their zeal, and they succeeded but too well. But neither time nor zeal prevailed; much was passed over, many monuments were only injured, and several withstood the attacks made upon them. Even during the storm, but still more afterwards, when its virulence abated, a few able men devoted to their country and to art, busied themselves in secret to save such monuments as they could, to get hold of those which were only half destroyed, and to put together many which had been broken in pieces. One of these men was Alexandre Lenoir, who was most active in establishing the *Musée des Monumens Français*. When the power fell into milder hands, people ventured to suggest that what had been thus saved should be opened to the public, and made one of the remarkable sights of the metropolis; the old convent *des Petits Augustins* was devoted to this purpose. Here wonderful things were to be seen, — monuments of kings and queens, figures in stone, paintings on glass, columns and mosaics, all of which gave a very high idea of the state of art in France in former centuries. The order of time was accurately observed; and to increase the effect, the various rooms in which the monuments stood were so arranged, that ornaments, windows, ceilings, and pavements were all, as nearly as possible, of the same century. What we saw gave us the highest opinion of French sculpture of former days, and the names of Jean Goujon and Germain Pilon must always be mentioned among those of the great masters of all times. The works of these men had a peculiar and independent character of their own, wholly unlike Grecian art. This sculpture, which was chiefly intended for churches, had an architectural character; it essentially belonged to buildings. In these plain and noble stones you may read religious sentiment, energy and courage, earnestness and the awe of death. Voluptuous beauty never was the aim of the artist; his object was to excite deep emotions, and to appeal to the imagination through the reason. The effect of the whole is not injured, but rather heightened, by the minute ornaments and careful handling of individual parts. The three monuments from the church of St. Denys, that of Louis XII. and Anne of

Brittany, the chapel of Francis I., and the tomb of the Valois, are certainly the most remarkable of their kind.

I must return, however, to the impression produced upon me by the whole, which indeed was strange enough. I thought that I saw the remains of a people that had long passed away, whose language was strange, to whose faith and feelings we were absolutely indifferent, and with whose race, glory, and greatness we had nothing in common. Thus we have Egyptian obelisks and monuments, mummies of Egyptian kings, as ornaments in our northern cities, and no one feels any emotion at seeing them. But a Frenchman who has a heart, and a recollection devoted to the history of his country,—what should he feel when he beholds the relics of its past history? The people see the monuments of their kings, of their statesmen, of their heroes, thrown out of their history, torn from their natural resting-places, with which their names are associated, and piled up within the narrow compass of a museum, ticketed and registered as things that once have been!

There is a great treasure of art in what was the Luxemburg palace, which is now converted into the palace of the senate, and where that august body is wont to assemble. Mary of Medici bought the palace from the Duke of Luxemburg, and the same name was still given to the beautiful building which the French architect, Debrosse erected after the pattern of the Pitti palace at Florence. Rubens was engaged by Mary of Medici to ornament the new palace with pictures, and he painted the chief events of her life in four-and-twenty compartments. These pictures were dispersed during the Revolution; some got into the National Museum, and others were for a long time missing: at length, the whole series has been again collected. The praise bestowed upon these pictures has been excessive, and they have been called Rubens's epic poem. I will not deny Rubens the merit of wonderful power of invention, and of bending the most refractory materials to his purpose, nor his free full manner of handling the pencil, and those who wish to study him must do so in these pictures; but, nevertheless, they do not please me: I left them without any feeling of excitement, and they had upon me the effect of a modern Latin ode: my former opinion of this extraordinary man was not changed. I was far more pleased by Lesueur's productions in another room; he has painted four-and-twenty pictures representing the life of Saint Bruno, and the establishment of the order of the Carthusians. The poor Carthusians were talked out of their property, during the first years of Louis XVI.'s reign; and the pictures were placed in the Louvre. Since that time they have made several peregrinations, and are consequently much injured. After the coarse strength and reality of life in Rubens, it was a comfort to fall back upon the pious gentle Lesueur, so well fitted to smooth away the feeling of disquiet which Rubens had raised. A third room contained Vernet's marine pieces, — fifteen views of French seaports. This painter proceeded to his work with prodigious energy, and with considerable success: his night scenes, his moonshines, his sea pieces, have a vehement and exciting power about them which, differing as they do from nature, still work powerfully on coarse minds. This was quite sufficient to insure him a great reputation; and the French of the eighteenth century knew as well how to puff and boast as those of the present day. Chamfort relates, that while Louis XV. was sitting for his portrait to the painter Latour, the latter wished to amuse the monarch, and ventured to make several very bold remarks; among others he mentioned the decay of the French navy: "Truly your Majesty has no marine!" whereupon the King gravely replied: "No marine! what are you saying? and Vernet? do you call that nothing?" and the King intended no joke.

There are likewise one Raffaelle and several pictures by Titian, Champagne, Ruysdael, Rembrandt, and Ostade in the Luxemburg, and it is said that the gallery will be still further increased. After these, two of David's pictures singularly displeased us — Brutus was a downright monster, and the Horatii looked like a copy of something on the French stage. What was good in David, the grandeur and firmness of his drawing, and the bold grouping of his figures did not satisfy us: his method of laying on the colours seemed essentially bad. It made Chamisso's heart bleed to be forced to condemn the leader and the glory of the modern French school, but there was no help for it.

We likewise visited the hall in which the senate sat, frequently under the presidence of the Emperor himself. A handsome flight of steps ornamented with statues of great generals and orators—Kleber, Hoche, Desaix, Mirabeau, Vergniaud, and others—led to a series of splendid rooms, of which this hall was the last. Notwithstanding the size of the rooms, every thing looked small and narrow; the Austrian colours which ornamented the walls of the room, made a strong impression on us, and recalled the bitter hostility of the two powers who were now allies, and pretended to be friends. The senate had just been sitting: the handsome arm-chairs of the senators stood in a semi-circle opposite to the Emperor's throne; we sat in some of them and found them still warm: the usher thought us rather bold, and would not permit us to sit down on the Emperor's throne. He took us, he said, for Austrians of rank, otherwise he would never have admitted us. The sentinel on duty below, at first denied us entrance, and told us somewhat roughly, that this was no day for the admission of strangers. We instantly gave way, and asked civilly for his advice how we were to act in order to obtain admission. The man then allowed us to enter, showed us where to find the usher, and gave us a few hints as to what we should say to him: all this without any prospect of gain, as it was strictly forbidden to give any thing to the sentinels. This sudden change of manner is usual with the common people, out of which class the soldiers are drawn, but we little expected it from a French sentinel in Napoleon's time.

The *Prix décennaux* established by the Emperor for the most distinguished and best productions of literature and art during the last ten years, gave us another opportunity of seeing and comparing pictures. The French were exceedingly excited by this distribution of prizes. The great and all-pervading interest which was shown by all classes about this exhibition, told well for the general cultivation of the people. The decision of those who distributed the prizes was severely and loudly criticised; but people were satisfied when they found that the Emperor was highly displeased with many of the decisions of the arbitrators: the populace always rejoices when those in power receive a check. We did not trouble our heads with the prizes given for literary merit—what should we care for people like Lemercier, Arnault, Jouy, and the rest? But we could not pass over the paintings. It was impossible to see David's works without confessing that he was a master in his own style. Gerard's and Guérin's pictures were much admired, and we recognised the bold strength in Gros's works, and the warmth of composition in those of Giraudet. But after devoting some time to these pictures, we always returned to the rooms where Raffaelle and others were to be seen, which soon made us forget that there was a modern school trying to make its way in the world.

The director of the *Musée d'Artillerie*, Monsieur Regnier himself, conducted us over this rich collection of ancient weapons and armour, of models, and all sorts of beautiful curiosities. Regnier was much esteemed as a man of scientific attainments, thoroughly well versed in the history of the treasures committed to his charge: it was said that the Emperor thought very highly of him. He was a man of some invention, and had taken out a patent for a sort of lock which made some noise at the time: every body praised his invention, and bought his locks. These consisted of broad steel rings—four, five, or eight deep—upon each of which the alphabet was engraved; these turned round on a cylinder of steel, and only separated where the letters, forming a particular word, were in a straight line with another. The word was selected from among a thousand, and the choice was the secret of the purchaser. Any one not knowing the word, might turn the rings round for years without succeeding in finding the right one. The workmanship was excellent, and Regnier was prouder of this than he was of the invention itself. The latter point might be contested. I had a vague recollection of having seen something of the sort before, but when I ventured to say so, my supicions were treated with scorn and indignation, and I was not able then to prove my assertions; but many years afterwards when a book, which as a boy I had often diligently read, fell into my hands, Regnier's lock was suddenly displayed! The book was called *Silvestri a Petrasancta Symbola Heroica*, printed at Amsterdam in 1682: there was an explanation at page 254, attached to a picture: these were the words:—" *Honorius de Bellis, serulæ innexæ orbibus volubilibus ac literatis circumscripsit hoc lemma :—Sorte aut labore.*" However, neither luck or labour would have done much towards discovering the secret of opening Regnier's locks from the variety of their combinations ; and their security seemed so great that the couriers' despatch-boxes were generally fastened with them.

The imperial library in the Rue Richelieu, one of the noisiest streets in all Paris, is not favourable for study. Moreover, the close neighbourhood of the opera-house is most dangerous to this valuable collection. It is said that no theatre comes to a natural end, but that they are all destined some day or other to destruction by fire. For this reason the Emperor intends to remove the library to some better situation. The Louvre is to be connected with the Tuileries on the side facing the town, with a gallery, similar to that towards the river. This new wing is intended to contain most of the collections which are now partly in the Louvre, partly in other places ; the Louvre will then be devoted exclusively to the service of the Emperor, and of the royal family, and to the reception of distinguished foreigners. In this case, however, the space enclosed between the Louvre and the Tuileries would be too large to remain empty : another reason for not leaving it vacant is, that unluckily the two buildings do not stand exactly opposite to each other ; and the triumphal arch in the Place du Carrousel, forms an unsightly angle. In order to conceal this defect, and at the same time to divide this great vacant space, Napoleon means to erect an enormous corner building in which nothing but iron and stone are to be used, wherein the books may for the future be kept perfectly fire-proof; even the book shelves are to be made of iron, and the building is to surpass any thing that was ever before erected of the sort. I heard the details of this plan from the mouth of Count Metternich, to whom the Emperor had related it during a conversation with him in the forenoon. The execution of this gigantic scheme is still far distant, whole streets must first be swept away, and the Louvre itself finished. But with Napoleon all that he wills is considered as completed, and his impatience goes so much faster than time, that he has already prepared for the Louvre upon which they are still at work, an inscription to the effect that it was completed by him ;

an untruth which the French imagine will always remain one, as the Louvre never can be finished. Even Napoleon shrank back with alarm from renovating Perrault's beautiful façade which runs all round the building. And at this very time the library is still in its old place.

This was naturally no time for study as far as I was concerned; nevertheless I found great objects of interest in the imperial library. The manuscripts, of which there were above 80,000, particularly attracted my attention. The librarians were most attentive, and not only procured me what I wished to see, but even assisted the subordinate officers in their search. Here I was shown the plunder which had been brought from Rome, Venice, Wolfenbüttel, and Vienna; from the latter place especially a number of Oriental manuscripts had been taken, the duplicates of which, where they existed, Von Hammer had succeeded in obtaining for Vienna. For this purpose he had expressly made the journey to Paris at his own cost. I then cared little for the letters of Henri IV., Francis I., or Louis XIV.; historical research was far from my thoughts: Fénélon's well corrected manuscripts of Telemaque, the Livre des Tournées of Count Réné of Provence, Greek and Roman manuscripts only excited a passing interest. On the other hand, a collection of Minnesinger's especially attracted me, I read a good deal of it, and commenced making extracts, and had some thoughts of editing the works of the poet Süsskind, called "The Jew of Trunberg," when I heard that a young scholar was already busily engaged on the same work, and that my labours were useless. My attention meanwhile had been called to a treasure which touched us Germans more nearly, and I devoted many hours to this new study. This was thirteen volumes of manuscript extracts and remarks by Winckelmann, which had been brought from Rome. These writings were invaluable towards acquiring a knowledge of the man, of his studies, and of his method of proceeding, even when the manuscript consisted merely of extracts from some worthless English spelling-book, which this great man had been forced to copy, at a great loss of his valuable time, for want of the few shillings wherewith to buy the book. All was written in that beautiful clear hand which had done him such service, for it was of great importance to him at Rome, as he says in his letters, that Cardinal Passionei expressed such high praise of his Greek writing, which, indeed, is exquisite. The first sketches of his history of ancient art are here preserved, with numerous alterations and transpositions; for example, the description of the Apollo Belvidere is written in several different ways. Besides this, there are half-finished letters, short extracts, remarks and observations written in a strong nervous language; in short, a mine of wealth containing traits of the highest importance for a just appreciation of character. After the second peace of Paris, these volumes of Winckelmann's were deposited in the royal library of Berlin, where they are more at home, and infinitely better placed than either at Paris or at Rome.

The library likewise contains other valuable collections, such as coins, cameos, and gems, engravings, Egyptian, Roman, and Middle Age antiquities. I looked at all these only in a hurried manner, as I had neither time nor inclination for closer inspection. What chiefly attracted my attention were the Apotheosis of Augustus, the largest gem which is extant, a sardonyx which was brought to France by Count Baldwyn of Flanders, the gem with the arrow-headed characters from Persepolis, the table of Isis, the so-called shield of Hannibal, the arms of Francis I., and the sword of Henri IV. A mutilated bronze seat, called Dagobert's chair, struck me from its inscription:—" *Ce fauteuil a été transporté à Boulogne pour la distribution des croix de la légion d'honneur, le 16 Août,* 1804." This trifling with antiquity and trying to mix up his own name with it, which Napoleon was so fond of doing, was ridiculous even to Frenchmen. The aping of Charlemagne which was so constant and so obvious, had some plausibility; but Napoleon and Dagobert—what on earth had they to do with each other? The scheme, too, failed in producing its effect; the soldiers laughed at the old chair, the authenticity of which is doubtful. The people knew nothing of Dagobert but what they had learnt from the popular ballad of "*Le bon roi Dagobert,*" and Napoleon got nothing but ridicule from this farce.

We found this association of Napoleon with Charlemagne again forced upon our attention in the church of Notre Dame.

The crown, the globe, the sceptre, and the hand of justice, belonging to Charlemagne, are placed in the treasure of the church, close beside the crowns of Napoleon and Josephine. That of Napoleon is a mere wreath of laurel worked in gold, extremely beautiful from its simplicity. Napoleon was continually alternating between the parts of Roman Imperator and King of France, and it must be confessed that he was more successful in the former character than in the latter. His eagles were a well-chosen emblem, which were not only instantly adopted by the army, but also found favour in the eyes of the people; whereas his attempt to revive the court dresses of the time of Louis XIV. appeared ridiculous to one-half of the nation, and odious to the other. His Ns, crowned and adorned with laurel, and the bees which he placed in profusion every where, especially in all public places where the symbols and mottoes of liberty had stood till now, were a coarse method of keeping himself continually before the attention of the public, but well calculated for the multitude. On several of the walls, however, we still saw caps of liberty, which had been forgotten, and mottoes which had not yet been effaced,—such as *Liberté, Egalité*, or *République une et indivisible;* for even the republic had taken care to place itself before the eyes of the people in this symbolical manner.

As I have mentioned the church of Nôtre Dame, I will here state that the impression produced by it is not comparable to that of Strasburg cathedral: nor did I find myself repaid for the trouble of ascending the tower. The view of Paris from the top of Montmartre is much finer than that from Nôtre Dame, the Panthéon, or the column in the Place Vendôme.

I made many excursions in the neighbourhood of Paris in the company of Austrians and sometimes of Frenchmen. We visited Versailles, Trianon, Marly, St. Germain, St. Cloud, Sevres, Malmaison, St. Denys, and Montmorency—the scenes of former greatness and splendour, which the Emperor longed to turn into monuments of his own power and greatness. But it was only at St. Cloud and Malmaison that he had succeeded in placing the interest of the present on a level with that of the past. The old royal palaces and gardens could never be made to speak of anything save their own times. The full stream of life that for centuries had flowed troubled and stormy through these places, was far too powerful in interest and importance to fade before what was now passing. The first scenes of the Revolution were vividly recalled by the sight of the spots on which they were enacted, and a walk through the palace and gardens of Versailles is in itself a course of history. When the imperial servant who showed us through the rooms told us where we were, the mere names spoke more powerfully to the imagination than the most eloquent discourse could have done. The *Salle de théâtre* at Versailles remained in exactly the same state in which it had been left after the fatal fêtes to the *garde du corps* of the 1st and 3d October, except that years of neglect and occasional pillage had robbed it of its splendour. The Emperor had a project of restoring Versailles, and some repairs were already begun there, but the estimates of the sum which would be required for its complete restoration were so enormous, that no one doubted that the Emperor would abandon the idea.

One inducement to go to St. Cloud was the theatre, to which Napoleon gave invitations. I am not aware of any dramatic enjoyment comparable to this: we sat in comfortable, handsome boxes close to the stage, and, owing to the smallness of the theatre, we saw Talma, Mademoiselle Raucourt, Fleury, Mademoiselle Mars, Baptiste, and many others to the best advantage. Opposite to the stage, sat the Emperor, surrounded by all the rank and wealth of his court. Between the acts refreshments were handed round, and we entered into conversation. It was impossible elsewhere to have so good an opportunity of observing the Emperor so closely and so completely at one's ease, or to see Talma to such perfection as on these evenings.

A whole book might be written about Talma: he is a great genius, far in advance of his age and nation. As the poet to the king, so is the artist to the hero, and the names of Napoleon and Talma are by no means unfit to be associated. The French stage has a character peculiar to itself; it is a structure which it has taken two centuries to raise from materials drawn from the inmost nature of the people whose pride and joy it is. Every thing that relates to it must be taken for granted; its first principles must be conceded; none can criticise it but those who have first given in their adhesion. I confess that I found it hard to acquiesce in this; but when I had done so, my humility was richly rewarded.

It was impossible to be at Malmaison without thinking of the Empress Josephine, whose brightest days were spent there. Even the beautiful picture gallery, consisting exclusively of master-pieces, while it rivets the attention, constantly reminds one of the absent owner of these treasures. She had left Paris before I got there, and I never saw her; but I will here insert a slight sketch of her by another hand. The following is an extract from the journal of an Austrian, who came to Paris a few months earlier than myself, and had left it before my arrival.

"I do not wonder that the poor Empress Josephine is so passionately fond of Malmaison. She arrived there in the middle of May in all her glory, and rejoicing to return home. When she was forced to go to Navarre she was in despair, and the people at Nanterre say, that they saw her cover her face with her pocket-handkerchief, sobbing violently as she passed through their town. Her departure had been ordered hastily, and without regard to her feelings. She was forced to travel without guards, without her usual attendants, accompanied only by gens d'armes. Her return to Malmaison was arranged with more decency, and she appeared content. The kings, the queens, and the Grand Duke of Würzburg frequently visited her, and the road between Paris and Malmaison was covered with carriages coming and going, gentlemen on horseback, couriers, &c. Every day she has twenty or thirty people to dinner: for instance, all the Talleyrands, Madame Juste de Noailles, and many others: at the same time she is said not to receive, and no strangers are presented to her: Count Metternich also visits her. She has not yet had an interview with the Emperor; but as soon as she has seen him she is going to Aix in Savoy. Bets are made as to whether she and the Empress Maria Louisa will meet before Josephine leaves Paris. I believe that the viceroy Eugene and his wife live at Malmaison, and also Princess Stephanie; at any rate she was staying there lately. The late empress is a good woman; every one pities her, and none say any harm of her. She never did an unkind thing to any one; but is very thoughtless, unable to occupy herself, except a little with botany, fond of being surrounded all day by company, charmed with the externals and splendour of a throne, passionately fond of ostentation, dress, and diamonds, without much talent, but gifted with great tact, wonderful grace, and the power of saying agreeable and flattering things to every one. She now finds her time hang heavy on hand, and this makes her unhappy. Madame d'Audenarde openly professes the greatest attachment to her, and cannot say enough in praise of her uncommon goodness, and of the admirable manner in which she endures her present lot. The ladies, who found her far more accessible and communicative than their present mistress, would gladly have her back again, especially those who, like Madame de Montmorency and Madame de Mortemar, expected that, in consideration of their names, an archduchess would treat them very differently from what Maria Louisa actually does. These women are furious, and they do not conceal it.

"Even now that the Empress Josephine lives in so retired a manner, the cabriolet of her hair-dresser, Leroi, may be seen upon the road every morning, and sometimes even twice a day. This Leroi especially must be filled with indignation against her successor: hitherto he had been the oracle of the Empress, the court, and the town, and had made a considerable fortune by his trade in millinery, and he must have thought himself tolerably secure against any reverse of fortune. Only a few days after the marriage he brought home some dresses to the new Empress. She found fault with them, as being cut too low in front. 'Ah! Madame,' said Leroi, 'so beautiful a bosom should not be hidden.' She rings:—'Turn out this impudent fellow directly, and let him never appear before me again.' Leroi was thunderstruck, and stood open-mouthed with astonishment: he had always been accustomed to flatter her predecessor a little, and his compliments had never been so ill received. His disgrace has made a great noise here.

"We went boldly up to Malmaison, and asked if we might see Madame d'Audenarde. A whole host of pages, of gentlemen-ushers, of footmen in gold lace, and of Basques,—for the Empress had some very handsomely dressed Basques attached to her household,—measured us from head to foot with astonishment for some time before they led us to the entresol where she lived.

Madame d'Audenarde received us with open arms: she is somewhat altered, and grown older, but still looks very well. She asked if we would like to see the gallery; and we told her, of all things. She immediately went to ask the Empress if she intended to visit the gallery that day. 'Yes; there are workmen about it, and several pictures have to be hung. Why do you ask?'—'In this case I will not venture to mention my reason for asking.'—'What is it, then?'—'Princess —— and Count —— have come to see me, and I should have liked much to have shown them the pictures.'—'Well, take them to the gallery, and I will join you there.' Madame d'Audenarde came back to fetch us, and we went thither with her. In a short time we stood face to face with the Empress, who received us most graciously, kindly led us about herself, and pointed out the best pictures, saying, 'My gallery needs your indulgence, as we are at work upon it,' and other things of the same kind. It is not possible to be more gracious and amiable than she appeared to us. At the end of a quarter of an hour she left us, quite fascinated by her. I thought her infinitely handsomer than I had expected, and her figure most beautiful: she was plainly, but well dressed.

"The gallery is well proportioned, beautifully but simply painted, and fitted up with great taste, and admirably lighted from above. The pictures are not numerous, but they are all master-pieces. As we were leaving the house, the Empress's carriages drove to the door: they were extremely light and elegant, entirely open, with a huge parasol in the middle of each, with beautiful horses, and handsome, well-dressed postillions. On our way home we met the Queen of Naples, with her faithful cavalier servente, the Grand Duke of Würzburg, who is said to be romantically in love with her. She is by no means cruel to him; but I believe that a certain great foreign minister enjoys a yet larger share of her favours. The worthy grand duke is very generally loved and respected. He is the only German prince who is still treated with some consideration.

"On the 15th June the Empress Josephine started on her journey to Aix, in Savoy. The Emperor only saw her once, and staid two hours walking with her in the garden at Malmaison. He is as much attached to her as ever. She wished to travel under the name of the Duchess of Navarre; but the Emperor forbade it, saying it would look as if she was no longer allowed the title of Empress: she had much better travel under the name of Madame d'Arberg, which she did."

Thus far my Austrian friend. In truth, Josephine was universally beloved, and she has left behind her in Parisian society, and even at court, many friends who speak openly in her favour. Nevertheless, Napoleon's immediate adherents, especially those who had not given up the principles of the Revolution, maintained that no one had done him more mischief than this woman. She had brought him into contact with the old aristocracy, and reconciled them to him; and his junction with that party, and with the old dynasties of Europe, had separated him from the nation, and that he would find. I heard such assertions made frequently by well-informed Frenchmen in 1810.

In the Tuileries, and on the Boulevards, the leaves were already fading in the middle of the summer, the Champs Elysées and the Bois de Boulogne had long ceased to be wood and field, and nothing was left for us to do but to go to the gardens of St. Cloud or to Montmorency. The latter place offered a peculiar attraction: there the memory of Jean Jacques Rousseau is associated with every thing one sees.

It is difficult to speak of Rousseau, as few are now-a-days acquainted with his writings, and his name is associated with the most arbitrary and unfounded representations. Who can judge him without an accurate knowledge of the sea of troubles in which his lot was cast, of every wave and current by which he was tossed through life, and a power of estimating their effects? or who shall dare to judge him save those who,—possessing a thorough knowledge of the conditions of his life, and of the times in which he lived,—can forget them all, and rise with him to the bright regions of free inspiration? For Rousseau, though inextricably mixed up with the outward life of his times, and often degraded by its influence, yet lived an inward life in immediate connection with nature, and felt a whole creation within himself. And now little minds incapable of imagining the existence of such an union with nature laugh at Rousseau's eccentricities, accuse him of vanity, and find in it the key to his whole character and writings, and especially to his confessions! Truly vanity is the last fault with which Rousseau can be reproached; nevertheless it is that which is usually made, for it is specious and commonplace; but this accusation has its treacherous side, and is apt to rebound on those who thoughtlessly employ it. Fichte has shown us how Rousseau should be judged; but the path he has opened has long remained untrodden both by Frenchmen and Germans: the time, however, will come when Rousseau's power will again be felt, and when his sentiments will again find response. Meanwhile he is the touchstone by which I try many of the most distinguished and best among men,—their judgment of Rousseau gives me the measure of their minds. The most frequent and pardonable errors are those of sheer ignorance; but where a tolerably intimate acquaintance with his works has led only to false conclusions and to narrow views, then I know that there are regions from which these men are for ever excluded, however high they may stand in other respects.

For an agreeable easy way of life with every sort of pleasure and charm, there is no better place than Paris. This all-powerful capital draws within its circle whatever is most distinguished and most admirable in all ways from all sides; every thing that the art and cultivation, not only of its own clever and active population, but also that of foreigners, far and near, can produce, in any branch of art or science, belongs to it immediately, and ministers to its pleasures and enjoyments. The commerce of Paris consists mainly in articles of luxury and superfluity. Taste in dress, furniture and houses, pomp and splendour of every sort, adornment of the person, cultivation of the mind, the pleasures of the table, conversation and novelties, dramatic art, music, dancing, every sort of talent and accomplishment, are all at work with zeal and success to render life in Paris perfect. Nowhere do cooks, mistresses, servants, and toadies understand their trade better: in short, every thing, even talent and learning, do their utmost to promote good and luxurious living. All their measures to satisfy in the cheapest, pleasantest, and most expeditious manner the thousand wants and necessities of mankind, are taken with the most consummate skill: to the merest trifle, to the most insignificant action a certain importance is given : add to this a polish of manner, which prevents what would otherwise be commonplace from even appearing to be so. You see that this generation, which lives only for the present hour, has the experience of centuries. Nothing but a long succession of generations always busied with the same objects, moving in the same direction, alike vain, active, industrious, madly extravagant, and ingeniously selfish, nothing but the constant concurrence of the greatest vices and the highest talents could compose a structure which now appears a whole, one and undivided, every part of which seems composed of the same materials, and animated by the selfsame spirit. Splendour and ostentation may be greater elsewhere, sensual pleasures may show themselves more openly, and in greater abundance; but nowhere does the enjoyment of life extend in the same manner to all classes; nowhere are the most trifling events of daily life so carefully studied ; nowhere is society so firmly held together by such slight bonds. Life is embellished and heightened by wit and address; but it is also subdued, and the oil of politeness floats smoothly upon the troubled waves. At the same time, I must own that the whole of Parisian life seemed to me rather calculated to guard against weariness and satiety by the constant change of a thousand pleasures and amusements, than to afford solid happiness, or any nobler gratifications. Nowhere does the duration of life appear to me a matter of so much indifference as in Paris; for ten years pass there as easily as one, while one comprises the occupations and amusements of ten.

And yet Paris is the focus whence for centuries, the most important historical movements have radiated. It is the scene of almost daily and violent convulsions, the theatre of the strongest passions and the strangest destinies. This uniform mass, all tending towards the same point, unanimous in sentiment and action, is the proper tool for those men gifted with powerful genius and commanding talents, who rise from the midst of it. This mass is traversed in all directions by electric currents, which in the common course of things diffuse only a genial and healthy warmth ; but when once set in motion, even its smallest veins contribute towards the creation of the most tremendous storms and explosions.

Besides the innumerable objects which in this place afford constant occupation to the senses and the attention, each day demands and receives something new, something to be looked at, wondered at, and talked about,— the product, theme, and subject of the passing day. It is the more easy to excite prodigious interest in these novelties as in so numerous and excitable a population, the mere number of lookers-on gives a certain importance to the most trivial matters, and that which in the beginning is nothing, soon becomes of consequence. *La foule s'y est portée,* is the phrase of the " Moniteur," and it means a good deal. If the importation of novelties could be stopped, and the Parisian be condemned to live without them, it would be almost as bad as cutting off the supply of provisions, for the old stock would not last long. Common emotions do not suffice to impart the necessary degree of animation to life in Paris, where weariness and satiety constantly lurk behind the thin veil of pleasure.

The necessity of making a sensation is visible in all directions. Whoever has any thing to sell, any service to offer, or any thing to advertise, must take some extraordinary means in order merely to be remarked. The signs, placards, and inscriptions which swarm in the most frequented streets, are truly laughable in this respect. Enormous placards, gigantic letters of all shapes and sizes, printed sloping forwards, backwards, or sideways, pictures with some sort of claim to good painting, others again monstrous caricatures, sometimes signs even more numerous than the wares which they indicate for sale— all this is necessary merely to keep the tradesmen's heads at all above water. The multitude of painted signs is, in many cases, as good as a comedy. In the Rue Richelieu I was walking with a friend lately arrived from Vienna, who was much struck with this extravagant expenditure of puffing: he stood still before a shop, looked at its external ornaments, and said gravely, seizing me by the arm:— " When a man has black-puddings for sale, who should think that he would hang out six black-puddings— twelve black-puddings— twenty black-puddings?"— he now stopped, and stretching out his hand, which until now had been resting on his chest, he exclaimed with a sort of explosion,— " a hundred black-puddings!" and he really had not exaggerated; the enormous quantity was ridiculous; and this was not only the case with the black-puddings which had struck my Viennese friend as so remarkable, but with other things as well. The tradesmen, however, are perfectly willing to be laughed at, provided the absurdities which they invent with great ingenuity answer the purpose of attracting customers. Near the Tuileries was a tobacconist's shop, where not only the sign itself but the whole front of the house was covered with magniloquent Latin sentences, exhorting customers to enter. But the most amusing of all was the inscription over a hair-dresser's shop in the Palais Royal, on which the owner had dedicated to himself the following inscription, repeated on tablets of the most various shapes and sizes :—

TELLIER
INVENTA EN L'AN DIX,
LES PERUQUES ELASTIQUES
IMITANT LA CHAIR.

What an event! and *en l'an dix!* what a monumental style. A schoolmaster attracts attention by a verse out of Virgil :—

"Disce puer, virtutem ex me, verumque laborem."

We were excessively amused, too, by a sign which was somewhat personal to us Germans. Since Napoleon's marriage, the Germans had risen in the estimation of the French, and were accordingly treated with greater respect; the French now rather courted them. A bad restaurant imagined that he had discovered the true bait for Germans, and over his dirty narrow shop, somewhere between the Tuileries and the Louvre, stood this inscription : —

Hier Be Finden sich die Deutschen
vor das gub Saurgrauth.*

This man accordingly had the pleasure of occasionally seeing, besides his regular customers, Germans of the higher classes look into his shop and leave a few francs there.

The busy Parisians were perfectly right in devoting all their energies to the attainment even of a momentary reputation;

---

* Hither the Germans resort for the good sauerkraut.

for the man who could produce any novelty, or make himself talked about, was certain of success: his fortune was made before the host of novelty seekers had tried the new invention and seen its defects: remonstrances could no longer injure him. There was even some honour in this; it was no small thing to have excited the attention of his fellow-citizens, and even to have duped them.

Look which way you would, you were perpetually reminded of the history of the day. There is a *Café de Jéna*, there is one *à l'Archiduc*, and *au duc d'Infantado*: the streets are named after battles; bridges, fountains, triumphal arches celebrate the victories of the conqueror whose name and arms are to be seen every where. The minor theatres daily produce new pieces, of which the materials are drawn from the events of the day. But, in reality, the Parisian takes but little interest in any great events which do not take place immediately under his very eyes. They are only valuable to him so far as they concern his own narrow circle, and provide him with holiday amusements. The indifference with which accounts of the Emperor's new victories are received is scarcely credible; the public value them as newspaper intelligence, but for nothing else. They are already tired of French glory; "*nous en avons assez*" is heard among people of all classes. The Emperor is constantly spoken of, but chiefly with reference to the trifling events of the day — balls, parades, court ceremonies, the favour or disgrace of such a one, and similar circumstances of small importance. The sight of a new uniform in the streets of Paris is a matter of far greater interest to a Parisian than a victory in Spain, or a battle in Calabria. This is far otherwise in the provinces, where Napoleon is judged more according to his actions. Most people agree that a constant succession of victories is necessary for the permanent security of his dominion, and it is by this alone that his opponents in France are kept in check. His enemies may be divided into two classes, Republicans and Royalists, each of which appear important, and may at any moment become dangerous. He is furious against both parties, and endeavours to detach individual members from each, and that not without success, for he has some most violent Jacobins in the service of the state, and some of the noblest of the emigrants are about his court. But he is only sure of their service as long as he is successful. Besides, there is always a large mass of both these factions which is not to be won over, and which for this very reason has become doubly important and dangerous. Many people think that it is a great error in Napoleon to fear the Faubourg St. Germain and the old noblesse more than the party which still clings to the Revolution; they say he will live to repent this error. It strikes me as remarkable how little the Emperor is feared: most people here have lived through far more terrible times, and have seen these terrors fade away, so that to them no tyranny seems lasting; they look upon all power as provisional, and recognise the government of the day only so long as it makes itself felt; beyond that no government in France can now reckon. It is certain that there still is much that is revolutionary among the people; the maxims of freedom and equality are by no means given up, the Jacobins are always silently at work, zealous adherents of the republic are to be found every where, even among the greatest names in the kingdom. It is true that these opinions are not supported by bayonets and cannon; but public opinion is the origin of all power, and the instruments wherewith to carry it into effect are sure to be found in time. In Germany, where the French yoke pressed so heavily, people can have no idea how little the French feel Napoleon's sway. I have heard men express their opinions very freely, not indeed in market-places, although even there much is allowed under cover of wit. The French people is not only witty, but wise from experience, and has always been remarkable for prudence and acuteness; the dust thrown in their eyes deceives merely the dregs of the people, and very often not these: moreover, those who try to appear grand are remembered of old; their former life is well known, and people laugh at their new titles and dignities.

I remember with particular pleasure an itinerant mountebank whom I saw arrange a little table on the Boulevards; after some wretched jokes had attracted a sufficient audience, the fellow began his oration. His voice was metallic and penetrating, his words were clearly heard, his tone and manner were bold and assured. He spoke with pride and importance of his calling—to remove stains—which he divided into three classes, and he then proceeded in detail, and with learned phrases to treat of his method for each variety of spots. He assured his audience with some pride that it was not every day that he came to the Boulevards, he had enough to do at home, but motives of philanthropy would induce him in future to sacrifice two days in the week to the public, as many an unfortunate wight would otherwise miss seeing him. "*Je pourrais aussi bien qu'un autre,*" such was his peroration, "*prendre le nom pompeux de professeur de physique amusante, mais un homme comme moi dédaigne un titre vain et barbare, qui ne se trouve pas même dans les dictionnaires.*" His balls cost two sous each, and he sold a great number: his oration had awakened confidence, and found favour among the people. A soldier or two of the imperial guard happened to come by; he immediately mentioned, as it were incidentally, that a whole regiment had made use of his balls with eminent success, and had attracted the Emperor's praise by the cleanliness of their appearance: on mention of the Emperor's name he respectfully took off his hat; "*Car Messieurs,*" said he, "*quand on nomme sa Majesté l'Empereur, il faut toujours ôter son châpeau.*" No one, however, did so; on the contrary, there was a general murmur, the soldiers went their way laughing, and the man's audience, which had hitherto been favourable to him, quitted him in displeasure.

Napoleon's only means of governing the French nation consisted in his army, in which all the discordant parties and different classes were fused together. It was remarked that it was only in the army that royalists and republicans were converted into true adherents of the Emperor; this was by no means the case with those about the court, or in the service of the state. Napoleon was well aware of this, and endeavoured to keep up the military spirit in the nation. He prescribed to the members of the Legion of Honour, "*de préférer toujours la noble poussière des camps au vain luxe de la grande ville:*" fine and proud words, to which, however, his own example frequently gave the lie; the pomp of his court, and his fêtes always had something vulgar; all his lavish expense failed in reproducing the easy luxurious state of society of former days. Nothing flattered him so much as to have the old noblesse about his court; the old titles sounded agreeably to his ear. The old word "court," on the other hand, corrupted a good number of the old families, and they could not resist the temptation: they endeavoured to conceal their confusion by being the first to ridicule it themselves. When Count de Ségur had become master of the ceremonies, his brother frequently signed "*Ségur sans cérémonie;*" nevertheless, he too accepted an office connected with the management of the theatres. One day, when he was at the rehearsal of an opera, where Elleviou the singer treated him with great insolence, Ségur said to him, "*Mais, mon cher Elleviou, vous oubliez tout-à-fait que depuis la révolution je suis devenu votre égal!*" Many were the witty sayings and answers like these, which were called forth by the strange position of parties in France at that time.

Political eloquence was completely crushed at this time in France. For want of the living I turned to the dead, and obtained the five volumes of "*Travaux de Mirabeau à l'Assemblée Nationale.*" The sort of academical eloquence which now prevailed in the National Institute, fashioned upon classical models, with all its hyper-refinements and gentle boldnesses, with its gliding over what was disagreeable, and other arts of literary tight-rope dancing, was an abomination to me, and many an earnest Frenchman who had known from former experience what power eloquence has, looked upon it with contempt. In times of oppression the small portion of freedom which is left must twist and endeavour to seek out all sorts of adventitious aid in subtlety of expression, poetical forms, wit and humour. But when this sort of cleverness gets the upper hand, when it becomes the only mode in which a man dares to utter his thoughts, then it is evident that it is not well with public life. The French were now in this predicament, and certain it is that they learnt much under this great oppression. The rich stream of eloquence which poured forth after the return of the Bourbons, although it did not yet venture beyond certain narrow limits, owed its origin to the school of laborious ingenuity, to which all speaking had been confined.

There seemed likewise to be but little left of pulpit eloquence, of which the French have had such glorious examples. I heard a funeral sermon preached at Saint Roch, over one of the victims of the Schwarzenberg ball. The congregation was numerous and distinguished, the preacher was obviously one of the best in Paris: he strained his voice and his intellect to the utmost, without producing much impression: it was an empty pompous affair, deficient in commanding thought, and it failed in exciting religious sentiment. The young clergy, who, in the pursuit of their calling, are following rhetorical studies, should not go to their churches where they would learn nothing of the sort, but to the Théâtre Français, where Talma's action and method of speaking would teach them what might be of service to them in their profession.

On the other hand, the eloquence of the bar was still in full force. An important case, in which all Paris took the greatest interest, gave me an opportunity of hearing some of the most distinguished members of the bar. The validity of a will was disputed, and besides a rich Dantzic merchant of the name of Sönniges, who was settled at Paris, there were two notaries who were placed with him at the bar. They were all three accused of having forged a will in favour of the first-named party, to the prejudice of a young nephew of the testator. The nephew had great connexions, so had the old merchant; the state of the case gave rise to considerable suspicion, and the publicity of an open trial caused prodigious excitement. The president, Hémart, who conducted the inquiry, was the same who had presided at General Moreau's trial, and who was supposed to have brought about his condemnation by unfair means. For this reason he was execrated: he knew this well, and appeared determined on this occasion to proceed more honestly. But his face had a bad expression, which reminded me of the men of blood in the times of the French Revolution. Still less was I pleased with the imperial procureur, who conducted the prosecution with zealous heat and great bitterness. The public were divided into two parties, who disputed violently for and against the accused. The Emperor had declared himself in favour of the young nephew, and some people sided with Napoleon, but a still greater number were in favour of the accused. It was evident that the will had been negligently drawn up, but without any fraudulent intention, and it was not worse than many other cases which frequently come before a court of law without entailing any bad consequences upon the parties concerned. The procureur strained every nerve to prove the fraudulent intention, while the two famous advocates, Chaùveau-Lagarde and Bellart, pleaded the cause of the accused. Their statements produced a great effect, and showed masterly talent, but they did not obtain a verdict in favour of their client, nor did the opposing counsel procure a severe sentence against him. The court steered a middle course, and the notaries only were severely punished. Napoleon publicly reproached the president for his want of vigour, saying, that the honour of the French bar was stained, and that it was he who had covered it with shame. How hard soever the anger of the Emperor was to bear, the old president showed by his conduct that public opinion had still greater terrors for him, and he now hoped to stand better with his fellow countrymen.

The impression made on men's minds by the tragical accident* which closed the festivities at Napoleon's marriage, did not prevent the French people from recommencing a fire of epigrams and witticisms on the subject, which we heard with secret satisfaction. The more strictly these things were forbidden, the greater was the pleasure of repeating them to others. Those puns especially are well known with which the famous comedian Brunet delighted the Parisians on this occasion. "*L'Empéreur n'aime que Joséphine et la chasse!*" is one of his boldest; another was, "*Jamais Archiduchesse d'Autriche, n'a fait un mariage civil,*" when the civil contract took place at St. Cloud, according to law. Brunet's exclamation, "*Le char l'attend,*" which he uttered, pointing to the arch of triumph upon the top of which stood the bronze horses from Venice harnessed to the empty triumphal chariot, must occur to every one that looked at it. Nearly every evening Brunet took some opportunity of amusing the audience at the Théâtre des Variétés with some such sayings. When, at last, it became too serious to be any longer borne, the prefect of the police, Count

---

* A number of people were killed by fireworks.

Dubois, sent for Brunet, and ordered him, threatening punishment in case of disobedience, to cease punning. Brunet replied, with a plaintive voice, "*Mais que voulez-vous que je fasse? c'est mon métier de faire des calembourgs, j'y gagne ma vie; voulez-vous donc que je scie du bois?*" Repeated imprisonments could not break this invincible habit, and Brunet's supply of puns was inexhaustible.

But the wittiest and most remarkable squib on Napoleon's marriage with Maria Louisa was a Poissarde song, to which I have already alluded; it was distributed in all directions, and learned by heart by thousands. Notwithstanding Napoleon's anger and all the efforts of the police, the author could never be discovered. Some hundred persons, who were guilty of copying or singing it, were imprisoned; but all attempts to trace the song to its source proved fruitless. It came to me, anonymously, by the post. It gives an idea of the state of mind of the people, who eagerly received and repeated these verses.

"AH! L' BIAU MARIAGE!

"AIR: 'REÇOIS DANS TON GALETAS.'

I.

"C'EST donc ben vrai qu' not' Emp'reur
Épous' un' princess' d'Autriche ;
Faut ben qu'un si grand seigneur
S'unisse avec queuq' zun d' riche,
Et pis c't' homme a sa raison
Pour prend' un' femm' d' bonn' maison (*bis*).

II.

"J'aurions ben gagé six francs
Qu'on n' li donn'rait pas c'te fille ;
Car il était d' pis longtemps
Si mal avec la famille,
Qu' leur fit deux fois prend' par peur
Jacq' Délog' pour procureur.

III.

"J' voyons des mariag' comm' ça
D' temps en temps a la Courtille;
Tout d'abord on ross' l' papa,
Pis on couch' avec la fille,
Et l' beaupèr' n' os' pas dir' non,
D' peur d'avoir z'encor l'ognon!

IV.

"Pour all' il s'est fait l'aut' jour
Peind' en bel habit d' dimanche,
Et des diamants tout autour,
Près d' sa figur' comm' ça tranche!
La p'tit luronn'! j'en somm' sûr,
Aim' mieux l' présent que l' futur.

V.

"Ah! comm' all' va s'amuser
C'te princess' qui nous arrive!
Nous allons boir' et danser,
N' s'enrouer à crier : Vive!
All' s'ra l'idol' d' la nation
J' l'ons lu dans l' proclamation.

VI.

"Stapendant sur mon honneur
J' plaignons c'te pauv' Joséphine,
All' fait cont' fortun' bon cœur,
J' savons ben qu' ça la taquine,
L' métier li semblait si bon!
V' la qu'on lui fait vend' son fond.

VII.

"Mais ent' nous, tout son malheur
Vient d' n'êt' pas en état d' grâce :
J' somm' si content d' nôt' Emp'reur,
Que j' voulons voir des chiens d' race ;
Il d' vait pour êt' sûr d' son fait,
Prend' un fill' qu'en eut d'jà fait.

VIII.

"D' ces deux rein' chacun' rendra
Tour-à-tour visit' a l'autre,
A la jeun' l'ancienn' dira :
'J'ai fait mon temps, fait' le vôtre,
Si vous n' travaillez pas mieux
A Malm'son y a plaç' pour deux.'

IX.

"J' tâch'rons d' nous placer 'n grand jour
Pour ben voir les réjou'ssances ;
D' pis qu' l'Emp'reur chang' tout' sa cour,
J' n'y ons pas tant d' connaissances,
Mais j'esp'rons ben par bonheur,
Raccrocher queuqu' dam' d'honneur."

Count Metternich gave most amusing breakfasts; the regular guests were numerous enough, and strangers were brought nearly every day. Count Metternich was fond of the excitement of conversation, and by no means avoided serious or even political discussions. At these breakfasts I met many of the most remarkable men of the day; among others, Dr. Gall, who had been forbidden to expound his theory in Vienna. I did not like him or his vulgar views of science and nature: he and I were always opposed: once, however, he appealed to me in a manner which amused me prodigiously. I found him one morning at Count Metternich's, engaged in a vehement discussion on the subject of religion with Count Sternberg, who had just come from Prague, and whose opinions were diametrically opposed to Gall's. The contest was carried on with great violence and harshness on both sides, when suddenly the disputants unanimously pronounced religion to be necessary, — "For," said Sternberg, turning to a bystander, "what would the world come to if the common people were not in some degree kept within bounds by religion?" "And," said Gall, addressing himself at the same instant to me, "what would become of us, if our princes and rulers were not somewhat held in check by religion?" Neither of the disputants heard what the other said, or knew by what various roads they had arrived at the same conclusion. But I was now furnished with a superfluity of arguments to convince me that, after all, religion was necessary.

Prince Schwarzenberg's dinners — and he generally dined at six or even seven — were grander than these breakfasts of Count Metternich's, but the company was less select. At Prince Schwarzenberg's, the society chiefly consisted of the great people about the French court, of the members of the diplomatic body, of the aristocracy of all countries, with a sprinkling even of their rulers,—in a word, of all the great world of Paris. It sometimes happened that only Austrians or other Germans were present, and then the most confidential tone prevailed at table; only German was talked, and the most easy merriment reigned in the whole society, which might almost be called a family circle. The prince himself, thoroughly imbued with kindness, the princess, endowed with a good understanding and practical good sense, full of zeal and interest for all that was going on, of an excellent wit, and causing good humour in others; then her charming children, and the devoted adherents and friends of the family, — all this formed a delightful picture of German domestic life: all pomp and circumstance paled before a noble simplicity of manner which would equally have adorned a palace or a hut. When Count Metternich happened to be present, the conversation grew more lively: it was impossible not to take part in all sorts of witty games; and even those who did not generally like mystifications, were carried away by the general fun and good-humour. An odd fish of a Frenchman acted scenes which Brunet himself might have envied, and which would have gained him most lively applause.

Notwithstanding all these attractions, I gradually avoided these dinners; they began too late, and lasted too long. I rather sought the company of my own friends, with whom, after walking about Paris in all directions, I adjourned to the Rocher de Cancale in the Palais Royal, or to the restaurant Very in the Tuileries, or sometimes, by way of a change, to Grignon's or Beauvillier's: by this proceeding we gained a good piece of the afternoon, and had the evenings to ourselves. So long as Chamisso was in Paris, I passed the chief part of my time with him: he had the great merit of being amused by the French, and of being able to laugh at their peculiarities, as if he himself were not one of them. This produced many most amusing scenes, which occurred without any seeking on our part. We were once walking in the gardens of the Palais Royal, when a young dramatic poet, an acquaintance of Chamisso's, joined us, and a sudden whim seized us to eat strawberries. Before we could well think where we were to get any, we saw some fine ones in the window of the Café de Valois. We immediately entered and ordered strawberries, sugar, and wine. The garçon brought us three plates, thinking that the strawberries would merely serve as dessert to an excellent breakfast, and waited for further orders; but when he saw that we ordered nothing else, he went to fetch the strawberries. The little dessert-plateful was soon emptied, and we asked for more: the fresh supply, likewise, quickly disappeared, chiefly by the instrumentality of Chamisso, and every moment we called out "*Garçon, des fraises!*" At length all the plates were emptied, and we were still calling "*Garçon, des fraises.*" Panic-stricken, he rushed to his master, and complained with grief and indignation. "*Mon Dieu! ils demandent encore des fraises!*" The master, like a general who receives unmoved the announcement of some fatal disaster, replied with solemn dignity, "*Eh bien! on leur en apportera,*" and some were brought from elsewhere. We laughed meanwhile like children, and, to do the garçon a pleasure, I again quietly asked for another portion, in the hope that he would be driven to desperation, and call down imprecations upon us. However, instead of this, he looked penetratingly at us, with that expression of mute astonishment which endeavours to comprehend an incomprehensible mystery—and then said in a tone it would be hopeless to try to imitate, "*J'y consens!*" None but a Parisian could in such a moment have found the exact words and the tone, so full of indignation, of persiflage, and yet so respectful, "*J'y consens!*" Chamisso compared it with the famous "*Qu'il mourût,*" and was incessantly repeating it. The poet confessed that the words had great dramatic force, and that the garçon was a hidden genius, and we ended by admiring and richly compensating him for his annoyances. But "*des fraises*" and "*J'y consens*" were phrases which we frequently repeated among ourselves. Chamisso was a dangerous companion in this respect; although he never played practical jokes himself, his uncommon relish of them induced others to do so to please him.

A trifling event gave us another example of the readiness and humour with which any Frenchman you may happen to meet in the street enters into every joke. An acquaintance had forced upon me a quantity of poems, accompanying them with a number of lies: the poems were written separately on large handsome sheets of paper, which I was carrying rolled up in my hand when I met a friend coming from the Museum. We unrolled the papers, and proceeded to read the first poem, which was wretched. I scornfully let the papers fall one by one to the ground as fast as I read them, till I reached the last. A well-bred young man who happened to be just behind us picked up some of the poems and handed them to me, saying, that we had lost some papers which he had been fortunate enough to find. I said to him: " *Quoi, Monsieur, vous voulez nous forcer de reprendre ces méchants vers? Mon Dieu! il n'y a donc pas moyen de se défaire de cela!*" I had scarce done speaking when I saw by the young man's face that he had perfectly understood the whole affair; he put on a humble mien, and said with an air of demure politeness, "*Oh! je vous fais mille excuses, Monsieur! veuillez être persuadé, que je n'ai pas eu de mauvaise intention.*" I now again threw away the papers, which fell into a puddle; but some fellow saw the white sheets of paper and picked them up again. "*On vous les présentera encore une fois!*" said the polite Frenchman, and we all three ran away as if a mad dog were at our heels.

The peculiar wit of the Parisians, and the talent which even the lower classes have of turning every phrase in a pointed agreeable manner, has the effect of inducing them to believe themselves the first people on earth, the wisest and most accomplished: they are wonderfully well satisfied with themselves. No praise is too coarse for their vanity, and they speak with the most open-hearted conviction of their own transcendent merits. A *garçon coiffeur* in the *Hôtel de l'Empire* entered the service of the Russian ambassador, Prince Kurakin, and once, while he was shaving me, he showed me a beautiful razor which he had bought for the prince: "*C'est déplorable,*" said he, "*comme la toilette du prince est mal fournie.*" He talked exactly as if he were extricating the prince from the deepest distress, and ended by saying: "*Mais que voulez-vous? C'est un Russe, ça n'a point de goût: ça n'a rien!*" It was impossible to take a walk through the streets, or to enter into an accidental conversation with a shopboy, or an apple-woman, without finding materials for some amusing anecdote.

At the same time I found the Parisians a melancholy people in spite of all their love of fun : the town appeared to me to be here and there merry, but, in reality, without joy. I was assured that there existed a race of honourable and excellent citizens, who lived in a retired manner, remote from the frivolities and vices of the great capital, and that in this class I should find real ease and happiness—the true French character, the " levissima Gallorum ingenia," of which Julius Cæsar speaks, tempered with good morals and kindness of heart. But this class lived by itself, and strangers seldom came in contact with these good bourgeois. What we did meet with was by no means engaging. We were told that Paris was rapidly declining, and that we ought not to judge of it by what we saw. The population had sunk from 900,000, which was the number before the Revolution, down to 575,000 inhabitants; trade and commerce were falling off, and spite of the apparent luxury and expensive habits, want and privation were very generally felt. We were likewise assured that what made the charm of the French—their real politeness—had disappeared, leaving only the outward forms. Moreover, the nation seemed likely to lose its national character ; Napoleon's eternal wars did much in this way; but the chief cause was to be traced up to the Revolution and to the reign of terror. All the charm of society which had formed the highest attraction and fame of Paris, was irretrievably destroyed.

Chamisso confirmed the latter assertion, and said that he knew no old-fashioned French house to which he could introduce us. The old style of society was beginning to revive in the Faubourg Saint-Germain ; but they were very exclusive, and the society was very limited. The great people of the Empire made the most of their advantages ; but it was all outward show ; the real and the solid were wanting. I had not the smallest wish to throw myself into this dreary waste of splendour; the few visits of ceremony which I could not avoid making, showed me clearly enough what was to be gained from this sort of society,—namely, tedium and disgust.

At the same time any one who was fortunate might still find some remnant of old Paris in the new. Madame de Genlis, among others, was in the habit of receiving at her house a select society of distinguished people in spite of the smallness of her means. Several artists and men of letters also opened their houses, and the conversation was said to be most entertaining. But these were the exceptions, and their influence over the rest of Paris was very small. The complaint of weariness and want of good society was very general in Paris.

Fortunately there was always the resource of the play: this, however, was no great temptation to me, and I seldom willingly exchanged the free air of heaven for the heavy lamp-oil atmosphere of a theatre, where one was forced to sit imprisoned a whole evening. The representations at Saint Cloud, where tragedies and the higher sort of dramas were acted, as I have before mentioned, were pleasant enough, and I made a point of going frequently to the opera. Nor did I neglect to see the popular opera of Cinderella at the Théâtre Feydeau, where Elleviou was undoubtedly the best performer. But what attracted us most of all was Brunet, at the Théâtre des Variétés: the Vaudeville, and other smaller theatres, afforded us no particular amusement. We stopped with much greater pleasure before the little peripatetic theatres on the Boulevards, to see Polichinelle and Bobèche, or went to Tivoli to witness the amusing little impromptu farces which were performed in the open air, and where we had an opportunity of seeing the true national character.

The diversions at Tivoli appeared to me to be in little a true picture of Paris life. From the moment of entering the gardens to that of quitting them, there was a constant succession of entertainments; every corner, every spare moment, had its peculiar amusement; from the most splendid fireworks, and the most clanging military band, down to the smallest optical delusions and most insignificant strumming of guitars, nothing was left untried as a means of passing away the time. These multiplied and diversified amusements, these attempts at and straining after pleasure, showed pretty clearly a general want of it. And, in truth, in the Tivoli gardens I never saw a happy face; all had a look of satiety and disappointment; a painful necessity of escaping the pressure of the present moment seemed to pervade them all.

In spite of the agreeable and exciting life I was leading, of the various objects I had to see and to admire, and of the happiness of my own personal existence, still I must confess that my stay in Paris gave me no satisfaction. The perpetual dissipation, the constant reception of new impressions without actual study or active cultivation of the mind, the easy mode of passing the hours without any special object in view, without any leading idea, — all this tired me to the last degree, and my general lassitude was increased by the occasional bright spots in this sort of existence. The crowd of people only made me more melancholy. Frequently, just at sunset, going from the Boulevard des Italiens beyond the Porte Saint Martin, where the Boulevard widens, I stopped to see the crowd shouldering one another, each one intent on his own individual object, and that generally one of interest, ambition, deceit, or seduction: a deep feeling of commiseration would then steal over me for this mass of individuals: they seemed to be wasting their lives in straining after something which they could never obtain. In the midst of this crowd, upon which shone the setting sun, the impression of melancholy which Paris made upon me was always the strongest.

Meanwhile my desire to return to Germany, to a German soil, and a German people, never left me. But another cause of uneasiness had preyed upon me during my whole stay at Paris, and my anxiety now became intolerable. For a long time I had heard nothing of Rahel, and my letters had remained unanswered. At last I heard that she had been ill. Paris now became odious to me, and I longed with impatience to quit it; but various delays intervened. At last the day of departure arrived, and I thought myself justified in saying, with Rousseau — "*Adieu, donc, Paris, ville célèbre, ville de bruit, de fumée et de boue; où les femmes ne croient plus à l'honneur, ni les hommes à la vertu. Adieu, Paris: nous cherchons l'amour, le bonheur, l'innocence; nous ne serons jamais assez loin de toi.*"

END OF PART I.

SKETCHES OF GERMAN LIFE,

AND

SCENES FROM THE

WAR OF LIBERATION IN GERMANY.

PART THE SECOND.

CHAPTER XIII.

The Castle of Steinfurt.—The reigning Count.—Life at the Castle.—The old Castle of Bentheim.—Torture Chamber.—The white Lady.—Superstitions in Westphalia.—The Castle Seer.—Münster and the Anabaptists.—Arrival of the French in Steinfurt.—The French Police. 1810, 1811.

THE solitude and quiet of Westphalia offered a striking contrast to the noise and splendour of Paris. The nature of the country, the manner in which it was inhabited and cultivated, gave it a lonely gloomy appearance. Wooded hills circumscribed the view, while in the valleys below a few patches of land were reclaimed with difficulty from the sandy, heathy soil. There were no villages; the farms were solitary, and for the most part concealed by trees, and at a distance from the road; the country thus looked less inhabited than it really was. The eager curiosity with which we were asked whether it was true, as they had heard, that Napoleon had divorced his first wife to marry the emperor of Austria's daughter, showed how separated these people were from the rest of the world. They did not believe it any more than they did the French victories, until the appointment of Frenchmen in lieu of their own countrymen as magistrates had made them comprehend that Münster was now under the dominion of strangers. However, no one doubted for a moment but that sooner or later the archduke Antony Victor would be installed as prince bishop. The people still looked forward to his advent, and mentioned his name oftener and with greater enthusiasm than they probably would have done had he ever really governed them.

Steinfurt or Burgsteinfurt, as it should properly be called, had been until now the principal seat of a reigning family; but it was now a French town, having its mayor, to whom the former rulers of the land as well as their late subjects were supposed to yield obedience. But the forms and personal influence of a government founded on the habit of centuries were not so easily changed, and every thing went on much as before, excepting that the body-guard of fifty men, which had formerly been armed and commanded by their colonel, now mounted guard without arms and without a commander, but still in their red uniforms.

The count's family inhabited the castle, which was close by the town: it had formerly been a place of some strength, and was surrounded by the small river Aa. On one side of the castle an extensive park, called the Bagno, had been laid out, at considerable expense, by the reigning count. It abounded in lakes, woods, waterfalls, fountains, grottoes, temples, kiosks, mosques and the like, and tolerably represented the taste of the last century. Every thing was intended to minister to courtly ceremonies and pleasures, and to show off to the utmost the pomp and magnificence of the ruler of the land. An immense concert-room had been built for the count's private band, brought at a great expense from Italy; occasionally the count himself played on the flute, which was brought to him on a silken cushion by a noble youth, whose chief duty this was. There were spacious saloons devoted to dancing and eating, and a suite of rooms was set apart for the reception of his subjects and any foreigners who might wish to be presented, with due solemnity, at court. Highly ornamented barges lay in a small bay on the lake, ready to transport the noble count, his family, and any illustrious strangers, with a proper guard, to the other side. In a part of the garden was an enormous chess-board: those engaged in the game ascended two platforms, from whence they directed the movements of the servants appointed to perform the functions of chessmen. On great occasions the fountains played, the waterfalls tumbled, and the inhabitants of Steinfurt and the country round who were admitted, thought it surpassed Versailles. The reigning count liked to give a high idea of his own power and importance by these extraordinary exhibitions, and the contemplation of his own splendour made him forget the smallness of the sphere over which his sway extended. Not only had he a court and body-guards, officials and servants, but he had taken care of the interests of his subjects in other ways. He had collected pictures, coins, statues, antiquities, and books: he sent those of his subjects who showed any turn that way to study in foreign lands, on the understanding that their native country — that is, the small province under the count's jurisdiction — should eventually profit by their acquirements. He issued an edict that no one should hold any office in his dominions who had not been educated at the high school of Steinfurt : neither were his possessions so very small — with the countship of Steinfurt he had inherited the larger property of Bentheim. This had been mortgaged to Hanover by the last possessor, and as Napoleon held Hanover, the mortgage-money was paid over to France. Besides this, the count possessed Alpen, on the Lower Rhine, Batenburg, in Holland, and had a right to take toll on the Maas. He was a good manager of his property, and, like his ancestors, had accumulated a treasure. His wealth and station had been so much in his favour, that at the dissolution of the German empire, when those who held immediately from the empire were subject to two different fates, — either to become sovereign princes or to descend into the lower grade of subjects, — it was generally supposed that Count von Bentheim would be one of the former and favoured class. Negotiations were opened with France, and nearly concluded by means of Talleyrand; maps of the principality, enlarged by the addition of the property of the mediatised princes, were drawn out, the sovereignty of the count was as good as acknowledged, when some new whim changed the posture of affairs, and every thing was thrown into uncertainty. The count immediately went to Paris to maintain his rights and just claims. He was received with due honours by Napoleon, and treated as a reigning prince, while his claims were less and less acknowledged, and the French were daily taking more complete possession of his own province. The worse his affairs grew at home, the less inclined the count seemed to return. He remained at Paris, which was the only spot where he was treated as a reigning prince, and where he hoped to succeed in his object. Here we found him petitioning, protesting, soliciting, paying court to Napoleon and his ministers: an accurate observer of all forms and ceremonies, but leading a retired and frugal life. He still kept up the old fashion of wearing red-heeled shoes, and attracted some attention in the Palais Royal by this and some other antiquated articles of dress: his secretary invariably marched before him. But people forgot these trifling absurdities when they knew him better, and found him intelligent, well informed, and accomplished. He remained at Paris on this footing for several years, while his affairs became worse and worse: at first he was mediatised, and subject to the Grand Duchy of Berg, then to France. As a subject of the French empire, he could hold no title but what was given him by the Emperor, and he found himself degraded to an equality with his former subjects. He remained at Paris indefatigably pursuing his claims until Napoleon's fall, when he returned home, was reinstated in many of his rights, and recompensed by the title of Prince of Alpen.

However, when we went to Steinfurt from Paris, such an event was beyond his most sanguine hopes. The family, daily expecting the return of their head, had settled down into a contented state of existence. Household cares distracted their attention, forming a strange contrast with many ceremonials which still existed. The gaily dressed trumpeters who summoned the family with shrill blasts of their trumpets to their daily meals, frequently interrupted the court ladies in their labours in the hen-roost, or the chancellor of the exchequer while counting the apples in the store-room. These scenes were the constant subject of laughter and amusement. The strong foundation of real worth and true nobility of thought supported these excellent people, whether they were sovereigns of the land or simple burghers.

We passed an agreeable life at the castle. The Bagno or the neighbouring country offered charming walks and drives, and we found endless subjects of conversation. Sunday was always considered a holyday; the officials were invited to dinner, and the most respectable inhabitants of the town came in the evening. The mayor, a certain Doctor Houth, regularly made his appearance. He had amassed a fortune in Holland, and, tired of practice, had settled in this village. His new office rather interfered with the enjoyment of ease and repose that he had promised himself. He had considerable acquirements, and was fond of reading, of music, and of pictures. His habit of thought and taste made him devoted to the family at the castle, and they again appreciated the friendly disposition of one who, by the nature of his office, might have given them much annoyance.

We made expeditions to Burghorst and Langenhorst, two convents for noble ladies, and selected one of the finest days to drive to Bentheim in a heavy coach and six. The road lay for about eight miles over the so-called Brechte, a tract of waste land, which, even during the thirty years' war, had been a fine forest. The country was hilly and romantic: one might imagine oneself transported from the plains of Westphalia into some mountainous country. The old feudal towers were seen at a distance crowning the top of the hill, under which nestled the small market town of Bentheim. The castle was built on high, rocky and uneven ground, and its massive walls and strong towers give it an appearance of prodigious strength. It is extremely probable that Drusus built a stronghold here to curb the Tubantes, who dwelt in this district; far and wide there was no spot so favourable for an encampment. Roman coins are frequently found there; the foundations of the castle are clearly Roman, and the whole length of rock facing the south is cased with large square stones of an older date than the middle ages. This side of the castle has nothing to fear from a storming party, and the heaviest artillery could scarcely make any impression upon it; a round tower to the south-west bears the marks of cannon balls directed without much effect against its thick walls by the French. On the south-eastern side there is a square tower, with even thicker walls: one of the watch-towers has been damaged by lightning. To the north there are no towers, as the precipice is so abrupt as to bid defiance to any attack on that side; here an old temple has been built into the castle: it is not known to which of the heathen gods it was dedicated. Two flights of stairs cut in the solid rock lead down to the most beautiful walks on the height, but outside the walls. Old trees rear their huge stems and heavy branches, and the ivy is thicker on the old castle walls than any I ever yet saw; the whole declivity down to the plain is overgrown with trees and bushes. From an old garden enclosed by a massive wall forming part of the outworks, there is a most beautiful view towards Steinfurt and far into Münster, while, from the towers, on the other side, the eye reaches across into Holland. To the west are several strange-looking rocks, one of which, that has somewhat the appearance of a round cushion standing on end and flattened at top, goes by the name of the "Devil's Pillow." According to popular tradition, he once slept upon this rock, and some lines are still pointed out as the marks of his ear on the soft stone. The vegetation on the rock was rank beyond measure; every hole and crevice afforded nourishment to coarse grass or parasitical plants, and the toilsome work of man was rapidly becoming a wilderness.

A room or two miserably furnished were prepared for our reception, and we had a joyous dinner, the place and its history affording us endless subjects for conversation. After dinner we visited the vaults and the chambers in the towers. We were shown horrible dungeons, a deep hole where the prisoners were starved to death, and a torture chamber in which the rusty instruments of torture lay scattered about; an old man still lived in the castle who had seen them used. One dark room was full of armour, lances, shields, and arrows. A number of old portraits in tolerable preservation represented the former heads of the family; the picture of the white lady who makes her appearance on important occasions, such as the death of any one of the family, was said to be lost; more likely it was not shown. But the old housekeeper maintained that she had seen the fearful apparition above ten times: — she might have passed for it herself, so dismal and ominous was her aspect.

We then visited a sulphur spring near the castle, and the quarries from which the stone for the town-house at Amsterdam was taken, and returned late, and filled with gloomy ideas, through the dark wilderness to Steinfurt, which appeared to us with its lights to be the newest and most cheerful spot on earth.

Before winter came several of the company left Steinfurt; the society became less numerous, and we were reduced to in-door amusements. I lived more in my own room, and made good use of the count's library, to which I had free access. I read a history of Westphalia, French memoirs without end, besides other works of greater historical value, and treatises on philosophy. But what attracted and delighted me beyond all the rest were the works of Johannes Tauler*, which I found in the library; not only his sermons, but his more important work on the imitation of Christ. This learned exposition of mystical truths could not have fallen into my hands at a more opportune moment; I can safely say that this book opened to me new and glorious views.

This produced in me an extraordinary state of excitement, and I passed whole nights reading and writing. I could not help being affected by the peculiar local colouring of the country and of the people among whom I was living. Catholic Westphalia stands in the same relation to the North of Germany as protestant Würtemberg to the South: catholicism, hemmed in by protestant countries, seems here to develop its utmost energy. Both in Westphalia and in Würtemberg superstition and religious madness have gone hand-in-hand with the strictest observances and the most fiery zeal. The people of Münster are remarkable for the strength of their belief; and the wonderful nun of Dülmen is the catholic counterpart to the prophetess of Prevorst. Pro-

---

* Johannes Tauler, a famous German mystic, called the Doctor Sublimis et Illuminatus, was born in 1294, and died at Strasburg in 1361. He was a Dominican, and his sermons, which had a prodigious effect on the common people, are remarkable for depth of thought, earnestness of purpose, and vigour of expression. They are the best specimens of German prose before Luther. His sermons were published in 1521, and reprinted in 1826 at Frankfort; and his mystic works by Casseder in 1823, and by Schlosser, at Frankfort, in 1833. — *Transl.*

phecies, tales of wonder, marvellous dreams and apparitions, are as common in Westphalia as in Würtemberg. One cause of the prevalence of this feeling is the peculiar nature of the country; another I would attribute to the race. In Westphalia the solitary mode of life, in remote, desolate-looking spots, renders this people peculiarly susceptible to gloomy ideas and impressions; the number of people who see visions and dream dreams, and to whom the hidden is revealed, is very great. Accidents, marriages, fires, sudden rises in fortune, and, lately, political events, are frequently foreseen: sometimes visionary foreign troops, in strange uniforms, are seen in full march; at other times the men are invisible, and only the tops of their bayonets are seen to glisten through the fog. Even children are subject to these fancies. I was told of a little child who, when she was scolded for her long absence, attributed it to being delayed by a long array of artillery and powder waggons; she had been seen standing on one side of the road, as if waiting till it was clear. The frequency and variety of these illusions must produce a deep impression, if not actual belief; the strongest understanding must, in the end, be affected by their constant repetition. I saw many people, who, by education, ought to have been above such superstitions, but in a corner of their hearts they believed them still. The Castle of Steinfurt itself was not wanting in legends and superstitions. No one could help feeling that they were still living on an old feudal soil, and that the modern drawing-rooms rested on gloomy dungeons, where bloody deeds and cruel horrors had once taken place. The way from one wing of the castle to the other, through the chapel, — which, by the way, could scarce be avoided, — always made me shudder; and an irregular sort of ante-room, paved with red tiles, offered no temptation to any one to stop there. One of the servants whom I frequently met in this very place annoyed me by the fixed expression with which he invariably followed all my motions. He was a tall, ill-looking fellow, with a pale, gloomy countenance, and was disagreeable without any particular fault being laid to him. He was supposed to possess the gift of prophecy to an eminent degree; but, owing to some unpleasant circumstances attending former exhibitions, he was seldom called upon to exercise his talents. Some thought that this gift was bestowed on him as a punishment, and that he had taken to drink as a consolation; others thought that drink might be the cause, and not the effect.

The night hours passed in study, and the religious frame of mind in which I then was prevented me from completely shaking off these impressions. I frequently fancied that my motions were watched, and that some one was listening at the door. Meanwhile I quietly pursued my avocations, finished some tales which I had begun at Tübingen, and worked hard at history. I collected my remarks and notes upon Paris into a readable shape, and had made some progress when I discovered, to my great annoyance, that some pages were missing. As my handwriting is peculiarly small, and I am in the habit of using scraps of paper, I thought that the MSS. might have got mixed with other papers: but the most careful search was fruitless: it was a riddle to me how they could have been lost. Unluckily the missing papers contained strong expressions against Napoleon, and the Poissarde ballad on his marriage, with the score of the tune. Those who remember that period can well imagine the danger of losing such papers; not I alone, but the excellent people with whom I then was, might be exposed to danger. I consulted Dr. Houth, who recommended me to try if the castle seer could discover where these papers were. I remembered the well-known history of Swedenborg, and agreed to try my luck. What happened was strange enough: the man at first would not answer, but turned his face away; at last he said dreamily, that the papers were a long way off: nor could we extract any thing further from him. This gave me some sort of clue: I might have inclosed these papers, by mistake, to Hamburg or Berlin; but it was not safe to ask, as no one trusted the post.

These thoughts, however, and the uncertainty of my future lot, distressed me less than the general uneasiness. A great portion of the north of Germany, including the grand-duchy of Berg, to which Steinfurt had been annexed, and even the Hanseatic towns, had become French departments, so that I was deprived of my last retreat at Hamburg. The news, too, from Berlin was disheartening. This impossibility of escape made me depend still more on my own resources for amusement. The winter passed agreeably in reading, while skating, dancing, and acting varied my occupations.

A journey to Münster gave me an opportunity of examining that most curious town. The history of the Anabaptists, which I had carefully read, is vividly brought to the mind by the sight of the iron cages in St. Lambert's tower, in which the mutilated bodies of three ringleaders of the Anabaptists were exposed. But a more agreeable sight was the picture of those who signed the peace of Westphalia: their remarkable faces contain a history in themselves. The French prefect who then resided at Münster was a certain Baron von Mylius; his brother was serving in the Austrian army. The family of Droste von Vischering, which was the most illustrious in Münster for antiquity and strict catholicism, had maintained its influence even under the French.

I had almost forgotten my suspicions at Steinfurt, when they suddenly returned with greater force. One evening I had quitted my room, leaving my candle burning. On my return I was astonished to find some one peering in through the keyhole; —it was one of the servants who had no business in this part of the house. My unexpected appearance and sharp questions frightened him not a little; but as there was nothing which I could impute to him beyond a stupid curiosity, I let him go with a reprimand. It was extremely probable that I had been frequently watched in this manner before; light footsteps and sounds of one listening may have acted on my susceptible nerves without my being exactly aware of the cause of my excitement. The discovery was unpleasant, and I could not help reverting to the loss of my papers, and connecting the one with the other. My suspicions were not unfounded.

Meanwhile strong detachments of French troops were marching towards the north of Germany. Their slow but continuous and regular advance gave some idea as to their destination. These were the troops intended for the Russian campaign, which Napoleon had long meditated, but still concealed under a pretence of great amity with the Russian court. One portion of the troops came through Steinfurt, and was quartered there for some time. Their company was not agreeable; the tone of superiority with which the French talked of their victories, and the manner in which they forced their society upon us, were equally painful. To avoid conversation as much as possible we played at billiards or at chess.

It was impossible on further acquaintance not to be struck by their different qualities and characters. The colonel was any thing but a good soldier: he was zealous and attached to the Emperor, but a man of no education; a fact which he was anxious as much as possible to conceal. Some of the young officers allowed their zeal for Napoleon to go so far as to consider him as the legitimate successor to the Bourbons. An old major, on the contrary, who had served under Bernadotte and Moreau, represented the revolution, and did not conceal how little the present state of affairs pleased him. In one of his walks with me he opened his heart, called Napoleon the oppressor of freedom, and inveighed against his whole system of government as one founded on arbitrary power, and productive of great immorality. Had I entertained any suspicion against him, it would have vanished the evening before the departure of the troops. I took a solitary walk with the major in the Bagno: the last evening we were to pass together caused him some emotion, and he pressed my hand, assuring me that he had a great respect for my opinions. He then startled me by the following words:—" You are young, and may live many years: keep, therefore, your opinions for better times. You are by no means prudent, and are needlessly running into danger. Why should you write letters? Remember, I want to know nothing, but simply wish to warn you; listen therefore to what I have to say, and take it as a mark of confidence. When I was last at Münster, an old comrade, now high in office, asked me how I liked Steinfurt, seeing that the French were much hated there. When I asked him why he thought so, I learned that he was accurately informed, by his spies here, of every thing that went on. It was well known that people were at work all night long writing and plotting against the French government. It is just possible, my young friend, that he may have meant you;—take care, therefore; for you cannot be aware of the scandalous means which our police will employ for these purposes. I recommend you to write no more letters as long as you remain here." I was somewhat disturbed by this warning. I had written very few letters; but the missing papers came across me, and I could not help suspecting that they had been stolen. In consequence of this honest well-meant warning, I burned or safely disposed of all papers which might have been dangerous.

Luckily, shortly after this arrived the time of our departure, and towards the end of June, 1811, we left Steinfurt. After passing a few weeks at Lich, at Laubach, and at Utpha in the Wetterall, we went to Frankfort on the Main. We then journeyed, without delay and without any adventures, to Vienna.

As soon as I had my papers safe in Austria, I completed my sketches of Paris. After several friends had read them, the Prussian Minister of Foreign Affairs, Count von Golz, borrowed them of me at Töplitz, in 1811, and I did not recover them till after his death, in 1834. I came upon traces of my lost MSS. in Hamburg, in 1813, when books and papers which had been found in the house of Count D'Aubignosc, the head of the French police, were brought to Russian head-quarters. In an old dusty parcel I discovered a paper, which I recognised as a passage from one of my sketches of Napoleon. It was headed, *Extrait d'une Lettre*. With it were two copies of Stägemann's ode to the Emperor Alexander.

The company in which my papers were found was honourable but dangerous. Luckily, however, the bundle of papers had been thrown on one side, and were now in our hands— witnesses of how much times had altered.

CHAPTER XIV.

Garrison Life in Prague. — The Prussian Minister Stein. — His Outlawry and Escape into Bohemia. — Stein's Character. — Vienna. — State of Public Opinion. — Prospect of War between France and Russia. — Birth of the King of Rome. — Ball at the French Ambassador's. — Festival at Prague. 1811.

AFTER the varied life which I led for so long, the routine garrison service, and whole manner of existence at Prague seemed dull and uniform. The pressure of the times was every where felt, the depreciation of paper money caused insecurity and loss on all sides; society hung loosely together, and in addition to the usual distinction of classes, another element — difference of race — made itself felt. But the natives who spoke German were not so completely separated from their Bohemian speaking brethren as other Germans were from both: — our ideas, habits, and customs were totally different, and in spite of our endeavours, always remained so. This was especially the case with the numerous officers who had quitted the north of Germany to enter the Austrian service. Forced to depend so much upon one another, we clung together as much as possible, but soon found that similarity of origin did not ensure community of tastes. Accident had dispersed those who would have been most agreeable to me, and I could have dispensed with the company of many who were left. On the other hand, I heard one German mentioned in Prague, for whom I had vainly enquired elsewhere, and to whom I felt myself strongly attracted. This was the late Prussian minister, Baron von Stein, outlawed by Napoleon, and highly honoured by all Germans who loved their country.

The French declaration of outlawry against Stein reached him at Berlin, where he was occupied with affairs of state. He fled into Austria. There his hatred and his hopes were amply fed during the war, and even the peace did not diminish his zeal. He was now waiting patiently at Prague to see what might happen. The place was well chosen for the purpose, and offered many opportunities for observation: and the society was pleasant enough for those who by birth and position belonged to the high aristocracy.

We heard several traits of Stein's unbending disposition, the acuteness of his intellect, and the vehemence of his expressions: these qualities won him esteem and confidence wherever the French were hated; he was considered as a hero, to whom his country might look with certainty. It is true that there were many Germans who did not implicitly trust so rash a spirit: many blamed his principles of action, accused him of prejudice against all that was old, and wished to see the liberation of Germany accomplished rather by measures dictated by prudence and moderation than by impetuous vehemence. Men who thought thus recalled the circumstances by which Stein had been brought to his present condition, and by which he had lost an opportunity for action, which would never occur again; the circumstances certainly do not speak in favour of his prudence, and were not generally known. The facts were these: The assessor Koppe was the bearer of dispatches from Königsberg to Berlin, and further northwards. Stein returned home from a dinner where a good deal of wine had been drunk, and found Koppe ready, and waiting only for final orders. Stein requested him to stop one moment longer, went to his standing desk and wrote a few hurried lines to Prince von Wittgenstein. Koppe received the letter and started. The matter was as good as forgotten, when suddenly news arrived that Koppe had been taken by the French and robbed of his dispatches. This caused some noise and anxiety, in the midst of which, Count von Golz, the minister of foreign affairs, confessed that he felt some anxiety about certain letters in which he had talked slightingly about Napoleon. "That was silly," said Stein, and when asked in his turn, what he had written, he answered: "Oh, the French may read all that I wrote." Shortly afterwards he read his own letter to Prince von Wittgenstein, printed in the "Moniteur," and was forced to confess that its contents, the import of which he had scarcely before considered, were dangerous and indiscreet. In the face of Napoleon's open hostility, Stein could no longer remain prime minister of Prussia. He sent in his resignation, but thought so little of any danger to himself as to proceed to Berlin. Here, however, he read unexpectedly in the "Moniteur" a decree of Napoleon's, dated from Madrid, by which "*le nommé Stein*" was declared an outlaw, on account of seditious practices against the French; nothing therefore was left for Stein but flight, and as escape to England was cut off, Austria alone offered a safe retreat. The French officials had already demanded that Stein's person should be given up to them, but did nothing to hinder his escape; the decree did not specify "*le nommé Stein*" as the minister, and this uncertainty was interpreted in his favour. Two days' grace were allowed him to settle his affairs, and he successfully made his way into Austria.

Such circumstances as these bring out a man's true character. Real greatness is independent of its accompanying defects: weaknesses and errors are forgiven. Popular opinion, guided by true instinct, bears its heroes harmless under misfortunes and failures, and does not hold them responsible for consequences. Blucher's reputation was not injured because he was forced to yield himself a prisoner with his forces at Lubeck; he was not the less a hero for this, nor was he less trusted afterwards. So we may say of Stein that this indiscretion, for which he was so much reproached, scarce lowered him at all in public estimation. People were sorry for what had happened, and laughed at it, but it did not diminish their respect and confidence in him; on the contrary, Stein's misfortunes stamped him as the uncompromising foe of the French; reconciliation was impossible; his very errors plainly showed how ready he was to expose himself at every opportunity. Stein lived respected and honoured by the best and worthiest people in Prague.

Through Stein I learnt many political events which had previously escaped my knowledge. Much of what was going on at Berlin and in the north of Germany was disclosed to me, and

I saw various ramifications spread over the country which could not remain without results. Stein had active correspondents, and was well informed of all that was passing.

The instructive and entertaining conversations which I had with Stein were too soon ended as other engagements required my presence at Vienna, where I had to see the Archduke Charles and many other persons of rank and importance. I found Count Metternich as obliging as he had been at Paris; I also had the good fortune to meet plenty of old and new acquaintances in Vienna, where it was just the season.

It struck me as a remarkable circumstance that men's opinions ran like two streams in two opposite directions — to unite them seemed impossible. As far as mere outward appearances went, there was friendship and alliance with France; the expression of public opinion led to this conclusion: men's private opinions, however, were decidedly in the contrary direction. The belief was universal and unalloyed by doubt, that this compulsion could not last long — that the yoke would speedily be thrown off. It was only a question when and how this was to be effected. Soldiers, and those who were idle like Stein and others were impatient; but those who most heavily felt the oppression of the times knew the necessity of a prudent delay. Great precaution had to be used in writing, and people avoided political topics in their letters. Nevertheless conversation was carried on with tolerable freedom from restraint; in fact, there was little to fear, as the existence of a spy or traitor among men all holding the same views would quickly have been discovered. The news from Spain of the ill success of the French could not be more eagerly received in England than it was in Austria; the hopes for Austria and Germany were nowhere more zealously entertained than in Vienna, and the prospect of war between France and Russia increased our excitement by the important question how Austria was to act on such an emergency. The thought of being compelled to join the French in their campaign against Russia was intolerable to some of us, while others maintained that for the sake of future good, we should think no abnegation too great, no trial too severe. These opinions, however, were not discussed as quietly then as now: there was always the possibility which, indeed, actually occurred, of men who had once fought under the same banner as brothers in arms, being arrayed in hostile ranks against one another. This naturally produced recrimination and mistrust. The idea of entering the Russian service was in many men's minds: those who were not bound by the ties of birth to the Austrian service did not consider themselves obliged to follow Austria in all her proceedings.

About this time the news reached Vienna of the birth of the King of Rome: this important event produced the most curious impressions, and brought the contradictions of that period into striking contrast. No one found fault with the real sympathy shown by those personally interested in this event; but, on the other hand, the public and official marks of joy were treated with scorn. By Count Metternich's special invitation, I attended a great ball given by the French ambassador Otto in celebration of the birth of Napoleon's heir, at which all the imperial court and high nobility of Vienna appeared in full splendour: but out of eight hundred who were invited, scarce six hundred appeared, and when the Emperor of Austria went away, a large portion of these left the rooms. But this ball was most remarkable when compared with another about which I purposely told all I knew — whilst I, strangely enough, was present on the 20th of May at the ball given by the French ambassador in honour of the young King of Rome, another was given on the 21st at Prague to celebrate the anniversary of the battle of Aspern. My colonel had boldly selected this particular day the better to oppose the direction public affairs inclined to take, by the commemoration of a victory which every one now appeared anxious to forget. He therefore gave his regiment, which had taken a distinguished part in the engagement, a military festival, at which all Prague was present, as it was given on the public walk on the Moldau, called the Bubnetsch or Baumgarten. Acting in accordance with his own liberal feelings, he was not afraid to do a thing which excited wonder and applause: he invited the common soldiers to join in the honours and pleasures which are generally reserved only for their officers. Several soldiers, who wore medals in honour of Aspern in their button-holes, were driven by the colonel and staff-officers in open carriages, and were seated in the places of honour at table. Good fare was not wanting: nor was there any lack of appropriate toasts, speeches, and songs. The impression made by this festival was felt to a great distance; this one regiment represented the feelings of the whole army and the German people. The freshness and originality of the idea gave universal satisfaction; even in higher quarters smiles of approbation rewarded the boldness of a whim which gave an index to the spirit of the times.

On my return to Prague I found every one still full of the spectacle, and many of my young comrades so excited as to imagine that I had brought from Vienna, if not an actual declaration of war, at any rate the certainty of its approaching outbreak: they hoped very shortly to take the field against the French. Instead of this, I could only tell them that I had been at a ball given in honour of the King of Rome, and that their military ardour would be forced to content itself with the prospect of reviews and field-days during the approaching summer.

CHAPTER. XV.

Töplitz. — The princely family of Clary. — The Prince de Ligne. — Life at Töplitz. — Troop of Bohemian Actors. — The French Spy. — The Disappearance of Mr. Bathurst. — The Englishman and the French Courier. — Beethoven. — Prague. — The Emigrants and Exiles at Prague. — Justus Gruner, the Head of the Prussian Police. — Napoleon at Dresden. — Arrest of Gruner, and Consternation of the others. — Arrival at Berlin. — News of the Burning of Moscow. — The Cossacks enter Berlin. 1811, 1812.

Rahel had requested me to join her at Dresden, on her way to Töplitz, and I left Prague full of joyful expectations: we reached Töplitz, and soon made ourselves comfortable in our several lodgings. Rahel knew the place well, but to me it was completely new; and in her company I visited the castle, gardens, and other walks. I will not dwell upon what has been so often described, but will turn at once to the company that was here assembled.

And, first, I must speak of the princely family of Clary, the owners of the country, round whom, as a common centre, the others revolved. Prince John Nepomucene was a quiet, sensible man, of simple, dignified appearance, accustomed to good company, well versed in literature, and a man of the world. He managed his property well, and took care that his castle and park, his gardens and buildings, his farms, forests, and chaces, should always be in good condition. He contrived that Töplitz, where a brilliant society always assembled, should be in every respect worthy of its company. His wife, Christina, was the Prince de Ligne's daughter, an amiable, guileless woman, who could speak nothing but French, and who joined a taste for literature with a love of wit and pleasure. She never had experienced pain or grief in her life, and certainly never caused any in others knowingly. Every thing had been done to smooth her way through life, and to meet her slightest wishes; as her father truly remarked, she remained a spoiled child into advanced life, without once having felt life's stern realities. Her eldest son Count Charles, and his wife, with a young family; two other daughters of the Prince de Ligne,—the one married to Count Palffy von Erdöd, the other to Baron von Spiegel,—lived at the castle. The chief star, however, in this society was the Prince de Ligne. Every word, every gesture of his was sprightly and cheerful. In him were united, to a remarkable degree, the honours of high birth, high station, and old age; and yet his wit was even more remarkable than his worldly advantages. In this circle a good humour incessantly prevailed, which did not allow grief or misfortune to weigh too heavily. Only one deep, settled grief had found its way there: no one could allude to it without exciting the most melancholy reflections. In the wars of the Revolution the Prince de Ligne had lost his dearly-loved eldest son, in the bloom of youth, and full of promise. But this grief had found a solace in the love he bore to this son's daughter, Titine, Countess O'Donnel.

We had a succession of most beautiful days. In the morning, after bathing, breakfasting, and walking, it was the custom to meet in the gardens of Prince Clary, where, generally, the family and some of the company played at bowls in the open air. Prince Charles disappeared, with his book, into some of the retired alleys, while others went in boats on the lake. The afternoons were spent in taking long walks, and we seldom returned home in time for the theatre in the castle, where a small troop of Bohemian actors played every evening. The incomparably witty and humorous Swoboda occasionally displayed his wonderful comic genius, and was pronounced by the celebrated Berlin actress, Mademoiselle Bethmann, to be one of the greatest actors of his day. The evenings were passed, most agreeably, in the castle gardens, and we met afterwards in the drawing-rooms, if there was no ball or other amusement announced for the day. When we returned home late, it was almost impossible to leave the open air: the bright stars in the dark heavens, the prolonged shadows, the stillness of the atmosphere, all these worked like magic on the spirits; and when Carolina Longhi, the celebrated Neapolitan harp-player, was heard practising at her open window, or Bohemian musicians played under those of the Duke of Weimar, it was impossible not to listen in utter oblivion of every thing else.

The visitors increased daily, and consisted principally of Austrians, Prussians, and Saxons: there were several Russians and Poles, and a few Frenchmen, but not one Englishman. Indeed, there were none on the whole continent except those who were prisoners in France or fighting in Spain and Portugal. One Englishman, who had lived a long time in Prague as a teacher, was forced to pass himself off as an American.

I was much disturbed by reports which reached me from Hamburg and from Berlin. Many things which should have been kept secret had been noised abroad, and had come to the enemy's ears; the uncertainty whether treachery had not been at work, not only gave great cause for alarm, but provoked suspicion and mistrust in all quarters. The French police, under Marshal Davoust in particular, became more active and watchful, and stretched their power over all the states of the Rhenish confederation. Arrests were made in the kingdom of Westphalia of which the Westphalian authorities knew nothing. We heard that Napoleon had demanded of Prussia that persons displeasing to him should not be tolerated there, and some few were to be delivered into his hands. It was said that he wished to have his rear cleared of enemies in the event of the campaign taking effect against Russia. My friends in the north of Germany were in great excitement; papers were burnt, residences changed, old connexions broken off, new and more secret ones formed. Austria had as yet kept out the French influence with considerable success: in Bohemia especially, every one lived in perfect security: the French civil and military officers knew but little of the interior of the country, and had no wish to enter further into it.

It was impossible altogether to shake off care, and we lived in constant suspicion, not only of friends and companions, but even of relations. I may here mention a Frenchman who limped about Töplitz for several weeks, and who had been ordered, as he said, to use the baths for his wounds. He was anxious to make acquaintances, and tried to worm himself into society. Nevertheless he was not liked, and was looked upon as a spy; and so he probably was, for the Duke of Rovigo mentions in his memoirs that he had a spy in Bohemia during that summer. I can only say that if this was the man, the Duke of Rovigo was ill served. No one would receive him. The Austrian officers, to whom he wished to attach himself, turned him into ridicule: one of them, a captain in the chasseurs, a certain Baron von Knorr, remarkable for humour and courage, and always ready to use either, had made it his business to tease this man, and was incessantly playing all manner of tricks upon him, which were worth their weight in gold. He once seriously represented to the Frenchman that it had a bad appearance first to limp with the right and then with the left leg: he ought to make up his mind at once as to which foot had been wounded, and in future only to limp with that one: for that he and others were determined to look closely to this, and not to bear any more changing about. The Frenchman was wise enough to take all this banter very well, vowing that it was quite a mistake to suppose that Germans did not understand a joke, — that they were masters in the art! However, the man was by no means without taste or knowledge, and was not ill-natured, — only he did not succeed well in a part for which he was singularly unfit. I do not believe that he did any one a mischief, but I cannot but think that he did little honour to the choice of him who sent him.

Among the personal events which arose out of these troubled times, the history of Mr. Bathurst, from the mystery which attended it, excited the greatest attention. He had been extremely active as English minister in Austria during the war of 1809: and after the peace of Vienna, as he saw no further use but considerable danger in staying any longer at his post, he determined to attempt the journey to England through Germany, rather than take the longer and no less dangerous way by Malta. His terror and anxiety lest he should fall into the hands of the French were excessive, and alarmed his Austrian acquaintance; but they comforted themselves with the knowledge that he was accompanied by trusty friends. Mr. Bathurst arrived on the 25th November, 1809, at Kletzke, the post station before Perleberg, in his carriage, with his secretary and a servant; he went under the feigned name of M. Koch. He got out of his carriage and asked for horses immediately, as he was in a great hurry. He inquired eagerly of those whom he met in the passengers' room about the state of the road, and whether he should encounter any French troops: he then drew out two pistols from his pocket, kept constantly looking at them, cocked and uncocked them, and this he continued to do for some time after the horses were put to: he was told that he would have to pay according to the tariff for keeping them waiting. This he did not mind; paid what was demanded; but it was some time before he entered the carriage and drove off. He reached Perleberg after dark, left his carriage, and asked to see the commandant, a certain M. von Klitzing: he went to this gentleman's house, which was lighted up for company, desired to see him alone, and when he was satisfied that no one was listening, and that he had to deal with a man of honour, he disclosed his real name, and requested to know if he could reach Hamburg in safety by that route? M. von Klitzing assured him that he could, and gave him all the necessary information; he remarked, however, that Mr. Bathurst was in a state of excitement bordering on madness. The traveller said that he was in great danger, that his life had twice been attempted by poison, but that he always carried its antidote about with him; that he greatly feared the French police, the soldiers, and douaniers, through whom he must manage somehow to pass. Somewhat quieted by the assurances of M. von Klitzing, Mr. Bathurst left the house with the commandant's best wishes, and went apparently to the posthouse. He was seen by the daughter of the former postmaster to go by the window; but from that moment he was never heard of again. Whether he left the town on foot to meet his carriage on the high-road, whether it was his wish to separate from his people, so as to pass through the country alone with greater security, whether he was killed and buried near or far from Perleberg, or seized and carried off — whether he reached the Mecklenberg coast, embarked thence and found a watery grave; — all this remains a mystery to this day.

His hat was found near Perleberg, on the banks of the Steknitz; but this one solitary trace proved nothing. The bed of this small river was laid bare as far as its junction with the Elbe, without any effect. When Mr. Bathurst's strange disappearance was made known in England, his wife appealed to Napoleon, who gave her special permission to superintend the search herself. I met her in Paris in 1810, at Schlabrendorf's*,

---

* Gustavus Count von Schlabrendorf was born at Stettin on the 22d

she had just returned from the Priegnitz, where all researches, conducted with a total disregard to expense, and with all the assistance which the local magistrates could afford, had produced no results. All the inquiries of subsequent years threw no light upon this mysterious affair, and even now, after a lapse of thirty years, it is as dark as ever. The general supposition was, that the unfortunate Mr. Bathurst was betrayed and fell a sacrifice to French intrigues, for in those days it was not unusual for people to disappear in this manner. I must own that such horrors were occasionally perpetrated on our side, as a necessary precaution against treason. I heard of one case which occurred almost under our very eyes. An Austrian general who arrived at Töplitz from Prague, told me what had happened to himself. An Englishman, travelling under a feigned name, made terms with a French courier to accompany him as far as Constantinople: he paid him beforehand a portion of the sum he had agreed to pay, and by his generosity won the man's favour. At Prague the Englishman was afraid that he had not sufficient money, and went to the general in question with his credentials

---

March, 1750. His father was Frederick the Great's minister in Silesia during the Seven Years' War. Without being either an author or a statesman, he had great influence on his generation. He travelled over France, and lived for six years in England, where he travelled with Stein. Just before the outbreak of the French Revolution he returned to Paris, where he remained until his death, in 1824. He was zealously and actively engaged in all that he thought for the good of mankind, and his eloquence enabled him to effect much. A great deal that in books and reports won for others applause and respect was originally picked up from his admirable conversation. As the friend of Condorcet, Mercier, and Brissot, he was imprisoned during the reign of terror. His conversation and kindness, his generosity and advice, were the comfort of his fellow-prisoners. Schlabrendorf escaped death by a sort of miracle. One day the cart came as usual for its freight of victims, and his name was called out. He soon was ready, with the exception of his boots, which could not be found. At length he said to the jailor, "Without boots, it is quite impossible for me to go. Let us see: you can call for me to-morrow; one day cannot be of much consequence." The cart proceeded without him. Next day Schlabrendorf, ready booted, was waiting; but his name was not called. The jailor was not a brute, and said nothing. Schlabrendorf remained in prison ignored until Robespierre's fall. After this, he devoted his mind and his money to the good of mankind. He lived for many years in the Hôtel des Deux Siciles, in a room he seldom quitted, and never locked. Without a servant, in shabby clothes, and in a meanly furnished apartment, he, like a second Diogenes, received the visits of men of all ranks and all nations. As he never concealed his opinions, the police ceased to trouble him; but he was for some time imprisoned during Napoleon's government. — *Transl.*

in order to obtain more. The general was satisfied, and gave him the money he demanded: he only asked him the object for which such a sum was required. The Englishman coolly answered, that he wanted the courier's dispatches, to obtain which he must kill him for security's sake. He saw that he could not do this in Bohemia, perhaps not in Hungary, but in Turkey some opportunity would probably occur. The general saw, at a glance, that the Englishman was perfectly capable of doing what he said; he stammered and shuddered, but could do nothing: no representation of his could shake the Englishman's determination. What times were these! when the most noble of causes, freedom and patriotism, were so intimately bound up with inhuman treachery, and when the one could not be separated from the other! May we never again see them return in Germany!

About this time I became acquainted with the musician who threw all others into the shade. It was Beethoven, of whose presence at Töplitz all had heard, but whom none had yet seen. His deafness made him avoid society, and his peculiarities, which were increased by solitude, rendered it less easy to become acquainted with him. He had, however, occasionally seen Rahel in the castle gardens, and had been struck by her countenance, which reminded him of some beloved face. Beethoven did for us what he had refused obstinately to do for others: once in Vienna bodily violence had been used in vain by a prince to force him to play before some company, but he now sat down to the pianoforte and played his yet unpublished pieces, or allowed his fancy to run wild.

The season was nearly ended, and by degrees all the company went away: Rahel, whom the baths had not benefited, left Töplitz towards the middle of September, on her way to Dresden, while I returned to Prague, where I had many things to do.

I will pass by a number of events and adventures which would afford the richest materials for romantic descriptions of life, and will note down those matters which have some reference to political affairs.

The pleasures of society did not prevent me from passing the greater part of the winter in study. In the spring the prospect of war between Russia and France became more imminent, and put every one in motion. But the greatest doubts prevailed in men's minds as to the future course they should adopt. It so happened that Prague contained several people who had the greatest cause to hate Napoleon. The Elector of Hessen-Cassel lived there as an exile with a considerable number of dependents and much property that he had been able to save: he was full of courage, and confidently looked for some change, which he was prepared to forward with all the means in his power. Many persons had joined the Austrian service only in order to fight against France, and were by no means inclined to fight for their enemies. Several French emigrants, the Prince de Rohan, Major de Trogoff, the Marquis de Favras, the son of the marquis of the same name, who was guillotined during the Revolution, and several others, most of whom were in the Austrian service, were living in Prague, as well as a nephew of Pozzo di Borgo, who hated his countryman Napoleon with the bitterest hatred. The number of malcontents increased daily. Major von Bose came from Saxony, then came Colonel Rühle von Lilienstern. The former head of the police, Justus Gruner, arrived from Berlin, and the bookseller and author Bran escaped to Prague from Hamburg under a feigned name. Marshal Davoust had ordered him to be shot for translating and publishing a work written by the Spanish minister Cevallos. He owed his life to the circumstance of the Leipsic police imagining that the strange name of Bran was a mistake for Brand, and to their arresting a man of that name. The real Bran took the hint and reached Bohemia before the error was discovered.

It had long been evident that Prussia could not well avoid an alliance with France, and it now appeared that an Austrian reinforcement would join the French troops. All were anxious to discover which regiments would be selected for a duty which every one wished heartily to avoid. When it was known that the brave and highly honoured Prince Charles von Schwarzenberg was to have the command of the troops destined to this service, people determined not to follow his example, but rather that of General Wintzingerode, Major Tettenborn, and

General von Wallmoden, who had all thrown up their commissions, and entered the Russian service.

Meanwhile Napoleon had assembled the French and allied troops from all quarters, and the huge horde was marching upon Russia through Prussia and Poland. Napoleon himself came with his wife to Dresden, where he was joined by the emperor and empress of Austria. During this meeting, upon which the eyes of the world were fixed, Prague acquired no small importance as a place of assembly for all parties holding views hostile to Napoleon, and as a good post of observation for English and Russian agents: it was near Dresden, without being within reach of Napoleon's arbitrary power.

Meanwhile the meeting at Dresden came to an end. Napoleon hastened to join his army on the frontiers of Russia. The emperor and empress of Austria, with Marie Louise, came to Prague, where every thing was prepared, on a scale of great magnificence, to receive our beloved ruler and his exalted guest: the war and all political cares and anxieties were forgotten for the moment.

I was determined to quit the Austrian service. If escape into Russia was out of the question, the north of Germany offered a wide field in which much might be done. Gruner encouraged me in this. In Berlin he had been at the head of an extensively spread system of police, and much had thus come to his knowledge. The most dangerous French spies had fallen into his nets, and had disappeared: his cunning and boldness had greatly injured the French, who knew him as their mortal enemy. When, in consequence of the Prussian alliance with France, French troops entered Prussia, Gruner did not think it wise to await their arrival in Berlin, but resigned his post, and fled into Bohemia. He was in constant communication with the Russians, and carried on an active correspondence over all Germany. One of his plans was to destroy all the stores and powder magazines in the rear of the French army, as soon as it had penetrated far enough into Russia. Gruner, however, did not sufficiently consider whom he trusted, and his correspondence was notoriously incautious. He imagined that his correspondence was inviolate, and his cipher undiscovered, at a time when his letters were opened and their contents well known. It was in vain that he was warned; he thought that he was deceiving those who were watching his motions. An audience with Prince Metternich, and several with General von Koller, instead of bringing him to reason, increased his rashness. The Austrian government saw the time approach when it could no longer protect him. The French authorities in Berlin and Hamburg had convincing proofs against him, and it was daily expected that they would demand his arrest in terms which could not be refused. To save him, therefore, from greater evils, the Austrian government took the initiative, arrested and sent Gruner as a state prisoner to Peterwardein. By this means his papers and his money escaped falling into the hands of the French. Gruner acknowledged, in the end, that this had been a most fortunate occurrence for him; but it was long before he could get rid of the bitter impression that the event at first produced on his mind.

This proceeding created consternation among those who were not in the secret. We used greater caution, and determined to trust no one but ourselves; in spite, however, of distinct warnings not to continue our journey, we left Prague, and succeeded in reaching Berlin without impediment.

As Berlin was garrisoned by French troops, we notified our arrival to Marshal Augereau and to General Durutte, the commandant, as well as to the Prussian authorities. Notwithstanding the apparently good reception that we met with, we soon remarked that our motions were closely watched. To this, however, we did not much object. After a few weeks' stay in Berlin my companion Willisen wished to visit his parents at Magdeburg; but scarce had he entered the frontiers of Westphalia, when he was arrested and imprisoned in the fortress of Cassel. We heard this, but could learn nothing further concerning him. This circumstance made my position more critical, and I did not dare to leave Berlin.

The news of the burning of Moscow now reached us: new hopes arose, the French shouts of victory ceased, reports of their retreat and utter demolition became rife, and were at length confirmed by the arrival of the miserable remnant of the once grand army. The Russians advanced, passed the Oder, and were soon before Berlin : Colonel Tettenborn and his cossacks chased the enemy through the streets for some hours, and in a few days the Russian troops entered the town.

Thus released from a painful constraint, and in full enjoyment of freedom and new life, I went to see Tettenborn, who offered me a commission in the Russian service, and confided to me his intention of attacking Hamburg.

CHAPTER XVI.

Tettenborn's early Life. — The Electoral Court at Mayence. — Flight of the Elector to Aschaffenburg. — Tettenborn joins the Army in the Netherlands. — Hohenlinden. — Tettenborn at Ulm. — Tettenborn at St. Petersburg. — The Retreat from Moscow. — The taking of Wilna. — The Advance of the Cossacks. — Failure of the Attack on Berlin. — Advance of the Russian Infantry, and Retreat of the French. 1812, 1813.

FREDERICK CHARLES VON TETTENBORN, one of the bravest leaders in the eventful war of 1813, was born on the 19th of February, 1778, at Spanheim, in the margravate of Baden.

In his thirteenth year young Tettenborn was sent to the electoral court at Mayence, and became one of the elector's pages. The pomp, magnificence, and social pleasures of that court are remembered even to this day. The elector and his followers passed their time in ever-varying amusements, utterly regardless of the spirit of innovation which was growing up, and which threatened the old state of things, a spirit which was rather encouraged than not, as entertaining. Their dangerous proximity to France, the spread of the French revolution, and even the war which was already declared, had made no impression on these frivolous voluptuaries; when suddenly the unexpected approach of the French in the autumn of 1792 woke them from their intoxicating dream of pleasure. On the approach of General Custine the elector with his women and favourites fled to Aschaffenburg: the rest of the court dispersed in various directions never again to re-assemble. Tettenborn waited till the French troops entered Mayence, and then returned to his father's house at Rastatt.

The turn which affairs had taken altered his father's views, and young Tettenborn was sent to Göttingen, whence he was shortly removed to Jena, in consequence of some youthful extravagances. Soon after this he was summoned home by his father's illness; and on the death of the latter, having no longer any one to control his military ardour, he quitted the university, and entered the Austrian service in 1794.

Tettenborn was sixteen when he entered a career which offered him every opportunity of displaying his military talents. The regiment which he joined was engaged against the French in the Netherlands, and took a distinguished part in all the actions of that campaign. There could not be a better school for war, nor one more likely to give great personal experience than the Austrian army of that day.

After a few months' service Tettenborn was made a lieutenant, and found numerous opportunities of showing his courage and of acquiring experience. The cavalry readily followed one who proved himself an able and determined leader, and whose courage was an example to the common soldier. Daring and success in these frequent encounters, of which history takes no note, are very often of more consequence than greater battles to the troops engaged in them. They learn in them to know the merit and value of their leaders.

The course of the campaign in the Netherlands and on the Rhine is well known. Tettenborn's regiment went through it all, and after various changes formed part of the army under the command of the brave Archduke Charles in 1799.

After an army has been dispersed or destroyed, there is little inclination to recognise any merit in the vanquished; but it is exactly during such a period of misfortune that the courage and endurance of individual troops and their leaders come most prominently into play. Without being able to give a different turn to the event, they place limits to the mischief, and recover in part what had been lost as a whole. In that unlucky campaign which led to the battle of Hohenlinden, many such individual traits of courage were displayed: the light troops especially distinguished themselves, and Tettenborn was the most active and successful of all. In the battle of Hohenlinden, Tettenborn was one of the last who left the field, and was in the rear guard which covered the retreat of the left wing.

He had meanwhile been promoted to the command of a

P

squadron, and retired out of active service to his quarters in Bohemia, with the reputation of a bold dashing officer. During peace his personal qualities won for him the love and respect of a large society, while he likewise enjoyed that of the narrower circle of his own regiment. With an agreeable, happy nature, a most winning courtesy, a fine person, and boundless generosity, Tettenborn could not fail to succeed in the brilliant society of Prague and Vienna, of Dresden or Berlin, and in the sumptuous country-houses of the Bohemian nobles. Women, play, and all the youthful passions gave rise to various adventures, of which he was the hero.

In 1805 the contest recommenced between France and Austria, and it soon became manifest, from the succession of defeats, that the hopes of Austria were again doomed to be deceived. Tettenborn remained in Ulm with one division of his regiment, while another had gone with the colonel to Bregenz. Thus he had the command of several reconnoitring and attacking parties, all of which he conducted to the satisfaction of his chiefs. But when General Mack, the commander-in-chief of the army, seized with an incomprehensible, blind, and sudden panic, saw no safety but in the surrender of Ulm, one portion of his army managed to escape this ignominy. The Archduke Ferdinand boldly determined to cut his way through the enemy with such of the cavalry as he could collect in the hurry of the moment, and to make his escape into Bohemia. Such was the confidence already reposed in Tettenborn that no one was deemed better fitted than he to lead the troops selected to form the advanced guard; and the important business of breaking through the French lines was entrusted to him. The whole undertaking, by dint of extraordinary skill and determined courage, succeeded. This movement in the rear of the French army was accompanied with incessant danger, until, after several forced marches and some engagements with the rear guard of the enemy, the Austrians at length reached the Bohemian frontiers. Tettenborn was then directed to cover the roads which lead from Waldmünchen into Bohemia, and, by skilful movements and constant skirmishing, he contrived for several weeks to maintain his position in the upper palatinate.

We will not follow Tettenborn's career in Petersburg or in Paris, whither after the treaty of Vienna he accompanied Prince Schwarzenberg as secretary and adjutant. It is sufficient to say that in 1812, when war appeared inevitable between France and Russia, and when it was evident that Austria would not take the field against France, Tettenborn, in order not to serve with the French, gave up his brilliant prospects, and made his way through Hungary into Russia. He entered the Russian service as lieutenant-colonel, and joined the troops of General von Wintzengerode, who had been ordered to cover the road from Twer.

After the retreat of the French from Moscow Tettenborn was sent thither with the advanced guard of Kutusoff's troops. Fearful scenes of violence were taking place in the midst of the smoking ruins, and he had great difficulty in restoring some sort of order. Tettenborn was then ordered to harass the French in every way during their retreat, and a separate detachment was given him for the purpose. He did this with such signal success, that the commander-in-chief, to enable him to pursue this object with greater advantage, increased the number of his troops very considerably. By this means Tettenborn had it in his power to render essential service to the Russians, as the circumstances of that memorable retreat enabled the leader of a flying body of horse to face many difficulties, which, in ordinary campaigns, and with a larger body of troops, would have been insuperable. He daily harassed the enemy during the retreat as far as the Beresina, hanging upon their rear, and taking a number of men, cannon, powder and baggage waggons. He was then sent to Lepel to disperse the Bavarians, but they had already retreated. He then pursued his march with all speed towards Wilna, where he arrived late in the evening, with his cavalry quite tired out: nevertheless he made 3000 prisoners and took possession of the suburbs.

Wilna had been one of the great stations of the French, and it was the point upon which the remains of the French army now directed their retreat: they hoped there to find reinforcements, military stores, and final relief from the horrors of hunger, cold, and death. But this expectation was vain; they found no safety there, no hope of opposing a successful resistance to the advancing Russians. The French were forced to continue their retreat under the same terrible wants and privations as before: even the Vistula scarcely seemed to oppose a barrier to their relentless pursuers. However, if Wilna could not long hold out against the regular attack of infantry, yet the town contained such numerous bodies of French troops, and such abundant provisions and stores, that the enemy could easily find time, before the arrival of the Russian infantry, to place every thing in a good state of defence, to destroy the useless stores, and to transport a large portion of their disorganised troops over the Vistula. It was, therefore, of the greatest importance to the ultimate success of the whole campaign, to give the French no breathing time. Tettenborn, accordingly, allowed no difficulties to stop him, and in spite of the doubts and advice of others, determined upon an immediate attack:—before daylight a company of chasseurs, whom he had caused to be transported on sleighs, stormed the gates of the town, and having taken them, he made his way by two different entrances into the principal streets at the head of three regiments of cossacks and four squadrons of huzzars. The French at first made a vigorous resistance, but when they found themselves attacked on all sides, they either laid down their arms or fled. The attack was so sudden that the French had no time to form any plans, and the town was soon in the hands of the Russians. The Jews, who every where in Poland were strongly opposed to the French, fell upon them in the rear, disarmed, and took many prisoners.

The loss sustained by the French was enormous. They lost at Wilna forty-eight guns, seven standards, 6000 prisoners, besides 24,000 sick who were in the hospitals. A large quantity of military stores likewise fell into the hands of the Russians. Thus, the last stronghold of the retreating army was utterly lost. "From this moment," said Napoleon, in a despatch he dictated to General Montholon, "began the real losses of this campaign. Nothing could be more unforeseen than this misfortune at Wilna."

Tettenborn gave up the town to General Tschaplitz, who had appeared with Admiral Tschitschakoff's advanced guard, and on the same day marched towards the Niemen, to prevent the junction of Marshal Macdonald, who was at Mittau, with Murat, who was collecting the scattered troops at Königsberg.

Tettenborn then proceeded to Tilsit, where he was received with the greatest joy by the inhabitants.

The armistice concluded between Prussia and Russia now permitted Tettenborn to use all his forces in the pursuit of Marshal Macdonald, who had continued his retreat, without even stopping in Königsberg.

Tettenborn kept his bed some days at Königsberg, owing to an attack of erysipelas in the foot, the consequence of over exertion and exposure to the cold in this extraordinary winter campaign. Meanwhile, it had been matter of doubt whether it would be advisable to continue the pursuit. First the Niemen, and subsequently the Vistula, were fixed upon as the utmost limits: it was feared that the further we advanced from the Russian frontiers, the smaller would be our advantages over the French. Moreover, the troops who were in immediate pursuit of the French were but few, and the numbers of those who were advancing behind them had been decreased by constant fighting, by losses during the march, and by being obliged to send detachments elsewhere. On the other hand, the French were every day drawing near their enormous stores, and were masters of great part of Germany. The possession of all the strong places from the Vistula to the Rhine gave the French the opportunity of collecting their scattered forces in perfect security, and of drawing reinforcements from France and its allies. These apprehensions, however, turned out to be vain. The French army was completely disorganised; fear and discouragement had a greater effect than war; resistance in the open field was despaired of; the army continued to retreat, and the pursuers rapidly followed. Under these circumstances, to which we must add the awakened spirit of Germany and the increased diplomatic activity, the Russians received general orders to advance, and it was uncertain where they were to stop.

In consequence of this change, Tettenborn, who meanwhile had become a colonel, was directed by General von Wittgenstein to cross the Vistula with his detachment, and to advance as far as he could. Tettenborn was so overjoyed in being the first to announce to his countrymen that the domination of the French was at an end, that, in spite of his erysipelas, he left Königsberg without delay, and pursued his march, by Konitz and Soldin, as far as the Oder. A considerable number of French troops still remained on the right bank of the Oder, the fortresses were strongly garrisoned, and the main body of the Russians were a long way in the rear. Nevertheless Tettenborn determined to cross over to the left bank of the Oder, so as to give the French no time to make new plans, and to counteract any they might already have devised.

He crossed the river at Wrietzen, and then advanced rapidly upon Berlin, which Marshal Augereau held with 10,000 French, and a numerous park of artillery. General Poinsot was sent with 2000 men as far as Werneuchen, about nine miles from Berlin, against the Russians, to keep them away from the town, which was already in a state of insurrection. As the French had no cavalry, and the Russians no infantry, both laboured under great disadvantages : one party could not maintain their ground in the field, while the other could not undertake any attack against towns or strong places. Tettenborn did not like to have advanced thus far for nothing, and invited General Tschernyscheff, who was still on the other side of the Oder, to join him. That general agreed, crossed the Oder with his cossacks and huzzars, and formed a junction with Tettenborn at Landsberg. Tettenborn left some troops behind at Werneuchen, so as to keep General Poinsot in ignorance as to his departure, while the two Russian commanders advanced upon Berlin.

The storming of Berlin was, however, prevented by some unfavourable circumstances ; but accident very nearly brought it about. The Russians had just reached Pankow, when a strong reconnoitering party of French happened to meet them, and Tettenborn sent some cossacks to drive them off. The French were thrown into confusion, and attempted to retreat into Berlin. Tettenborn, however, pursued them with such impetuosity as to enter the town with them, mastering the guard at the gate. In an instant Berlin was full of cossacks, and had become the scene of battle. Tettenborn advanced as far as the Alexander-platz, where some French troops had assembled, and were offering a vigorous and steady resistance. The cossacks meanwhile had made about 500 prisoners, and seized many horses; and, to the consternation of the French, and the joy of the inhabitants of Berlin, were galloping through the streets. Although the French had 8000 men in Berlin, many of whom were under arms; although cannon was placed on several of the bridges, and in various places; yet such was the surprise of the enemy, that for some time all these preparations were useless : many a musket was fired into the air, and the shots seldom reached the cossacks. The people were excited, and might at any moment rise against the French; there wanted only a leader to make a good use of the opportunity. But as the cossacks were not assisted by the Russian troops, who remained outside the town, Marshal Augereau found time to collect his troops in the Wilhelmstrasse, and advanced with such numbers, supported by artillery, as to force Tettenborn to quit the town, of which he had held possession for three hours. He retreated almost without loss; and the French, in spite of their superior numbers, did not venture to follow him.

Although this bold stroke failed in its object, it produced a very strong impression in favour of the Russian arms, and showed what might be done if all were inspired with the same determined spirit; and the affair was looked upon as one of the most brilliant feats of arms of the campaign. The whole exploit cost the lives of a few cossacks, who lost their way in the streets, and found their retreat cut off.

After Marshal Augereau had withdrawn General Poinsot from Werneuchen, he held possession of Berlin and of the left bank of the Spree for several days, in order to collect all the scattered troops which the Viceroy of Italy, Pince Eugene, was bringing from the Oder. By this means he found himself at the head of 16,000 men. With these reinforcements, and being now provided with some cavalry, the French ventured to make frequent sallies from Berlin, and bloody encounters daily took place before the gates, in which the few remaining French guards were destroyed by the cossacks. This state of things continued until the Russian infantry had crossed the Oder and were advancing upon Berlin, whereupon the French fell back upon Magdeberg and Wittemberg. Tettenborn entered Berlin at the head of his troops, and was received with loud acclamations. The cossacks attacked the retreating French, whose rear guard they reached before it quitted the town, and followed closely upon their traces.

Tettenborn was again obliged to keep his bed at Berlin, as the erysipelas had been much increased by exposure to cold and excitement; but this did not prevent his restless spirit from devising new schemes. For some time the attention of the Russians had been directed towards Hamburg: besides the motives for an attack in that quarter in a military point of view, the political ones were equally strong; among these might be mentioned the effect to be produced upon Denmark, the advantage of opening a communication with England, and the impression which the opening of this important commercial town must make in St. Petersburg. It was well known that discontent prevailed in Hamburg; and that the French, who had only a small force there, did not in the least expect an attack. Nevertheless, this expedition against Hamburg would never have taken effect, cogent as were the reasons in its favour, had not Tettenborn been present, the best and most enterprising partizan leader of the day, who did not hesitate to advance with a small detachment some hundred miles from head quarters, and to commence a series of operations, the result of which no one could foresee. He described his plans and resources, and showed what measures he thought necessary for their success — and all were approved. He received the proper orders and instructions, and on the 12th March he left Berlin, at the head of five regiments of cossacks, two squadrons of huzzars, two of dragoons, and two pieces of light artillery. A report, which greatly exaggerated the number of his troops, went before him, raising the spirits of his friends as much as it depressed that of his enemies.

CHAPTER XVII.

State of the North of Germany in 1813.—Riots in Hamburg.—Executions.—Excitement of the People.—Tettenborn at Ludwigslust.—Encounters General Morand.—Arrival of the cossacks in Hamburg.—Tettenborn's Triumphal Entry into the Town.—Joy of the Inhabitants.—Tettenborn's Measures for the Defence of Hamburg.—Spread of the Insurrection.—Inefficiency of the Hamburg Authorities.—The Approach of the French.—Their Defeat at Lüneburg.—The French quit the Elbe.—Negotiation with Denmark.—The French advance upon Lüneburg and Haarburg.—Fresh Preparations for the Defence of Hamburg.—Attack upon Wilhelmsburg.—The Danes enter Hamburg, but receive Orders to withdraw again.—They are succeeded by the Swedes, who are likewise ordered to withdraw.—Desperate Condition of Hamburg.—Tettenborn retreats to Lauenburg.

The excitement which prevailed throughout the whole of the north of Germany in the beginning of 1813 had reached its height, and some violent commotions could not but arise out of this state of suspense. The hatred against the French domination had been fearfully increased by every means which severity, interference, cunning, and bribery could devise; this manifested itself more openly when the miserable remnant of the grand army announced a defeat in Russia for which neither the experience nor the imagination of man could find a parallel. Further statements, instead of diminishing, added to the loss of the French. Napoleon had brought upon his own army a destruction more complete than any he had inflicted on his enemies. Every one now felt that the day of freedom had arrived: the only difficulty was how to take advantage of it. Those countries more especially which had become French or Westphalian departments had the greatest inducement to throw off the yoke; but deprived of their legitimate rulers, without connection or confidence in one another, they felt their own weakness and separation too severely to take up arms except in conjunction with others. They therefore looked with the greater eagerness to the approach of the victorious Russians.

But the impatience of the oppressed people was too great to allow them to wait even for this. The long-repressed hatred broke its bounds in a French province, in a town far removed from Russian assistance,—in Hamburg—where the French domination was more peculiarly intolerable from the degree of freedom which the town had previously enjoyed. A riot occurred on the 24th of February, before the Altona gate, from the following trifling cause: a large crowd had collected, owing to the harsh manner in which the French douaniers had searched those entering the town; at length, full of confidence in their strength, the mob proceeded to attack these hated ministers of a foreign power, mastered and disarmed them, destroyed the guard-house, and tore down a long row of strong palisades which served to bar the entrance into the town. The victorious people then rushed furiously through all the streets of Hamburg, vowed death and destruction to the French, sought out the French employés, who for the most part had fled or concealed themselves, plundered their dwellings, demolished all the insignia of the French government, and called down execration on Napoleon and his abettors. But as the excited masses were not guided by any one who could give this passionate outbreak any fixed plan or purpose, the tumult by degrees spent its force in the darkness of the night. On the following day business was resumed, as if nothing had happened. Some few Danish huzzars, who had been called into the town at the pressing invitation of the French officials, restored order in some measure, and protected the authorities, without acting harshly towards the people, who, perceiving this, treated the soldiers well, in order to prove to them that they did not consider them in the same light as the French. The latter could not show themselves without being exposed to ill usage. Even the French were forced to admit, much to their shame and annoyance, that, in the midst of all this hostility against them among the lower orders, there was something more than coarse violence and love of plunder,—there was a general hatred, which could neither be kept down nor appeased. No man's property was injured, no excess of any kind was committed by the people, that was not directed against French domination. During the plundering of some store of money, people almost in rags had thrown out the booty to be scrambled for by the mob in the streets, and the money was for the most part restored on the following day.

Nevertheless, by good management, activity, and prudence, the French were still enabled to retain possession of their power, and shortly afterwards completely to regain the upper hand. They summoned the principal citizens to their councils, entrusted them with considerable powers, and restored to them the weapons of which they had previously been deprived. The citizens were by no means anxious to undertake military duty: they were well aware that their arms were restored to them less with a view to their own security than to that of the French authorities: nevertheless, they received the weapons, which were almost forced upon their acceptance, in the hope of soon being able to use them after their own fashion, and against their real enemies. Meanwhile, however, they were content to strengthen their enemies, who had now succeeded in filling men's minds with such distrust of one another, that the French ventured to seize and, after a short trial, to shoot a certain number of the ringleaders in the riot. This, however, had the effect of rousing the people from their state of torpor, and on the following day it was impossible to continue the executions. The whole population was in fearful excitement. The position of the French daily became more precarious: they felt that they could trust neither their Danish allies, nor the citizens of Hamburg: there were no French troops near at hand, nor were any expected to arrive from a distance. Convinced that they could not maintain possession of Hamburg, and yet fearful of being accused of yielding too soon, they gave way by turns to terror, anger, hope, and anxiety; they did not even venture to send out scouts, for fear of putting the people on their guard. Meanwhile, this state of suspense was fast approaching its termination.

On the 14th of March, Tettenborn had reached Ludwigslust, at the head of an advanced body of cossacks, and by his prudent, but determined conduct, had compelled the duke of Mecklenburg-Schwerin to desert the French alliance and to declare for Russia. This first example of a German prince, who dared to throw off the forced dominion of a foreign ruler, and to subject himself to every sort of danger for the sake of his country's honour and freedom, showed to all the north of Germany what should be done, and had great effect in Hamburg; it proved that a decisive day was not far distant.

After this important gain, Tettenborn advanced further, and had reached Lauenburg on the 15th, when he received accounts which, for the moment, interfered with his whole plan, and made him doubt whether the attempt upon Hamburg should not be at once given up.

While Tettenborn was advancing upon Hamburg by way of Mecklenburg, the French general, Morand, was likewise marching through the same country towards the Elbe, where the two lines of march must intersect one another; Morand had 2500 infantry, a small body of cavalry, composed chiefly of douaniers, and sixteen pieces of artillery. He had quitted Swedish Pomerania according to orders, and was sufficiently strong to stop the advance of the Russians. On arriving at Mölln, he had been alarmed at the unexpected sight of the cossacks, and ordered his troops to halt. Tettenborn did not dare to leave him in his rear, and had no choice left but to attack him at once: this, however, was dangerous, as the Russians had nothing but cavalry. Morand, however, did not wait for the attack, but, uncertain as to the strength and object of the Russians, retreated during the night upon Bergedorf, where he was joined by the French authorities, the douaniers, and others from Hamburg, whose terror had prevented them from staying any longer in the rebellious city. The French were most advantageously placed between the Russians and Hamburg, but they did not appear to be aware of the advantage of their position. Morand thought himself strong enough to be able to maintain possession of Hamburg as a good place of refuge, and meant to advance upon the town. But the Danes, alarmed lest Holstein should become the seat of war, had sent a body of troops and some pieces of artillery to protect their frontiers, and refused to allow the French to pass through their territory, in which lay the high road. On the other hand, the cross roads appeared impracticable, as the dykes had been cut by the people of Hamburg.

Under these circumstances, Morand could at any rate have

defended Bergedorf and the Vierländer, and as he had by this time learned that the Russians had nothing but cavalry, he sent 500 men and eight cannon next morning to Escheburg to oppose the Russians, who were advancing from Lauenburg. Tettenborn ordered Lieutenant Colonel Constantine von Benkendorf to attack the enemy, and harass him all the day until nightfall. The country was extremely unfavourable to the Russians: from Escheburg to Bergedorf there is but one narrow road, which was in the possession of the enemy. Towards the left, where flowed the Elbe, the country was impassable for cavalry from bogs and broken ground, and on the right it was necessary to make a large circuit. However, the cossacks found means to surmount these difficulties. Tettenborn ordered a number to dismount and to fight on foot: they crept through the broken ground close to the enemy's cannon, avoiding their fire and setting up a shout of derision, while they themselves picked off several of the French artillery men.

While these cossacks were giving the enemy employment in front, Tettenborn had sent another division some way round to Bergedorf, where Morand's head quarters were. The out-posts, to whom such an attack was wholly unexpected, were beaten back into the town, where they carried dismay and confusion with them. The French naturally concluded that the advanced troops at Escheburg were destroyed. But when Morand saw bodies of cossacks on his right flank, threatening to cut off his communication with the Elbe, he thought it more prudent not to wait for this contingency. He had already sent his heavy baggage to the other side of the Elbe, by Zollenspieker, and early on the 17th of March he himself took the same direction, in order to place his troops on the left bank of the Elbe. Tettenborn followed close upon his heels, and harassed their retreat to such a degree as to force the French to halt at about a mile from Zollenspieker. They planted a battery of six guns upon a dyke, which commanded the only road by which the Russians could advance. The cossacks again dismounted, took their carbines, and kept up the fight until Tettenborn could bring his two guns to bear upon the French from the dyke on which he was. He had only occasion to fire one, as the moment the French perceived that the Russians had cannon with them, they lost all heart for further resistance, and attempted to reach the boats which were to transport them across the river as fast as they could. In this confusion many men were cut down by the fiery cossacks, and the French lost the six pieces of cannon which were ready shipped, but could not be carried off.

The road to Hamburg was now open, and not a Frenchman was left on the right bank of the Elbe. The inhabitants of the town and of the surrounding country had passed the time while the contest was going on in the most anxious suspense. Some few, who had ridden from Hamburg to the Russian quarters at Escheburg, had witnessed the successful attack, and the account they gave on their return had excited the whole population to the most vehement joy: this was much increased by the arrival, on the 17th, of a party of cossacks in Hamburg. The mayor and his assistants now sent a deputation to the Russian commander, inviting him to take possession of the town, and recommending themselves to his favourable consideration. Tettenborn received the deputation in Bergedorf, whither he had gone after the defeat of Morand. They laid before him their ardent wishes that he would free them from the yoke of the French domination. It was now that Tettenborn, by his prudence and decision, opened the way for the freedom and independence of Hamburg, — an admirable example to the rest of Germany. He declared that the Russians might do what was requested of them by the deputation, but they might also treat Hamburg as a town taken from the enemy; the latter would probably be more to the advantage of the Russian arms, but such considerations were of no weight with him; the interests of Russia were identical with those of Germany, and these required that Hamburg should effect its own deliverance. They were therefore instantly to dismiss the French authorities, and to replace those who were in power before: he would not set foot in the town as a friend until this were done. With this answer he dismissed the deputation, among whom were several who had been in office under the old state of things. Tettenborn's orders were hardly made known before they were carried into execution. The mayor, and others appointed by the French, laid down their offices, the old forms were reestablished, and the freedom of the city was openly proclaimed.

A fresh deputation was now sent to Tettenborn with a report of what had occurred; these he recognised as true citizens of Hamburg, and promised them the Russian protection and assistance.

About mid-day of the 18th March, Tettenborn made his public entry into the city. Never was there a finer sight; the whole population lost itself in the one common feeling of joy for its recovered freedom, and cast off the whole weight of many years of oppression and misery. From the depths of their heart they gave vent to their long-restrained feelings in loud and joyous excitement. None had ever seen such an outpouring of passionate joy as was manifested by the people, nor were Germans deemed capable of so much emotion. The most trifling occurrences of this day were rendered touching and important by the feeling which everywhere prevailed. Thirty citizens had advanced to a distance of ten miles to meet the Russian troops; they rode at their head with loud shouts of joy till they entered the city. The nearer they approached the greater became the crowd, which took up and repeated the loud huzzahs. A guard of honour on horseback, placed at the so-called Letzen-Heller,—where the byeroad along which the Russians were advancing from Bergedorf joins the mainroad, which till then runs through the Danish territory,— was waiting to place itself at the head of the cavalcade: this was increased by the guild of archers. Every garden, every country-house, every lane, was filled with people; an interminable swarm of human beings met the eye in all directions. The approaching band was greeted with loud huzzahs in front, while the cheers were repeated in their rear and on all sides. Betweenwhiles the ear caught the voices of the cossacks singing their national airs. Before the gate, Tettenborn received the keys from the hands of the town authorities. At the gate itself maidens clad in white crowned him with flowers, bidding him welcome as their saviour and deliverer, while the mob loudly shouted applause. The joy and excitement had now reached its height. The crush in the town was enormous. The people formed one vast stream, which, like a river restrained within its banks, slowly forced its way through the narrow streets, and was occasionally choked up by the impediments it encountered. Every church bell was rung, guns and pistols were incessantly fired off, and every one seemed drunk with joy. "Long live the Emperor Alexander, our deliverer, our saviour!" "Huzzah," and "long live Tettenborn!" and "Wittgenstein!" "Long life to the Russians and to the cossacks!"—these cries so filled the air, that every building shook with the sound. Flags and streamers fluttered from every window; women and girls waved their handkerchiefs, hats wreathed with green were carried on swords and pikes, or thrown up into the air. Some forced themselves, to the danger of their limbs, between the horses, crowning them also with leaves, which were carried in all directions by the wind; the people even went so far as to kiss the horses in their excess of rapture. Some laughed and cried for joy, old and young raised their hands to heaven, strangers as well as acquaintances embraced, and wished each other joy, every one made friends with his bitterest enemy — a sudden fit of brotherly love took possession of all men. In many streets, pictures of the Emperor Alexander had been hung up crowned with laurel. Tettenborn drew up his horse, saluted each picture as he passed, and gave a huzzah for the emperor, which was caught up and repeated by the mob. At length, in the midst of a thousand different manifestations of delight from the crowd, Tettenborn reached his house, where the noise continued uninterrupted. This scene was the more impressive, as he who received this eager applause was not a foreign prince or commander, but a German — an adventurous leader of strange-looking horsemen, who followed him rather on account of his heroic courage than from any feeling of obedience; moreover, he was not at the head of a strong body of troops, but of a mere detachment: the times seemed almost to have returned when great things were done by small numbers, or even by the strength of one right arm. There was an illumination at night, and the zeal of the people found means to repeat, by various devices, the feelings of the day. The applause was continued in the theatre as soon as Tettenborn and his officers appeared in their box; the spectators stood up, women and all, and sung the popular song,

"To Hamburg's success!" without which the piece was not suffered to begin. This was some play improvised for the occasion, and every clap-trap was rapturously applauded. The famous actress, Sophie Schröder, came upon the stage with a Russian cockade, and was received with a storm of joy. When Tettenborn left the theatre, his horses were taken out of the carriage, and he was dragged home by the people, who then carried him on their shoulders into his house. Thus ended the greatest day of his life: he had been the hero of the people, and his name was borne far over land and sea.

On the following day appeared two proclamations, in one of which Tettenborn declared Hamburg a free port, while the other directed the seizure of all French property. He gave up to the city the goods in the custom house, which were valued at 400,000 thalers, or about 60,000*l.*, so that the property might be restored to its original possessors. This business, as well as every thing else concerning the internal management of the city, was entrusted to the old corporation. By this impartial conduct Tettenborn laid a fresh claim to the gratitude of the citizens of Hamburg, and his fame magnified on all sides.

As soon as these matters were settled, Tettenborn turned his whole attention to military arrangements. There was no time for delay; the most important business was to make preparations to meet the enemy, and to raise the population against the French. Appearances in Hamburg favoured the notion that it was no longer necessary to give the French a thought: many of the inhabitants were fully impressed with this idea, which, indeed, was now common over all Germany, where it had taken the place of the former belief in the invincible power of the French. In order to rouse them to exertion, Tettenborn issued a proclamation, on the 19th of March, in which he exhorted the people of Hamburg to draw the sword, and to chase the foreigner from the German soil, calling down shame and execration on those who, in such times as these, remained with their hands folded.

He then announced to the municipal authorities, that he had the Emperor's authority for raising a body of volunteers, both infantry and cavalry, to be called the Hanseatic Legion, who were to fight as the allies of Russia and Prussia during the remainder of the war. On the 20th of March the lists for names were opened both at Hamburg and Lübeck, which latter town Lieutenant-Colonel von Benkendorf had entered with a Russian detachment, and where he had been received with a joy and enthusiasm equal to that which had welcomed Tettenborn to Hamburg.

The numbers who entered their names as volunteers were enormous. At the end of a few days the lists contained some thousand names; several competitors were rejected whose age and infirmity had nowise damped their zeal. Distinguished young men, who had been most carefully educated, and had been used to all sorts of luxuries, enlisted as common soldiers. Many who had shortly before paid large sums to avoid the French conscription, now offered their services with joy and alacrity.

From the very first Tettenborn had told the authorities that he would have nothing to do with the payment of the legion, but would readily suggest what was necessary, leaving the rest to them. A sum of 200,000 thalers, or about 30,000*l.*, was voted for the costs of arming the troops, and a commission appointed to see to its proper expenditure. Considering the importance of the object, the smallness of the sum is remarkable. It is, moreover, worthy of remark, that the town council at first proposed only half, and that the citizens who had to pay it at once doubled the sum. But differences of opinion now showed themselves in this, and subsequently in other matters, causing the most disastrous results: they were immediately perceived, but could not be checked. The old constituted authorities were so dilatory in reforming the abuses of all sorts, that the most precious time was lost, and nothing was done. Delays occurred, difficulties were discovered, objections found, where business, if rightly treated, would have done itself. Tettenborn, at a great sacrifice of time and labour, had to direct every thing himself: he was obliged to enter into the most trifling details, and, in the end, he had to use his authority to insure things being done at all. Instead of making alliances at once with England, Denmark, and Prussia, it was only after long delays that the senate even thought of sending delegates to the Emperor Alexander. The senate was altogether unequal to what was required of it, and the energies of the people were wasted for want of union. A delay of six months might have given the senate time to combine the resources of the city into a well-organised and effective whole: but this time was not granted to the people of Hamburg.

To return to matters which occupied men's thoughts and minds in Hamburg. In spite of all obstacles, the raising of the Hanseatic Legion continued. The cannon taken from the enemy, together with some which originally belonged to the town, suggested the formation of a division of artillery, to be incorporated with the Legion. They sent to England for such arms as were wanting; gun carriages and powder waggons were built, a laboratory was established, horses were collected, all sorts of arms were made and furbished up, and other materials of war procured as rapidly as possible. This town, so rich in other resources, had scarce any appliances for war: much that was wanted had to be brought, under great difficulties, from the Danish provinces: the total ignorance of its citizens as to military affairs threw innumerable obstacles in the way, which could only be removed by incessant attention and indefatigable self-devotion. Very few officers who had seen service, and no non-commissioned officers, could be found for the newly-raised troops, which therefore had to be taught the very elements of military tactics from books. Besides the Hanseatic Legion, a battalion of Lauenburgers was raised, but these men were mostly without arms: another battalion, formed chiefly of men from Bremen and Verden, was in like manner raised in Stade, while Count Von Kielmansegge enlisted some Hanoverian chasseurs for the service of Hamburg.

Meanwhile the insurrection had spread in Haarburg, Lüneburg, Stade, and along the whole strip of country bordering the Elbe, and the people every where demanded and obtained from Tettenborn arms, instructions, and assistance. French soldiers, douaniers, even gensd'armes and officers, were daily brought in as prisoners, and it was difficult to restrain the fury of the populace, more especially against the douaniers, whom they pelted with stones and dirt. Bold fellows came from Zollenspieker, from the Billwärder, from Ochsenwärder, and the Vierländer, offering to raise the landsturm or militia, and received Tettenborn's authority and advice for so doing. Even in these provinces the weakness and inefficiency of the authorities threw many difficulties in the way which could not be surmounted without the exercise of occasional severity. The old officials, most of whom had continued to act under the French government, again resumed their duties; and did not always, with the change of the office, change the opinions which a foreign rule had instilled into them: many were the claims which had to be adjusted. The Russian general had to give his attention to subjects connected with commerce and navigation, although these were matters purely within the competence of the municipality.

The seizure of French property, and the strict watch which it was necessary to keep upon the numerous French families living in and near Hamburg, gave Tettenborn much trouble: some of these had been long settled there; but a mixed rabble from all countries, who had found their way into Hamburg during the French occupation, had lately joined them. To turn them out would have required considerable time, especially as the population of Hamburg is much mixed, and it is extremely difficult at any time to keep a sharp look out upon all parts of the town. Moreover the Hamburg government, like most free states, was very indifferent about the strangers in their town, and left all matters connected with the police entirely in the hands of the Russians.

Meanwhile some English troops from Heligoland had taken possession of Cuxhaven, and the insurrection of the peasants near Bremerlehe was promoted by all the means in their power. Tettenborn immediately placed himself in communication with the officer commanding these troops, but learnt to his mortification that, a short time before, the store of arms at Heligoland had been reshipped to England. This was a misfortune which nothing could repair. Tettenborn, however, determined to turn the connection with England to some account, and sent a Russian officer, accompanied by a Don cossack, with despatches to the Prince Regent and the Russian ambassador in London, where the appearance of the first cossack who had ever been seen in that city caused great amazement.

The Danes, from their proximity, were naturally the object of much attention to the Russians, and to the people of Hamburg. In spite of its adoption of the policy of Russia and Prussia, Denmark had two great difficulties to contend with: the Russians were allied to the English and to the Swedes; the Danes hated the former for the injuries they had lately inflicted on Denmark, and the latter for the views they were supposed to have upon Norway. The navigation of the Elbe could not be obtained without the consent of the Danes, and yet it was essential that English ships should have free access to Hamburg. The boundary between the Hamburg and the Danish territories existed only in name, and the communication between Altona and Hamburg was constant.

All these manifold duties and endless details rested entirely upon Tettenborn: he had to unite military with diplomatic talents, to attend to business of different sorts, to reconcile the prejudices of various races and governments, to decide upon political and commercial matters, to temper the immoderate zeal as well as to rouse the sluggishness of the authorities, to give audiences, to listen to consultations, to make reports, in short to be constantly occupied in one way or another. His officers in head-quarters were at work from early dawn till late at night; he himself gave the example of untiring zeal and incessant exertion. He had the art to see and seize upon material points with unerring judgment, to make a good use of accidents, to overcome obstacles, or even to turn them to advantage: with the most mature consideration few could devise better schemes than Tettenborn on the impulse of the moment.

A great number of distinguished officers had collected round Tettenborn, drawn towards him partly by his character and the fame attached to his name, partly by the cause which he had undertaken. All this called to mind old times, when troops followed their leader more from affection than from discipline. Besides the Russian officers who more immediately belonged to his little army or to his staff, there were many others who had obtained leave from their superiors to fight under his banner. Men of noble family came from Russia, Austria, Oldenburg, Hanover, from Mecklenburg and from the neighbouring districts; but the Russians were the most numerous. Albert de Staël, a lieutenant in a Swedish regiment of hussars, had been sent on special service to Hamburg, and obtained permission to remain some time with Tettenborn. Many of these volunteers had commissions given them in the newly raised troops, but the greater number of their officers were taken from among the inhabitants themselves. This numerous and brilliant company was daily increased by the visits of officers, who, belonging to other detachments, stopped awhile with Tettenborn, to take part in the battles and expeditions.

The variety and quantity of business to be got through required more hands than could be found, especially where so many were wanted for active service. In this, however, the cossacks left little to be done, and gave the newly-raised troops sufficient time to learn their trade. For the various and heavy duties of government, for the constantly recurring negociations and deliberations, for the obtaining supplies, for calculating the advantages or disadvantages arising from ever-varying circumstances — for all these labours there were but few men left. Unfortunately many duties requiring the supervision and watch of the higher authorities were left to the discretion of subordinates, and errors were frequently committed, which were not discovered until it was too late to remedy them: all this Tettenborn had to learn by bitter experience.

The same things occurred in Lübeck as in Hamburg, excepting that the change was made more quietly from the population being smaller and less crowded together. The spirit of order and the intelligence of the inhabitants of Lübeck appeared even in the troops which this town contributed to the Hanseatic Legion; the men were superior in manner and bearing to those of Hamburg. The numbers who offered to serve proved the spirit which prevailed in Lübeck. The zeal for the good cause was not only shown in the amount but in the nature of the contributions which poured in from all sides to assist in procuring arms: the women zealously co-operated by offering their last remaining jewels, which indeed could never adorn them so well as the noble sentiments which they now displayed.

Meanwhile Tettenborn had sent one half of his cavalry across the Elbe on the road towards Bremen. The French general Morand, who had needlessly drawn back his troops as far as the

CHAP. XVII.] THE APPROACH OF THE FRENCH. 223

Weser, now seemed inclined to retrieve his error, and advanced, most probably in obedience to higher instructions, towards the Elbe: he even hinted that he intended again to occupy Hamburg. The cossacks hovered about the closed ranks of the infantry, giving them plenty of occupation and annoyance, without, however, stopping their march. As the enemy advanced the cossacks gave way, and the French re-entered the districts which had taken arms against them. The news of the approach of the French excited the greatest consternation and anxiety in Hamburg; those who escaped from the left bank of the Elbe brought dismay and terror with them. All men had given themselves up too completely to the intoxication of happiness not to be utterly unprepared for a change so sudden as this: they were so overwhelmed by it that it was necessary, in order to calm their fears, to say some words of comfort, if they could be uttered with any show of truth. Tettenborn, therefore, issued a proclamation on the 27th of March, in which he declared that the tocsin was sounded in all directions, that the peasantry were up in arms, led by officers and supported by 600 cossacks, and that he would answer for their success. He urged the men of Hamburg not to fear 20,000 of the enemy, much less the few hundreds without cavalry, who would soon be surrounded and cut to pieces. He further told them that the enemy was not in a condition to undertake any enterprise: on the contrary, that the Russian generals Tschernyscheff, Benkendorff, and Dörnberg, had already crossed the Elbe on the 23d, had driven back all the enemy's outposts, and had advanced their own as far as Salzwedel.

Never was an assurance of this sort so brilliantly verified. People were quite willing to hope, but no one expected the fulfilment of these promises. When it was known that a good many Saxon troops were in Morand's army, Tettenborn published an address to them, calling upon them to leave the enemy. He told them that they were deceived and betrayed, that they were surrounded by thousands of cossacks and chasseurs, and that the peasants were every where up in arms: moreover, that the Russian and Prussian army was advancing upon their country; that Davoust had blown up their beautiful bridge in Dresden, to revenge a few stones thrown against General

Regnier's windows, and a few threats uttered against some insolent Frenchmen. He ended by telling them that every one taken with arms in his hands would be sent into Siberia, while those who left the enemy would be treated as brothers.

But before Tettenborn could form the citizens of Hamburg into a burgher guard, the enemy met with a sudden reverse. The English-Hanoverian general Dörnberg, at the head of a body of 2000 Russians and Prussians, had crossed the Elbe at Werben on the 14th of March, but had been forced, by the superior numbers of the enemy, to retreat to the right bank of the river. Meanwhile General Morand had advanced with 3000 men and eleven guns to Lüneburg, whence the inhabitants, with the assistance of fifty cossacks, had shortly before driven out a French squadron which had attempted to take possession of the town. A hard fate seemed to await the unfortunate city, and no help appeared at hand. The French had scarce entered the town before they singled out their victims, who were to be shot in the forenoon of the 2d of April. But General Dörnberg had meanwhile formed a junction with Tschernyscheff and Benkendorf, recrossed the Elbe, and advanced straight upon Lüneburg. They entered the town just in time to hinder the enemy's intentions, and proceeded to attack them with vigour. The French defended themselves bravely, but when General Morand was mortally wounded, and no way of escape was left, the enemy laid down their arms. Tettenborn had meanwhile sent a body of 600 cossacks to the rear of the French, thus cutting off their retreat in that direction. A more complete victory, and a more brilliant affair, can scarcely be conceived. The troops showed the greatest courage, and had not only beaten but destroyed an enemy superior in numbers, and in a strong position. The inhabitants had borne a share in the engagement, and had cut down several Frenchmen. The intrepidity of a Lüneburg girl, Johanna Stegen, was much admired: during the heaviest fire she carried powder and shot to the Prussian chasseurs.

Dörnberg's victory at Lüneburg caused the greatest joy in Hamburg: even the most faint-hearted were reassured, and inspired with fresh zeal for the affairs of their country. This event gave an impulse to every thing which had been kept in a state of suspense and uncertainty. The two delegates now seriously thought of starting on their journey to see the Emperor Alexander.

Nevertheless, this failure of the French in their attempt to fix themselves firmly in the district of the Lower Elbe caused Tettenborn to fear that they might try again, and meet with better success. Moreover, the progress of the war in Saxony no longer afforded those brilliant hopes, which had been cherished, of soon seeing Germany free as far as the Rhine. Hamburg was thus exposed to considerable danger, and it became necessary to strain every nerve to maintain a conquest which the cossacks had so brilliantly achieved. But no reinforcements could be obtained from Saxony; and Tettenborn was obliged to fall back upon those resources which he had himself called into existence. Besides the 500 Mecklenburg grenadiers whom he had procured by his own personal influence from the Duke of Mecklenburg, a body of 200 Russians was sent to join him. Of the Hanoverian troops who were being organised as speedily as possible under Tettenborn's inspection, some were not yet fit for service, while others had already gone to the Elbe, where they were destined to form a special division of the northern army, under the command of General Count Von Walmoden. These considerations induced Tettenborn to redouble his activity, so as to get the Hanseatic troops ready to take the field. A citizen of Hamburg had at his own expense equipped a squadron chiefly composed of butchers' apprentices, he having once been a master butcher himself. As he was utterly unfit for the command, some petty office in the staff was given him, by which his vanity was more hurt than flattered. A battery of six pieces and another of horse artillery were organised by Captains Wertheim and Spooreman, but besides these two officers who served as volunteers not a third was to be found in all Hamburg fit for this duty! It was equally difficult to procure artillerymen capable of serving the guns, as mere raw recruits would not do in this as in other branches of the army. Nearly every thing connected with this service was wanting, and had to be obtained elsewhere at great cost and trouble. Not only was there a deficiency of muskets, but even sabres and pistols were obtained with great difficulty. In the hurry the foot soldiers were at first armed with pikes, and some squadrons of horse received lances, which they afterwards kept in preference to sabres.

The burgher guard, armed at first chiefly with pikes and some few muskets, was constantly exercised, and gradually learned its business: whatever was ridiculous about it quickly disappeared before the serious nature of its purpose. Had there been but 1000 Prussians, or other experienced soldiers among them, the recruits, who required only instruction and example, would soon have been equal to old soldiers. But the troops which could serve as an example to the Hanseatic Legion and to the burgher guard were but few, and were, moreover, generally employed elsewhere.

General Morand's movement, which had ended in the defeat at Lüneburg, was not so totally without plan as it would at first appear. It was subsequently proved that other troops were to have advanced simultaneously from the Elbe, and that Lüneburg was the point where they were to meet. General Montbrun entered Lüneburg on the 4th April, with 4000 men, Davoust was to follow with the main body, but instead of General Morand they found traces of his defeat. Dörnberg had fallen back upon Boitzenberg in order to defend the passage of the Elbe, which he suspected the enemy would attempt. Hamburg was again in danger: the city might be called unfortified in spite of its walls, as the breast-works and gates were destroyed, and the bridges bricked up: there was no cannon, and the garrison consisted mainly of cavalry; thus the inhabitants were filled with alarm. Tettenborn immediately took such measures as the circumstances seemed to require: the troops were got ready, the weak points guarded, and where the country could be flooded, every thing was prepared for laying it under water at a moment's notice. Most fortunately also at this juncture some thousand muskets arrived from England, which were immediately distributed among the troops. Meanwhile, the cossacks were frequently engaged in successful skirmishes, and prisoners and stragglers were constantly brought into Hamburg. The enemy did not find it advisable to remain longer on the Elbe, when the communication in his rear was in danger of being interrupted every moment: they had General Morand's example before their eyes; they, therefore, quitted the river. General Montbrun evacuated Lüneburg on the 9th April, and Marshal Davoust, carefully destroying the bridges behind him, retired with all his troops behind the Aller. Tettenborn then sent the greater portion of the Russian cavalry, with two squadrons of Hanseatic horse, and two pieces of cannon towards the river, as far as the gates of Bremen.

This alarm showed the importance of protecting Hamburg from a surprise, and it was resolved to put the town into a proper state of defence. The execution of this project was not easy. Tettenborn directed Major von Pfuel carefully to inspect the place, and to fix upon the spots where works should be erected. The first line of defence was the Elbe itself, with its several islands, from the Zollenspieker to Haarburg. But it was difficult with so few troops to defend every point, and it was feared that after repeated attacks the enemy might break through a line extending some fifteen or twenty miles. The whole country is a series of lowlands, protected against the water by dykes, and intersected by numerous ditches. The district called the Billwärder could be laid under water, and would form the second line of defence, in which the position at Eichbaum was of the utmost importance. However, the chief point was the defence of the town itself, by walls and outworks; some of these were old, some were now added. The district of the Hammer Brook, which was completely flooded, rendered Hamburg inapproachable on that side as long as the bridge on the Bill was held, and here every precaution was taken. On every point which could be threatened outworks were thrown up, and a few guns planted, which, however insufficient, gave the place an appearance of defence. The main fortifications and the sally-ports were again surmounted with breast-works; outworks covered the approaches into the town, the drawbridges which had been bricked up were restored to their former condition, the earth was dug out and the moat deepened. Some forts were likewise raised on the so-called Feddel, an island on the other side of the Grasbrook.

All these works were carried on with untiring zeal to their final completion: it was wonderful how so much could have been done in so short a time. The French themselves, unwilling as they were to give the Russians credit for any thing, could not help openly praising what had been effected.

Meanwhile, in other branches of public business with which the Russian authorities were not so intimately connected, and over which they could not therefore exercise a wholesome control, the want of activity, zeal and attention, produced positive confusion, and a remedy for this state of things was sought in vain. Every one seemed perfectly aware of what was wanting, all recognised the error where it appeared, all were quite willing to assist, but were prevented from coming publicly forward by the want of a leader.

Meanwhile the Danes had made overtures to Tettenborn; and endeavoured to obtain the friendship of the Russians by courtesy. The navigation of the Elbe was not only opened to Russians and Hamburgers, but even to the English. Ships sailed to England from Altona; the hostilities between Denmark and England seemed forgotten. Even later, when the Elbe was no longer safe, owing to the number of the French privateers, the letters for England were conveyed without obstruction through Holstein to the mouth of the Elbe. But the friendly disposition of the Danes was further shown by the announcement which the Danish colonel made to Tettenborn, that he was instructed to offer all the troops under his command, whenever the general wished for them, to garrison Hamburg or Lübeck.

The meaning of this last proposal was shortly explained by a letter of Prince Sergius Dolgorouky, who had been sent by the Emperor Alexander, on the 23d of March, to negotiate with the Danish cabinet. The emperor had given instructions to his minister to propose to Denmark ample compensation for the loss of Norway, which had been ceded by treaty to Sweden, on condition that Denmark should immediately renounce the French alliance, and join her forces to those of Russia and Prussia. The Danish court entered into this arrangement, and wished to secure the Hanse Towns as part of the indemnity. Prince Dolgorouky rejoiced at the speedy success of his mission, and most desirous of at once giving the allies such an increase of forces, promised the Danes the temporary occupation of Hamburg and Lübeck: he urged Tettenborn to give the Danish troops immediate possession of these two towns, and by this means to secure their immediate services against the French. Tettenborn, by no means disposed to act in a hurry, refused to sanction a step which he could not approve, and sent a courier to head quarters to report the true position of affairs. The Emperor Alexander praised Tettenborn's correct views and prudent reserve, and ordered him to keep possession of both towns; adding, that Prince Dolgorouky, in his zeal, had exceeded his instructions. Tettenborn hereupon thanked the Danish commander with great politeness for his offer, stating that he would avail himself of it whenever circumstances should require it.

While all this was going on, after a long and most disadvantageous cessation of hostilities, there were symptoms on the Upper Elbe of great disquiet; every thing indicated a decisive advance of the army. The Swedes still held back, the Danes stood ready, but neither seemed likely to take any share in the campaign. The troops of the northern allies appeared to be a superfluous addition to the already sufficient garrison of Hamburg; the insurrection in the provinces beyond the Elbe promised plenty of materials for new armies, and rapid progress was made in raising recruits in Mecklenburg, Hamburg, and Lübeck. These and other like considerations may have been the reason why it was not considered necessary to send more troops to the Lower Elbe. On the other hand, Count Wallmoden entered Hamburg on the 17th of April, with the intention of taking the command of one division of the northern allied army; but as he found no troops save the few divisions of Tettenborn, Dörnberg, and Benkendorf, and the newly-organised, half-armed, and untried recruits, who could be of little use without an admixture of old soldiers, he had no desire to interfere, and allowed Tettenborn to manage matters in Hamburg as before. Wallmoden proceeded first to Lauenburg, and then further up the Elbe, whence he afterwards made some successful expeditions against General Sebastiani and Marshal Davoust.

Tettenborn seldom missed inspecting the Hanseatic Legion, or the Burgher Guard, and daily visited the fortifications; but these duties by no means made him lose sight of the enemy, and he sent a strong body of cavalry, with two pieces of artillery, towards the Weser. General Vandamme had been despatched by Napoleon to Bremen, where the appearance of Russian and Hanseatic troops before the gates of the town enraged him; but as he had little or no cavalry he could do nothing. The skirmishes generally ended to the advantage of the Russians, and prisoners were daily brought into Hamburg from these quarters. Tettenborn looked forward with impatience to the day when he could lead the newly-raised troops to the relief of Bremen, which had suffered so much from the enemy's hands, and restore it to the condition of a Hanse town.

Tettenborn had laboured incessantly and vigourously at the formation of these troops. In the hope of speedily seeing them in a condition to be at once led against the enemy, the colours, which had been worked by the fair hands of noble maidens of Hamburg, were ordered to be solemnly presented to the troops on the 21st of April, in the church of St. Michael. The worthy senior preacher of Hamburg, Dr. Rambach, conducted the ceremony in the presence of Wallmoden, Tettenborn, the senate, and a large though chosen assembly; all the troops in Hamburg were drawn out on parade, and the general feeling of patriotism was increased and strengthened by the pious impression produced by the holy services of the church.

Vandamme, meanwhile, suspecting that the Russians had no infantry, from their not following up their advantages, determined no longer to submit to the disgrace of being pent up in Bremen by a horde of cossacks. He advanced on the 22d of April against Ottersberg, with 3000 infantry and six guns, and drove back the advanced posts upon the main body at Rothenburg: the cossacks could make no impression on the dense masses of infantry; and although they hovered round and harassed them, they could not prevent their advance. But scarcely had Benkendorf rallied the troops, which had been driven back upon Rothenburg, when he fell with impetuosity upon the advancing French at the head of his whole cavalry and a few pieces of artillery, put the enemy to flight, and pursued them without intermission to the gates of Bremen. The fire of his guns was directed against the retreating French, killing and wounding above 300 men, while the cossacks took above 100 prisoners, and all the baggage which had accompanied the expedition.

This check, however, did not prevent the enemy, confident of their great superioty in infantry and artillery, from making so decisive a movement as to compel the Russians to retire altogether from the left bank of the Elbe. The latter, fortunately, had timely notice of the intentions of the French. The Hanoverian post-master at Soltau had killed a French courier, who gave himself out as the bearer of important despatches, and sent the papers to Tettenborn at Hamburg. From these it appeared that the enemy meditated a repetition, only with a larger number of troops, of the attack which had formerly failed owing to Morand's discomfiture at Lüneburg. Marshal Davoust advanced with 12,000 from the Weser on Lüneburg, while General Sebastiani marched with 8000 men from his position half way down the Elbe, towards Giffhorn. The whole of the allied forces in this district were not equal to one of these French divisions, still less would they be able to compete with the enemy when they had effected their junction; the Russian cavalry were therefore obliged immediately to fall back from the Weser upon the right bank of the Elbe, if they wished to escape being cut off. To prevent the enemy from attempting to follow, all the boats were brought over to the right bank of the Elbe or destroyed. The islands and fords were closely watched, and here and there protected by cannon.

Marshal Davoust had now joined his forces with those of General Sebastiani, and they both remained for some time, undetermined what to do, in the neighbourhood of Haarburg and Lüneburg. But as they did not venture to pass the Elbe, nothing further remained for General Sebastiani to do but to return with his troops to Magdeburg, while Marshal Davoust retained possession of Lüneburg and Winsen, watching and threatening the principal passages over the Elbe. He likewise sent strong detachments to Stade and Cuxhaven, so as to secure these two places, whereupon the English retired on board an English man-of-war which was lying off Cuxhaven.

From this time Hamburg was exposed to terrible trials, and its destruction became daily more imminent. The French were so superior in numbers that it was impossible to carry on a successful defence by means of attacking parties; the besieged were doomed for a long time merely to measure their movements and proceedings by those of the enemy.

The French advanced towards the Elbe with great caution: several days passed before Davoust ventured to remove his head-quarters from Winsen to Haarburg. Tettenborn had carefully removed from the opposite side of the Elbe all possible means of transport, in order to throw all the difficulties he could in their way; but the wide district from Cuxhaven to Haarburg, with all its islands, rivers, and creeks, had not undergone so vigilant a search but that some vessels escaped detection, or were perhaps conveyed back to the other side of the river. Moreover, it was almost impossible to ensure obedience in a district of which every inhabitant is by nature a sailor, and even the daily necessaries of life are conveyed by the peasantry to market in boats. In most places the Russians could merely give the orders, without being able to spare men to see them carried into execution; and a large portion of the coast, — the whole length of Holstein, belonging to Denmark, — was not bound to obey the Russian commander. Notwithstanding this, the French at first found great difficulty in obtaining any boats, and when they had succeeded in getting together a few, they saw them carried off by a detachment of Mecklenburgers despatched for the purpose by Tettenborn. However this did not deter them from procuring others; and from the zeal with which they transported them in carts from the interior it was easy to judge how much in earnest they were. They had seized a certain number of boats from the Este, and had pressed the peasantry of the surrounding country into their service to convey these boats to Haarburg. During the night of the 5th of May about 100 Mecklenburgers effected a landing in spite of the fire of the French, and put them to flight with the loss of several killed and wounded. The people whom the French had pressed into their service were set at liberty and allowed to return to their homes, but the vessels were taken away. A schipper, who had a Frenchman on board to superintend his going to Haarburg, shut him in the cabin while he was sea-sick, and said that, as the French talked of going to Hamburg, he would take his passenger there at once. At length, after endless trouble and repeated annoyances, the enemy got together a few vessels; and as these were not enough, they constructed a certain number of rafts to assist in transporting the troops over to the other side. Marshal Davoust now returned to Bremen, leaving the management of the affair to Vandamme.

Tettenborn's task was to defend Hamburg to the last extremity; the importance of the town, duty towards the inhabitants, and the orders from head-quarters left him no choice, as long as there was any chance of holding out. Tettenborn now sent the greater portion of the cavalry out of the town, where they were only in the way, and distributed the infantry, consisting of about 3300, in various positions about the island of Wilhelmsburg, the Ochsenwärder, the Zollenspieker, and the Hooper fortress. There were only about 3000 of the burgher guard out of the nominal 7200 who could be turned out properly armed. Of the heavy cannon which still remained in the arsenal, two four-and-twenty-pounders were mounted on gun carriages; one was planted at the Zollenspieker, the other on the extremity of the island of Wilhelmsburg looking towards Haarburg: at each of these places were likewise planted two smaller cannons and a howitzer. Several vessels were armed and manned as speedily as possible: a cutter with six small guns lay off Haarburg, another vessel of the same force off the Zollenspieker, and the Haarburg yacht, carrying eight guns, lay in the harbour. The men on board these vessels knew as little of the duties in a vessel of war as their commanders, and this circumstance lessened their value in a service where more than any other skill and judgment are necessary to render courage available. Meanwhile every thing was prepared to flood the country when required, and the fortifications were vigorously continued; Tettenborn also sent reports of the straits in which Hamburg was placed to Wallmoden, to the imperial head-quarters, to London, and to Stralsund, where the Crown Prince of Sweden was hourly expected. The troops of the latter power were already in Mecklenburg, and were almost equal in number to the French. From England they expected a fleet of gun-boats which Tettenborn had earnestly demanded, as necessary to ensure the command of the Elbe and its many islands.

Every movement of the French army was watched from the top of St. Michael's tower; their drilling, and all their preparations were observed; even the number of cannon counted before they were conveyed to the batteries. Tettenborn thought that he could impede their labour by feigned attacks: he disturbed them at drill by occasionally throwing a few four-and-twenty-pounders into their camp, or sending out small detachments to alarm them on the other side of the Elbe.

The chances of war, however, soon outweighed these small advantages with reverses which no care or prudence could altogether prevent. By an unlucky accident, the cutter which lay off Haarburg was lost; during the ebb tide she grounded, and a party of French crept up the vessel's sides, overpowered the watch, and took the ship's company prisoners. To prevent the vessel from being of any use to the French, who immediately manned and attempted to get her afloat, the garrison at Wilhelmsburg knocked her to pieces with their four-and-twenty-pounders. The greater part of the crew were either killed or wounded, and their groans were distinctly heard.

Hamburg was now in a very dangerous position. The number of the French troops daily increased, and with their number, their boldness. They were for the most part untried new soldiers, but unfortunately the troops to whom the defence of Hamburg was entrusted were in the same predicament: the French, moreover, had the advantage of numbers, and of being the attacking party. The inhabitants of Hamburg, who instead of the pleasures and enjoyments of freedom had only its labours and tribulations, nevertheless still showed considerable zeal. But the most clear-sighted had their doubts as to the issue, and thought escape hopeless: the women and children began to leave the town, and the merchant-vessels went to Altona for safety. Trade was entirely at a stand-still; no one thought of any thing save arms and war; the lower classes especially were most zealous and active, and determined to resist to the utmost.

The confidence of the more intelligent sunk still lower when the slow advance of the allied army was announced: we first heard that a desperate battle had been fought, and then that the allies had retreated. The enemy, who had been driven back upon Bremen, again appeared in sight of Hamburg, which, in connexion with these reports, had a most depressing effect upon men's minds. It was known that Russia and Prussia were in active negotiation with Austria, and hopes were entertained that the alliance against Napoleon would be strengthened by the junction of this power. But the incessant delays tried men's patience: negotiations were endlessly protracted; those in command of the army—able as they were—seemed to pursue that system of delays which had so often ruined former enterprises. Ill-disposed people attempted even to throw suspicion on the intentions of the allies: the negotiations of Prince Dolgorouky at Copenhagen were canvassed, and there were not wanting some who maintained that Hamburg and Lübeck were actually given up to the Danes. These doubts and suspicions had a most mischievous effect in Hamburg: the former zeal was replaced by timid reserve; nay, many even endeavoured to make terms for themselves with the enemy. Most of the inhabitants, however, had gone too far to do this with any hope of success.

Tettenborn was exceedingly hampered by all these matters. The allies, moved by mature consideration, and influenced by the negotiations with Austria, had agreed among themselves no longer to excite insurrections and popular movements in Germany, but in future only to call forth the zeal and strength of the people on the advance of the allied army, and under the control of government. On this principle no attempt was made to excite the population in the districts to the rear of the French army, where, though deprived of regular troops, the people were quite ready to rise against the French: on the contrary, their ready ardour was damped. But to announce this openly was almost impossible, especially as the French had the greatest dread of these popular insurrections: indeed, it was chiefly by this means that Hamburg still maintained its independence. As Tettenborn could seldom give the people of Hamburg certain and encouraging news, as he was not authorised to rouse their zeal, and had no wish to deceive them, he was forced, at a time when they most wanted such encouragement, to be sparing with his proclamations and addresses.

In this posture of affairs the town was suddenly alarmed by hearing that the enemy had effected a landing at Wilhelmsburg, and was in full advance upon Hamburg, driving our scattered troops before him. The island of Wilhelmsburg is very flat, and so cut up by ditches that troops and artillery could only move along the dykes which, running in various directions, protect the land from the sea: in bad weather the dykes even are impassable. Owing to this, Tettenborn had always considered this southern point of the island as quite untenable in the event of an attack, from its distance from any position whence it could be succoured. But as he had been forced to plant some artillery there, so as to command Haarburg and the Elbe, he had ordered the artillerymen, in the event of their being unable to save their guns, to spike them on the spot. The northern part of the island and the so-called Feddel were the easiest to defend, and there several works had been erected. During the night of the 8th of May, General Vandamme, under cover of the darkness, had, by means of rafts, transported a strong detachment to the island of Wilhelmsburg: moreover, he had collected about 5500 men at Haarburg. Under these circumstances Count von Kielmansegge, who had the command of the island, drew back his advanced posts, and determined to concentrate his forces for the defence of the Feddel. But the enemy had unluckily surprised the outposts, and had thus been able to advance before we were even aware of their landing. The disorder produced among the raw troops, who ran away, after firing a few shots, might have entailed the loss of the whole island; the exertions of a few able officers were for a long time vain, and in the noise and turmoil the Feddel itself was near falling into the enemy's hands. The French, however, did not venture to advance so rapidly; and on being vigorously attacked by some reinforcements sent by Tettenborn, they fell back, setting fire to several houses and a mill to cover their retreat. The French were then pursued until they got under the protection of their guns, and in a short time the whole island, except the southern point, which was exposed to their fire, was cleared of them.

The French, at the same time, made an attempt upon the Ochsenwürder, and spread their forces in all directions, after overpowering the 600 men placed to defend that position; but afraid of being cut off in their turn, they did not make a long resistance against the troops sent to attack them, and retreated with a loss of 200 men.

Both these skirmishes had ended in our favour, but success could not blind either the inhabitants of Hamburg, or Tettenborn and his officers, to the weakness and difficulty of their position. Neither could this be kept altogether from the enemy's knowledge; and the French could repeat the attempt a hundred times without much disadvantage; it only cost them a few men, of whom they had a superfluity, while on the side of the Russians, even victory was fatal by diminishing the small number of their troops, and one failure at the Zollenspieker, the Ochsenwärder, or the Wilhelmsburg, would at once endanger the safety of the town. Tettenborn announced this state of affairs in all places whence he expected to receive reinforcements and support, while at the same time he made the most of the materials in his own hands.

Every thing had remained perfectly quiet during the forenoon of the 10th of May, when suddenly an alarming report arose about mid-day that some 7000 Frenchmen had established themselves in the Billwarder, and were then advancing upon the gate called the Steinthor. The drums beat an alarm in every street, the tocsin sounded, cavalry dashed here and there, all seized their arms, while crowds of fugitives, with women and children, bag and baggage, poured out of the gate on the road towards Altona, which was considered the nearest place of safety. The burgher guard assembled on parade in greater numbers than at any time when they had been summoned for drill. The peaceable, commercial, and luxurious town of Hamburg seemed now to have nothing but steel instead of gold. When all were ready to march against the enemy, it was discovered that the noise only arose from a slight skirmish, in which a few shots had been exchanged, and that not a Frenchman was to be found on the Hamburg side of the Elbe. Meanwhile Tettenborn had ridden to the so-called Letzer Heller, which seemed the point most threatened, and made all arrangements necessary to meet the coming danger; but every thing remained perfectly quiet. The Danes, although their zeal had cooled in the meanwhile, and they were aware that some change had taken place in the views of their court, had as yet received no positive counter orders, and were bound by former promises to assist in the defence of Hamburg. Tettenborn, fully aware of the insufficiency of his own means, and without hope of obtaining succours from any other quarter, was compelled by this tumult to demand assistance of the Danes, which he would only have done in the utmost need, from fear of not being able to get rid of his new allies when once they had entered the town. Tettenborn commenced the negotiation with Lieutenant-Colonel von Huffner, the commandant at Altona, and with General von Wegener, who commanded 3000 men in the district of Schiffbeck, and succeeded so well in spite of manifold difficulties, that General von Wegener entered Hamburg in the evening, and promised to afford all that Tettenborn required.

On the following day, the 11th of May, every thing remained perfectly quiet. Lieutenant-Colonel Revest, one of General Vandamme's staff, came with proposals from the French authorities, and was met by two Russian officers at the entrance of the harbour, whence they accompanied him to the Baumhaus. His request to see Tettenborn was at once refused, and he was forced to content himself with delivering a letter from General Vandamme, and saying what he had to say to the two officers. He began with the most pompous mention of the victory which Napoleon had gained at Lützen, and ended with the demand that the Russians should give up possession of Hamburg, so as not to expose this important town to destruction. Tettenborn found the letter after returning from a round of inspection, and refused to see the French officer, but returned an answer to the letter which he had brought. The people were rejoiced that Tettenborn would not give him an audience; and although the object of his mission was not known, it was currently reported that his demands had been bluntly refused.

On the 11th the Danes actually entered Hamburg, to the unspeakable delight of the inhabitants, who now thought themselves safe from harm. The citizens were most zealous in their attentions to the Danes; but that they were bivouacking, they seemed like guests invited to be made much of, with such profusion were they served with the best of every thing. They now came as friends in need ready to help; and indeed the troops had no other wish than at once to come to blows with those to whom they had been so long united by an odious alliance, which forced them to restrain in public the hatred they cherished in secret.

General Vandamme now attacked our troops on the Wilhelmsburg, who could not maintain their position a quarter of an hour against the overwhelming force of the enemy, and retreated towards the Feddel. A gun had been placed on the dyke, but it could not be employed against the enemy, as our own men were in the way. The Danes were accused of having been the first to fly: Tettenborn had intentionally placed them in the front of the attack. The Hanseatic troops were the last to leave the field, and consequently lost most men, among them their leader, who with a number of others could not be received on board the vessel, and was taken prisoner. The Danes and the burgher guard lost several men; the Danes who were taken prisoners were sent back by General Vandamme, with the declaration that France was not at war with Denmark. The guns which were lost were of no value.

Meanwhile the second Hanseatic battalion had gone over from the Ochsenwärder to the island of Wilhelmsburg, in order to attack the French in the rear: this was at first attended with some success; but the enemy, reinforced by a brigade, advanced in large numbers upon the Hanseatic troops, forcing them to retreat, which they did in good order for about four miles, to their landing place, where some made good their retreat in boats; but the remaining troops, with the water behind them and the enemy in front and on both sides, were forced to surrender when they had shot away all their powder.

The unfavourable termination of these skirmishes cannot be wondered at, considering the superior number of the enemy. And yet it was the merest accident — for accidents play so important a part in war — that the day did not end to the disadvantage of the French.

As the enemy was now in possession of the whole island of

Wilhelmsburg, and of the adjoining Feddel, he could from his new position throw shells and bombs into the town, and this produced considerable alarm. The two Hanseatic battalions were nearly destroyed, the small remnant of them was scattered and exhausted. This failure produced general sadness: the citizens had fits of excitement, in which they were eager to recapture the Feddel and the Wilhelmsburg, but with their utter ignorance of military affairs, a thousand cares and anxieties tormented them. On all sides dangerous and important posts had to be maintained, for which we had not sufficient troops, nor could we depend on those we had. The smallest success of the enemy might now decide the fate of the war. The regular troops defended the outworks, while the citizens kept the harbour, the gates, and the whole interior of the city. Such was the state of things after the unfortunate loss of the island of Wilhelmsburg — it was not consolatory, neither was it totally hopeless.

However, this state of things did not last long, and on the very 12th May on which the above-named skirmish took place Tettenborn received the most disheartening information. The Danish minister, Count Joachim von Bernstorff, not only was not received in England, but had been abruptly ordered to retire, and the English cabinet had declared that it would only negotiate with Denmark in conjunction with Sweden. The effect of such a proceeding was obvious; Denmark would inevitably form an alliance with France, at any rate recal her troops from Hamburg. In five or six days the order might be expected, for Count von Bernstorff had already reached Glückstadt, and was on his way to Copenhagen. Tettenborn's first care was to keep this news secret as long as possible, so as to keep the Danish troops in Hamburg until the last moment, and to prevent the citizens from being utterly cast down: his next object was to devise some means by which he could replace this inevitable loss. He sent the most pressing messages to Wallmoden and to head-quarters, but owing to more urgent necessities nearer home, the events at Hamburg were forgotten, and Wallmoden had received orders to direct his whole attention to the Elbe, and to the country round Magdeburg. The Crown Prince of Sweden had not yet arrived, but was expected at Stralsund;

nothing, therefore, remained but to obtain some Swedish troops for the safety of Hamburg.

Meanwhile the French were not backward in taking advantage of their successes. After establishing themselves in Wilhelmsburg, and thus approaching the town on that side, they made an attempt upon the Zollenspieker, so as to cut off the only means of communication between Tettenborn and Wallmoden; in this, however, they failed.

The alternations between despair and joy caused by these events kept us in a state of terrible suspense. The fate that was hanging over the town excited every one to unusual activity. The number of men employed in repairing the fortifications was doubled and trebled; the burgher guard pressed all whom they met in the streets into this service; no one was now seen going about unarmed; the gates were carefully guarded, every horse and cart retained for the use of the town, and no person allowed to leave Hamburg, so that none should escape their share of work. Those against whom there was a shadow of suspicion were seized and placed in the guardhouse, which was speedily filled with prisoners. The citizens did all this of their own impulse and zeal, which, to say the truth, was frequently useless and mischievous. It is, however, a remarkable fact, that although these masses of armed men, taken too from all classes of society, were kept under scarcely any restraint; no excesses of any kind were committed in spite of such strong temptations, and no case of disorderly conduct occurred. The general, the greater part of his officers, all the regular troops, and most of the burgher guard, were outside the town; the senate and the authorities kept in the back ground, and did no one thing out of their province, or made one suggestion during all these stormy days. What they ought to have done, among other things, supplying the troops with rations, they shamefully neglected; in many outposts the men were four-and-twenty hours without food; that too in a town which was amply supplied, in proportion to the small number of troops: nay, their own fellow-citizens, who were exposed to every sort of discomfort and privation at distant outposts, were equally forgotten.

Early in the morning of the 14th May, the outposts imagined

that they saw through the haze large masses of infantry on the Feddel marching towards the shore to embark ; they likewise thought that they could perceive cannon. The tocsin and the drums called the citizens to arms, while the flight of defenceless inhabitants to Altona and the country round increased the general confusion. The batteries on the Grasbrook kept up an incessant firing, and the terrible uncertainty, whether the enemy had already landed and was then actually advancing, made the inhabitants quite desperate. The several military posts were more than ever filled with armed men, as even those who generally avoided military service were now in their places. When the haze dispersed, there was not an enemy to be seen on the Feddel; the French were lying quietly under cover of the dykes, and not a trace of a battery was discovered. Thus all lived in anxious suspense ; the slightest cause was sufficient to rouse them to violent excitement ; all clearly saw the approaching evil, and the insufficiency of the means to meet it.

The people of Hamburg still flattered themselves with the hope that the Danes would assist them, and that the Swedes, or a strong reinforcement of Russian or Prussian troops, would arrive: the victory achieved by the Russians and Prussians at Gross-Göschen, and its possible effects in bettering their condition on the lower Elbe, raised their spirits. The best informed, however, had long given over all hopes of any of these possible accidents. On the other hand, a population of 150,000 offered materials for excellent resistance, and Hamburg was not lost as long as it did not despair itself; and the burgher guard was a very small fraction of the population. This corps was completely exhausted at the end of a few days, by constant bivouack in rainy weather and by over-work. Most of them would have been willing enough to have been led by Tettenborn into battle, there to seek a bloody death or freedom ; but this was neither possible nor advisable. The formation of the country, requiring to be guarded at endless points, and cut up on all sides by water, dams, and other impediments, prevented the employment of large masses, and even the personal guidance of their leader. Circumstances thus forced upon the people of Hamburg the hardest part of war, which consists in the patient endurance of unceasing troubles and privations, in the willing performance of small individual services, rather than in the exertions of actual warfare, or the excitement of danger.

Tettenborn soon saw his fears confirmed. The Danish government was no sooner informed of the refusal which Count Bernstorff had experienced in England, than orders were sent to the Danish troops to withdraw, and to leave Hamburg to its fate. This order reached Hamburg on the 18th of May, and was to be instantly carried into effect and communicated to the French. Tettenborn did all in his power by entreaties, and by representations, to obtain some delay. He urged Denmark's position with reference to the allies, the hostilities which had already taken place against France, the French blood but just shed in the Wilhelmsburg by the Danes, the honour of the Danish troops, and the consternation with which they received their orders to quit Hamburg — in short, nothing was left untried, which eloquence could suggest, to obtain a respite of at least four-and-twenty hours. Tettenborn at last succeeded, and the Danes promised not to inform the French of the withdrawal of their troops before the expiration of this time. This short interval was employed in sending couriers to General Döbbeln, and to other quarters whence Tettenborn hoped at some future time to receive succours, and where the news of what had occurred would be of considerable importance. When at length, on the evening of the 19th of May, just as it was getting dark, the Danish troops broke up their quarters and removed their guns, — all hearts sunk. Even with the Danes the people of Hamburg had not felt secure in the presence of a vastly superior enemy; but now, deprived of their assistance, the inhabitants gave up all hopes. To comfort them, Tettenborn announced the immediate approach of the Swedes, whom General Döbbeln had actually promised to send, — a promise which most people, however, thought extremely problematical. To make matters worse, the French cannonaded the town heavily all night. The actual mischief which they did was inconsiderable; but the whole city was alarmed at the thunder of the artillery, and at the sight of the shells. Left to its own resources, Hamburg must have yielded to a vigorous attack in this terrible night; and this was expected every moment. Redoubled vigilance was exercised, the out-posts were strengthened, and the officers were most active. They were determined that the French should not enter Hamburg without great loss: although their superiority in point of numbers rendered their ultimate success certain, we hoped to maintain the contest for some time, and, perhaps, to destroy the enemy in the streets. But no attack was made, and the cannonading ceased towards morning. By the following day many of the inhabitants of Hamburg had already fled; Altona was full of fugitives, carrying their most precious chattels with them: many fled to escape the vengeance of the enemy far into Holstein, some even to Copenhagen and London: they thought that this time the French would not confine their hostilities to Hamburg, but would seize people in Altona, and the neighbouring Danish territory.

The whole of the following day and night, and the next day again, every thing remained quiet. It was incomprehensible why the French, during this interval, made no attack; on the contrary, the firing even stopped, and yet no time could have been more favourable than this, when the town must have fallen an easy prey. But the French must have had bad information, or have distrusted the Danes. These days were passed in a state of constant suspense; our anxiety was increased by the non-arrival of assistance, and we thought with terror that the enemy could not long remain ignorant of our condition. At length the long-wished-for moment appeared, and on the evening of the 21st, three Swedish battalions, sent by General Döbbeln, arrived. Tettenborn rode to meet them beyond the gates, where likewise a division of the burgher guard and a vast concourse of people had assembled to greet their deliverers. The Hamburgers once more breathed freely, and thought that after passing safely through such a trial they had nothing further to fear.

It was high time for these troops to come. As if some magic influence had restrained the French until fresh troops could be opposed to them, the enemy renewed their attack upon Hamburg that very night, but without much effect. We put out the fires caused by the bombardment before they became serious; a few citizens were wounded in the streets, but the garrison on duty did not lose a man. Tettenborn inspected and ordered every thing, and incited every one to activity by his presence. He hoped that he should be able to maintain Hamburg until further reinforcements should arrive.

The following days again passed quietly, but, in the midst of the anxious suspense, every one was forced to be in constant readiness; the burgher guard was always on duty, and the majority of the people was incessantly employed in working at the fortifications; all trade was at an end.

Meanwhile the Danes looked upon the advance of the Swedes as threatening to themselves: from Hamburg the Swedes could reach Altona in ten minutes; the Danes therefore drew back their troops and artillery towards Blankanese. They acted as if they were in momentary fear of a hostile attack, and as though they could not trust the Russians now that the Swedes had joined them. The Swedes, on their part, showed some uneasiness about the Danes, who had the advantage in position and in numbers. The Crown Prince of Sweden, who had reached Stralsund on the 17th, shared their apprehensions: he thought that the Swedish troops in Hamburg were in an awkward position. He disapproved of General Döbbeln's proceeding, and immediately recalled the Swedish troops. The Swedes left Hamburg on the evening of the 25th of May, and it is scarce possible to describe the consternation of the citizens, and the dejection which seized upon the troops.

The most pressing instances were made to the Crown Prince of Sweden; the importance of the town, its present condition and impending fate, were urged upon him as an inducement to march to its assistance. If Hamburg were saved, it would be the brightest example for all Germany; if it fell, the effect would be fatal. The Crown Prince was reminded of the especial interest which he must feel for Hamburg from the intimate terms on which in former times, when he was simply Marshal Bernadotte, he had lived with the inhabitants. The senate had sent delegates to the Crown Prince immediately on his landing at Stralsund, but it was of no avail. Nothing, therefore, was left but to draw some reinforcement from Wallmoden, who sent one Prussian battalion of tried veterans, who had decided the fate of the battle at Lüneburg. On the 27th of May this battalion entered Hamburg, and brought a gleam of hope to the inhabitants, who thought that at length they were sure of these troops at least.

Strangely enough, the enemy remained perfectly quiet after the departure of the Swedes, as they had after that of the Danes : no attack was made on the town; even the cannonade ceased. The French thought that they should obtain possession of Hamburg more easily than by storming it, and looked to the Danes to spare them this trouble. The negotiations between Altona and Haarburg became daily more frequent. President von Kaas arrived from Copenhagen on his way to Napoleon's head-quarters, and staid some time at Haarburg with Marshal Davoust. It was suspected that the negotiation tended not only to a neutrality, but to a perfect alliance on the part of Denmark with France. The intimate relations subsisting between Altona and Hamburg, which two towns might almost be reckoned one, and the bonds of commerce which united them more strongly than any political tie could unite Altona with Denmark, made the inhabitants of Hamburg acquainted with the most secret proceedings of the Danish cabinet. It was currently reported that the combined forces of France and Denmark were to attack the town, or to obtain possession of it by more gentle means, granting free egress to the Russians. The unfortunate Hamburgers thus saw the very troops which had lately been their allies and protectors now turned into their bitterest foes : the Danes were the more dangerous, as fewer preparations for defence existed towards the Danish territory, as it was imagined that the Danes would, at any rate, act a neutral part after they had ceased to be allies. The outworks raised against the French were now strong enough, with the protection of the Elbe; but the unfinished works on the Danish side offered many weak points. The powder likewise began to fail. There was enough to supply the infantry for a few days, but not more than a round or two was left for the artillery. Tettenborn now received a formal notice that the burgher guard was no longer to be depended upon, and that they would not fight against the Danes. The people of Hamburg were in a fearful predicament: without the chance of appeasing Napoleon, exposed to the attacks of a superior and revengeful enemy,

DESPERATE CONDITION OF HAMBURG.

they saw one support after another fail them, one hope after another vanish. Although the wealth and prosperity of the inhabitants of Hamburg by no means consisted in their town but in their zeal and activity, the citizens shuddered at the thought of leaving nothing but blackened ruins upon which the enemy might wreak his vengeance. When Tettenborn had nothing to propose but tar-barrels and firebrands, the unhappy people withdrew in despair.

Once more a moment's sunshine appeared in Hamburg. The Crown Prince of Sweden had taken to heart the desperate condition of Hamburg, and had at length promised immediate assistance. On the 27th of May General von Rosen came to Tettenborn from the Crown Prince, and announced the advance of some Swedish troops. One portion was destined to relieve Hamburg, the rest were to join Wallmoden's division, and to assist him in a vigorous expedition against Haarburg, on the other side of the Elbe, in order, by attacking the French in the rear, to prevent their threatened movement on Hamburg. Nothing could have been better, and every thing was arranged, when General von Boye entered, and demanded from the Danes a safe conduct for the Swedish troops.

During these negotiations, the French by an unexpected attack broke the lull, which had now lasted for some days. Early on the 29th, before break of day, they every where drove back the weak outposts on the Ochsenwärder, and spread themselves over the island before Tettenborn even knew of their attack. He immediately hurried to the spot, put himself at the head of the troops who had fallen back, but who now, inspired by his presence, held out against the enemy's fire for some time. But as the French had come in considerable numbers, and it was evident that they intended to cut off the Russians in that quarter, Tettenborn ordered the Prussian battalion to occupy the important position of Eichbaum, and to maintain it until Wallmoden's attack should force the French to withdraw their troops. He himself fixed his head-quarters at Billkirche.

Tettenborn's position was worse than ever: in order to defend the Ochsenwärder, the town had been almost deprived of troops, and the only hope was that the French would not make an attack on Hamburg just at that moment. Every one was expecting with the utmost anxiety the arrival of the Swedes, and the ratification of the terms demanded of the Danes. Tettenborn received accounts from both quarters at the same moment the Swedes, instead of coming to his assistance, had retired further inland; the Danes, on the other hand, had advanced nearer, and were ready at a moment's notice to strike a decisive blow. Their position at Altona and elsewhere was threatening, their object evidently hostile: they had but to make one step, and Hamburg, with all the troops in the town, were lost beyond hope.

The answer to General von Boye's request for eight-and-forty hours' notice was, that the Danes would allow only two hours to intervene before hostilities commenced. Meanwhile it was discovered that a treaty had been signed between the Danes and the French, by which the Danish troops in Holstein were placed entirely at Marshal Davoust's disposal. Every moment Hamburg might expect to be attacked either by the Danes or by the French from the Danish territory. The Swedish general declared that to send his troops to Hamburg under such circumstances would simply be to deliver them at once as prisoners of war: he therefore, in proportion as the Danes advanced, drew back the Swedes still further inland. Under these circumstances, with the misunderstanding existing among the citizens — the want of ammunition, the small number of troops, — the retirement of the Swedes, and the hostility of the Danes — Tettenborn was compelled, on the 30th May, to order Major Von Pfuel to quit Hamburg, and to retreat with the few remaining troops through the Billwärder towards Bergedorf. The senate had of its own accord previously deliberated as to the necessity of yielding, and delegates were now sent to Altona, requesting the mediation of the Danes.

The burgher guard was formally dissolved, and such of the citizens as had taken a decided part in the late occurrences escaped into the Danish territory, or prepared for flight. The departure of the troops took place in perfect order and quiet. The batteries in the Grasbrook answered a few shots which the French fired against the town from their quarters on the Feddel.

The signal for marching was given in Altona, and the Danish troops began to advance.

The whole narrow pass of the Billwärder for eight miles was guarded by Danish troops with a large park of artillery: the artillerymen stood by their guns with lighted matches. The artillery was most advantageously placed behind barricades along the whole length of the road. An hour later, and the Danes would most probably have received orders to attack, and the small body of retreating troops would have been either destroyed or taken prisoners in the narrow pass of the Billwärder. General von Schulenburg did not even abide by his promise of giving two hours' notice, but commenced hostilities instantly. The Danes entered Hamburg, and being upon the rear of the Russian force, exchanged a few shots with the cossacks near Bergedorf. From this place the Prussian battalion formed the rear-guard, and reminded the French that it was not owing to their own bravery that Hamburg was again in their hands. At the Nettlenburg sluice the French had crossed over in considerable numbers, on foot bridges and planks which they laid across the water, driving back the Prussian skirmishers. Lieutenant Colonel von Borck hurried to the spot: after forcibly addressing his men, and ordering them not to fire, he placed himself at their head, and charged the enemy with the bayonet, driving all before him. There was not a shot fired, but above 400 of the enemy were drowned or bayonetted; a few only escaped across the river. Not one of the eighty Prussians who performed this feat was even wounded.

Tettenborn reached Lauenberg on the 31st May, without further loss, and joined Wallmoden. Before he could act on the offensive, came the news of an armistice having been concluded. I leave to eye-witnesses whose grief may give force to their description to relate what happened in Hamburg after the Danes gave up possession of the town to the French.

CHAPTER XVIII.

State of the North of Germany. — Tettenborn in Mecklenburg. — Newspaper started in the Camp. — Johanna Stegen, the Maid of Lüneburg. — Eleonora Prochaska, of the Lützen Free Corps. — Tettenborn's Expedition against Bremen. — Difficulties of the March. — Bremen is invested. — Death of Colonel Thullier, the Commandant, and Surrender of the Town to Tettenborn. — The Fortifications destroyed and the Town evacuated. — The Battle of Leipsic, and its Effects. — The Crown Prince of Sweden enters Bremen. — Campaign in Holstein and Schleswig. — Armistice with Denmark.

THE fall of Hamburg was the last of a series of military events which, instead of answering the confident anticipations which had at first been formed, turned men's hopes to despair and doubt. Although the battles of Gross-Görschen and Bautzen, the skirmishes at Magdeburg, Halle, and Haynau had covered the allied armies with laurels, they nevertheless found themselves driven back upon the Oder, while the French threatened to overrun Silesia. The Russians and the Prussians were painfully aware of the difficulties to which they were exposed. The Swedes had retired to the coasts of the German Ocean, where they awaited the ratification of the hard terms which they imposed upon the allies for joining them against Napoleon. Austria was arming, but its accession to the alliance was not yet declared, and the delay and uncertainty produced anxiety and disquiet. The French, again in full possession of Saxony and of a part of Silesia, made the greatest exertions in all the countries subjected to their sway, and their army increased daily in number and in confidence. The divided command in the allied armies was mischievous and dangerous compared with the absolute military sway of the greatest conqueror of the age. A settled despair prevailed over the whole north of Germany, and with the fall of Hamburg the last gleam of hope disappeared.

Nevertheless the courage and determination of the troops were not extinguished: hopeless as our condition was, we still wished for war, and preferred the chance of being driven back upon the Dwina to seeing the campaign ended by a disgraceful peace made on the banks of the Elbe. With this disposition, preparations were made for a fierce and obstinate contest.

Tettenborn had done his utmost in the defence of Hamburg: he had got together, borrowed, and invented every means of resistance; had contended — often with singular success — against innumerable obstacles; and on the very verge of destruction had saved the troops committed to his charge. His only comfort lay in the prospect of fresh enterprises and contests, no longer behind walls and ditches, but in the open field at the head of his cavalry, in an element peculiarly his own.

During the days which immediately followed the surrender of Hamburg he had collected his troops in Lauenburg; but he soon saw how vain was the attempt to defend this district, and determined therefore to annoy the French by boldly pushing on into the territories of Hanover and Brunswick as far as the Weser and the Harz, and threatening their positions on the upper as well as on the lower Elbe.

We will not follow Tettenborn in his campaign against Davoust in Mecklenburg, but will merely mention that the French were incessantly harassed by the straggling parties who unexpectedly appeared first in one place then in another, joined forces, separated again, and were found at one moment equal to any troops sent against them, and at another were discovered to have suddenly vanished. The enemy's couriers were taken, their outposts and waggons were daily seized, and the whole country was rendered unsafe for them. The rapidity of our movements made it impossible to know our strength: when all the cossacks who had been seen in various places during one day were counted up, the numbers seemed incredible. Our patrols went as far as Celle and Zeven, intercepting the couriers who plied between Hamburg and Bremen, forcing them at last to go a long way round, by Stade and Bremerlehe.

One great cause of annoyance to the French was a newspaper from the camp, which was first published in Lüneburg. The eagerness which the people showed for news of what was going on, made it imperative upon us to print hasty accounts of the chief events of the campaign, so as to satisfy their zeal and curiosity as speedily as possible. The quantity of matter which poured in on all sides soon compelled us to publish our intelligence daily: it only wanted a name to become a regular newspaper. The frequent mention of what was going on in our immediate neighbourhood made Marshal Davoust one of the chief objects of remark in the paper, which being published wherever Tettenborn's head-quarters happened to be, soon had a great circulation, and was received with the greatest favour and curiosity. Nor were satirical effusions wanting, in which the humour and wit of our camp found a vent. The French had been accustomed until now to have a monopoly of this species of warfare, and were furious to see themselves equalled, nay even surpassed. This newspaper was always published wherever we were, and at last ceased with its sixteenth number in France, where it appeared in French, and its last words were devoted to Marshal Davoust.

We cannot omit mentioning Johanna Stegen, the maid of Lüneburg, who, during the battle fought between General von Dörnberg and the French General Morand, coolly brought cartridges in her apron, in the midst of the fight, to those Prussian chasseurs who had expended all their ammunition. When the French again became masters of Lüneburg, she was compelled to hide herself, and was afterwards subject to many annoyances and threats not only from strangers, but even from her own countrymen, until at length her deeds were gradually forgotten in the occurrences of every-day life. But Tettenborn sought her out, and made her sit at his table as a companion in arms: her behaviour there was as unaffected and decorous as it had been courageous in the field of battle. In order that she might not be again exposed to the enemy's revenge, she was invited to settle at Berlin. It is a sign of the spirit which animated this war, that even women felt themselves urged by a noble impulse to take part in it. A girl of Potsdam, of the name of Eleonora Prochaska, was induced by love of adventure and of her country to quit her former quiet mode of life, assumed a man's dress, and joined the Lützen free corps, under the feigned name of Augustus Renz. She was wounded by a musket shot at the very commencement of the battle of the Görde, but the courageous girl refused to go to the rear until a second shot in the thigh compelled her to quit the field and her disguise. She discovered her sex to an officer, by whose means she was treated with proper care and due respect. She died of her wounds in the course of a few days, lamented by all her companions in arms, whose love and esteem she had won in an eminent degree.

Tettenborn had long conceived a plan for advancing to the Weser, with a flying troop of cossacks, in order to attack Bremen. The difficulties which stood in the way of this enterprise were enormous. Taking into consideration the circuitous route, it was at least from eighty to one hundred miles from Boitzenburg to Bremen, and it would require four days severe marching through almost impassable districts. The slightest hint conveyed to the enemy of our movement would have ensured the failure of its object. Bremen itself was a fortified town, with walls and a ditch, the gates were protected with a chevaux de frise; between Bremen and Haarburg lay the well-fortified town of Rothenburg, defended by a strong garrison. Marshal Davoust could easily send a considerable number of troops from Hamburg to attack us on one side, and cut off our retreat, while the garrisons of Bremen, Nienburg, and Minden, could advance against us on the other. The only way to avoid all these dangers was to keep the plan a profound secret until it was executed; but the distance we had to go, and the length of time which the expedition must take, gave but little hopes of this. Tettenborn was not a man likely to be stopped by difficulties: the plan which he conceived with great boldness, he carried out with consummate prudence; and as he possessed in an eminent degree both these qualities, he obtained a well-deserved success in all he undertook.

On the evening of the 9th October, Tettenborn assembled on the left bank of the Elbe, near Bleckede, the troops which he had selected for his expedition to the Weser. These consisted of 800 cossacks, and as many Prussian chasseurs, a portion of whom were conveyed in covered carts: he took with him also four guns of the Hanseatic horse artillery and two howitzers. Tettenborn broke up his quarters early on the 10th of October, and started on his march. The second day they reached Soltau; the third day's march was through Visselhövede to Verden, which town we reached about midday on the 12th. The infantry soon found the carts an impediment rather than a service to them: they had to make their way through the deep morasses and pathless wilds of the Lüneburg heath, in the midst of incessant rain, and to contend with all the difficulties of a march purposely directed through by-ways, so as to enable them to reach their destination unperceived: the guns, too, had to be dragged, with indescribable labour, over this broken country in forced marches: the cossacks, in small parties, scoured the country far and wide in advance. From Visselhövede, Tettenborn had sent Colonel von Pfuel with a strong detachment of chasseurs and cossacks and one cannon against Rothenburg, to attack this important post simultaneously with Bremen, and prevent the garrison from sending assistance to Bremen, or information to Haarburg. Major Denisoff went in advance with another detachment of cossacks to the Weser, which they crossed near Hoya by swimming, thus cutting off any communication with Bremen on the other side. The straggling parties of cossacks prevented the French from approaching the line of march, and allowed no one to break through their wide circle. By means of this device the utmost the enemy could learn was that here and there a few cossacks had been seen, which gave them but little cause for uneasiness, as the French had long been used to see these troops at great distances from the main body to which they were attached. The few French gensdarmes or douaniers, who attempted at our approach to escape or to slip unperceived through the hands of the cossacks, were discovered and taken.

Our troops were only allowed a rest of three hours in Verden, and we recommenced our march at nightfall, so as to reach Bremen with the early dawn. The sixteen miles of road, from Verden to Bremen, was one continued deep sand, which wore out man and horse, especially after the great fatigues they had already undergone. The infantry could march but very slowly, and Tettenborn, who was in advance with the cossacks, was obliged to wait a considerable time in Arbergen for the classeurs, who were a long way behind. During the journey a post-boy had ridden into the midst of our troops, asking eagerly for the general. He was taken before Tettenborn, whom he imagined to be a French general, as he had no conception that any Russian troops could have advanced so far, and delivered to him a letter from the captain of a French outpost at Ottersberg, informing the commander in Bremen of the approach of Russian troops. A few men were sent to Ottersberg to seize upon the outpost.

It was past seven o'clock in the morning of the 13th October when our troops approached Bremen. The enemy, alarmed at the report that cossacks had been seen, thought at first that they had only to do with these, and as a reinforcement of 1200 Swiss had entered the town a few days before, they sent into the suburbs and to the neighbouring village of Hastett strong detachments of these troops, who commenced skirmishing with the cossacks. As every moment's delay gave the enemy time for thought and defence, Tettenborn determined to attack them at once. He brought the cannon to bear as speedily as possible; and after a few discharges he galloped up the streets at the head of his cossacks, cutting down and making prisoners all those who were dispersed about as skirmishers in the gardens or houses. He reckoned most correctly upon the effect which the unexpected sound of artillery would have upon the French; they were convinced that they were attacked by a large force, and immediately took to flight. The fugitives did not stop till they found themselves safe behind their walls, whence a brisk fire was poured upon the cossacks, who charged up to the Oster gate, but found the drawbridge up. About 300 prisoners, among whom were several officers, fell into our hands: most of these men surrendered under circumstances in which half their number might have prevented our further advance for a whole day.

Nevertheless, with all this we had not gained much: the garrison was numerous; their position, behind walls and ditches, more secure than our own, and it was difficult, without the co-operation of the inhabitants, to take the town, as the favourable moment for a surprise had passed.

The cossacks had distributed themselves all round the town,

and guarded every approach to it; even on the left bank of the Weser every outlet was watched. It soon appeared, however, that we could not reckon much on any assistance from the citizens. The French commandant, Colonel Thullier, an old tried soldier and a man of sense, had taken every precaution to keep an unruly populace in check. Numerous patrols drove the people into their houses, which were ordered to be closed.

After about 200 grenades had been thrown into the town, Tettenborn caused the fire from the large guns to cease, and the discharge of small arms only continued with various success. He took up his head-quarters in Hastett, and kept Bremen closely invested, recalled Colonel von Pfuel from Rothenburg, examined the best places for an attack, and prepared every thing for carrying the town by storm. Towards evening the cossacks swam over from the other side of the Weser, and returned in the same manner with despatches, to the extreme amazement of the enemy, who saw from the ramparts that the river was no obstacle to these horsemen. Our men made good use of the brief cessation of hostilities to take some rest, to which they had long been strangers; their repose, however, was short, for early next morning the fire of musketry recommenced, and by one of those accidents which so often decide the fate of a war, on this very morning Colonel Thullier was killed on the rampart. This event, which we only learnt in the afternoon, was of the greatest importance to us, as it was not easy to find any one to equal Colonel Thullier in perseverance and courage. Meanwhile Colonel Pfuel had arrived, and all the troops were now before Bremen; every thing was prepared for storming the town, and the following morning before daybreak was the appointed time. In order to leave nothing untried, Tettenborn now summoned the town to surrender, and, contrary to all expectation, a French officer demanded an interview with the Russian general, to treat about the capitulation. The death of Colonel Thullier had completely extinguished the courage of the French authorities; the troops, who for the most part were Swiss, showed no great desire for fighting, and the citizens began to be turbulent. The money and stores which happened to be in the town made it difficult to arrange the terms, as the French authorities did not like the idea of giving all these up, and had hopes of saving something by delay. The French officer requested to see Tettenborn, whom he knew by sight, to convince himself that this general was really present, a fact which had been doubted. When it was certainly known in the town that General Tettenborn was before their gates, no one thought of offering further resistance. Much time passed in discussing the terms of capitulation, until Tettenborn announced, that if they were not signed within an hour the town would be stormed. This speedily brought matters to an issue, and Colonel Pfuel and Major Devallant, the new French commandant, agreed upon the terms of surrender. The garrison were to march out with all the honours of war, giving their promise not to serve against us within a year. We knew very well that most of the Swiss would immediately enter our service, and that the others would disperse. All the money, provisions, cannon, and military stores were to be delivered up to us; the cavalry were to give up their horses, and to march off on foot. We found fourteen pieces of cannon and two mortars of immense size, intended for the defence of Hamburg.

About ten o'clock in the forenoon of the 15th of October, the Prussian chasseurs took possession of the Oster gate, and one hour later, after the French troops had marched out with martial music, of the town itself. When the French saw the small body of infantry to whom they had yielded, a murmur arose among them that the terms of surrender had been obtained by stratagem, and ought not to be kept; several French veterans spoke their opinions pretty loudly on this subject. But Tettenborn had the cannons loaded with grape shot, and threatened to blow them to pieces on the slightest resistance. The populace also now broke loose, — they had hardly been kept within bounds during the negotiation. They rushed with wild cries of joy to the gates and ramparts, and filled the streets near the Hotel de Ville; the French authorities, with Count Arberg, the prefet, at their head, saw with terror the increasing tumult among the people. Already a wretched douanier, who had imprudently shown himself in his uniform, had received such violence at the hands of the mob that he died from its effects. The prefet sent a messenger to Tettenborn, beseeching him, in the most urgent manner, to come speedily, and by his presence to give some protection to the terror-stricken authorities. Tettenborn now entered the town at the head of the cossacks amid loud shouts of joy; the streets and windows were full of people; wreaths of flowers were showered down, handkerchiefs waived, and the huzzahs were deafening.

The taking of Bremen, and the presence of Russian troops on both sides of the Weser, in the rear of Marshal Davoust's French and Danish army, caused great joy and excitement far and wide among the inhabitants: the French authorities, on the other hand, were terror-stricken, and thought themselves no longer safe at their posts. Marshal Davoust was now separated from all other French detachments, and had to depend entirely upon himself. From its strength and population, from being the centre of government, and forming the connecting link between Hamburg and Holland, the town of Bremen was essential to the French; to us its possession, opening the communication with England, was most important, not to mention the minor consideration of the cannon, stores, money, and booty, which we had obtained. Tettenborn sent his infantry, and the cannon he had seized, back to Lüneburg; but as he neither wished totally to leave Bremen to its fate, nor yet to disobey the orders he had received from Wallmoden to return to the Steckniss, he fixed his head-quarters on the 18th October at Verden, near enough to Bremen for him to keep the town by means of a detachment of cossacks, and not too far to prevent his junction with Wallmoden by two forced marches, in case of urgent necessity. He left Major von Schultz in Bremen as commandant, to see that the walls and the ditches were levelled, and the report that 2000 French were marching on Bremen from Osnabrück, made it advisable to hurry the work of demolition. As Tettenborn now had nothing but cavalry, he was more at liberty to act on an emergency; even should the enemy advance against him at once from Cassel, Haarburg, and Minden, he could find a safe retreat in the wild heaths of Hanover.

As the French troops approached Bremen, Tettenborn desired the cossacks to evacuate the town. Meanwhile the bridge at Celle over the Aller was repaired as quickly as possible, as it might be necessary, instead of retreating, to make a bold dash into Hanover or Brunswick.

On the 22d of October the French re-entered Bremen. The account of Blücher's victory at Gross-kugel, and of the great victory of Leipsic, was now received, and the rounds which were fired on this occasion prepared the enemy for the information they received on the following day. The French, thinking it no longer advisable to stay near the Weser, again left Bremen on the 26th of October, after holding the town only four days.

Tettenborn now sent strong detachments to great distances, to Oldenburg, Emden, Osnabrück, Münster, and other towns, in order to leave the French no peace, and to drive them out of the country as speedily as possible. The French had retreated from Bremen to Münster, after being joined in Osnabrück by the garrison of Minden, and with these forces General Carra-Saint-Cyr intended to push on towards the Rhine. But we will not narrate all the separate skirmishes and surprises which took place; the French in the hurry of flight were compelled to leave behind them every thing which the government or the troops themselves had collected in money or stores. The people every where received our men with the greatest joy; in many places the plundering gensdarmes and douaniers had been driven out before our arrival. Tettenborn, although suffering from illness, directed all these expeditions from his head-quarters at Verden, where he remained until the 4th of November, when he returned to Bremen.

The results of the battle of Leipsic became every day more and more apparent. In order even to retreat, it was necessary for Napoleon to obtain a victory. Numerous armies pushed forward in all directions into the newly recovered provinces, gathering fresh strength during their advance, while the enemy's forces gradually melted away. All the provinces between the Elbe and the Weser, the coasts of the German ocean as far as Holland, and the country along the Rhine extending to Switzerland, saw with joy not unmixed with terror, the old chains in which they had so long languished, at length broken. Large bodies of our troops forced their way through all impediments, towards the Rhine; nothing stopped them; and victory was this time the occasion of a thousand blessings. The army of the Crown Prince of Sweden was in the north of

Germany: the Swedes were marching upon Hanover, the Prussians through Minden into Westphalia, while the Russians were following the course of the Weser towards Bremen. But while Napoleon's beaten and disorganised troops fled towards France, there to draw fresh strength and courage, and while all Germany was directing its full force thither, a dangerous foe still remained in the north. The time was now come for the Crown Prince of Sweden to lead the allied army against the Danes, and in the common enemy to conquer his own especial foe. It was surmised that Marshal Davoust, in consequence of what had occurred, would concentrate his troops in and near Hamburg, and attempt to make his way through Holland. Wallmoden therefore turned his whole attention to this quarter, and endeavoured at any rate, if he could not altogether stop his retreat, to prevent the enemy from escaping unscathed. With the same view Tettenborn defended the Weser. We afterwards learnt that Napoleon had directed Davoust to march his troops through Holland, but that the latter had thought this no longer possible.

The Russian and Prussian troops soon approached nearer, and all fear of Davoust vanished. On the 12th of November General Wintzingerode, at the head of his division of the Russian army, entered Bremen, and was followed, six days later, by the Crown Prince of Sweden. The favourable accounts from Holland, where the people every where rose upon the French, and drove them out of the country, the surrender of the forts of Bremerlehe and Blexen, and the evacuation of Stade, left no more difficulties in the way of proceeding at once with the expedition which had been arranged against Denmark. All our troops commenced their march from the Weser back to the Elbe, with the exception of the Prussians under General Bülow, who entered upon a new field of glory in the Netherlands, and of a portion of General Wintzingerode's division, with which this general crossed the Rhine by Dusseldorf.

While preparations were going on for the campaign against Denmark, a change took place in Tettenborn's position. The Crown Prince of Sweden took him under his own immediate command. After consulting with him several times, the Crown Prince gave him nothing but general directions, leaving to his own discretion the manner of carrying these orders into execution, or modifying them according to circumstances. Tettenborn was in future to keep only his cossacks, with whom he could move more freely, and could, thus unencumbered, undertake the boldest enterprises. These cossacks now united all the advantages of regular troops with those peculiar to themselves: they had become used to obedience and to stricter discipline in the presence of the enemy, and were not only fully equal to cope with any cavalry, but in broken marshy ground they were as good for skirmishing on foot as the best sharpshooters.

We will not, however, follow Tettenborn's movements in Holstein, into the heart of which he penetrated through the most horrible country where the horses frequently sank up to their bellies in the morasses near the Eider, or had to scramble through deep ditches, and wade through sedgy water and half-formed ice. After Holstein had been overrun and Schleswig was on the point of being attacked, the news of an armistice, brought about by the intervention of Austria, gave the troops a welcome and necessary rest. The Danes could hope for no foreign aid, and a popular insurrection in their favour was out of the question. The subjects of Denmark in Holstein and Schleswig were heart and soul for us: they thought ours the cause of freedom. Many earnestly hoped that peace would not be concluded, trusting, in the course of the war, to be separated from Denmark, and to become an integral part of Germany.

CHAPTER XIX

The Allies enter France. — Napoleon's Resources. — The Allies at Chalons and Rheims. — State of Affairs. — The Army of Silesia under Blücher and the Main Army under Schwarzenberg. — Blücher's Advance upon Meaux. — The Battle of Laon. — Excitement of the French Peasantry against the Allies. — Difficulty of Communication. — The Attack upon Rheims. — The French retake it. — Tettenborn evacuates Epernay. — The Action at Arcis-sur-Aube. — Epernay is retaken by Tettenborn. — Junction of Blücher and Schwarzenberg. — Determination of the Allies to march upon Paris. — They encounter and beat Marshals Marmont and Mortier. — The Battle of Saint Dizier. — Napoleon learns the Advance of the Allies upon Paris. — The Allies enter Paris, 1813-14.

AFTER many delays and difficult negotiations, peace was at length concluded, and we left the duchy of Schleswig by forced marches. We crossed the Eider at Friedrichstadt, then halted a few days, waiting for the King of Denmark's approval of the terms on which the peace had been signed; and on the 24th of January we commenced our march. By this peace we had gained a new ally, and 10,000 Danes were added to the army, with which the Crown Prince of Sweden advanced towards the Rhine, while the conduct of the siege of Hamburg was left to General Benningsen's Prussian army, which dropped down from the upper Elbe.

After some few difficulties, the allied armies entered France from all sides, in a line that extended from the Netherlands to Switzerland, and moved slowly on, in large masses, towards Paris as their central point. The wish for peace became stronger with every step we took; the sight of Basle excited a longing for a second treaty of Basle, the likelihood of which, however, was by no means promoted by the threatening aspect of the cannon of Hüningen, a fortress still in the hands of the French. The line of fortresses which we left threatening our rear was dangerous enough even if our troops were victorious, and alarmed those who had not yet made up their minds to stake all upon this one venture. But such was the impulse given to this movement that all difficulties were overcome, and the troops advanced boldly forwards to a war of which the issue could only be decided in the heart of France. It was, indeed, essential to carry a patriotic spirit with us into an enterprise, the result of which, in spite of all favouring hopes, was by no means certain, and which had become more perilous than ever. The Emperor Napoleon devoted all the energies of his iron will, and all the resources of his subjects, to the one object of opposing the advance of the allied troops. He represented to the French nation their glory on the one side, and their ruin on the other. On his own adopted soil he appeared more formidable than ever to his opponents. He collected round him his chosen troops from Spain; he made use of all the arts of persuasion in his power to excite the people against us, and succeeded in so doing, although the feeling of the French had already begun to waver. And what had we to oppose to this? Moreau was dead; the idea of the Bourbons was far removed from both parties; and we were still negotiating with Napoleon!

Under these circumstances, the appearance of the Crown Prince of Sweden in France might bring about most important changes in the posture of affairs. He intended to enter France by Soissons, and had prepared every thing for a campaign which subsequent events prevented him from carrying into effect in person. Tettenborn had been ordered by the Crown Prince to penetrate between the army of the North, — of which the larger portion, under General Wintzingerode and Bülow, had already entered France, — and the army of Silesia, commanded by Blücher, so as to maintain a communication between them, and to act on their front or their flank, according to circumstances.

After our troops, by dint of forced marches, had reached the Rhine on the 11th of February, we rested some days in Bonn, and then proceeded by way of Andernach, Kaisersesch, and Wittlich, to Treves. The troops were forced, by the vile mountain roads, to halt some days in Treves; this rest was more necessary, as the next day's march, by still more impassable tracks in mountainous districts, forming a part of the forest of Ardennes, would lead us under the fortresses of Luxenburg and Montmedy, and between Sedan and Verdun.

Tettenborn left Treves on the 19th of February, and marched to Stenay, where he intended to cross the Meuse. The whole of this march was conducted with the greatest circumspection, as not only were the reports as to the state of the country exceedingly disquieting, but the garrisons of the various fortresses could at any moment make sudden sallies and had it in their power, by occupying the defiles and narrow passes, to impede the progress of our troops, which consisted entirely of cavalry. The bridge at Stenay, which had been destroyed by the French from Montmedy, was soon repaired, and on the 23d of February our troops crossed the Meuse. On the following day we had some sharp skirmishing in the woods with the gensdarmes; they attacked our advanced posts with great boldness, and only retreated when they perceived that it was more than a straggling party which they had to contend with. The inhabitants had been lately provided by the government with arms and military stores, and had been incited to resist our advance.

At length, on the 25th of February, we fell in with the first Russian troops, without having lost a single man: in the evening we entered Rheims, where General Wintzingerode had fixed his head-quarters. The state of affairs was shortly this: Blücher had made good his retreat upon Chalons, and the army of Silesia, by its junction with the main army of Prince Schwarzenberg, was able to make head against the enemy. Napoleon moved his large masses of troops, uncertain where to direct his blow, in front of the two German armies, but appeared by no means disposed to risk all in a general engagement. Never had we longed so earnestly for the army of the Crown Prince of Sweden as we did now, when a force like his, under such a leader, placed on Napoleon's left flank, would have distracted his attention, and impeded the freedom of his movements.

The greater portion, however, of the army of the north was still in the Netherlands; and only two divisions, the Russians under Wintzingerode, and the Prussians under Bülow, had advanced into France, the one to Rheims the other to Soissons; they were unsupported and without any reserve upon which to fall back, and were far too weak, in the event of Napoleon attacking them with all his force, not to be compelled to fall back immediately upon the Netherlands. Wintzingerode had taken his measures with great skill: he had evacuated Soissons, which he had taken by storm, so as to turn all his attention to the Marne and the Aube. General Alexander von Benkendorf, who commanded the Russian advanced posts on this side, held Epernay, and sent out exploring parties, who, however, returned without coming upon any traces of the French. The silence and uncertainty which had prevailed as to all military events, since Napoleon's first victories over Blücher, caused great uneasiness, which was much increased by the negotiations which were still going on with Napoleon at Chatillon, and by the many signs we could perceive of hesitation on the part of the allies. Napoleon's untiring spirit of enterprise, and still more his perfect confidence in himself as a leader, had a prodigious effect, although the falling off of his armies began to deprive him of his power to injure us.

After Wintzingerode had given his opinion that Tettenborn's original destination was admirably adapted for present circumstances, and had given him full liberty to act on his own judgment and responsibility, Tettenborn advanced towards the Marne. On the 26th of February, General von Benkendorf, after having been for some time in utter uncertainty as to what was going on in the allied camp, received notice that Blücher had left the French army standing opposite to Prince Schwarzenberg's forces; that the Prussian general had of his own accord given up his communication with Schwarzenberg, and had gone by forced marches to Meaux in the direction of Paris. This bold and admirable movement—perhaps the best in the whole campaign—was at first misunderstood, and created some uneasiness, as it was imagined that not alone the main army of Prince Schwarzenberg, but also that the separate divisions under Wintzingerode and Bülow would be thus left an easy prey to Napoleon's superior forces. But by this bold movement Napoleon's flank was threatened, as well as Paris, and this the French Emperor could not allow; the utmost uncertainty, however, still prevailed as to Napoleon's movements. Tettenborn instantly made his plan, and left Rheims early next morning with his horde of cossacks, crossed the Marne at Epernay, and marched directly upon the Aube towards Arcis, with the determination not to stop until he came across some traces of the French, with the certainty of finding Napoleon either on his way back to Paris, or still in his former position. He therefore sent a detachment of cossacks under Captain Bismark along the road that crossed our path diagonally between Arcis to Sezanne, and that very night he came in contact with the French. Other parties were now sent out in all directions; and, as many of Napoleon's Mamelukes and of the Imperial guard were taken prisoners, there could no longer be any doubt that Napoleon was here with his chosen troops.

The cossacks drew back in good order, turning upon the enemy from time to time. Napoleon's movements being thus discovered, and his intentions made clear, couriers were despatched to Schwarzenberg to the left and to Blücher to the right, informing the one of Napoleon's departure with his guards, and warning the latter of his approach. Napoleon thus saw his intentions frustrated of surprising Blücher, and keeping Schwarzenberg in ignorance of the smallness of the force left opposed to him.

Tettenborn hung upon the right flank of the French Emperor during the following days, and sent out parties in front and in the rear to obtain the most accurate information of the direction in which the French were marching. It was soon discovered that the French forces were taking the direction of La Ferté-sous-Jouarre, where they would probably cross the Marne, whither Tettenborn determined to follow him.

On our way to Montmirail an advanced party of cossacks captured a French courier who had been sent from Paris to Troyes: not finding the French Emperor there, he had turned back, and was then on his road following Napoleon towards the Marne. His papers were as remarkable as they were numerous. All the current despatches of the day from the ministers of war and of the interior, lists of the troops and national guards, reports of Lord Wellington's progress in the south-west of France, accounts of the ill success of the attempts to arm the people, and many other papers developing the true condition of Napoleon's affairs, fell into our hands. The most remarkable, however, were some extracts from private letters, which had been opened at the post-office at Paris: all people, from Napoleon's sisters down to the most insignificant officials or shopkeepers, were liable to have their letters subjected to this secret examination: by this means praise and blame, complaints and hopes, reached the Emperor's ears in abundance, and the daily bag of letters thus supplied him with a number of victims whom he could immolate sooner or later to his revenge. From a letter of Queen Hortense we learnt that at one moment Napoleon himself had given up all as lost—namely, after the battle of Brienne; but that he had soon gathered fresh hope, and had completely recovered his old confidence after the defeat of the army of Silesia; he had, moreover, now succeeded in exciting the people in his favour.

We were perfectly ignorant of Blücher's movements during the following days, but from our position on the right bank of the Marne we were able to observe all Napoleon's movements. By forced marches Napoleon had distanced the cossacks, and Tettenborn found himself in the rear instead of on the flank of the French army, which now attacked and compelled us to fall back; he therefore endeavoured to form a junction with Wintzingerode near Rheims. But on approaching Rheims he learnt that the French had attacked and taken the town early that very morning, and with the assistance of the inhabitants had made the small Russian garrison prisoners of war.

As Rheims was in the hands of the French, nothing was left for us but to endeavour to reach Epernay by the best way we could, and to place ourselves in safety on the other side of the Marne. Completely cut off from Wintzingerode's division, as well as from Blücher's, without any hope of reaching those troops in time for the contest which was now inevitable, Tettenborn thought he could in no way fulfil his mission better than by remaining in Napoleon's rear, whence he could observe his movements, and give Prince Schwarzenberg accurate information of all that was going on.

Blücher had sent forward several parties from Meaux as far Ligny, about six hours' march from Paris, when the approach of the French Emperor on his left flank compelled him to fall back in order to join Generals Wintzingerode and Bülow; by this means he would be in a condition to bring 100,000 men into the field against Napoleon, who, having meanwhile united his troops with those of Marshals Marmont and Mortier, appeared desirous to force Blücher into an engagement. As Soissons had already surrendered to General Bülow on the 3rd of March, Blücher expected to form a junction with the two divisions of the northern army without impediment. But Napoleon, by one of his usual rapid movements, endeavoured to turn the extreme left of our army, and by threatening to cut off the communication in our rear compelled Blücher to leave the advantageous position he had taken between Soissons and Vailly and to advance with all speed to Laon, where on the 9th of March the two armies encountered each other. The French took the villages of Semilly and Ardon, which lay close to Laon, in the direction of Soissons; but General Wintzingerode recaptured them in the forenoon. The chief attack of the French was now directed against the left wing of the allied army towards Corbeny, where the Prussian troops were placed. The enemy advanced in the afternoon from Féthieux, and sent strong divisions of horse to the right in order to cut off our line of communication with the Netherlands in the rear. A most murderous struggle took place at Athies, upon which village the Prussians had been forced to fall back, and where they made a stand: the battle there lasted till the evening, when it was still undecided, as both parties remained in possession of different portions of the village. But towards the close of the day the Prussians made an unexpected attack upon the enemy, who had already retired to rest; and, after a short resistance, during which the Prussians charged with the bayonet up to the mouths of the enemy's guns, we succeeded in utterly discomfiting the French. Marmont's division and General Arrighi's cavalry were routed, sixteen cannon taken, and 3000 men made prisoners. Meanwhile, the French Emperor had remained opposite to Blücher's division before Laon, and on the 10th of March, Napoleon repeatedly attacked him and then the town of Laon, with all the rage and despair which he could instil into his tired soldiers. In his zeal he himself sprang off his horse and pointed a gun: but all his exertions were vain, his attacks were repulsed in every quarter; and, with the conviction that he could do nothing more, he at length withdrew his troops out of the murderous fire. Several days passed in a sort of doubtful quiet, during which Napoleon meditated fresh plans, and endeavoured to find fresh opportunities for attack. The expectation of what he would do next kept all men in a state of great suspense. Blücher was ill, and no one but he dared to take the initiative against so formidable an opponent: Napoleon therefore was left undisturbed.

This was a most anxious time: towards the north, the army of Silesia, after so many marches and battles, was detained in inactivity by Blücher's illness; while towards the south the main army, under Prince Schwarzenberg, was waiting with some anxiety to be attacked by Napoleon in its turn. Between these two armies their wily opponent for some time played his game. Every one watched in great suspense for his next movement, and vigorous attempts were made to establish some communication between the two allied armies: it was of the greatest importance to procure accurate information. No one was so well fitted for this as Tettenborn, who was then actually in the rear of the French army, and who, from his position on the Marne, was incredibly active, and despatched his cossacks in all directions against the enemy. To the right, through Epernay, he kept up a communication with Saint Priest, who was still in the neighbourhood of Rheims; and to the left, through Vertus, with General Kaissaroff, who now commanded the cossacks in Fère-Champenoise in lieu of Hettman Platoff. Saint Priest was attached to Blücher's army, Kaissaroff to that of Prince Schwarzenberg, and by this means some sort of communication, — a very loose one it is true, — was kept up between the two. However, the carelessness with respect to delivering letters, which was almost unavoidable where they had to pass through so many hands, frequently rendered the information useless when it arrived, and many letters never reached their destination at all. Moreover, a circumstance which happened rendered the procuring information, and the forwarding it to various persons, exceedingly difficult and dangerous.

Napoleon's incessant marching and countermarching, if it had no other effect, certainly had this — that by dint of great exertions he succeeded in stirring up the peasantry more and more against us. At first this was confined to the particular spot where he happened to be with his army; there the inhabitants were forced to make common cause with his soldiers: they invariably tried to avoid imperilling their lives and their properties by taking any part in the war, but Napoleon's will was not to be trifled with; he ill-treated the mayors, bullied and punished the communes who did not obey his requisitions, and at length brought matters to such a crisis, that people preferred having the appearance and merit of revolting against us of their own accord to yielding to necessity; for one of the two they must do. When once under arms, and guilty of fighting against us, there was seldom any retreat for them, and the common people of France were then forced for the sake of their own safety to persevere in that which they had most unwillingly commenced. The excesses committed by our troops, of which the French papers gave such awful descriptions, and Napoleon never ceased talking, were not only extremely exaggerated, but were even inferior to those which the French soldiers allowed themselves in their own country. However, the impression of terror which these constant representations excited in the minds of the people gradually began to tell, and to produce those very excesses and disorders which before were mere invention. Nothing could be more imprudent than the conduct of that portion of the French people who did not take up arms against us. The doors and windows in every town or village which we entered were barricaded, the inhabitants had disappeared, and the authorities had absconded. When, after a long search, the mayor happened to be discovered, he invariably said that the village contained nothing to supply the wants of the troops,— that the constant plundering to which they had been subject had exhausted their means; time was requested in order that search might be made in the neighbouring villages, whether peradventure something might be discovered there. In this manner many hours elapsed, during which we got nothing but good words; and when, after waiting a long time, no provisions or fodder made their appearance, the soldiers, who ran the risk of losing their hour of rest and refreshment, and naturally became impatient, searched for themselves, and found, in most cases, a superfluity of all they wanted. This conduct of the authorities made our men take matters with a high hand, and in a spirit of revenge they seized upon whatever they could find in the people's kitchens and cellars, where, with different treatment, they would have been content with a crust of bread. If a cossack took up a bundle of straw, there were loud screams of plunder; if he asked for a kettle for the camp, there were noisy complaints of personal violence, until at length plundering and personal violence became very general, caused entirely by such conduct. The guides were often led by the army with a rope round their necks; but this precaution, which the "Moniteur" described as degrading to humanity, was adopted in consequence of the guides so frequently running away, and had been taught to the cossacks by the French in Russia. Sometimes the tricks of the French peasantry were exceedingly laughable: for example, if by chance we came suddenly upon a party of them in the road, there was scarcely an instance in all Champagne, that, to escape being taken as guides, they did not all begin to limp. In those places where the mayors and citizens prudently supplied the wants of the troops with alacrity, nothing but good order and friendliness prevailed. Most of the authorities, however, acted in a manner which was fatal to them. The inhabitants of the villages fled to the woods, where their wives, children, and the best part of their property were concealed; the men, armed with rifles and muskets, prowled about the edges of the woods, endeavouring to cut off some straggling party, or to seize a stray waggon or a courier. Escaped prisoners, veterans, foresters, gensdarmes, even officers, joined these parties, and brought them into some sort of discipline, for which every Frenchman is so naturally disposed. These armed bands received support and advice from the various fortresses. Parties of regular troops followed the rear of our force, and found in every village plenty of men ready to join their ranks. The French peasants, who almost invariably wear blue smock-frocks, were often taken for troops of the line. If they laid aside their arms, they had the appearance of peaceful peasants; while, on the other hand, hundreds of French soldiers could go about undiscovered, with their uniforms hidden under their blue smock-frocks. This state of things extended from Lyons far into Picardy, in our front, on our flanks, but more especially in our rear. The manner in which the French people rose against us was a remarkable instance of the power which Napoleon's untiring energy and determination exercised over men's minds: this insurrection was carried on without excitement, almost against their wishes and feelings; Napoleon himself had, at first, despaired of bringing it about. It was no longer possible for any courier to traverse the country without a body of 100 horse, and every order required a whole party for its safe conveyance. All the usual means of communication were broken up, the government of the whole country was dissolved, and it was extremely difficult to procure provisions, or to find any means of conveyance. In every village, in every wood, numerous enemies lay hidden. Had our provisions and supplies failed, — had the insurrection around us increased, — and had Napoleon made head against us, these blue smock frocks would have done us infinite mischief in our retreat. Wherever Tettenborn appeared, the tocsin sounded in every village; and his communication with General Kaissaroff was kept up at a great expense of human life. Above a thousand armed peasants were dispersed about the woods between Epernay and Rheims, on the other side of the Marne, and in the brushwood between Epernay and Montmirail on this side of that river.

General Kaissaroff took a French courier prisoner on the 10th of March, and discovered by his papers that it was Napoleon's plan, as soon as he had beaten his opponents at Laon, to march immediately by Chalons towards Arcis sur Aube, with the intention of falling upon and destroying the right flank of the allied main army. It did not seem likely that Napoleon would undertake a new enterprise after the repulses he had encountered: nevertheless, Tettenborn took up a position on the rear of Napoleon's army along the Marne, and kept so vigilant a watch that no movement on their side could escape him. From the 10th to the 14th of March he daily sent out parties of observation, who, with unexampled boldness, penetrated to the inner lines of the French army, and scoured the whole country from Epernay towards Rheims, as far as Soissons and other points on the Aisne. Patrols went daily along both banks of the Marne towards Château Thierry. The information which Tettenborn acquired by these means confirmed him in his opinion that it was not Napoleon's intention to fall back again upon the lower Marne. On the 10th and 11th a number of troops marched upon Soissons, whither all the national guards of the district were ordered to proceed. Napoleon's evident intention, therefore, was to renew the attack upon Blücher with greater vigour than before.

Our parties were now engaged in creeping silently through woods, or in fighting against the armed peasantry in these villages, and occasionally in skirmishing with the enemy in the open field, frequently with great success. But in spite of all the skill and boldness of the cossacks, Tettenborn could scarcely have carried on these expeditions with such signal success with them alone: their ignorance of the language, of the customs of the country, and even their want of higher intelligence, would have thrown invincible impediments in his way. But Tettenborn took measures to supply this defect. Every party of cossacks was commanded by German officers, whom the cossacks followed as willingly as they did their own.

Meanwhile General Count Saint Priest, in order not to remain idle with his 11,000 men, had attacked Rheims early in the morning of the 12th of March, and, after a short opposition, had retaken the town, which was wholly unfortified, and but weakly garrisoned. The French cavalry and the greater part of the infantry, altogether about 1000 men and eleven cannon, fell into the hands of the Russians, who lost but few men. Count Saint Priest now sent out parties against Fismes and Bery au Bac, to form a junction with Blücher; these, however, were driven back by the enemy's posts. Napoleon, whose original schemes had been delayed, but by no means given up, did not long suffer the Prussians to remain on his right flank on the road he intended to take. On the following day, the 13th of March, he sent Marshal Marmont against Rheims. Count Saint Priest had neglected the most obvious precautions: the consequence was, that our troops were unexpectedly attacked by the enemy: some retreated in good order upon the Aisne, while the rest were scattered in the direction of the Marne. Saint Priest himself paid the penalty of his neglect with his life: he was shot down as he was attempting to get his men into order. The town of Rheims, 10 cannon, and 2000 prisoners remained in the hands of Marshal Marmont.

On receiving the intelligence of this disaster Tettenborn could no longer remain where he was in Port à Bainson, as he foresaw that this advance of the enemy was not an isolated movement, but was connected with other military combinations. He drew in all his straggling parties, and marched towards Epernay, to keep a vigilant eye upon the Upper Marne. Those who had escaped from Rheims said with one accord, that a very large body of men had appeared there, and were on the point of pursuing our troops by both roads to Chalons and Epernay. We were, therefore, liable to be attacked at Epernay even should the enemy have no further object in view than to spread out his flank as far as this town, and clear the country round of enemies. At the moment when he most wanted it Tettenborn was reinforced by two squadrons of Silesian landwehr, or militia, which Blücher had despatched under Major von Falkenhausen, to keep open his communication with the main army. This distinguished officer willingly joined his forces with those under Tettenborn, who had much the same duties to perform. On the following forenoon French troops made their appearance on the wooded heights on the road from Rheims, and advanced into the valley of the Marne. Our advanced posts were driven in, after a slight skirmish, and the enemy, consisting of about 300 infantry and three squadrons of horse, approached the bridge of Epernay. When they had come near enough, Tettenborn despatched a regiment of cossacks against them, who overtook and cut in pieces the cavalry, while the infantry laid down their arms. During this combat an accident happened, which, under less favourable circumstances, might have had most serious consequences. The stone bridge over the Marne could be blown into the air at any moment that the advance of the French might render this necessary. By some unfortunate accident the powder ignited and the bridge was blown up, whilst our cossacks were still on the other side of the river in full pursuit of the enemy. Tettenborn immediately sent two cannon into the plains before Epernay, to protect the cossacks in case they might be driven back, while he hastily repaired the bridge, one side of which, sufficient to admit one cossack at a time, was still left standing. Not long after this battle we again saw the wooded heights covered with troops, but this time in far greater numbers: enormous bodies of cavalry followed in endless succession, mixed with artillery and infantry. It was now quite evident that the enemy was making a strong movement in our direction, and would soon force a passage across the river. Nevertheless, Tettenborn determined to dispute the passage as long as possible. He defended the bridge with two guns, until the enemy brought a great number to bear upon it, and it was not till evening that Tettenborn retreated without loss. The French could only use the bridge for foot soldiers that evening, and their cavalry were forced to pass the night in the plains on the other side of the river.

There could no longer be any doubt that Napoleon, in accordance with his original plan, would advance by Chalons and Epernay towards Arcis-sur-Aube. In order to obtain perfect certainty on this point, Tettenborn during the night sent a party of cossacks to Chalons, to get information as to the state of things there. He himself withdrew from the Marne towards Velie, on the brook Somme Soudé, whence at an equal distance from Chalons and Epernay he could watch the enemy's motions, and avoid any attack by retreating in time to the strongly fortified town of Vitry. On the following morning, the 16th of March, Tettenborn received information from the parties who had now returned, that General Davidoff, who held possession of Chalons with 2000 Russians and numerous artillery, had not waited for the approach of the French, but had retired with all his troops to Vitry. Upon this the French, whose numbers they could not exactly calculate, but which must have been very inconsiderable, had entered Chalons without opposition. Tettenborn, who had instructed Schwarzenberg but a few days before of the advance of the enemy, now hurried forward to confirm his previous statement. He likewise communicated this important news to General Kaissaroff, who was still at Fère-Champenoise and Sezanne. Tettenborn himself withdrew his troops out of Napoleon's line of march to Cosle, in order, if possible, to keep up the communication with Blücher's army, and at the same time to remain on the enemy's flank. During the whole of this march we fell in with the advanced posts of the allied army, who had pushed forward to some considerable distance on this side, to gain early intelligence of the enemy, as the allies had been prepared by previous circumstances to expect their approach. There happened to be no light cavalry on this flank of the main army, and the regiment of guards had been forced to do duty as outposts: Tettenborn's arrival with his cossacks was therefore doubly welcome. He now found himself attached to Schwarzenberg's main army, where he remained two whole days, supplying the advanced line of outposts.

The contradictory orders which he received from various quarters added to his difficulties. Tettenborn had obstinately maintained that the enemy would advance with all his force upon the Aube; but as this advance was delayed for some days, doubt was thrown on his supposition, and unfortunately he was not allowed to make more active inquiries.

Under the impression that the taking of Chalons and Epernay arose merely from an isolated side movement of the enemy, and would have no further consequences, the Russian General Lambert received orders from head-quarters to join his forces to those of Generals Tettenborn and Davidoff, and to make an attempt to retake Chalons. On the 18th of March, therefore, Tettenborn left Cosle, and intended to advance by the left bank of the Marne to Chalons. Meanwhile intelligence was received that the French were marching in great strength through Vitry towards Somme-sous, consequently towards the Aube, and a brisk firing was heard in the direction of Vitry. General Lambert, accordingly, now altered his former plan, and trusted to Tettenborn alone the attempt upon Chalons, and to keep open the communication with Blücher, while he himself returned to Vitry, so as not to leave that important post exposed on the anticipated general advance of the enemy. Tettenborn, accordingly, forded the Marne with all his troops, and now proceeded down the right bank towards Chalons.

Napoleon had left Marshals Marmont and Mortier at Soissons with sufficient forces to hold Blücher in check, and had taken the road towards the south with 30,000 of his best troops, and a considerable reinforcement of recruits from Paris: he now intended to attack the allied army. He marched in four divisions, which crossed the Marne at La Fertè-sous-Jouarre, Château Thierry, Epernay, and Chalons. By deploying his troops, Napoleon hoped to compel ours to fall back, in order not to be forced into an action; he would thus gain ground without a victory, and at his next advance he hoped to reach the Meuse. His plan was a very simple one,—invariably to direct his chief attack against our centre, and to throw his troops boldly forward between our two flanks, and, by separating them, to compel our forces more by fear than by actual necessity to retreat. By this manœuvre he hoped now to clear Champagne of his enemies on both sides. He would have succeeded completely in his object had not an accident brought about an action at Arcis-sur-Aube. When Napoleon's advance was no longer doubtful, Schwarzenberg's army quitted its position and went up the Aube towards Bar-sur-Aube, where he fixed his head-quarters on the 20th of March. The order sent by Schwarzenberg for the troops on the Seine to join him was by some unlucky accident, never delivered; and these troops must inevitably have been cut off and lost, were not the enemy held in check at Arcis. Schwarzenberg, therefore, now advanced with all his forces against the enemy, whom he found in the plains by Plancy and Arcis, on this side of the river: he immediately attacked the French, as no other course was left open to him. After a contest which lasted three days, without coming to a regular engagement, Napoleon retired from Arcis on the 22d of March with the loss of eleven cannon and many prisoners. He had found Arcis a second Laon.

Meanwhile Tettenborn discovered that the enemy had evacuated Chalons, and on the evening of the 20th of March he took possession of the town. He proceeded to send out parties on all sides to gain information, more especially in the direction of Rheims and Epernay. On the following day he succeeded in reopening the communication with the army of the north: Tettenborn's outposts fell in with Wintzingerode's troops in Rheims. Blücher now advanced with all his troops towards the Marne, and wished to secure all the bridges, in order to destroy them should the enemy happen to return, meaning to reserve for his own use the bridge at Epernay. However, the French, with 800 infantry and three squadrons of horse, still held this town. Tettenborn, therefore, sent two regiments of cossacks to drive them out. General Vincent, who commanded at Epernay, advanced out of the town with his cavalry, and held his ground for some time, until, after some false attacks, the cossacks unexpectedly rushed upon him, completely routed the three squadrons, and drove them into Epernay. The infantry who defended the entrance of the town were cut to pieces, and the French were chased and butchered all through the streets into the open fields: General Vincent managed to escape into the woods with a very small number of his troops. During this brilliant affair the advanced guard of General Wintzingerode made its appearance on the other side of the Marne, and entered Epernay by the bridge which had been repaired.

On the 22nd March the intelligence which Tettenborn gathered from his scouts, induced him to suspect that Napoleon, in consequence of the unfavourable issue of the battle at Arcis-sur-Aube, would return towards the Marne, most likely to Vitry, where the river was fordable, whence he could without difficulty gain the road to Nancy, or place himself in the rear of our main army. It was a matter of the gravest importance to obtain certain and rapid information on this point, as it might effect a complete change in the conduct of the whole campaign. Tettenborn, therefore, sent out parties to scour the country on either side of the Marne, both towards Vitry, in order to discover the march of the enemy, and towards Cosle and Somme-sous, suspecting that, perhaps, the enemy had already crossed the Marne, in which case he hoped to gain intelligence in Napoleon's rear, and to intercept couriers. A courier was intercepted after a long chase, and his despatches, which were of the highest importance, forwarded that same evening to Chalons. Besides a corrected copy of the bulletin of the battle at Arcis, which announced the victory in such terms as to leave no doubt that the advantage had been on our side, there were a considerable number of remarkable letters: for example, Marshal Lefevre wrote to his wife that Napoleon and his staff had been in great danger at Arcis from an attack of a regiment of Hungarian hussars, who had come so close to his person that Napoleon had grasped his pistols, and had had a horse shot under him. However, it was Napoleon's wish that this should not be known, and so forth. The chief thing, however, was a letter in Napoleon's own hand to Marie Louise, in which he expressly said that, without having exactly gained a victory at Arcis, he had been so far successful that he was then pushing forward his army in order to approach his strong places, and to keep the two allied armies separate at the same time that he drew the allies further from Paris.

According to the information thus obtained, no time was to be lost. General Wintzingerode took all the cavalry of his division, about 7000 horse, together with forty-six horse artillery, and started on the 23d March from Epernay on the road to Vitry: he ordered Tettenborn to join him from Chalons, and on the following day he marched towards the fortified town of Vitry. The communication between the two main armies was now established without impediment through the towns of Vertus and Fère-Champenoise in Napoleon's rear; and both Blücher and Schwarzenberg, informed of all that was going on, agreed to attack Napoleon from both sides with all their united forces, and thus, if possible, to put an end to the war with one blow. Blücher, therefore, marched from Rheims to Chalons, Schwarzenberg from Arcis-sur-Aube to Vitry, in search of Napoleon: instead of falling back before him at some distance from one another, and thus giving Napoleon plenty of room, as he had expected, they boldly formed a junction of their several divisions behind him. We hoped that Napoleon might turn back when he found his expectations foiled, and we then should have fought him in the great plains between the Marne and the Aube, where our numerous cavalry could have been brought in large masses against the very inferior cavalry of the French. But Napoleon was already on his way to Saint-Dizier, and had only left a small division behind him, which occupied the villages along the road, close to Vitry.

On the 24th of March Schwarzenberg reached Vitry, where he was joined by the Emperor of Russia and by the King of Prussia. It was then resolved to march immediately, with united forces, upon Paris, the road to which was open, and to leave the pursuit of Napoleon to the cavalry and horse artillery of General Wintzingerode, who was to harass Napoleon's troops. Taking into consideration all the circumstances of the case, it is impossible not to give to this determination the praise of great boldness. Napoleon had nothing but chosen troops with him, and could form a junction with the numerous garrisons in his fortified towns. General Maison, in the Netherlands, had already joined his forces to those of General Carnot, who was then threatening Brussels, and might at any moment render assistance to Napoleon. Behind us the whole country was in a state of insurrection, which would naturally be increased by the approach of Napoleon. Marshal Augereau was at the head of numerous forces at Lyons, and could send troops from thence. Meanwhile our armies plunged deeper and deeper into the heart of France, — were separated from the sources whence they drew their supplies, — were in the midst of a desolated country, without any point upon which they could fall back for their supplies or support, — and were shortly about to appear before the capital of the kingdom, the population of which were perfectly capable of giving employment to, and even destroying, a whole army. All this was sufficient to excite the greatest anxiety; but in their determination the allies clearly took the right course, even had the results been less successful. Paris and Napoleon had now lost the importance which they mutually gave to one another.

The large armies broke up their quarters near the Aube and the Marne on the 24th and 25th of March, on their way to Paris. On the 25th, near Fère-Champenoise, they encountered the united troops of Marshals Marmont and Mortier, who were on their way from Soissons to join Napoleon. After a short but bloody engagement the two marshals were beaten, their troops destroyed, and the march on Paris was resumed.

On the evening of the 24th of March Wintzingerode advanced with all his cavalry from Vitry towards Saint-Dizier, whither Napoleon had directed his march, true to his intention of drawing the allies away from Paris, and approaching his own fortresses. The command of the advanced guard was entrusted to Tettenborn, who had five regiments of cossacks, one of hussars, and eight pieces of horse artillery under him.

The French had withdrawn from the neighbourhood of Vitry during that afternoon, and we only came up with them at nightfall in the village of Thièblemont, where we had some sharp skirmishing with the infantry. On the following day the pursuit was continued with increased vigour, and we overtook a still larger division of the enemy at Saint-Dizier, where a brisk engagement took place. The enemy held possession of Saint-Dizier with infantry, so as to cover the march of the other troops who were there recrossing and marching along the Marne. From the direction which these troops were taking, it appeared certain that Napoleon intended again to attack our main armies; he must, therefore, have received some intelligence of the direction they were taking towards Paris. On the other side of the river we saw compact masses of troops coming straight towards us, having changed their line of march; they advanced down to the banks, and then marched away up the heights on the left. Tettenborn immediately brought his guns close to the bank of the river, and commenced pouring a murderous fire of cannon-balls and grenades upon the nearest French troops, which retreated into the woods with the loss of many men. As a regiment of cossacks now crossed the Marne, and threatened to cut off the troops in Saint-Dizier, these men, who had bravely stood their ground until now, likewise fled to the woods. However, the French were not long exposed to this fire, as a portion of their artillery, placed on the heights of Valcour, commanding the road which lay through a narrow gorge, soon silenced our guns. The French held the heights of Valcour until evening, and then pursued their retreat towards Wassy. Tettenborn followed close at their heels, and drove them out of the village of Humbecourt, but found it impossible to penetrate further, as the adjoining villages were full of infantry, who offered the most obstinate resistance; a sure sign that the main body of the French army was close by, and could not suffer our troops to approach any nearer. The skirmishing continued all the night, during which we saw the whole surface of the country between us and Wassy lighted up with numerous watch-fires, which stretched a long way to our right along the wood, almost reaching our quarters. Tettenborn passed the night in Eclaron, while General Wintzingerode fixed his head-quarters in Saint-Dizier, and sent a considerable number of troops from Vitry towards Montier-en-Der, so as to secure our right flank.

Early on the morning of the 26th of March Tettenborn found the villages which the French held on the previous day by no means deserted: on the contrary, the enemy advanced against us. We could clearly perceive large masses of troops in the distance, drawing nearer every moment, followed by still greater numbers; among them were considerable bodies of cavalry. The French, who were about 30,000 men, advanced against us on all sides, forcing the cossacks to retreat: considerable bodies of cavalry showed themselves on both sides of us. On first seeing these masses of troops, Tettenborn assured Wintzingerode that the whole French army had turned and was marching against us. The advance of the French was so rapid, and their numbers so great, that to form any plan was useless. The danger was imminent, the nature of the ground prevented our employing even one regiment of cossacks with any advantage, and in our rear was the gorge through the village of Valcour, which the enemy only had to take possession of before we did, and our retreat was completely cut off. Nothing, therefore, remained but to retreat immediately across the Marne, which Tettenborn did, remaining as long as he could on the left bank of the river, to give Wintzingerode time to take such measures as he might think necessary. Whilst Wintzingerode was still doubtful whether Napoleon was actually approaching with his whole force, and hesitated to give full belief to Tettenborn's statements, he saw General Tschernyscheff suddenly driven back from Montier-en-Der, while he himself was attacked at the same moment. The French poured their forces upon us with incredible rapidity; troop followed troop, the whole plain was covered, and in a few minutes the engagement commenced on all sides. A large number of guns were brought on the plain and pointed against Saint-Dizier. The country was flat, but cut up with vineyards and hedges, and too much hemmed in on all sides by woods and low bottoms for our numerous cavalry to be used with any advantage. It was still possible by a rapid retreat to avoid an action which must end to our disadvantage. Tettenborn tried to impress this upon others; but, unfortunately, 700 Russian chasseurs were stationed in Saint-Dizier; and as these were the only infantry which Wintzingerode had with him, he delayed his retreat in the hope of saving them. He therefore ordered Tettenborn to defend the road to Vitry, while Wintzingerode maintained himself in Saint-Dizier, intending to fall back upon Bar-le-Duc in case of necessity.

Meanwhile the enemy had crossed the Marne between Valcour and Saint-Dizier, with large bodies of cavalry, infantry, and some artillery, and advanced without impediment towards the road to Vitry: the guns planted on the heights of Valcour had protected this movement. The Russian cavalry and horse artillery were distributed in the plain behind this road; in their rear was the wood, in their front the enemy, who poured a heavy fire into our ranks. The baggage and led horses had not yet been sent to the rear, and caused considerable disorder. On one side of this road to the right, Tettenborn stood his ground with about 1000 horse, of which four squadrons were huzzars, the rest cossacks. A body of at least 10,000 French cavalry had already crossed the Marne, and had forced their way between Tettenborn and Wintzingerode. Tettenborn was in momentary expectation of seeing these masses suddenly deploy and throw his men into utter confusion. Meanwhile bodies of infantry and artillery continued to cross the river, and to form. It was no use to think now of retreating, as the cavalry was close upon us; a resolute front could scarcely check them, much less a retreating foe. Tettenborn, therefore, boldly formed his 1000 men into a compact body, with which he charged the masses of French with reckless courage, just as they were about to deploy. The huzzars and cossacks fell with the utmost intrepidity upon the French, and drove them before them: the first line was broken, then the second; and the contest was most bloody. But fresh masses of French cavalry deployed on both sides of him; more and more troops came from the back-ground,—the inequality of numbers was too great, and the greatest bravery of no avail. Our troops came within the range of the enemy's guns, and could no longer bear up against this unequal contest: in our turn we were put to the rout, and chased along the road to Vitry; here the baggage and led horses, flying in all directions, caused indescribable confusion. Tettenborn, who with his officers had maintained the contest to the last, and had been in great personal danger, got his troops again into some order at the village of Perthe, skirmished a little with the enemy that same evening, and retreated during the night by Marolles to Vitry. His whole loss consisted of only forty men. The rest of Wintzingerode's cavalry, who were drawn up on the plains by Saint-Dizier, and who had waited till the French attacked them, without taking the initiative, had a far greater number of men killed, besides losing many cannon. After a heroic defence of Saint-Dizier, Wintzingerode left that town on the same evening and retreated to Bar-le-Duc, hotly pursued by the French, whom, however, he beat off when they pressed upon him too closely.

This battle, in spite of its unfavourable issue, was most successful in its results: it led Napoleon into an error by which he lost three entire days, during all which time his capital was in imminent danger. Napoleon was convinced that Schwarzenberg's whole army was on his traces, and Wintzingerode had taken care to strengthen this surmise by hiring rooms at Saint-Dizier for the Emperor of Russia and for the King of Prussia, and by giving out that his cavalry was merely the advanced guard of the main army. Napoleon, who learned all this from some of his devoted adherents in Saint-Dizier, halted at Wassy, recalled those troops which had already marched forwards, and thought that he would fight a battle where the ground and the circumstances would be in his favour. Even on the day after this action Napoleon could not be brought to believe that he was mistaken, and had been striking at a shadow; he persisted in advancing against Vitry, where the small garrison prepared to meet the storm. There, however, he suddenly learnt Marmont's and Mortier's defeat, and the advance of the allies upon Paris: he now hastily collected his weary, half-famished troops, and made forced marches by Troyes, Sens, and Fontainebleau, to relieve his threatened capital. A part of his troops dropped down with fatigue on the road, a number of horses perished, and many pieces of cannon were thrown into the rivers, as the want of horses was felt more and more every day. Spite of all, Napoleon came just too late; the news of the surrender of Paris reached him on his arrival at Fontainebleau.

Whatever might have been the ultimate result, it is certain that Paris would not have surrendered so quickly had Napoleon arrived at the right moment; the storming of the city, with the certainty of a general rising of the people, would have been attended with great peril. Napoleon reinforced by 100,000 national guards from Paris and its immediate neighbourhood, might have carried on the war with fresh hope and renewed vigour. These considerations induced the Emperor Alexander to use the most flattering expressions to Wintzingerode; attributing to him the actual presence of the allies in Paris. Tettenborn's charge, although the advantages he first gained were speedily again lost, was reckoned one of his most brilliant feats; its results were invaluable, as it helped to confirm Napoleon's erroneous impressions, and made him lose the most precious time.

After Wintzingerode and Tettenborn had effected a junction at Chalons, they advanced on the 28th March by Saint-Dizier and Montier-en-Der to Troyes, which town they reached on the 30th, without, however, coming up with Napoleon's rear guard. They found many traces of his march along the road. From one station beyond Troyes Napoleon had left the troops to pursue their march alone, and had hurried on to Fontainebleau on post-horses, accompanied by only one adjutant.

From Troyes Tettenborn went by Villeneuve l'Archeveque on the Yonne, to Sens, which town was still held by the enemy, and had lately been re-inforced by troops under General Allix. After an ineffectual attempt to induce the inhabitants to surrender, Tettenborn determined to find some other passage over the Yonne, so as to advance upon Fontainebleau. But further hostilities were speedily put an end to by the news of the allies having entered Paris, and of Napoleon's abdication: there were even reports current of the return of the Bourbons.

On reaching Bray on the Seine, we received orders to march without delay towards Auxerre, to hinder Napoleon from carrying into execution a plan which he may have conceived, of escaping to the south of France, where he could still have formed a formidable army out of the numerous troops in that district. At Villeneuve-le-Roi, however, we learnt that Napoleon was staying quietly at Fontainebleau, and received orders to return to Bray. The troops were then removed to Sens and Pont-sur-Yonne, whence they directed their march back towards the Rhine, as peace with France was certain, and the terms ready for signature.

From Bray I was sent with special instructions to the Russian General Diebitsch, and to General Wintzingerode at Paris. Tettenborn himself shortly came thither by invitation, with most of his officers. This capital now offered to us a remarkable spectacle: it contained soldiers from almost every country in Europe, as well as its chief rulers, from whose victories and future alliance the face of the world would most probably undergo great changes. The French revolution seemed to be completely nullified by the re-establishment of the Bourbons and the announcement of the new constitution called the Charte. Nevertheless, signs were not wanting that France still contained the elements of fresh outbreaks which the new government would find it no easy matter to destroy. Napoleon's military dominion still lived in the wreck of his army, in the measures and ordinances which he had established, and which were still maintained. The revolutionary maxims and opinions which had only been kept under by Napoleon were daily becoming more rife, and rising into opposition against those powers which appeared willing to restore matters to the state in which they were before the revolution, in spite of the Charte. However, the rapidity with which new and strange events succeeded one another, the pressure of public affairs, by which all eyes were now directed to the cabinets of London and Vienna,— the whirl of daily life, which occupied all minds, did not allow time for much reflection on the excitable condition of the French nation, which then seemed a matter of secondary importance.

CHAPTER XX.

State of Paris in 1814. — Rapid Change in the Parisians. — Scheme to seize upon the Emperor of Russia and the King of Prussia. — Defeated by Count Schlabrendorf. — The Count d'Artois enters Paris. — Plan of a Constitution. — Chateaubriand, Benjamin Constant, and Count Gregoire. — Louis XVIII. enters Paris. — Ballad on the King. — Madame de Stael. — Death of the Empress Josephine.

My communications with General Diebitsch were soon finished: not so the business with General Wintzingerode. I found him still much excited about the affair at Saint-Dizier: the Emperor Alexander, it is true, had made a great merit of his services in that he had drawn upon himself Napoleon's army, and had thus enabled the allies to march upon Paris. But this praise had somewhat the air of a back-handed blow; and Wintzingerode always considered that, if he had been better supported, he might have rendered the same service, with the additional advantage of having been enabled to hold his ground against Napoleon.

I lodged at the well-known Hôtel de l'Empire, and immediately began to revisit the old familiar places, which had changed so much that most of them were quite new to me. Not only is Paris full of foreigners, who walked proudly about, but the French appeared to have a totally different bearing from that of former times. With the belief in their own military supremacy they had lost most of their other characteristics, — their dogmatical opinions, their self-sufficiency, the quick clear comprehension of their own position, which had given them such signal advantages in all practical matters — all were gone, and it seemed doubtful how they were be recovered. Napoleon's star had sunk, that was quite cain; some few of his adherents looked sadly and wistfully after him, but the mass had entirely deserted him. The partizans of the Bourbons were loud in their rejoicings, and no one disturbed them: but among themselves there were many divisions and anxieties. But few had kept perfectly true to the cause: most of them, and these the noblest and most intelligent, had committed greater or lesser errors which needed forgiveness; and while the exceptions claimed for themselves the greatest rewards, and meted out punishment to the others, they still felt the necessity of conceding something to the new-born zeal of the latter party, and of allowing them some share in the spoil. Politicians, on the other hand, wished to start from the present, and to consider only the future: in their eyes opinions and devotion went for only so much as they might serve present purposes, and it soon became evident that the real strength lay with them. The old nobility and the officials who had served under the Emperor, whom they now deserted, had the advantage of possession, and were best fitted to promote order in the new state of things. The friends of liberty and the republicans, at least those few who had not given in their adhesion to the Emperor, were dispersed and stood in the background; they were scarcely mentioned. The mass of the people had no opinions of their own, but waited impatiently for what was to turn up, and were perfectly disposed to be contented with moderate measures, provided order were firmly established, and there remained a hope that the governing powers would yield somewhat to the exigencies of the times. This expectation was very general, and people looked with confidence to the Allied Sovereigns: they had conducted their own affairs well and wisely, their moderation was evident, and the Emperor Alexander talked in a strain which reminded men of the most beautiful speeches of the early days of the revolution. People were convinced that good must come out of so much that was noble. The mass of the people would have been content to be ruled by young Napoleon under the regency of his mother or by the Crown Prince of Sweden. The restoration of the Bourbons, which immediately took place, was viewed with mixed feelings of indifference and confidence, and it was obvious, that this was less popular than either of the two other alternatives.

What has been said above only held good for the space of the first eight or ten days, after which a complete and rapid revulsion took place. There was no more uncertainty, wavering to be seen anywhere, collectively or individually: people ceased to feel the effects of the blow, and began to recover their senses; the French recollected what they were, took an accurate measure of the foreigners, of their enemies and others, and within a few weeks the advantages of position and of daily intercourse were again all on the side of the French. A strong feeling of nationality arose out of this turmoil of contradictions and adverse parties, which was directed with success against all foreigners in Paris. All the strength, all the peculiarities of the French nation were actively employed in this work; the French stood before us in the position of enemies, who had unexpectedly built up a wall before morning to replace one which had been knocked down the preceding night: they had safely entrenched themselves within the strong lines of nationality,— a work at which all classes had laboured silently, but zealously: this feeling of nationality could not be overcome, and inspired respect and admiration. In truth, it soon appeared as if we had come to Paris, not for our own especial business, but simply to please the French, as if the main object was to give them satisfaction, to gain their approval, and to obtain from them some testimony to the possession, on our part, of mental refinement and of good manners. We felt, and not without some disgust, that in the same degree in which their affairs prospered, ours languished; we felt that we Germans, split into different races and parties, were far behind the French in nationality, that our wants were not attended to, our soldiers—and that in a conquered country—were ill-quartered and not cared for. But in this we had no reproach to make against the French; on the contrary, we were forced to recognise that in all this they set before us an admirable example.

The Allies had advanced into Paris with a comparatively small force, were surrounded with French troops, which had capitulated, it is true, but which were continually coming into contact with others who might yet be considered hostile to us. The masses which were still at Fontainebleau with Napoleon might advance: the Parisian national guard had not been disarmed; the populace was in a violent state of excitement; several thousands of Napoleon's officers, unattached and most anxious for fresh employment, some of them recovering or just recovered from wounds and sickness, were prowling about the town in all directions: all this and the small number of allied troops, the insignificance of the measures taken for the safety of the Emperor of Russia and the King of Prussia, occasioned the formation of a bold scheme to seize upon both these sovereigns. Five hundred officers had bound themselves by oath to carry this project into execution: they were to penetrate into the dwellings of these two monarchs, while the populace was to rise in masses, to fire the town in several places, and even if Paris were thereby burnt to the ground, they did not consider this too high a price to pay for the liberation of France: meanwhile the troops at Fontainebleau were to advance at a given signal. Schlabrendorf sent accurate information of the plot, of which he had immediate notice, to the King of Prussia, who directed the necessary measures for frustrating the attempt to be immediately taken. A few bodies of armed men made their appearance in the streets, but were quickly dispersed, and the troops which were on their way into Paris were driven back. The first moment was the only one to be feared: when this had gone by and the intended plot had failed, there was no fear of a second attempt; for such plots opportunity and the requisite courage seldom recur. Although Schlabrendorf had thus rendered essential service to his sovereign and to the cause of the Allies, he still remained in other respects the steady friend of the French. He wished to secure to them all the advantages of the revolution, to lose none of the good which had been so dearly bought. He saw much to blame in the conduct of the Allied Sovereigns, and spoke out with a freedom and boldness which, joined to the impetuous flow of his extraordinary eloquence, astonished all who heard him, especially as he talked to Frenchmen of all parties and to Germans of all ranks and conditions, and his rooms during many hours of the day were filled with visitors. He was reminded that many of his expressions were dangerous, that those then in power were, in certain cases, stricter than Napoleon himself; but he continued to say every thing that came into his head.

Schlabrendorf was my constant refuge, and a day seldom passed without my seeing him. The society at his house was always numerous and mixed; no one interfered with what he said; but, as he invariably took all the conversation to himself, the worst that could happen was to be made answerable for what one had heard. This danger the most distinguished persons willingly incurred: Hardenberg, the Humboldts, Gneisenau, and other Prussians, were constantly with him. But there were many other resources: the history of the world, the affairs of Europe, the termination of a terrible revolution, the commencement of a new order of things, the taming and remodelling of a most excitable and powerful nation; all this was to be seen in Paris, and these elements were working and fermenting together. There was no longer any doubt as to the future system of government to be established in France: no impediment was opposed to the return of the Bourbons. The Count d'Artois, for whom the old title of Monsieur had been revived, had entered Paris as the forerunner and representative of his brother, and had been received with great ceremony by the magistrates and the national guard. Every one was convinced that the new government would have a constitutional form; the only doubt, and one which caused much anxiety, was how far the reforms would be carried. The senate had sketched out and made public the plan of a constitution, in the expectation that the king of their choice would not dare to refuse it; but this body was deficient in weight and wanted the confidence of the public, and it had an ill appearance to stand thus between the king and his people. It was the ruin of the senate and of the new constitution that they had taken care in it to secure the dotation of their own members.

Perfect freedom of the press prevailed at this time in Paris; it was not authorised by law, but so it was. There was no one to interfere with it, no one to act the part of censor. Even during the iron reign of the Empire, in the very last days of its existence, and just before the Allies entered Paris, Chateaubriand, at the peril of his very life, had placed his vehement diatribe against Napoleon in the printer's hands, and it appeared simultaneously with the great events which it announced as probable. It was received with the greatest enthusiasm by the royalists and by the foreigners in Paris, and the accusations against Napoleon found a ready audience in many Frenchmen; but the pompous and flattering declamation in favour of the returning Bourbons excited distrust and suspicion, or was received with cold indifference. Benjamin Constant likewise published a paper to prove that Napoleon was the curse of France, and that every thing depended on the reestablishment of royalty. Constant had handled his subject with greater vigour and power of thought than the imaginative Chateaubriand; but he too was accused of flattering the incoming dynasty, and many of his enemies talked of reprinting a publication of his which had appeared eight years before, called *Des Reactions Politiques*, in which he wished to prove that the return of the Bourbons was not a thing to be desired, and could never be for the benefit of France! But besides these works of a high and noble purpose, appeared a host of low and mean pamphlets in which Bonaparte and his whole family, his adherents, and his reign, were covered with ridicule, and all the faults of his government, those of which he was guilty as well as those of which he was innocent, were dragged into light, and worked up to inflame men's minds and passions against him. It formed a complete literature in itself, odious to any one of decent taste or of good understanding. I saw to my annoyance that these publications were eagerly devoured by my countrymen!

Several pamphlets written with great power and in a totally different spirit appeared on the side of freedom. One of the earliest and best was that of the Senator Gregoire, formerly bishop of Blois, who, spite of his revolutionary zeal and of his being subsequently ennobled by the title of count, had always remained a strict Catholic and a staunch republican. He criticised the proposed constitution of the senate in the most cutting manner, and promulgated political maxims which had not been heard of for many years. Several other pamphlets written in the same spirit, some anonymous and others under their authors' names, followed in rapid succession; and when people heard such opinions expressed in such terms, they felt that the revolution was not yet crushed.

In the course of time Louis XVIII. arrived in Paris, and French affairs now began every day to wear a more settled aspect. The emigrants rushed from their hiding-places, and took possession, not of their lost possessions, for that was impossible, but of the monarch's favour, of influence, and of the vacant offices. The clergy struggled hard with them to obtain their share of the advantages which the times seemed to offer; but they had to proceed with some show of prudence and decency, as the king was not favourable to them, and cared for their formulas no further than they had political influence. He was a philosopher in the French sense of that word, which is what we Germans should call a free-thinker, and rejected all belief inculcated by a church. Wonderful to relate, this side of the king's character had been sedulously puffed as a means of gaining adherents for him among the mass of the French nation, and not without success, as it seemed to give an assurance that the priesthood would not be allowed to have a mischievous preponderance in state affairs. But the general feeling towards him was cold and suspicious; even the royalists, at least the most ardent among them, had rather trust their affairs in the hands of the Count D'Artois and of the Duchess d'Angoulême than in those of the king. Among the people the king's air and manner produced no good effect; on the contrary, they were the subject of ridicule and caricature. One of the numerous squibs which appeared against him happens to be preserved among my papers: it was distributed among the crowd on the Boulevards on the day of the king's entry into Paris, and as it contains more fun than malice, I will insert it here.

LOUIS XVIII.

Air: " Quand l'amour naquit à Cythère."

Je vous revois, peuple fidèle,
   Qui m'avez donné mon congé,
Pardon . . . ma goutte habituelle
   M'ôte le peu d'esprit qui j'ai;
Les grands rois, les hommes de tête,
   Font le malheur de leur pays;
Pour être bon faut être bête,
      (le peuple s'écrie)
Vive le roi! Vive Louis!

Vous étiez las de la victoire;
   Vous n'en aurez plus sous ma loi,
On vit bien plus longtemps sans gloire,
   J'ai soixante ans,—regardez moi!

> Je ne puis souffrir la vaillance,
>   Ça me fait mal de voir le sang,
> J'arrive avec mon innocence,
>   Mes vertus et mon ruban blanc.
>
> Bon jour, ma brillante noblesse !
>   Jadis vous m'avez planté là ;
> Mais aujourd'hui le péril cesse,
>   Je vous reconnais . . . vous voilà !
> Venez, ferme appui de mon trône,
>   Recevez le ruban de moi !
>   (les nobles s'écrient)
> Nous savons tous ce qu'en vaut l'aune,
>   Vive Louis !   Vive le roi !

Among other shining lights Madame de Stael now made her appearance in Paris. She had taken a large house, and began receiving people in an evening. She had been ill-looked upon in former times by the royalists and emigrants, and the Bourbons had an old grudge against her; but the long persecution she had endured from Napoleon was considered in the light of an atonement, and latterly this clever woman had done some service to the royalist cause. Meanwhile her old friends of the time of the revolution were not lost; those of the empire had no longer any cause to avoid her society, and all foreigners strove who should pay her most attention and homage. In her journeys through Europe she had done much socially, politically, and in matters connected with literature, and had associated her distinguished name with hopes and expectations which were now for the most part fulfilled. The Emperor of Russia paid her the greatest attention, and frequently went to her evening parties ; other great people, such as the Duke of Wellington, with a host of warriors and diplomatists of all nations, followed his example : literary men and artists had a prescriptive right to go there. She held a sort of court; and if the Bourbons had their restoration, certainly Madame de Stael had hers. I could not deny myself the pleasure of seeing such a society, and I had been personally invited. I was introduced by August Wilhelm von Schlegel one forenoon into a room looking on the garden. Madame de Stael, in a light morning dress, came out of the garden holding in her hand a branch

which she had plucked from an orange tree. She received me
like an old acquaintance. I knew enough of her not to be surprised at any thing; but I did not expect to find such simplicity
and natural ease, as no one had described her to me as possessing
these pleasing qualities. Schlegel reminded her that I had been
a comrade of her son Albert, and she wished to hear all that I had
to say of him, — how we had lived, what people had thought,
and what expectations they had formed of him. I had to detail
all the circumstances of the duel in which he was killed: she
wept bitterly, but it did her heart good to hear that he had
acted with courage, and had never shrunk from danger. This
first visit was very short; fresh people were announced, and I
took my leave of her after she had invited me to her evening
parties: Schlegel accompanied me in order to learn more fully
how I liked his friend. I perfectly satisfied him; but I could
not conceal from myself that Madame de Stael — interesting and
admirable as she was — did not exactly please me: I missed the
charm of sensibility, the expression of deep feeling: — kindness,
softness, and talent the possession of which I could not deny,
did not make up for the want of the former qualities. Her
manner made upon me the impression of a contradiction, which
allowed of no softening down: she was both a princess and a
bourgeoise; and it was matter of serious doubt to me which
of the two characters was assumed: perhaps both were. Her
book on Germany, the whole edition of which, with the exception of a few copies which had been saved, had been destroyed
by Napoleon, was now reprinted; several editions had been
struck off, and it was generally read and praised. I had seen
the book on a former occasion, and I could not judge it more
favourably now than then. Much in it annoyed me: the evident want of philosophy was only equalled by the arrogance
with which the restless author imagined that she comprehended
every thing at a glance: in matters of taste it was easy to perceive how implicitly she had adopted the opinions expressed by
others. I then thought that these sins outweighed all the rest
of the merit which the work had; but I afterwards fully appreciated its worth, and defended it with success against Tieck's
objections. It cannot be denied that the book had a prodigious

effect, and produced consequences which should be thankfully recognised by Germans and French.

In order to complete the picture I turned from the personal to the literary,—from Madame de Staël to her novel of Delphine, which I was told was the ideal of the author, and was intended to represent her own feelings and mode of thought. But this did not satisfy me: there was always something in spite of the undoubted talent—of the power of thought and passion—to disturb and to prevent me from being thoroughly pleased. I never could be quite sure of any fact, and even now I can only describe my meaning by saying that I did not feel on a firm natural soil.

I went only once to Madame de Staël's evening parties: a brilliant, shifting, but unusually silent society filled the rooms: every body was listening with attention and deference to the voices of one or two individuals who spoke very low. The Emperor of Russia was present, and walked about without any ceremony: Madame de Staël was the only person who preserved perfect freedom of manner towards him, and she alone kept up the conversation. I pushed a little way into the room and heard the hostess turn the conversation on the subject of the slave-trade, and her illustrious guest called it, with some indignation, "infamous." A Portuguese—I forget whether it was the Marquis Marialva—ventured to hint to the Emperor that serfdom still prevailed in his own dominions. The Emperor was taken aback for one moment, but immediately recovered his self-possession, and said with noble firmness, "You are quite right: serfdom exists in Russia, but the difference between serfs and negro slaves is very great: however, I will not now dispute this point, but declare that the existence of serfdom is an evil which must be abolished, and that, with God's blessing, it shall cease during my reign." A murmur of applause ran through the whole assembly; for the Emperor had spoken these words aloud, and they were instantly repeated and commented upon. Meanwhile I had been pushed back again, and saw no chance of even making my bow to Madame de Staël; the heat was most oppressive, and I determined to go away at once. At the door I met Bartholdy, who was likewise going: he appeared to be but little edified by the Emperor's expressions, and not at all by the assembly, where, he said, unless a man had the title of prince or duke, and three or four orders on his breast, he only stood to endure all sorts of mortifications, without deriving either profit or amusement: and that he certainly would never go again. Without exactly thinking thus, I was contented with this one visit, and never saw Madame de Stael again, which I have often since bitterly regretted.

The great events which had occurred, and the individual and minor questions which arose out of them, kept all Paris in a constant state of excitement: this was further increased by the number and variety of the unusual concourse of strangers. Such excitement works strongly on mankind, but it is not uncommon for it suddenly to cease after reaching a certain point, and to pass into a languid state of weary indifference. This change was already beginning to be felt by most people, and it brought with it the seeds of disease. Spring had commenced, and the contest going on in the atmosphere between heat and cold was so violent, that it was sufficient only to breathe this air to be ill. Sickness was universal. Strangers and natives were all affected by it, especially our young troops, who were distributed about in bad quarters. Every one was now beginning to leave Paris, some on their road to Germany, others to England, whither Hardenberg, Blücher, and Gneisenau accompanied the King of Prussia.

The peace with France was now as good as concluded, and only awaited signature. The terms, however, satisfied neither the French nor the Germans. The English alone seemed to have attained their object, and next to them the Russians. Many questions which concerned Germany were referred to the decision of the Congress to be held during the summer at Vienna.

Little was heard of Napoleon, who remained perfectly quiet in the island of Elba. The Austrian, Count Carl von Clam-Martinitz, who accompanied him to Elba, told me of the wonderful things which occurred on the road, and of the hatred which was everywhere manifested against Napoleon. All men imagined that his game was lost, and no one thought of the Convention of Fontainebleau, the stipulations of which the

Bourbons refused to acknowledge. Suddenly, however, the name of Napoleon was again brought to men's minds by a tragic event. The Empress Josephine died at Malmaison, on the 29th of May, of the prevailing disease. The Emperor of Russia had treated her with especial favour; the Bourbons had taken her up, and she was to have appeared on the following day at the court of Louis XVIII. While the splendour of her husband — of one who had deserted her in the pride of fortune — was gradually sinking, the star of the repudiated Empress was beginning to rise. Her death was deplored sincerely by many Frenchmen. People thought of the impression which this event must make on Napoleon. Many recognised in it the hand of Nemesis, warning Napoleon that his good fortune was gone, and delivering him over to the terrors of remorse. Others, on the contrary, saw in it the punishment which Josephine deserved by making friends with her husband's foes: some went so far as to accuse her of having been the principal cause of Napoleon's fall: she it was, they said, who had nourished those ideas in him which led him to favour the Faubourg Saint Germain, and which ended in making him wish for a second marriage.

CHAPTER XXI.

Viennese Life and Society. — The Prince de Ligne. — Cardinal Consalvi. — Stein. — Baron Cotta. — Dr. Bollmann. — The Opening of the Congress. — Difficulties and Impediments. — The Influence of France. — Entertainments in Vienna. — Lord Stewart. — Death of the Prince de Ligne. — Prince Metternich. — Baron Wessenburg. — Gentz. — Frederick Schlegel. — Prince Hardenberg and Baron William Humboldt. — Counts Stackelberg and Nesselrode. — Lord Castlereagh. — Prince Talleyrand. — Sir Sidney Smith and the Knights of Malta. — The Question touching Saxony and Poland. — French Intrigues. — Life in Vienna. — The Collection in the Castle of Ambras. — Difficulties in Congress. — Funeral Service for Louis XVI. — The Arrival of the Duke of Wellington. — Murat and Sicily. — Napoleon's Escape from Elba. — Its Effect in Vienna. — Napoleon's Progress. — Murat defeated. — War with France inevitable. — Termination of the Congress of Vienna.

AFTER I had fulfilled my mission in Hamburg, and had been married at Berlin, I again started on my journey to Vienna, where I was to meet the Prussian Chancellor, Prince Hardenberg. I was obliged to hurry, as I had to go round by Frankfurt on the Main, to join General Tettenborn and Baron Ompteda. We then proceeded on our way to Vienna, which we reached in the beginning of October.

It is not my purpose here to give a history of the proceedings of the Congress of Vienna; a complete description of all the personages and events of which it was composed would be too difficult; but I can bring together some few fragments out of the store of my own personal observations and impressions.

I had often seen Vienna before, and always under most favourable circumstances, but this time I scarcely recognised it. The population seemed doubled: there was constant throng and motion; there were endless crowds of the highest and most illustrious guests, of the most distinguished men of all nations, and all classes. Europe had sent hither the most remarkable men who sat on thrones or who were about courts, the pillars of states, the heads of the political and military world, the most distinguished for wit, beauty, and birth, for art and taste, in all the pride of victory, in all the freshness of hope, of zeal which I might almost call infatuation, in all the excitement arising from highly-wrought expectations of a general as well as of a personal nature. This throng of strangers was mixed up with the original inhabitants of the imperial city: the latter, owing to their luxurious love of pleasure, which had a local as well as a general character, to their pomp and agreeability, and to their power, were too strong to receive any impression from without. On the contrary, the Viennese, with a sort of gentle violence, forced their modes of thought, their habits, and ways of speaking, upon the strangers within their gates. I need scarcely say that the imperial court had prepared the most brilliant reception and kept open table for all its illustrious guests, their numerous dependants and retainers. To the astonishment of all men, this, occasionally varied by grand festivals on special occasions, was kept up for months, and without any parade or apparent trouble. All this, however, foreigners and natives could easily have pictured to themselves; but what I must mention as remarkable, and what no one could have conceived had he not witnessed it, was the atmosphere of Viennese life, the element in which the days slipped away, the jovial sensual luxury, the strong out-pouring of fun and laughter, the happy good humour having its origin in comfortable ease, the half Italian *dolce far niente*, and its concomitant half Italian humour, the simple expressive dialect running so glibly from the tongue, and so abounding in witty repartees — a dialect which has impressed some of its peculiarities upon all other German tongues, — this, together with many other ways and doings of this Phæacian sort of life, belongs so peculiarly to the Congress of Vienna, — to its individual physiognomy, — that without noticing it no picture would be true. It would be difficult to maintain that this element penetrated into the political negotiations and resolutions, or that its presence could be there traced, as no peculiar local nationality can preserve its integrity in opposition to diplomatic skill and acumen. But this element must undoubtedly have affected all those who breathed its atmosphere, and in this manner have re-acted upon the business which these persons transacted.

It was no easy matter to make one's way and find one's place in this throng of people. But most fortunately rooms had been secured for us in one of the best hotels of the city long before. I had the advantage of being already tolerably well acquainted with Vienna. I renewed a number of former friendships, and unexpectedly found acquaintances whom I had known in other places, or made new ones of whom there were more than enough. There was no lack of splendour or festivity, and those who opened their houses to receive company contended for the honour of entertaining the foreigners. There were, of course, various gradations of society: in some circles only the very highest were admitted; in others the high and the rich aristocracy met together; there were others where this aristocracy mixed with the men of business, and these again were admitted under some special circumstances, or on the occasion of some great festival, into the houses of the great.

The crowds of people at the Prince de Ligne's were more than his small rooms could hold. The charming old man was, as usual, a spendthrift in wit, and kept up a constant fire of fun and humour. But lightly and amusingly as he touched upon the topics of the day with his old-fashioned French wit, no one could help feeling that the present were very different from former times. The light-hearted old man felt too well how vain are the spirits and pretensions of youth unaccompanied by its strength. He who had distinguished himself for courage and gallantry in the court of Catherine the Great; he who had been her most brilliant and favoured lover, seemed out of place while flattering her grandson, the Emperor Alexander, and shining with his borrowed light. There appeared to be a sort of attraction between them; but the heroes of such different ages could recognise each other's merits more easily than they could unite in friendship; and the Prince de Ligne, indefatigable as he was, was nevertheless compelled in the end to give way to younger people. More neglected by the great than his youthful recollections led him to expect, he still maintained his supremacy in humour, was admirably witty, and uttered the happiest sarcasms imaginable to keep the world aware that his spirit was still there. In spite of the hostile position he had taken up, his rooms were never empty. I there saw people of the most opposite characters surprised to find themselves thrown together. Meanwhile other duties drew me away from this French sort of circle after I had been there several times.

The house of the lovely and witty countess whom I have mentioned in a previous chapter, and who, after the fashion of Viennese coteries, was nicknamed " the Queen," attracted me far more than that of the Prince de Ligne. By the magic of her grace she ruled over a large number of slaves, of whom I was fortunate enough to be one. At her house were to be found the most distinguished Viennese, and the society was sufficiently mixed to make it agreeable. Among others who frequently went thither, I may mention Prince Philip of Hessen-Homburg, Gentz, the Princes Esterhazy and Liechtenstein, Counts Neipperg and Wallmoden, the Duchess of Sagan and her sisters. But even here the influence of the Congress was felt: the friendly German tone was gradually changed for a French one, a change materially brought about by Prince Eugene Beauharnais, who was a daily visiter at the house. This admixture, agreeable as it was in some respects, had a bad effect upon the native society, and took from it much of its former charm. The number of foreigners oppressed Viennese society, and many longed for the time when the increased splendour caused by their presence should cease. Baroness Fanny von Arnstein's house was the one most visited by foreigners; there were to be found assembled the highest members of the diplomatic body,— Cardinal Consalvi, Prince Hardenberg, the Duke of Wellington, the Marquis Marialva, and the like.

Soon after my arrival in Vienna I had a long interview with Prince Hardenberg, which decided the position I was to hold in the service of Prussia. I was to begin my diplomatic career attached to the Prussian embassy in Vienna, but I was first to transact some special business which Prince Hardenberg would give me. In a short time I received a mass of papers and documents touching German affairs, upon which the prince requested me to draw up a report. Shortly after I was relieved of this labour, in order that I might apply myself to another work, upon which the Chancellor laid great stress. This matter related to the claims of Prussia upon Saxony, which had been settled by former arrangements, but which were now strongly contested on many sides, and threatened to be a most difficult and thorny subject. It appeared to be of the greatest importance to work upon public opinion through the press, especially as the opposite party had already done so with great effect. The Rhenish Mercury* had rendered good service in this respect; Prince Hardenberg had likewise caused a pamphlet to be written by the privy councillor Hoffmann, called "Prussia and Saxony," and another was nearly ready from the pen of Niebuhr. But these were not thought sufficient: Hoffmann's pamphlet was too statistical and dry, Niebuhr's was expected to be too hard and stiff, and a third was wanted, written in a more flowing and popular style. Prince Hardenberg entrusted me with this work, saying in the most flattering manner that it was mainly upon Stein's recommendation. The subject required a thorough insight into the state of political affairs, and both Stein and Hardenberg gave me the benefit of their knowledge, the former in a way which none other could have dared to do it, using the most violent expressions, while Hardenberg, on the contrary, dismissed me after a two hours' audience, during which the subject was explained to me with the utmost precision and clearness, and I commenced writing without having once to ask for any further explanation.

Besides the great powers who dwelt in palaces, and to whose dinners and evening parties welcome and unwelcome guests thronged, there were others who were contented with the smallest space where they might indulge in privacy and free conversation. Doctor Cotta and his wife had, one might say, pitched a tent, so small and transient was their dwelling; but this tent was the centre of much that was going on. Cotta had come to Vienna as the representative of the German booksellers, in order to arrange some measure for securing a general copyright for all the German states; but under this humble guise he had many other objects in view, touching German affairs

* In which Görres wrote his brilliant papers.—*Trans.*

in general; many were the warnings and recommendations which found their way through him into the Augsburg Gazette, and into the Hamburg Observer. While he enjoyed the personal intimacy of several sovereigns and of the greatest statesmen, his prudence and reserve, together with the power given him by the press, caused him to be trusted with the most important matters. This remarkable man, in spite of his wealth and influence, was simple and homely in his habits, always went afoot, attended to every thing himself, allowed nothing to stand in his way, and how small soever was the business on which he was engaged, he invariably looked to what was great and good in the end.

Among other remarkable men who came to Rahel's house — for she had now joined me in Vienna — was Dr. Bollmann, who had just arrived fresh from London, viâ Paris, and had found means while in England to bestow some attention upon literature and poetry, as well as upon commerce and manufactures: he was the first to mention the names of Lord Byron and of Walter Scott in Vienna, and to praise their poems. Some few in Germany might already have heard of them; but they were quite unknown to the generality of the Viennese world, and remained so for some time, as people had but little time to bestow upon literature. Bollmann had brought letters of introduction from Schlabrendorf, who took great interest in the newly opened intercourse between France and Germany.

I will mention some of the chief persons with whom I lived on terms of intimacy: — of the host of petitioners and memorialists — of people great and small — of attachés and plenipotentiaries secret or acknowledged — of spies and listeners — of busybodies of all sorts who were there assembled, — it would be beyond my purpose to speak. In the first class were the highest princely families, the whole of the mediatized princes, and the Frankfurt Jews. Just below them might be found a sprinkling of great and small, of highflying adventurers, of diligent men of letters, and of financiers from those of the highest grade down to the lowest usurers. The power of the house of Rothschild was only then beginning, or it would have seized upon much that was distributed among other houses: but the support it gave to the claims of the Frankfurt Jews in particular, and to those of the Jews in general, to be admitted to the rights of citizenship, did infinite service.

I must first mention three people who step in my way like restless shadows: Jassoy, a Frankfurt doctor of canon law, cheerful and easy in his manners, and having great knowledge of life, was one of them. He had much to do; among other things he managed some important business for the house of Metternich. In the second place I will name Wiesel, who came accidentally to the Congress of Vienna, and without any ulterior object in view. The third person is the Russian Colonel Karl von Nostitz, who had been adjutant to Prince Louis Ferdinand. These three, dissimilar in all other respects, had this in common — a clear insight into other people's follies and weaknesses, boundless hatred for all self-deception, a longing and determination to place the naked truth, however hateful, before their own eyes, and, consequently, a distrust and doubt of all that chiefly influences the world. These three men were the incarnation of the negative principle — of satire and of scorn; no person, no event of the day, was safe from their unsparing and biting satire: they used this weapon with a rude vigour which no description can pourtray. They were the Aristophanic salt of the Congress, the Mephistophelian acid, which, while it destroys what is false, attacks also what is noble and sacred. To live much with such spirits, whose searching proof so little in this world could stand, was not without its pleasures, although accompanied with danger. Wiesel was the only one who remained in Vienna during the whole time of the Congress, Jassoy and Nostitz went away, one at the very commencement, the other in the middle, of its sitting. But a description of the Congress would have been incomplete without the mention of their names.

It is time, however, to return to our main subject. Our progress has been somewhat like that of the Congress itself, which had much extraneous matter to clear away before it could proceed to business. At the peace of Paris, the 1st of August had been fixed for the opening of the Congress, but it was put off for two months longer, chiefly on account of English affairs, and the 1st of October was then named as the day. But as much even then remained to be done, a statement was inserted in the papers on the 8th of October announcing the 1st of November as the day for the commencement of real business: this was done to allow time for the arrangement of the various knotty questions to be brought before the Congress. But on the 1st of November appeared a fresh statement, which announced that the Congress was busy examining the powers of the delegates, preparatory to entering upon its business. While those upon whom the whole negotiation depended were endeavouring to clear away the difficulties which beset them, it did not escape the public that there was a hitch somewhere.

The difficulties lay deeply involved in the subject itself, and not in any want of will or of capacity in the members of the Congress. When we look back to former congresses, — to the impediments arising from mere technical formalities, — to the endless time wasted in this manner at Münster, Osnabrück, Nimeguen, and Utrecht, — we must concede that the Congress of Vienna got rapidly over these matters of secondary importance, arranging some at once, and putting others aside. Still, the old forms in which courts and states had been accustomed, from time immemorial, to transact business, could not be altogether abandoned: they had been in use time out of mind in diplomatic affairs, and were obliged to be tolerated in spite of their present inconveniences. Nothing could have been easier than for the four great allied powers who carried on the war against Napoleon to have combined, and to have made their will the law of the others. They could not have failed to agree, and only had to keep away any pressure from without. But these powers did not think themselves justified, after breaking the neck of one tyranny which had burdened Europe, to set up another, nor would their co-allies have borne it willingly. Moreover, a number of questions, with which they themselves had very little concern, could not be decided by the mere will of these powers: claims had to be weighed, rights to be recognised, compensations to be awarded. They could not avoid holding consultations, in which the claims of the great who were any way injured were adjusted, and the complaints of their inferiors listened to. It was no small matter to devise

DIFFICULTIES AND IMPEDIMENTS.

the means of meeting contingencies which had never before occurred: to cut the Gordian knot by a mere order was impossible.

The Congress of Vienna arose out of the peace of Paris, and the eight powers who had signed, or been parties to, that treaty stood in the first rank. But admission and voice did not give equal rights; each court had only the weight belonging to its power, its position and circumstances. It was not to be thought of for a moment that Sweden should have the same influence in the Congress as Russia; or that Spain, wasted and desolated by war, should be on the same footing as victorious England. Then came this additional difficulty, that states, which perhaps had done great service to the common cause, and which, from their size and importance, appeared fully entitled to it, were not admitted among the eight great powers. This was the case with Denmark, the Netherlands, Sardinia, and the pope: to the latter, at this moment, public opinion was extremely favourable. The interests of Germany, which was in a state of great confusion, were represented in the council only by Austria and Prussia. The most contending claims were set up, the most various and entangled requisitions were put forth. In order to see their way at all, the five courts of Vienna, Berlin, Munich, Hanover and Stuttgart took the question into their own hands, to the great annoyance of the middling and smaller states, who saw themselves excluded from this council.

The political questions of greater and more general importance were treated, according to old diplomatic forms, by the exchange of notes between the great powers. The subjects which did not immediately touch these great questions, but which concerned particular provinces or classes, and some matters of more general interest, were referred to select committees, formed of the plenipotentiaries of the great courts, where business was carried on by boards or by protocols. Besides questions touching German provinces and constitutions, there were many other most important matters to be decided for other countries, and in addition to the committees for these special objects, there were others for putting down the slave trade and the Algerine pirates.

Even when the distribution of the duties to be performed

was accomplished, it was some time before business got into a proper train. First of all, the political question as to the future territories of the great powers had to be arranged among themselves. The data upon which they were to proceed seemed fixed; but upon closer examination many points appeared doubtful, and others now became uncertain. The heads of the cabinets who had conducted affairs until now knew perfectly well what they individually and collectively wanted, and the special concessions which they demanded from France, and which they had arranged among themselves, clearly proved what their pretensions and expectations were. Actual superiority will always be recognised in this world under all circumstances, and when the rights of the inferior powers, and their advantages, as was undoubtedly the case in this Congress, are attended to by those in power, the latter will always naturally find obedience. Such was the general feeling with regard to the Congress, and no one ventured to deny the dictatorship exercised by the four great powers when united. It would doubtless have been very much for the benefit of Europe, and especially of Germany, if the decision of all questions had been left in that high region, without the disturbing influence of the narrow jealousies and busy meddling of inferior courts: opposition would have been fruitless, and would soon have ceased. However, affairs turned out very differently. Differences were observed among the allied powers, which, by a little management, could easily be worked into actual division. There was no lack of such arts, and soon the treating powers stood in an hostile attitude, and instead of a frank interchange of mutual help and advantage, the only result was a few scanty concessions made with reluctance and distrust.

Two kinds of influences were working in this direction. On the one hand, Germans expected the most extraordinary things from the promised Congress. They were in a remarkable position, widely differing from that of any of the other nations in alliance with whom they had obtained the hard-earned victory. Russia and England, Sweden, Prussia, and Austria stood much in their former conditions, and needed only to seize, and turn to their own purposes, the fruits of the victory. Poland and Italy, long without any independence of their own, and having had a semblance of it bestowed upon them by Napoleon, followed the fortune of the conquerors, by which they imagined that they could not lose. Spain, Portugal, and Denmark stood, though not quite so securely, upon their former footing. The Netherlands rejoiced in a newly-acquired position, Switzerland in a partial reform and a promised security. In Germany every thing was in a state of disruption; some few things had been reconstructed, others had been irretrievably broken up and lost. The French domination had been felt most severely in Germany, but its effects had varied in different states according to times and circumstances. All the changes which had taken place during the last thirty years could be clearly traced in their course, producing every where infinite varieties of confusion, and agreeing only in this, that while the old fabric was destroyed, the new one was not yet raised: justice, oppression, conquest, merit, advantage and loss were every where wonderfully mixed together. The French rule had lasted too long, and left too many traces behind, to allow any one to declare it and its results null and void; and when this was attempted, it produced only shame and confusion. To restore, accordingly, the old forms was impossible as a general rule, and equally impossible in individual cases, as the connection of each state with all the others as a whole, upon which so much depended, was irrecoverably gone. If the emperor and the empire could not be revived, neither could the former diets or imperial chambers be re-established, as one depended upon the other. So much of the new element had been received and adopted by the Allies before it was certain on which side victory would turn; and it had, moreover, taken such strong root, that justice and necessity imposed on governments the duty of discreetly and prudently meeting the difficulty halfway. Moreover, the great powers by no means wished to see the old state of things restored: it was against their interests.

If, on the one hand, the weight of German influences and necessities pressed heavily on the Congress — if a new and popular element showed itself; on the other, a political power began to be felt, which, increasing rapidly and unexpectedly, complicated the negotiations, and threatened to place great obstacles in their way. This was the influence of regenerated France. Unquestionably the victors would have had full power and right to refuse to conquered France the privilege of being in any way a party to the negotiations, which were the termination of those events by which, without the aid of and against France, the latter country had been placed where it then was. Indeed, it would have appeared unwise and dangerous to have admitted unconditionally into the ranks of the treating powers a country still in a state of fermentation, standing in many respects in a hostile attitude towards the rest of Europe. But the sincerity of the reconciliation seemed to justify this mark of confidence; the restored house of Bourbon almost demanded it; and not alone generosity, but prudential motives, spoke in favour of this concession. It was of the greatest importance that the new arrangements which were to be the groundwork of the future political state of Europe should have the sanction and approval of a country which, from its nature and position, must very shortly again become one of the great powers. Either alternative presented insuperable difficulties; but it by no means follows that they were overlooked: the cabinets were not often deficient in prudence and forethought with respect to things that were important to themselves. But no one was prepared for the part which France took, and the influence it obtained. In this respect the adjournment of the Congress was especially mischievous. The short delay—the lapse of one summer, during which the allied armies separated and returned to their distant homes — was quite sufficient to combine the French, already excited by shame for the past and hope for the future, into a united people fully prepared for war. Had the Congress begun, as had been arranged, some months earlier, and could it have concluded its sittings quickly, it is most likely that France would have played a very insignificant part, and its share in the negotiations would have been merely a matter of form. But when time was given for further preparation, the gain was entirely on the side of those in Germany and France who were opposed to the pre-determined views and objects of the Congress, while the treating powers could only lose by this ill-advised delay. However, to be just, we must not blame individuals, but circumstances themselves, and the collective body of negotiators, none of whom, supposing them to have foreseen all the mischief arising from it, had it in their power to control the rest: indeed, in many respects delay seemed desirable, or at any rate not dangerous.

But while affairs were at a stand-still, or at least while the various difficulties were but just beginning to be unravelled, Vienna was full of life, and events were rapidly succeeding one another. The presence of the greatest rulers, of so many royal and princely persons, of high-born women surrounded by the flower of the most distinguished families from all countries, gave ample opportunity to the old imperial city to display all its pomps and luxuries, day after day. Festival succeeded festival; the love of display, amusement, and dancing asserted its full power. The old Prince de Ligne said:—"*Le congrès danse bien, mais il ne marche pas;*" and this *mot* spread like wildfire in Vienna and over all Europe, to the amusement even of those who felt its truth.

A splendid entertainment was given in the Prater on the 18th October, in commemoration of the battle of Leipsic. The highest officers and the privates ate at one common table, and every one in Vienna took part in the spectacle. Sixteen thousand men dined in the open air: the weather was fine, and the feast was prolonged far into the night. The sovereigns seemed, by this commemoration of a victory gained by their allied troops, to give a fresh pledge of their mutual agreement. This was further confirmed by the royal progress to Pesth, which lasted six days, and gave rise to many jealous remarks.

But the most brilliant of all festivals was one given by Prince Metternich, to which the great world of Vienna sent all its most remarkable and attractive members. This entertainment was for a time the talk of all who had seen it, until a second one, the splendour and beauty of which surpassed all previous ones, was given in the Circus, which was brilliantly ornamented and lighted for the occasion: this was a carrousel, in which the Austrian nobility, by their splendid dresses and their dexterity in feats of arms, carried back the imagination to the fabled days of chivalry.

Not alone every evening, but every day there was something to be seen. Early in the morning the troops were exercised, and the parade was frequently honoured by the presence of the allied monarchs with a brilliant retinue. At mid-day the choicest bands of music, for which Vienna has ever been famous, played in public places. So long as the weather was fine the Bastion was the favourite haunt: there were to be seen the Emperor Alexander and Prince Eugene Beauharnais walking arm in arm; Prince Metternich and the Duke of Coburg, the handsomest men of their day; while Lord and Lady Castlereagh walked about in the bright sunshine, dressed as if for a masquerade, and utterly unconscious that they were the observed of all observers. The two Archduchesses,—Catharina, the widowed duchess of Oldenburg, and Maria, the hereditary grand-duchess of Saxe-Weimar, both sisters of the Emperor Alexander,—were admirable specimens of high birth, female beauty, and gentle manners; and those who had the opportunity of seeing much of the Archduchess Catherina discovered in her great elevation of mind and an excellent understanding, which gave us the greater pleasure, as she was shortly again to become a German princess by her marriage with the King of Würtemberg, — a marriage which unfortunately was soon dissolved by death. The Grand Duke of Weimar was more fortunate; and even now his court is blessed by the presence of an earnest and gentle spirit—the best attribute of a noble woman,—of whom Goethe once wrote to me with perfect truth, that she would have ennobled any condition in life, and that even in the highest she would have excited personal admiration. On the Bastion were likewise to be seen the Archduke Charles, who, although he did not command in the last war, was still covered with glory; the brave, chivalrous, liberal-minded Prince William of Prussia; the Crown Prince of Würtemberg, distinguished by his military achievements, generally walking with Stein; the Crown Prince of Bavaria— too early snatched from this world—with Field-Marshal von Wrede, the victor at Hanau; the Grand Duke of Baden, young, pale, ill-looked upon, and marked out, as it were, for sacrifice; the Duchess de Sagan with her sisters; the Count and Countess Bernstorff, the latter one of the first beauties of the Congress; Counts Capo d'Istrias and Pozzo di Borgo; Cardinal Consalvi walking with Bartholdy, who pointed out to him the various personages and their business; the young Marquis de

Custine and the Count de Noailles; the Grand Duke of Weimar, even there the most affable of princes, full of intellectual activity and kindly feeling:—but any attempt at further description were vain. To sum up in a few words, all Vienna and the whole Congress were to be seen pushing their way through the crowd. The Bastion might be called a diplomatic Bourse; and indeed affairs were there much discussed: it was observed, however, that neither Gentz nor Humboldt were ever seen there.

An adventure of the English minister, Lord Stewart, Lord Castlereagh's brother, gave rise to much conversation at the time: Lord Stewart fell out with a Viennese hackney-coachman, and soon proceeded to blows in the public street—a contest which lasted some time to the intense delight of the spectators, until the combatants were at last separated, each claiming the victory. The esteem in which the English general was held by his countrymen was in no degree abated by this adventure, or by many others of which report made him the hero; and many envied the English this liberty of overstepping the conventional with impunity.

In the middle of the Congress a death occurred which awakened general interest. The Prince de Ligne, who at first had only a slight illness, but who from the very commencement had said, jestingly, that he would provide for the Congress, satiated by other amusements, something quite new, namely, the funeral of an Austrian field-marshal, made his jest come true: he left a world which he had long entertained, but which he no longer recognised as his own, earnestly as he had endeavoured to maintain his place in it by the exercise of his wit and humour. His loss was honestly felt, and many regretted that they had not sought to profit more by the last rays of his genius. With him ended a whole century, which was now left without a representative.

After so many digressions, I must devote a few words to the business which now really commenced. But first I will bring before the reader a few portraits of those to whom the negotiations were entrusted, and by whose prudence and ability they were brought to an issue. I will not give a catalogue of all who were present, but merely select the names of those who struck me most at the time.

At the head of the Congress, excluding of course the crowned heads from the diplomatic category, stood Prince Metternich. Every one recognised in him the future president of this august assembly, which, in fact, shortly elected him to that post. As Austria acted the part of host, and those who were invited were under her charge, the minister, in addition to the weight and influence belonging to his office, and which he had enjoyed both in Paris and London, and to his own personal character, now exercised all the rights of a host towards his guests. I have elsewhere spoken of the importance of Prince Metternich as a statesman, and of the charm of his appearance and manner; but it was in times subsequent to the Congress of Vienna, and this, therefore, is no place for its insertion. I must here confine myself to a slight sketch of a few points of character which showed themselves during the Congress.

The personal importance of Prince Metternich was proved by this circumstance. The Emperor Alexander, who of all sovereigns took most part personally in political negotiations, scarcely stood in a higher position than Prince Metternich, to whom all the other plenipotentiaries resigned the first place. The Emperor of Russia and the Austrian minister contended for some time in the same field for the prize. At first they were on admirable terms together; and had this continued they would have overcome all opposition in the Congress. But differences of opinion arose, which were followed by a complete rupture. Nevertheless they fully recognised each other's merits, and the most perfect confidence was subsequently restored between them.

Baron von Wessenberg held the second place in the councils of Austria. He belonged to the class of well-informed, clear-sighted, hard-working men, by whom so much is done. The unbending nature of his character stood in his way in cases where business could only be advanced by knowing when and how to yield. A man who will not give way at certain times soon becomes inconvenient, and ends by being gradually put on one side.

No one was more useful or more active at this time than Gentz. As I have written more fully about him elsewhere*, I can add but little here. Gentz's influence was far greater than belonged to his nominal rank of Austrian privy-councillor, and he enjoyed a European reputation. His position in the Austrian government gave him considerable importance; but as the framer of the protocols of the Congress, as member of so many committees and commissions, as a sound adviser and clear exponent, he was of the utmost service and importance to the highest persons, and the first statesmen treated him on a footing of equality at this time. There could be no doubt as to Gentz's influence and powers; and the parties interested in the decisions of the Congress knew it full well, and sought to reap for themselves the fruits of his intellect and talent. He was capable of embracing large views and of defending a variety of interests, while his mode of speaking was most instructive to friends and foes. But when matters were to be definitively settled, his brilliant powers failed him; and instead of being European or English, at any rate German, his sympathies were purely Austrian. On this account he incurred bitter hatred from those whose expectations he had raised and disappointed. Nevertheless, Gagern, who was brought into immediate contact with Gentz, expressly testified, that he was one of the most important, active, and able men at the Congress; and Humboldt said that in his hands nothing had an unfinished look, but all things immediately assumed a convenient and durable form.

If I here mention Frederick Schlegel, it is not that he was employed in any diplomatic capacity, but that his name is important in connection with that of Gentz. Like the latter, Schlegel was from the North of Germany: distinguished for his literary attainments, he had been pressed into the service of Austria. When these two men lived in Berlin, they hated each other cordially: the anti-revolutionary Gentz was an object of intense disgust to Schlegel, who was a strong advocate

---

* Bildnissen aus Rahels umgang, pp. 155—260. (Portraits from Rahel's acquaintances.)

for republican freedom. But now Schlegel not only honoured the political opinions of his former opponent, but even exaggerated them; he looked upon his rival as a superior, whose favour and patronage he needed. Gentz, who was not revengeful, looked only to Schlegel's present good intentions, and thought that at any rate this writer's name might be of use, although his services might be doubtful, and Gentz still viewed his opinions with distrust. Gentz remained a Protestant, and was Austrian only with regard to politics; while Schlegel had turned Catholic, and had devoted himself to the Catholic party in Austria, and could not conceal that on all occasions in which the affairs of church and state ran counter to each other he would endeavour to promote the former. But at Vienna, the honesty of Schlegel's Catholic convictions was doubted, and the Prussian convert was strongly suspected of being an ambitious hypocrite by his Viennese brethren. But the unfeigned respect which was paid to Schlegel as a writer by the learned at Vienna, and the warranty which this gave for the truth and earnestness of his conversion, helped to keep up a name to which some blame attached on account of the notorious novel of Lucinde. In this respect, the support which William Humboldt, the Prussian minister, gave to Schlegel was of the greatest importance to him. But Humboldt, likewise, had many former misdemeanours to forgive in Schlegel, which he did with the greatest generosity. Schlegel was not exactly employed in public affairs; but, owing to the attention which his work on Ancient and Modern Literature had excited, he possessed considerable influence. He and his gifted wife had a large circle of acquaintance; every one connected with the arts and literature of the Middle Ages, all the so-called romantic school, and those ardent spirits who were attracted by Eastern lore—for Schlegel was the first who introduced the study of Sanscrit,—as well as those belonging to the Catholic Church, found a footing in the society which met in Schlegel's house. Many diplomatists gained information, and listened to advice, which they did not always follow; the authorities of the German Catholic Church there fed their hopes, and even Cardinal Consalvi, the pope's nuntio, made great use of the opportunity thus afforded him, to gain information and experience.

Between Gentz and Schlegel may be placed Adam von Müller, who, without the knowledge of business possessed by Gentz, had such skill and readiness, that he could perform all manner of work, and his flowing style, in many cases, surpassed that of his master. Müller for some time enjoyed the especial favour of Prince Metternich, who saw in him one who might replace Gentz. But he had the weakness to be vehemently annoyed at opinions which were opposite to his own, and tried every means in his power to convert those with whom he lived to his own way of thinking; and in this endeavour, hoping to inspire confidence by showing it, he told, not only his own secrets, but those of Gentz and Schlegel.

Prussia was most ably represented at the Congress of Vienna. The Chancellor Prince Hardenberg had the unusual advantage of being not only at the head of foreign affairs, but of all other departments of government. His age, his great experience in life and diplomacy, the career he had run with such eminent success, his vigorous circumspect intellect, and his amiable character, all combined to secure to him respect and importance. Many were the distinguished statesmen then assembled in Vienna, men remarkable for their services and personal advantages; but among the aged diplomatists there was not one who could compete with Prince Hardenberg any more than among those in the full power of manhood was any one to be found able to cope with Prince Metternich. Hardenberg, in spite of his white hair, was still a handsome man; and it was easy to see that he must formerly have had great success among women, and that even now he had rather to meet their advances than to pursue them. He suffered under an infirmity which generally makes those afflicted by it irritable, and which, though a great inconvenience to him, did not disturb his good humour, and had but little effect upon his lively and brilliant perception. He was deaf, more or less according to circumstances, but always sufficiently so to be annoying to himself and to others, and he could only hear those voices which were strange to him when they were raised to a high pitch.

Baron William von Humboldt was Hardenberg's associate as Prussian minister to the Congress. During the whole time that the Congress lasted, the most intimate and perfect confidence prevailed between them, and each served to bring out the good qualities of the other. Humboldt, subordinate to the chancellor as chancellor, but almost his equal from his position as plenipotentiary, and greatly his superior in intellect and genius, fulfilled willingly and most admirably the various duties which his mixed office forced upon him. In any other person a constant endeavour to be first would necessarily have entailed upon him the second rank, whilst Humboldt's moderation and steadfastness secured to him a position fully equal to the first in rank. Their relative position was unlike that equally remarkable one between Blücher and Gneisenau, which had arisen and lasted with such advantage to the state during the war. Their immediate business brought the two diplomatists nearer to each other; they could exchange duties, and thus had far stronger cause for jealousy than the two warriors could have. But Humboldt's assistance was as essential to Hardenberg, for carrying out his plans, as the leading idea of the chancellor was necessary before Humboldt's diligence and knowledge of detail could be brought into play. There was a constant emulation between these two men on every fresh occasion for exertion. The work which Humboldt performed during the Congress, the prudence, care, zeal, and untiring activity which he exhibited, are beyond all belief; and he required the same from his subordinates and assistants. The chancellor bore the burden of all matters of state in all their branches; but diplomatic affairs chiefly took up his attention, and in this branch he did much alone and unassisted. Many of the most important notes, more especially when the contest respecting Saxony was at its height, were written during sleepless nights by his own hand, and were masterpieces of prudence, judgment, and energy: a peculiar charm and clearness of style marked these productions as his.

Prince von Rasumoffsky, Count von Stackelberg, and Count Nesselrode took part in the discussion, on behalf of Russia; but the personal influence of the Emperor himself made itself felt the whole time. Counts Capo d'Istrias and Pozzo di Borgo were not yet in the first rank, to which, however, they were fast advancing. There were likewise a great many Russian diplomatists and generals, and their conduct and manner had considerable effect on the Congress.

For England appeared Lord Castlereagh and his brother Lord Stewart, then Lords Clancarty and Cathcart, and later still the Duke of Wellington. Lord Castlereagh was without any personal charm; his views were narrow, his opinions appeared mainly to depend upon the impressions he received from others, and his actions were rather those of an agent than of a statesman. He talked a good deal without saying much: it was well known that he did not shine in Parliament as a speaker. His favourite expression, "features," was constantly on his lips, to Humboldt's great amusement, who never missed such little traits. The difficulties which he foresaw he should have to meet in Parliament on his return to England had great influence on his decision as to what he agreed to or what he opposed, and did infinite mischief in many cases. Lord Clancarty was a careful, diligent, hard-working man, who arranged his materials well, and put many matters into good order.

The interests of France were represented by four names, but that of Prince Talleyrand overtopped them all. So much has been written about this arch-diplomatist, from Thiers on the one hand, who has traced all his secret motives with the utmost precision, to those zealous moralists on the other, who call him a rogue without further periphrasis, that it would be difficult to say any thing new about him. The part he had to play at the Congress of Vienna had two distinct tendencies, first to dissever and then to unite, and he played them both with admirable success. Talleyrand belonged to that class of men whose life conducts them through various changes to mere selfishness in the end. The feeling for liberty which really animated him in former days was not strong enough to withstand temptation; equally transient was the display of patriotism and public spirit which he assumed, in order to give a favourable colour to the share he took in the government under Napoleon, and of the reality of which he tried to persuade himself and others. He now served the Bourbons, as he had formerly served Napoleon, from motives of personal interest. This disposition led him to become avaricious in proportion to the privations which he had endured in former times of poverty, and his chief rule of action seemed to be to avoid a return of those evils at all events. His whole manner still savoured of the priesthood to which he had once belonged: the reserve, the quiet, the social ease, the impressive earnestness and admirable wit which were all united in him, had much of the essence of priestcraft. His real superiority over others was not borne out by his outward demeanour; of this he was aware, and he therefore kept a strict guard over his manner. He no longer felt any enthusiasm for the ideas of his youth, but this did not prevent him from still liking them, and he would have preferred seeing them triumphant, had it suited his interest at the same time. It was very doubtful whether he was acting honestly by the Bourbons, at any rate he most likely leaned towards the Orleans faction. He held fast to his old friends with a sincere heart and a true spirit; things must have been bad, indeed, to have made him deny them. He patronised authors and the learned class as much as he could, and endeavoured to gain them over to himself, for he knew how to value their influence. The great experience and knowledge which he brought into public affairs, and the acuteness with which he always perceived and insisted upon the most important topics, would have given him greater influence than he actually had, were it not that the better sort of people distrusted him, and that his duplicity deprived him of the confidence even of those whose interests he represented. He worked but little, and with great unwillingness; and his chief talent lay in making others, even men of the highest importance, work for and under him. On the whole, he understood better how to make use of those who were on his side than of those who were opposed to him. Where something had to be done, he let nothing interfere; he knew neither hate nor love, he was never swayed by the impressions of the moment, but pursued resolutely and directly the course which he had marked out for himself. No foreign influence made the least impression upon him; and it would have been difficult to have influenced him, were it not that he loved money and feared war.

Besides Talleyrand, the Duke de Dalberg, Count Latour du Pin, and Count Alexis de Noailles, represented the interests of France. It looked like an insult to see a Dalberg in the service of France now, as in the time of Napoleon; and the duke, in whom the Bonapartist did not seem quite extinct, had to endure many bitter affronts on the subject.

Circumstances were unfavourable to those who advocated the claims of the Knights of Malta to that island. Public opinion was in their favour; but as Malta was irrevocably in the power of England, and no other spot could be found for the Order, the whole affair fell to the ground. Admiral Sir Sidney Smith, without powers from other quarters, endeavoured to promote a measure closely connected with the re-establishment of the Knights of Malta; namely, the destruction of the African pirates. The personal character of this naval hero and public opinion were strongly in favour of his proposal, but his own countrymen were accused of secretly working against it adoption.

Meanwhile the question as to the fates of Poland and Saxony caused the greatest excitement: the interest on this point daily increased. All the allied powers had already agreed that Saxony should be united to Prussia; others had nothing to object to this project but what they were permitted to say. But another question was the union of Poland and Russia. The Emperor Alexander had never given up his claims on this point, and had always said in general terms that Russia, Prussia, and Austria were severally to receive their compensations in Poland, in Germany, and Italy. This had been agreed upon on all points; the only question was the amount of the compensation. The Russian power appeared in the splendour of victory to increase every day; and to see its territory advanced to the Vistula caused the greatest anxiety in others. Austria and England were the first to exchange their views on this subject; then France — at first gently, but afterwards much more strongly — uttered a similar remonstrance. Supposing Prussia to join the other allies, Russia would stand quite alone, and it was then hoped by a general opposition to put some limits to the demands of that power. In this point of view, the questions touching Poland and Saxony were closely related; but the claims of Prussia upon Saxony would have been less contested, had the former power assisted the others in placing some bounds to Russia's views upon Poland. It was, however, impossible to expect such a rupture between Prussia and Russia; the personal liking of the two sovereigns for each other, the victories which the two armies had won together, and even the general state of politics, more especially as regarded Prussia, caused the most intimate union between them. The opposition which the other powers made to the claims of Russia with respect to Poland was now extended to those which Prussia had upon Saxony.

This Saxon question, however, forced itself on the Congress, and became the battle-ground upon which all parties met. France here found a favourable opportunity to obtain fresh political influence. It suited the position of the Bourbons to represent the hereditary rights of sovereigns as inalienable, and it flattered the national feelings of the French, to save in the king of Saxony a true ally, not only of Napoleon, but of France, at the same time that the gains of the hated conqueror were diminished. In Saxony itself the old connections and old influences, which had been kept under by war, were at work, and were strengthened by the continued state of indecision in which every thing remained. In the rest of Germany arose doubts and discussions which people had scarce dreamt of before. Bavaria, in particular, appeared to look upon the increasing strength and greatness of Prussia with a jealous eye. Thus fresh obstacles were thrown in the way of the adjustment of a political question already uncertain and hard to arrange.

Meanwhile the claim of Prussia was firmly grounded in public opinion, and met with a good reception in Germany. Hatred to France such as animated Stein, the idea that Prussia ought to be strong and great, so as to form the centre of a powerful unassailable German kingdom, the hope of raising up a strong national spirit, which had been excited even in Saxony by the events of the last war, not to mention various other influences and motives, spoke loudly in favour of Prussia. Every one had the greatest confidence in the warriors and statesmen who were at the head of Prussian affairs: it seemed to be for the general advantage to join with them.

The disunion which this subject produced in the cabinets of Austria and Prussia was still kept within bounds, and both Metternich and Hardenberg used all their personal influence to prevent its producing any bad effect on other constitutional questions. Neither did England manifest any bitterness against Prussia. But Lord Castlereagh, who shortly before had declared the yielding of Saxony to Prussia to be right and advantageous, now made this lame excuse for holding the opposite opinion, that he had to consider the discussions likely to arise in the British Parliament on the termination of the Congress. England and Austria, however, spoke out with great vehemence and hostility against Russia, and the Emperor Alexander several times appeared disposed to break off all further negotiation.

The Emperor of Russia recognised the intimate connection of his interests with those of Prussia, and was most anxious to strengthen the tie by a close alliance. It was an important fact as regarded the political state of the question, that Russian and Prussian troops then occupied those countries whose ultimate fate was under discussion. Poland, at least that portion of it which had been erected by Napoleon into the Duchy of Warsaw, was naturally in the hands of those Russian troops by whom alone its conquest had been effected. But Saxony, which had been conquered by the Allies, had in the general distribution likewise been given into the charge of the Russian authorities. The Emperor Alexander, in order to make his future intentions clear and to show that he was in earnest, had already some time previously offered to yield possession of Saxony to Prussia: this actually took place on the 8th of November. The public announcement of Prince Repnin, the Russian governor-general, that the country was in future to be governed by Prussia, was based on the consent which the other allied powers had formerly expressed. But at this time, and under altered circumstances, the consent of the Allies to such a proceeding, which, however, they could not hinder, would be difficult to obtain.

The negotiations daily became more acrimonious, the divisions more apparent; an open rupture was feared, and the anxiety was general. The influence of France was exerted with great skill to our disadvantage, and an attempt was made to prevent the Allies from coming to any arrangement. By forming some new alliance, France hoped to become the mediator between the negotiating powers. Prince Talleyrand directed his attention to all sides, but devoted most of his energy to forming an English connection, which he thought would enable him more easily to win over the others. And, to say truth, he had no very hard game to play with Lord Castlereagh; mental superiority exercised its usual power. If France and England agreed, Austria could not, under the circumstances of the case, fail to join them. The states of second or third rate importance felt the effects of this: the Netherlands, Hanover, and Bavaria joined the new alliance. The French already assumed a threatening tone; the newspapers announced the movements of troops towards the Rhine: the marshals were even named who were destined to take the command. It seemed fabulous that this should be done in the name of a family so lately reinstated, and which, moreover, owed every thing to the Allies,—by the Bourbons, who were scarcely yet secure on the throne. This gave ample proof of Talleyrand's talent, and great praise was due to him for so soon changing weakness into strength. But while obtaining this brilliant success, he saw but one side of the case: he blindly left out of the question the small hold that the Bourbons had on the soil of France: he forgot the yawning abyss of the revolution, he did not see the sword of Napoleon already drawn, but devoted all his energies to making France appear formidable in a diplomatic point of view to those very powers to whom he would have to apply for support and assistance whenever real danger should arise. In truth, if in all this Talleyrand proved himself an able negotiator, he by no means showed himself to be a great statesman. Even without the unexpected event, the shock of which overset all men's plans and expectations, Talleyrand's policy could not have stood, and a European war would certainly have endangered the safety of the Bourbons, if not of France.

There was a strong feeling in Saxony as well as elsewhere in favour of Prussia: the far-sighted and energetic spirits were all on its side. The change of opinion which afterwards took place was as natural an occurrence as the change of the seasons, and was brought about by the usual train of circumstances. The prospects of Russia with respect to Poland were equally favourable. The Emperor Alexander had come forward as the protector, first of the Polish army, and then of the whole nation, and appeared destined to do what Napoleon had only vaguely promised. The Poles felt that their nationality could only be revived under his mighty hand; they recognised the possibility of their regeneration through him. The Emperor was the personal friend of Prince Adam Czartoriski, who was his adviser in all affairs concerning Poland; and the name of this stanch friend of Poland was the best pledge of the sincerity of his intentions with regard to that country. The Emperor sent his brother, the Grand Duke Constantine, to Warsaw, at the head of such Polish troops as had survived the last war; a choice which at any rate was justified by the love which this prince showed for the Poles. To the strong feeling against the union of Poland with Russia, which daily became more apparent in Vienna, it was easy to give the interpretation that these objections were really directed against the existence and prosperity of the Polish nation. If it should come to a war, this feeling might summon the whole strength and nationality of Poland into the field, with greater force than ever. In fact, on the 11th of December, the Grand Duke issued a proclamation calling upon the Poles to take up arms for the defence of their country, and for the maintenance of their independence: it could not have been more strongly worded had war been actually declared. This outbreak had a prodigious effect upon the Congress; and the danger of a contest which would bring such energies into play, in case matters came to an extremity, was fully recognised. Meanwhile, however, the opposing parties had prudently drawn in and moderated their excessive zeal under the pressure of such powerful circumstances. At the very moment when the Grand Duke's proclamation became known in Vienna, there already were fewer divisions in the council, and all parties were less disposed to attach undue weight to any accidental event.

The every-day life of Vienna was most happily calculated to relieve the oppression and fatigue which had been produced on men's minds by all these misunderstandings and the destruction of their hopes. Viennese life carries along with it whatever it touches: the daily necessities of life, which elsewhere are matters of indifference,— the eating, drinking, walking, looking about,—all this here became somehow or other a luxury and an enjoyment. In the highest society, of course, there was a constant succession of brilliant assemblies and festivities; and as the curiosity of the populace was excited by this display, so in like manner did the life of the people exercise its attraction upon the upper classes. Crowned heads were not ashamed to take part in the enjoyments of the middle classes; the most pampered palates were contented with the homely but abundant fare of a suburban tavern. The smaller theatres were filled mostly with people of the upper class, while the lower orders thronged to the larger theatres, with the mutual desire of seeing each other. Neither politics, nor the state of the funds, were thought of amidst the pleasures of a Viennese winter.

The Prince de Ligne was dead; but his style of wit survived, and many subjects of ridicule upon which it could be exercised were to be found. The sight of all this motley crowd, the violent contrasts to which it gave rise, the plentiful indulgence of the senses, and the sparing exercise of the intellect, the polish of manners, and the coarseness of sentiment, challenged the attention of all men, and there was not one who, in his own way, was not amused by a spectacle in which he himself was one of the actors. As some doubts existed whether the negotiations would end in a peace,—and well-thinking men could scarce endure the thoughts of a war, one, too, between Allies,—it was proposed by some who took the possibility much to heart, that, in the event of a war, all the diplomatists who had vainly laboured at establishing peace should be driven without mercy into the field, and be formed into a company of chasseurs, under some veteran leader who would not spare them: bets ran high, that in this case there would be no war. It now became the fashion, and one that has since continued, to say all that is bad of diplomatists, who until then had been a highly honoured and tenderly treated class: they were now depreciated, ridiculed, and caricatured.

Let us now turn to subjects of a purer interest,—to the arts. The wealth of Vienna in this respect was boundless, and excited the astonishment of every lover of art. Those who once entered upon the study of antiquities, pictures, sculpture, and such works, found no end to their inquiries and pleasures. There was but little noise made about these things; they were there as a matter of course, either in the Imperial Gallery, or in the equally rich collections of private families, proudly awaiting the inspection of the solitary artist, rather than the gaze of the vulgar. No one was more alive to these works of art, or more anxious to discover, and when discovered to enjoy them, than the Duke of Saxe Weimar, who still found time, in the midst of all the occupations imposed upon him by his station, to satisfy his eager zeal and interest in all that was important. In his company we saw a collection of arms, jewels, and works of art, which had lately been brought to Vienna from the castle of Ambras, in the Tyrol, where they had lain forgotten for ages: the most curious things were discovered in this collection. Goethe's translation of Cellini's life had made all German readers inquire with eagerness after the famous salt-cellar of the Florentine artist; but no one, not even Goethe, had the slightest knowledge where it was, and this precious work of art had been given up as lost. The duke was triumphant when he had it in his power to announce to Goethe the discovery of this treasure in a state of perfect preservation, and the fact that he had seen it with his own eyes. This salt-cellar had been discovered in the collection at Ambras; and when we consider, not indeed the beauty of the workmanship, for this too often fails to inspire respect, but the value of the gold, it is inconceivable how it escaped destruction so long.

On all sides music offered its attractions; and concerts, churches, operas, salons, artists, and dilettanti did their best to amuse the public. Prince Antony Radzivill, who had already made some progress in composing music to Goethe's Faust, induced me to call with him upon Beethoven; but the great composer's deafness had much increased since I had seen him last, and with it his dislike to society: moreover, he would have nothing to do with great people, and expressed his hatred towards them in no measured terms. But when I reminded him that Prince Radzivill was brother-in-law to Prince Louis Ferdinand of Prussia, whose untimely death Beethoven had so much deplored, and whose musical works he so highly esteemed, he agreed to receive the prince's visit. I gave up all thought of taking the savage musician to Rahel, as society annoyed him, and there was no doing any thing with him alone if he would not play. His name, well known and honoured as it was, had not reached that pinnacle of fame to which it subsequently attained: and the motley crowd then assembled at Vienna preferred the ease and charm of the Italian to the depth and earnestness of the German school.

Meanwhile the negotiations, which had gone on smoothly for a time, again became difficult, and Prussia was forced to declare herself strongly. It was even said that Hardenberg would leave the Congress, in which Prussia would no longer take part. It was a subject of alarm to all those persons who had hoped such great things for Germany from the union of Prussia and Austria, and had clung to this hope, to see that Austria now appeared to head the opposition begun by France and countenanced by England. But others who took narrower views were exceedingly wroth, and were ready to maintain what they thought their rights and their honour at the point of the sword. Reports of war became rife, people began to inquire into the numbers and the position of the troops, and endeavoured to take an accurate measure of the new impending danger.

In Berlin, where the long duration of the Congress was a subject of ridicule, it was said that Blücher and not Hardenberg should conduct the matter, and the aged warrior was as impatient as the rest of the world. Sharp expressions of this sort were uttered in Vienna, and produced their effect: songs, in the same sense, were circulated about the town. In this state of anxious uncertainty a new year commenced.

The tone of Prussia, firm and strong before, now became threatening; and, owing to some expression of Hardenberg's, which left the others no power of making any reservation, England, France, and Austria made a formal covenant, and bound themselves mutually to assist each other, by a treaty signed on the 3rd January, 1815. The negotiations had been carried on in secret, and the agreement was likewise intended to be kept so.

This alliance took place at the very height of the divisions in the Congress; but from that moment the divisions decreased.

The position which they had assumed seemed to the chief actors already sufficiently dangerous, and a retreat appeared advisable. Russia, whose power and independence could least be called in question, was the first to give way. The Emperor Alexander abated his claims with regard to Poland, the shares of Austria and Prussia were considerably enlarged; Thorn and Cracow were to be free cities, and even Thorn was eventually ceded to Prussia. By this means the negotiation with reference to Saxony assumed a different aspect, and the two questions of Saxony and Poland were thus solved, after considerable difficulty, in a peaceful manner.

On the 21st of January a remarkable scene took place. The restoration of the Bourbons had caused the anniversary of Louis XVI.'s death to be kept in France as a day of general mourning, which was done with much ostentation and party feeling. The ministers abroad were directed to keep this day holy, and Talleyrand was forced to do the bidding of his government. The funeral service was read by his desire in the church of St. Stephen, and all the members of the Congress were invited to attend. The celebration of this event in France, dictated more by party hate than by real feeling, was unwise; but in Vienna the proceeding, if not offensive, was at least ill-timed. It was unnecessary in the presence of so many princes thus to recal the memory of an event which had better have been buried in oblivion. Matters were discussed which it would have been more prudent to have left alone; even the person of Louis the XVIII. was not spared. Talleyrand's position was awkward and painful enough: people thought of the execution of the Duke d'Enghien, in which transaction some thought he had had a share; moreover, he had always lived on terms of friendship with the judges of Louis XVI.

Meanwhile the Duke of Wellington arrived in Vienna from London, as plenipotentiary in the room of Lord Castlereagh, who returned to England, bearing with him one result of the Congress — the abolition of negro slavery, — a subject in which his countrymen felt the liveliest interest. The celebrated warrior had far greater talents for diplomacy than his predecessor: he knew how to listen; and although he was not so loquacious, what he said was more to the point. If the duke was sent to impose upon the other powers by his reputation as a warrior, and to silence them by his authoritative tone, he certainly failed in this respect; but every one soon perceived that an able and well-informed negotiator had joined the Congress in the person of the Duke of Wellington. The duke found at Vienna an old comrade in the Prussian general Grolman, who had served under him in the Peninsular war. This circumstance was doubtless favourable to a good understanding with Prussia: at any rate the two soldiers were on the most friendly terms with each other, and the Duke of Wellington took every opportunity of showing respect to Grolman personally, and in him to his country.

The French endeavoured to make something out of the difficulties with regard to Saxony, but others had meanwhile arisen which promised to be still more beneficial to them. At the Emperor's fall, two only of those who had risen with Napoleon — Bernadotte and Murat — had saved themselves, and their success was owing to their taking part with the Allies; moreover, Murat's sincerity was doubtful. The Bourbons could not endure seeing this upstart where he was, and Talleyrand formally proposed to reinstate the old family, which still reigned in Sicily, on the throne of Naples. The presence of the ministers who separately represented Naples and Sicily at the Congress formed a strange contradiction: it was clear that this state of things could not fail to produce mischief. Talleyrand's proposal created great excitement, and was strenuously supported by many who, at the same time, expressed a wish that Napoleon should be removed to some more distant spot than Elba. However, the agreements which had been made gave a strong support to Murat's representatives, who behaved as if they were the victors, while the Sicilian ministers had all the appearance of being vanquished. How it would have ended had Murat understood his own game, is difficult to say: most likely, however, he would not have escaped a fate which his folly only hastened. But, excited by the open hostility of the Bourbons, and but little assured by the treaty under which he reigned in Naples, especially when he appealed to his conscience and to his actions, Murat thought to maintain himself on the throne by his own force: with the dream of conquering Italy he entered into secret negotiations with Napoleon. His preparations, apparently directed against France, but in reality against Austria, could not long remain unobserved. Large bodies of Austrians quietly marched into Italy; and as soon as any movement took place on the side of Naples, there was an Austrian army already prepared to meet any contingency.

We now heard frequent mention of the Carbonari—a society which directed its chief views towards compassing the unity of Italy. Whether Murat was at their head—whether he gave strength to their views, or owed much to their support—this, together with surmises as to the forms, rules, and extent of this brotherhood, were topics of incessant conversation; but none gave credit to the Carbonari for the activity which they displayed, or for the importance to which they subsequently attained.

While anxious looks were turned towards the South, and matters did not much brighten in the North, Vienna remained the same: there was a constant succession of balls and amusements: the same people who had entered the lists against each other in the morning as bitter enemies were to be found in the evening mixing in the same scenes of festivity. The long duration of the Congress put no stop to the prodigality and splendour of Viennese hospitality: the sources from which all this expenditure flowed seemed inexhaustible. The great world obeyed every call that was made upon it, and always showed fresh zeal and energy. The number of visitors increased, foreigners continued to arrive, and gave additional liveliness to the scene. Even the change of the seasons brought the charm of novelty; as the weather became warmer, excursions were made on horseback or in splendid carriages, instead of in sledges. The crowds now sauntered about on the Prater and the Augarten, or were seen on the road to Schönbrunn or Baden.

But we have now to speak of other things. The month of March had commenced, and matters went on smoothly enough.

The King of Saxony had arrived in Presburg, and the Allies, who were now unanimous against the partition of Saxony, were smoothing the way for his junction with them. In Vienna people were still talking of a royal progress which the court, or rather all the assembled courts, had made; every one was amusing himself, working or idling as usual, when suddenly, on the 7th of March, the intelligence that Napoleon had left Elba on the 26th of February, and had been seen steering northwards with six vessels, burst like a thunder-cloud over our heads. Prince Metternich received the first intimation of this event early in the morning: the ministers of the five powers had been engaged in a conference in his rooms until three in the morning. As the heads of all the cabinets were then in Vienna, Prince Metternich had ordered his servant not to awake him, in case a courier arrived late. Notwithstanding this order, the servant gave him a despatch which a courier brought in at six o'clock, and which was marked "Immediate." The Prince read the words, "Imperial Consulate of Genoa," on the envelope: as he had been scarcely two hours in bed, and stood in great need of sleep, he laid the despatch, which he considered unimportant, unopened by his bed-side, and turned, to sleep again. But once disturbed, this was not so easy, and at about half-past seven o'clock he made up his mind to open the despatch. To his astonishment he read in six lines that the English commissary Campbell had just arrived at Genoa, to inquire whether Napoleon had landed there, as he had disappeared from Elba. On receiving an answer in the negative, the English frigate had again set sail. In a few minutes Prince Metternich was dressed, and before eight was with the Emperor Francis. The Emperor read the despatch, and said, with great coolness and composure, both which qualities he possessed on occasions like the present,—"Napoleon seems inclined to play the adventurer—that is his affair: ours is to secure to the world that peace which he has so long disturbed. Go without delay to the Emperor of Russia and to the King of Prussia, and say to them, that I am ready to order my army to march back into France immediately. I have no doubt that the two monarchs will agree with me in every particular." Shortly after eight the Prince was with the Emperor

Alexander, who dismissed him with the same words as the Emperor Francis: a quarter of an hour later he received the same declaration from the mouth of King Frederick William of Prussia. By nine he was back again in his own house, where he had already requested Field Marshal Prince Schwarzenberg to meet him. At ten o'clock the ministers of the four great powers met him by appointment, and at the same hour adjutants were sent in all directions, ordering the troops, who were already marching towards their several homes, to halt. The ministers were ignorant of what had occurred, when they entered Prince Metternich's apartment. Talleyrand came first, and read the despatch from Genoa. He was perfectly cool; and the following laconic conversation ensued:—Talleyrand. "*Savez vous où va Napoleon?*"—Metternich. "*Le rapport n'en dit rien.*"—Talleyrand. "*Il débarquera sur quelque côte d'Italie et se jettera en Suisse.*"—Metternich. "*Il ira droit à Paris!*" As every thing had been settled between Prince Metternich and the sovereigns within the hour, and war had already been determined upon, nothing now remained to be done but to arrange how this was to be conducted, and this presented no difficulties.

In the course of the forenoon arrived an English courier who had left Genoa early on the 2nd of March; shortly after him came an Austrian with intelligence as late as the evening of that same day. Towards mid-day the occurrence was known all over Vienna, and it is impossible to describe the effect that the news had upon all men. Every one felt that this was a crisis which might be fatal to Napoleon; that by him all things were reversed, all order rendered insecure, and all movement suspended. There were, however, some minds which were not disordered by the event. The Emperor Alexander said that it was a trifling matter if it were treated as such. Prince Metternich retained his equanimity: he had immediately seen that France was in greater danger than Italy; and even Gentz looked upon the common danger with courage. Humboldt exclaimed—"Capital! this will cause some movement!"

The French, and Talleyrand at the head of them, endeavoured to put on an air of the utmost indifference. This, whether true or assumed, was the prevalent tone on the evening of this eventful day, when all the high and distinguished world of Vienna met to witness a play at the palace. Talleyrand feared most for Italy, where he thought that Napoleon would be most likely to succeed: he concluded that in France Napoleon's attempt would be nipped in the bud. And yet most men guessed that France was his destination. On the 10th of March an Austrian courier from Genoa brought the intelligence that Napoleon had actually landed in France, and had attempted to take the castle of Antibes by storm. On the 13th another Austrian courier came with news down to the 5th. Talleyrand, and with him the Duke de Dalberg, now began to feel alarm, especially as a courier arrived from Paris with despatches dated the 5th, on which day nothing was known there of what had occurred. According to credible witnesses, Talleyrand was for a moment visibly upset, and fixed his eyes dully on vacancy: but this was only at first, for in a short time he regained his composure, his clearness of intellect, and his activity. The Italians rejoiced that Napoleon had directed his steps to France, and exclaimed with vehemence, that it was an extraordinary blessing that heaven had conducted the evil doer whither he would infallibly meet with his due reward. On all sides, as soon as people had had time to collect their thoughts, and to speak to and encourage one another, their passions broke all bounds, and they gave vent to their rage and hatred in the wildest terms. The women vied with the men in depreciating the hero of the day, who by his unexpected appearance had thus disturbed and alarmed them.

This state of things was turned to account by Talleyrand, in order to bring about measures, the failure of which could nowise be dangerous to himself or make his position worse; but which, if successful, would secure to him profit and renown. It is the common opinion, that he was the originator, or at any rate the vigorous promoter, of the strong terms in which the powers assembled in the Congress on the 13th of March, condemned Napoleon's proceedings, placed him beyond the pale of the law, and held him up to public execration. The effect of this declaration was at first very great: but it was rapidly weakened by the reports which reached Vienna from France announcing Napoleon's rapid progress. Instead of seeing him surrounded and taken prisoner, we heard that Grenoble had opened its gates to receive him, that the troops had gone over, and that the Bourbons were weakly and unadvisedly thinking of flight. The Congress now rapidly wound up the discussions about Saxony, and overcame the king of Saxony's objections by the earnestness of their representations, in all which Talleyrand had a very great share, but with this ceased the French influence on the Congress. When Napoleon reached Lyons, and Marshal Ney, of whom the most extravagant expectations were formed, instead of effecting any thing, went over to Napoleon with all his troops, every one was forced to confess that any opposition to the returning Emperor was fruitless, that Paris would open its gates to him, and that the cause of the Bourbons was lost. The interests of France naturally ceased to be represented at the Congress; and when Austria, Russia, England, and Prussia bound themselves, on the 25th of March, to begin the war afresh, Talleyrand's signature and co-operation were no longer required.

After Napoleon had reached Paris without striking a blow, and the supreme power had once more fallen into his hands, people began to breathe again after the terror, delusion, and disappointment under which they had lately suffered, and began to look seriously at the new and unheard-of position in which they were placed. I can confidently assert that any thing more wonderful or romantic, more important in its effects, than this progress of Napoleon from Cannes to Paris was never yet known in history. People imagined the most extraordinary things to account for the miracle, but shut their eyes to the simple chain of events which brought it all about. One thing, however, could not be denied, that France and Napoleon were now once more united against us, and that we had to deal with them some way or other, either by war or by peace.

I say peace, for this contingency was forced upon men's minds, in spite of the declarations and alliances which had been made before the full importance of the event had been seen and felt. In truth, Napoleon, in the full possession of power, and borne on the stream of popular excitement, acted with more moderation than was expected of him, and offered to recognise the terms of the peace of Paris. Such an offer required deliberation; the state of Europe, and the relations existing between the several powers, demanded mature consideration. England clearly showed that in the forthcoming war, although willing to fight against Napoleon, she would not do so merely for the sake of putting the Bourbons on the throne; and if this were not the object, the other powers would rather see Napoleon's dynasty take its place among the sovereign houses of Europe than have France again subject to the excitement of republican movements. Napoleon's connection with Austria might also induce the latter power to look favourably upon him. Napoleon seized with avidity upon this possibility, and made use of it for the purpose of dazzling the French by promises, and of making the most pressing overtures to Austria.

Napoleon's attempt was based upon two suppositions: the one was, that France was tired of the Bourbons, which seemed to him so certain, and self-evident, that he scarcely gave himself time to prove or examine the second, which was that the members of the Congress could not agree, and would separate in disunion. Napoleon was well informed as to the first point, but not with regard to the second. The sovereigns had already determined to leave Vienna; the days of their stay were numbered, and their departure was close at hand. But the separation of the rulers would not have interfered with the conclusion of peace; on the contrary, the negotiation had never been in a better train, or more certain of being continued. Napoleon's return would have had a totally different effect, and his political cunning a much larger field of action, had the heads of the Congress not been assembled, and had the intelligence of his escape reached each one separately. It would have been difficult for ministers at a distance from each other to have made common cause, and to have taken general measures, and nothing could have made up for the rapidity and energy with which they had now acted from being all together. But the condition of France was what determined him; no time was to be lost, and Napoleon could hardly have ventured to delay his expedition, even had he been better informed of the state of affairs in Vienna.

Napoleon's return fixed public attention upon his wife and child, who had been at Vienna during the sitting of the Congress, and were just then at Schönbrunn. A bold plan was laid at

Paris to carry off the young prince from Schönbrunn, but it failed at the critical moment. The affair made a great noise, but only had the effect of insuring a stricter watch for the future.

But it was not only upon Austria that Napoleon was secretly at work: he endeavoured to convince the other powers of all the advantages which would accrue from an alliance with him, or at any rate from maintaining peace. It is easy to imagine the connections which he wished to establish and the inducements which he held out. But he everywhere found his expectations deceived: Murat alone followed Napoleon's dangerous incitement, which suited his unquiet spirit. Prince Eugene Beauharnais, who received pressing exhortations to join his Emperor, his leader, and his father, remained true to his word not to leave Vienna, and deserved the confidence which all, more especially the Emperor Alexander, placed in his honour. Just about this time these two were seen constantly walking arm in arm on the ramparts, and this alone sufficed to allay all suspicion. The Poles likewise remained true to the Emperor Alexander, and Napoleon could not re-awaken their old confidence in him, nor could he gain followers anywhere in Germany, in spite of the multitude of the discontented produced by the new state of things. It is remarkable that Napoleon was not above holding out every sort of bribe to his old ally, Talleyrand: he even thought it possible to resume their old friendship. The prudent, cunning, polished Monteron, who was sent by Fouché to try the ground at Vienna, soon found that nothing was to be done there, and that it was more prudent to be on the side of the Allies than on that of Napoleon.

Meanwhile, every-day life kept its old course, and society went on as if nothing had happened; but this was not the case with public business. The re-appearance of the common enemy strengthened the bonds of union among the great powers, who, forgetting their disputes, now had in view only the great object of crushing the revolutionary military power in France. The preparations for war, the general arming, the re-organisation of large masses of men, the marching of troops, the arrangements for the commissariat, were now the chief subjects of consideration. The high military authorities of the other powers who were at Vienna held frequent consultations with the Duke of Wellington: the ministers of war and of finance met together to concert measures.

At the same time it was necessary to watch the state of public feeling, to allay discontent, to produce a good understanding, and to excite the zeal of the people in favour of war. Nowhere were opinions stronger or energy greater than in Prussia: the whole nation, ready to make any sacrifice, forgetful of every thing in their warlike excitement, rose to the call that was made upon it; the troops of the line were raised to their full complement, the landwehr, or militia, were under arms, and the free corps of chasseurs rejoined their ranks. The Prussian troops were the first in the field.

Murat brought upon himself the first shock of arms: the Austrians, who alone were interested in Italian matters, attacked Murat, who thought that he was deceiving the others, while he himself was the only one who was blinded. He plotted with Napoleon at the same time that he assured the Allies of his loyalty to them. He then invaded the Pontifical states, and advanced against the Austrians. From the very first he was repulsed; and after a series of reverses, the campaign was ended in a few weeks. On the 22d May the Austrians took possession of Naples, and promised to reinstate the old dynasty. Murat sought safety in France.

This first act was happily ended before the real contest with France could begin, and its successful termination raised the confidence of the allies. Nevertheless people felt that this trifling gain was nothing, so long as the chief blow had not been struck; it was a very different matter to deal with Napoleon, backed by the French, than with Murat and the Neapolitans. The news from France was by no means satisfactory. Whoever came from Paris, whether Bourbonists or Bonapartists, confirmed the truth of the great preparations which were making for a war which Napoleon wished to avoid, but which he saw to be inevitable. The party of the Bourbons was annihilated; nothing, therefore, was to be expected in that quarter. The prevailing tendency was revolutionary and republican, and this was more to be dreaded than Napoleon himself, who could scarce stem the tide: indeed, he was compelled to yield in a degree. Carnot and Fouché were forced upon him as ministers rather than chosen by him, and their names had much significance abroad.

During this interval, in which people had leisure to consider the various circumstances of the times, the question very naturally arose, whether it was not possible, considering its peculiar connection with Napoleon, for Austria to sanction his governing France, taking upon herself the part of a mediator between him and the other powers. The court and the cabinet never countenanced this plan; but men of some note spoke their views on this point publicly, and the idea was widely spread among that numerous class which is just above the people. It is perfectly credible that Gentz himself, in a moment of weakness, may have thought it possible to escape the horrors and uncertainties of war by this means.

At any rate the powers at the Congress had not judged it superfluous to reconsider the position they had taken up with regard to Napoleon and France in all its various bearings, and to make their decision public. After mature deliberation they found that their former decision ought to be maintained, and that the only thing to be done was to declare war against Napoleon without delay, and with all their united forces.

The Congress, however, could not separate without coming to some determination upon the many important questions still left undecided, more especially those concerning German affairs. The question as to Saxony was seriously taken into consideration, and brought to a conclusion by general consent, on the 18th May. German affairs, however, continued to be conducted in a dilatory and tedious manner in spite of the impending war, and it was the 8th June before they could be finally settled. And even then Würtemberg and Baden refused for some time to sign. Those who drew up the terms declared their work to be imperfect, hurried, and requiring future alteration. But all the resolutions touching constitutional and territorial questions, with all their explanations and amendments, were brought together in one document, which on the 9th June received the signature of all the plenipotentiaries, as the act of the Congress of Vienna. The German states were afterwards required to sign. But now the Spanish minister Don Gomez Labrador refused, after having specified his reasons in a note he delivered to Prince Metternich. Consequently, of the eight powers who were originally associated together, only seven signed. Moreover, the Cardinal Consalvi made a protest, in the name of the pope, against all measures passed by the Congress in any way tending to the detriment of the Catholic church.

Thus ended the Congress of Vienna. But the broken threads were still left to be afterwards gathered up, and it is not my purpose here to inquire what the Congress did, or what it neglected to do. . . . . Meanwhile, from all districts, far and near, troops were incessantly in motion towards the Rhine and the Netherlands: in Belgium, the Duke of Wellington assembled the allied forces of England, Hanover, and the Netherlands, while Blücher was collecting the Prussian troops. The Russian and Austrian armies were bearing down towards the Upper and Lower Rhine. Many of the princes, statesmen, and generals, who had been staying in Vienna, now returned to their respective homes, or to their regiments. The great rulers fixed the day of their departure, and at length quitted Vienna to meet again in the field of battle.

THE END.

LONDON:
SPOTTISWOODE and SHAW,
New-street-Square.

www.ingramcontent.com/pod-product-compliance
Lightning Source LLC
Chambersburg PA
CBHW030323240426
43673CB00040B/1256